Adobe®
Photoshop® CS2
for the Web
HANDS-ON TRAINING

Includes Exercise Files & Demo Movies

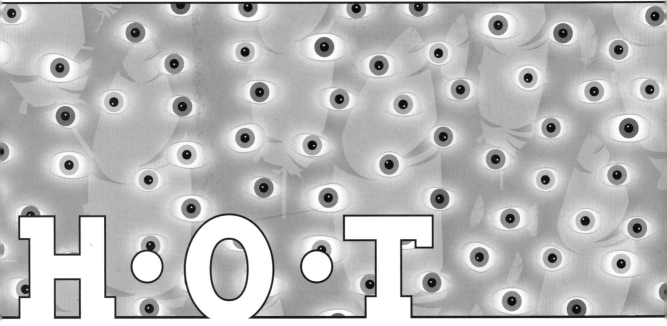

H·O·T

Tanya Staples

Adobe Photoshop CS2 for the Web | H·O·T
Hands-On Training

By Tanya Staples

lynda.com/books | Peachpit Press
1249 Eighth Street • Berkeley, CA • 94710
800.283.9444 • 510.524.2178 •
510.524.2221 (fax)
http://www.lynda.com/books
http://www.peachpit.com

lynda.com/books is published
in association with Peachpit Press,
a division of Pearson Education
Copyright ©2005 by lynda.com

ISBN: 0-321-33171-0

0 9 8 7 6 5 4 3 2 1

Printed and bound in the
United States of America

H•O•T | Credits

Original Design: Ali Karp, Alink Newmedia (alink@earthlink.net)

Editor: Karyn Johnson

Copyeditor: Darren Meiss

Production Coordinator: Myrna Vladic

Compositors: Rick Gordon, Deborah Roberti

Beta testers: Adam Fischer, Matthew Halely

Proofreader: Liz Welch

Cover Illustration: Bruce Heavin (bruce@stink.com)

Indexer: Julie Bess, JBIndexing Inc.

H•O•T | Colophon

The original design for *Adobe Photoshop CS2 for the Web H•O•T* was sketched on paper. The layout was heavily influenced by online communication—merging a traditional book format with a modern Web aesthetic.

The text in *Adobe Photoshop CS2 for the Web H•O•T* was set in Akzidenz Grotesk from Adobe and Triplex from Emigre. The cover illustration was painted in Adobe Photoshop and Adobe Illustrator.

This book was created using QuarkXPress, Microsoft Office, and *Adobe Photoshop CS2* on an Apple Macintosh using Mac OS X. It was printed on 60 lb. Influence Matte at Courier.

Photoshop CS2 for the Web | H•O•T _____ **Table of Contents**

Introduction

HOT

PCS2Web HOT CD-ROM

A Note from Lynda

In my opinion, most people buy computer books to learn, yet it is amazing how few of these books are actually written by teachers. Tanya Staples and I take pride in the fact that this book was written by experienced teachers, who are familiar with training students in this subject matter. In this book, you will find carefully developed lessons and exercises to help you learn Photoshop CS2 and ImageReady CS2—two of the most well-respected graphics applications on the planet.

This book is targeted toward the beginning- to intermediate-level Web designers and Web developers who are looking for great tools to create graphics and Web content. The premise of the hands-on exercise approach is to get you up to speed quickly with Photoshop CS2 and ImageReady CS2 while actively working through the lessons in the book. It's one thing to read about a product, and another experience entirely to try the product and get measurable results. Our motto is, "Read the book, follow the exercises, and you'll learn the product." I have received countless testimonials to this fact, and it is our goal to make sure it remains true for all of our hands-on training books.

Many exercise-based books take a paint-by-numbers approach to teaching. Although this approach works, it's often difficult to figure out how to apply those lessons to a real-world situation, or to understand why or when you would use the technique again. What sets this book apart is that the lessons contain lots of background information and insights into each given subject, which are designed to help you understand the process as well as the exercise.

At times, pictures are worth a lot more than words. When necessary, we have also included short QuickTime movies to show any processes that are difficult to explain with words. These files are located on the **PCS2Web HOT CD-ROM** inside a folder called **movies**. It's our style to approach teaching from many different angles, because we know some people are visual learners, others like to read, and still others like to get out there and try things. This book combines a lot of teaching approaches so you can learn Photoshop CS2 and ImageReady CS2 to create Web graphics as thoroughly as you want to.

This book didn't set out to cover every single aspect of Photoshop CS2 or ImageReady CS2. The manual, and many other reference books are great for that! What we saw missing from the bookshelves was a process-oriented tutorial that taught readers core principles, techniques, and tips in a hands-on training format. We've been making Web graphics since 1995, and it used to be a lot tougher than it is today. Photoshop CS2 and ImageReady CS2 are oriented toward making Web graphics faster to download and easier to create. In addition, ImageReady CS2 even writes JavaScript and HTML code, which is something traditional imaging programs have seldom broached.

I welcome your comments at **pscs2webhot@lynda.com**. Please visit our Web site at **http://www.lynda.com**. The support URL for this book is **http://www.lynda.com/info/books/pscs2web/**.

Tanya and I hope this book will raise your skills in Web design and digital imaging. If it does, we will have accomplished the job we set out to do!

Lynda Weinman

NOTE | About lynda.com/books and lynda.com

lynda.com/books is dedicated to helping designers and developers understand design tools and principles. lynda.com offers hands-on workshops, training seminars, conferences, on-site training, training videos, training CDs, and "expert tips" for design and development. To learn more about our training programs, books, and products, visit our Web site at **http://www.lynda.com**.

About Tanya

Tanya Staples is a freelance author and educator teaching traditional and digital art. She has a bachelor's degree in fine art and art history and a bachelor's degree in education. Tanya is the author of *Photoshop CS and ImageReady CS for the Web HOT* as well as numerous Adobe Photoshop, Corel Painter, Jasc Paint Shop Pro, and Apple Keynote video-based training titles in the lynda.com Online Training Library. As the former program manager for the Corel Painter product line, Tanya designed, taught, and wrote about graphics software. Tanya lives in Ottawa, Canada with her husband Matt and son Erik.

Snapshots

Tanya and Lynda take a break to smile for the camera.

Acknowledgments from Tanya

This book would not have been possible without the support of many dedicated, enthusiastic, and talented individuals.

My deepest thanks and appreciation to

You, the reader. I hope you enjoy this book as much as I enjoyed creating it for you.

Lynda Weinman, my mentor and my friend, for the great opportunities you've given me. You are an incredible inspiration, and I'm so grateful for everything you have done for me.

Garo Green, for keeping me on track. It has been a blast working with you.

Domenique Sillett, for creating the incredible imagery in this book. You are a fantastic designer and a wonderful friend.

The beta testers and copyeditor, **Adam Fischer**, **Matthew Hately**, and **Darren Meiss**, for your hard work, dedication, and attention to detail.

Michael Ninness for your fantastic advice and suggestions. It has been a pleasure working with you!

The folks at Adobe, for making another fantastic version of Photoshop and ImageReady!

My parents, **Barry and Pat Staples**, for taking such great care of Erik while I worked on this book.

Patricia, Ifoma, and Myles Smart for your constant encouragement and support, for our lunch dates on Mondays, and for spending so much time with Erik while I worked on this book. You are amazing friends. I'm so grateful to have you in our lives and for the opportunity to raise our boys together.

My son, **Erik**, for being such an amazing baby and for understanding when mommy had to get some work done! You are my sunshine!

My husband, **Matthew** for your patience, love, and support. Thank you for taking care of life while I buried myself in another book.

How This Book Works

This book has several components, including step-by-step exercises, commentary, notes, tips, warnings, and movies. Step-by-step exercises are numbered, and filenames and command keys are bolded so they pop out more easily. When you see italicized text, it signifies commentary.

- At the beginning of each exercise you'll see the notation **[PS]** if the exercise takes place in Photoshop CS2, **[IR]** if the exercise takes place in ImageReady CS2, or **[BRIDGE]** if the exercise takes place in Bridge.

- Whenever you're being instructed to go to a menu or to multiple menu items, it's stated like this: **File > Open**.

- Code is in a monospace font: **<HTML></HTML>**.

- URLs are in a bold font: **http://www.lynda.com**.

- Macintosh and Windows interface screen captures: The screen captures in the book were taken on a Macintosh, as I do most of my design work and writing on a Mac. I also own and use a Windows computer, and I noted important differences when they occurred.

What's on the CD-ROM?

Exercise Files and the HOT CD-ROM

The files required to complete the exercises are located inside a folder called **exercise_files** on the **PCS2Web HOT CD-ROM**. These files are divided into chapter folders, and you should copy each chapter folder to your Desktop before you begin the exercises for the chapter. Unfortunately, when files originate from a CD-ROM, under some Windows operating systems, it defaults to making them write-protected, meaning that you cannot alter them. You will need to alter them to follow the exercises, so please read the "Making Exercise Files Editable on Windows Computer" section on page xvi.

QuickTime Files on the PCS2Web HOT CD-ROM

There is a folder on the **PCS2Web HOT CD-ROM** called **movies**, which contains several QuickTime tutorial movies for some of the exercises in this book. These movies are intended to help you understand some of the more difficult exercises in this book by watching me perform them. If you like these movies, you should definitely check out the **Photoshop CS2 for the Web Training Essentials CD-ROM** at **http://www.lynda.com**, which contains several hours worth of QuickTime movies about creating Web graphics in Photoshop CS2 and ImageReady CS2.

Making Exercise Files Editable on Windows Computers

By default, when you copy files from a CD-ROM to a Windows 2000 computer, they are set to read-only (write protected). This will cause a problem with the exercise files because you will need to edit and save some of them. To remove the read-only property, follow these steps:

Note: You do not need to follow these steps if you are using Windows XP Home Edition or Windows XP Professional Edition.

1. Open the exercises_files folder on the **PCS2Web HOT CD-ROM**, and copy one of the subfolders (such as **chap_02**) to your **Desktop**.

2. Open the **chap_02** folder you copied to your **Desktop**, and choose **Edit > Select All**.

3. Right-click one of the selected files and choose **Properties** from the shortcut menu.

4. In the **Properties** dialog box, click the **General** tab. Turn off the **Read-Only** option to disable the read-only properties for the selected files in the **chap_02** folder.

Making File Extensions Visible on Windows Computers

By default, you cannot see file extensions, such as .gif, .jpg, or .psd, on Windows computers. Fortunately, you can change this setting!

1. Double-click the **My Computer** icon on your **Desktop**.

Note: If you (or someone else) have changed the name, it will not say **My Computer**.

2. Select **Tools > Folder Options**. The **Folder Options** dialog box opens automatically.

3. Click the **View** tab.

4. Turn off the **Hide extensions for known file types** option. This makes all file extensions visible.

Photoshop CS2 and ImageReady CS2 System Requirements

This book requires you use either a Macintosh (Mac OS X v10.2.8 or later) or Windows 2000/XP. You will also need a color monitor capable of 1024 × 768 resolution and a CD-ROM drive. Here are the minimum system requirements you need to run Photoshop CS2 and ImageReady CS2.

Macintosh:

- PowerPC G3, G4, or G5 processor

- Mac OS X v10.2.8 through v10.3.8 (10.3.4 through 10.3.8 recommended)

- 320 MB RAM (384 MB recommended)

- 750 MB available hard disk space

- 1024 × 768 monitor resolution with 16-bit video card

- CD-ROM drive

- Internet or phone connection required for product activation

Windows:

- Intel Xeon, Xeon Dual, Intel Centrino, or Pentium III or 4 processor

- Microsoft Windows 2000 with Service Pack 4 or Windows XP with Service Pack 1 or 2

- 320 MB RAM (384 MB recommended)

- 650 MB available hard disk space

- 1024 × 768 monitor resolution with 16-bit video card

- CD-ROM drive

- Internet or phone connection required for product activation

Getting Demo Versions of Software

If you'd like to try the software programs used in this book, you can download demo versions as follows:

- Adobe Photoshop CS2 and Adobe ImageReady CS2: **www.adobe.com**

- Adobe GoLive CS2: **www.adobe.com**

- Adobe Illustrator CS2: **www.adobe.com**

- Macromedia Flash MX 2004: **www.macromedia.com**

- Macromedia Dreamweaver MX 2004: **www.macromedia.com**

I

Getting Started

| Creating Web Graphics in Photoshop CS2 and ImageReady CS2 |
| When to Use Photoshop CS2 vs. When to Use ImageReady CS2 |

This chapter offers an overview of the Web features in Photoshop CS2 and ImageReady CS2. Here you'll find ideas for the kind of Web graphics you can create with these programs, advice on when to use each program, and an introduction to new Web features in Photoshop CS2 and ImageReady CS2. The information in this chapter builds a foundation for what you'll learn in the hands-on exercises in the chapters that follow.

chap_01

PCS2Web HOT CD-ROM

Creating Web Graphics in Photoshop CS2 and ImageReady CS2

You can use Photoshop CS2 and ImageReady CS2 to create a variety of images for the Web. This section lists some examples of the kinds of Web graphics and content you can create. You'll get a chance to explore projects like the following in the chapters to come.

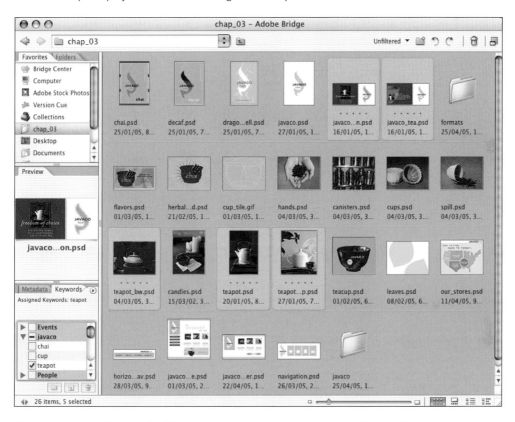

Organize assets: Use Adobe Bridge to view, organize, flag, rate, and keyword your images in Chapter 3, "*Organizing Assets.*"

Create type: Create and edit vector-based type in Chapter 6, "*Creating Type.*" Type created in Photoshop CS2 or ImageReady CS2 is great for Web buttons or banners that require fancy fonts or special type effects.

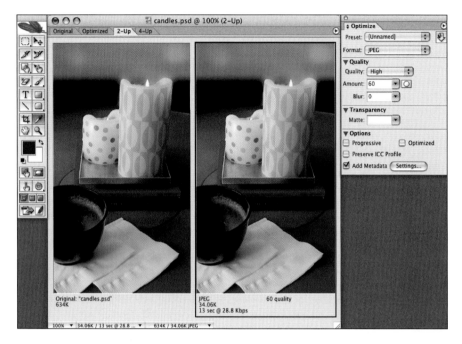

Optimize images for the Web: Learn techniques for optimizing photographs, logos, and graphic images in Chapter 7, "*Optimizing Images.*"

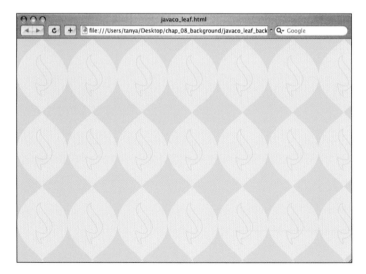

Create Web backgrounds: Create symmetrical and nonsymmetrical background images, define images as background images, and save the required HTML code to make background images work in a Web browser in Chapter 8, "*Creating Web Backgrounds.*"

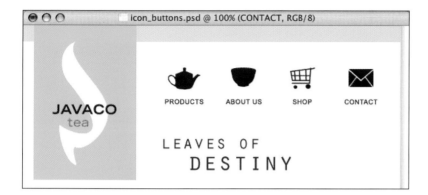

Design effective navigation: Learn how to create unique Web buttons, navigation bars, tabbed navigation, and iconic navigation with the shape tools and layer styles in Chapter 9, "*Designing Navigation.*"

Create animated GIFs: Create and save animated GIFs using the new animation features in Photoshop CS2 in Chapter 11, "*Creating Animated GIFs.*"

Slice: Slice images, edit slices, optimize slices, and save the required HTML code to make sliced images work in a Web browser in Chapter 12, "*Slicing.*"

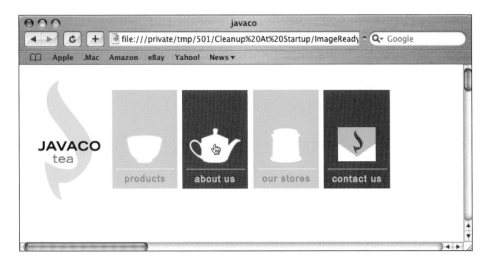

Create rollovers: Create simple Web buttons with rollovers, remote rollovers, and selected states, and save the required JavaScript and HTML code to make rollovers work in a Web browser in Chapter 13, *"Creating Rollovers."*

Create image maps: Create multiple hot spots in a single image and save the required HTML code to make image maps work in a Web browser in Chapter 14, *"Creating Image Maps."*

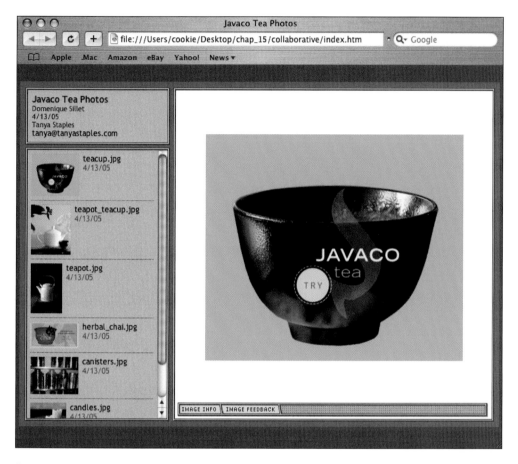

Create Web photo galleries: Create Web photo galleries to display images. Photoshop CS2 automatically creates all the elements for the Web site, optimizes the images, writes the HTML code, and designs the navigation buttons. Assemble Web photo galleries in Chapter 15, "*Creating Web Photo Galleries.*"

When to Use Photoshop CS2 vs. When to Use ImageReady CS2

When you're creating Web graphics, when should you use Photoshop CS2 and when you should use ImageReady CS2? Although Photoshop CS2 and ImageReady CS2 have many common features, there are many features exclusive to each program. Here are some recommendations:

- **Creating simple Web graphics:** Use either Photoshop CS2 or ImageReady CS2 to create simple Web graphics such as Web buttons and background images.

- **Performing complex image-editing tasks:** Use Photoshop CS2 to perform complex image-editing tasks, such as retouching a photograph or making a collage. The reason is simple—Photoshop CS2 has more sophisticated image-editing tools than ImageReady CS2.

- **Designing full Web page layouts:** Use Photoshop CS2 to create full Web page layouts. Photoshop CS2 has more advanced image-editing and creation tools. When you've finished designing the layout, you can always jump to ImageReady CS2 to create rollovers or animations and save the required JavaScript or HTML code required to make the Web page work.

- **Organizing assets:** Use Adobe Bridge when you want to organize, sort, or assign keywords to images.

- **Optimizing images:** Use the program you have open at the time. The Save For Web dialog box in Photoshop CS2 is similar to the Optimize palette in ImageReady CS2; however, ImageReady CS2 gives you better access to the original image if you want to make changes during the optimization process.

- **Slicing images:** Use ImageReady CS2 when you're slicing an image. Although Photoshop CS2 gives you access to the slice tools, you don't have access to the Slice, Table, or Web Content palettes, which you'll need for performing complex slicing tasks and creating rollovers.

- **Creating rollovers:** Use ImageReady CS2 to create rollovers. ImageReady CS2 gives you access to the Web Content palette and all the controls you need to create rollovers. It also writes the JavaScript and HTML code required to make the rollovers work in a Web browser. Although Photoshop CS2 does not have the features for creating rollovers, you can design the artwork in Photoshop CS2 and use ImageReady CS2 to create and save the rollovers.

- **Creating image maps:** Use ImageReady CS2 if you want to create image maps. ImageReady CS2 gives you access to image map creation tools and lets you save the required HTML code to make image maps work in a Web browser.

- **Creating animated GIFs:** Use Photoshop CS2 or ImageReady CS2 if you want to create and save animations as animated GIFs. The animation features—new to Photoshop CS2—are identical to those found in ImageReady CS2.

- **Creating Web photo galleries:** Use Photoshop CS2 or Adobe Bridge if you want to create a Web photo gallery from a series of images.

Don't worry if you're still unsure about which program to use when. You'll get hands-on experience completing all these tasks in the appropriate program as you work through the book. Plus, you can always glance back at the following handy reference chart.

When to Use Photoshop CS2 vs. When to Use ImageReady CS2	
Task	**Program**
Creating simple Web graphics such as buttons or backgrounds	Photoshop CS2 or ImageReady CS2
Performing complex image-editing tasks such as retouching and manipulating photographs or creating collages	Photoshop CS2
Designing navigation or full Web page layouts	Photoshop CS2
Organizing images	Adobe Bridge
Optimizing images	Photoshop CS2 or ImageReady CS2
Slicing simple images	Photoshop CS2 or ImageReady CS2
Slicing complex images, editing slices, or using slices for rollovers	ImageReady CS2
Creating rollovers	ImageReady CS2
Creating image maps	ImageReady CS2
Creating animated GIFs	Photoshop CS2 or ImageReady CS2
Creating Web photo galleries	Adobe Bridge

Now that you've had a chance to see what Photoshop CS2 and ImageReady CS2 are all about, it's time to get started with the hands-on exercises. In the chapters that follow, you'll learn practical techniques for using Photoshop CS2 and ImageReady CS2 to design Web graphics and content. Enjoy! ;-)

2

Understanding the Interface

The Welcome Screen	Interface Overview
Customizing Palette Locations	Saving Custom Palette Locations
Customizing Keyboard Shortcuts	Customizing Menus
Saving Custom Workspaces

chap_02

PCS2Web HOT CD-ROM

Adobe has always been known for consistent, easy-to-use interfaces across products, platforms, and versions. Photoshop CS2 and ImageReady CS2 are no exception. This chapter guides you through the basic components of the Photoshop CS2 and ImageReady CS2 interface and teaches you how to customize your workspace to suit your preferences and workflow.

This chapter begins with an overview of the main interface components: the Welcome Screen, the Toolbox, the Options bar, and the palettes. You'll also learn how to customize the interface by docking and undocking palettes, saving custom workspaces, creating custom keyboard shortcuts, and customizing menu options.

You might be anxious to start in on some of the step-by-step exercises in later chapters, but you should review this chapter first to understand the key elements of the Photoshop CS2 and ImageReady CS2 interfaces.

The Welcome Screen

When you open Photoshop CS2 or ImageReady CS2 for the first time, you'll see the Welcome Screen, which is designed to give you quick access to tutorials, tips and tricks, color management, and new feature information.

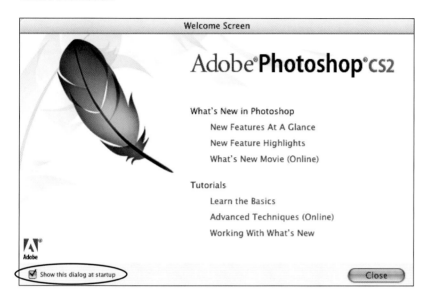

To view information from the Welcome Screen, click a text link (items in blue) and follow the instructions onscreen. **Note:** Some of the content is online, and you will need to have an active Internet connection to view the information.

If you close the Welcome Screen, you can reopen it by choosing **Help > Welcome Screen**.

If you do not want the Welcome Screen to appear each time you launch Photoshop CS2 or ImageReady CS2, uncheck the **Show this dialog at startup** option located in the lower-left corner of the Welcome Screen.

Interface Overview

Photoshop CS2 and ImageReady CS2 are separate applications that ship together. Fortunately, from an interface perspective, you're in for an easy learning curve because Photoshop CS2 and ImageReady CS2 share similar Toolboxes, palettes, and menu items, which are organized in the same logical way.

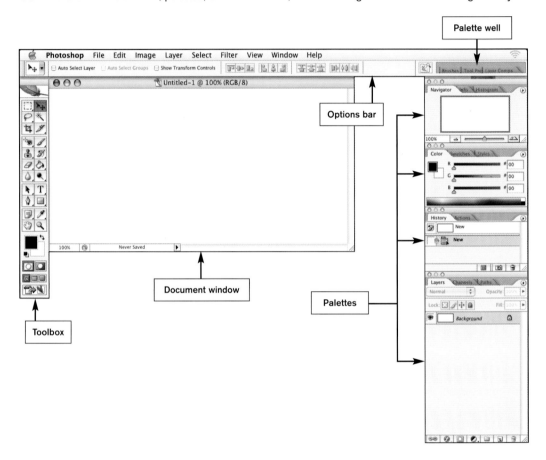

Photoshop CS2 interface

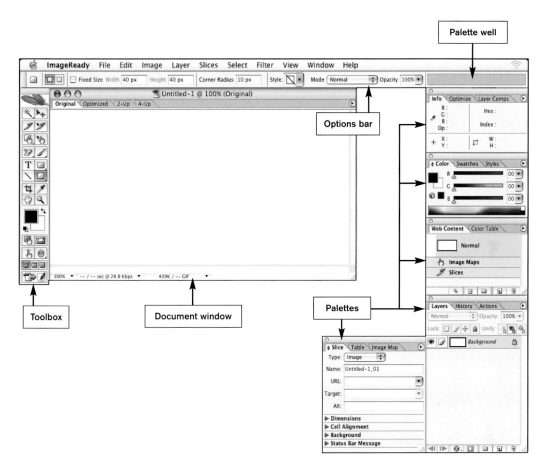

ImageReady CS2 interface

When you first open Photoshop CS2 or ImageReady CS2, the Toolbox, Options bar, and key palettes are turned on by default. Even though different palettes are turned on in Photoshop CS2 and ImageReady CS2, you can see from first glance these programs share similar interfaces. If you know Photoshop CS2 already, you'll have a huge advantage when learning ImageReady CS2.

Tip: Pressing the **Tab** key in Photoshop CS2 or ImageReady CS2 toggles the palettes on and off.

The Toolbox

Photoshop CS2 Toolbox   *ImageReady CS2 Toolbox*

The Toolboxes in Photoshop CS2 and ImageReady CS2 are vertical and are docked to the upper-left corner of the screen by default. In both programs, you can undock and move the Toolbox to any location onscreen. Many of the tools have an associated keyboard shortcut, which is listed in parentheses in the tooltip. You can access the tooltips by hovering your mouse over a tool, without clicking.

Toolbox Fly-Out Menus

When you see a small arrow on the lower-right corner of a tool in the Photoshop CS2 and ImageReady CS2 Toolboxes, it indicates hidden tools in fly-out menus. To show the hidden tools, click the arrow, and the additional tool choices will appear to the left or right side of the Toolbox.

Here is an example of a fly-out menu in Photoshop CS2. The small arrow on the lower-right corner of the tool indicates hidden tools reside in the associated fly-out menu. To access the fly-out menu, click the tool and hold down the mouse button until the fly-out menu appears. Keep holding down the mouse button, and move the cursor over the fly-out menu to make the tool selection. The letter on the right side of the fly-out menu is the keyboard shortcut for the tool.

The Options Bar

The Options bar contains settings for each tool in the Toolbox. The Options bar is context-sensitive, and it changes depending on which tool is selected in the Toolbox. By default, the Options bar is docked to the top of the screen, below the application menu. The Options bar works the same way in Photoshop CS2 and ImageReady CS2.

Here are two examples showing the Options bar. In the first example, the Move tool is selected in Photoshop CS2. In the second example, the Slice tool is selected in Photoshop CS2. Notice the contents of the Options bar are different for each tool.

The Palettes

Photoshop CS2 and ImageReady CS2 let you manage the interface through a series of palettes. Each palette is identified by a tab in the upper-left corner. By default, the palettes are docked together in groups. To make a palette appear at the front of the group, click the palette's tab. To help you customize your workspace so only the palettes you need are visible, Photoshop CS2 and ImageReady CS2 let you display each palette individually or as part of a group in any combination. You'll learn how to customize palettes into groups later in this chapter.

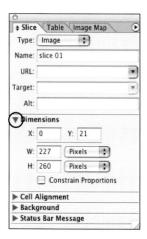

Some of the palettes in ImageReady CS2 (not Photoshop CS2), such as the one shown in the illustration above, contain fixed drop-down panels so you can hide and show areas of the palette. This helps reduce the amount of space the palettes take up onscreen. You can expand or contract these panels by clicking the small arrow to the left of the palette name. To expand or contract all of the drop-down panels at once, hold down the **Cmd** (Mac) or **Ctrl** (Windows) key and click any of the arrows in the palette group.

Jumping Between Photoshop CS2 and ImageReady CS2

When you're designing Web graphics, you'll often need to go between Photoshop CS2 and ImageReady CS2 quickly. The Edit In button, located at the bottom of the Photoshop CS2 and ImageReady CS2 Toolbox, lets you switch quickly between the two programs.

The Edit In ImageReady CS2 button in Photoshop CS2

The Edit In Photoshop CS2 button in ImageReady CS2

When you have an open image and click the Edit In button, the same image reopens in the other program.

 MOVIE | interface_tour.mov

To learn more about the Interface in Photoshop CS2 or ImageReady CS2, check out **interface_tour.mov** from the **movies** folder on the **PCS2Web HOT CD-ROM**.

I. [PS/IR] Customizing Palette Locations

Photoshop CS2 and ImageReady CS2 let you reorganize your workspace by docking and undocking palettes individually, vertically, and in custom palette groups. You'll find this technique helpful if you're working with a unique combination of palettes and don't want to crowd your workspace with palettes you don't use.

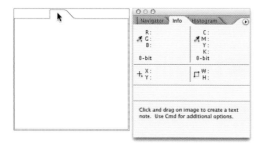

1. In Photoshop CS2 or ImageReady CS2, make sure the **Info** palette is visible. If it's not, choose **Window > Info**. Click and drag the **Info** palette tab to the center of your screen so it is floating on its own. Notice as you move the palette, a dotted line appears around the edges.

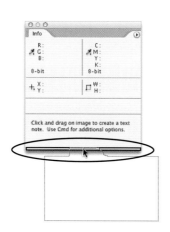
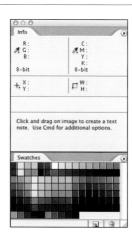

2. Make sure the **Swatches** palette is visible. If it's not, choose **Window > Swatches**. Click and drag the **Swatches** palette tab to the bottom of the **Info** palette until you see a black line appear at the bottom of the **Info** palette.

*The **Info** palette and the **Swatches** palette should now be docked together vertically. You will find it helpful to dock palettes vertically if you are using just a few palettes at a time or if you want to see all the contents of the palettes you have open. Next, you'll learn how to group palettes into palette groups.*

3. Make sure the **Layers** palette and **Layer Comps** palette are visible. If not, choose **Window >** **Layers** and **Window > Layer Comps**. **Note:** In Photoshop CS2, the **Layer Comps** palette is docked inside the palette well by default. In ImageReady CS2, the **Layer Comps** palette is docked beside the **Optimize** palette by default.

4. Click and drag the **Layers** palette tab to the center of your screen so it is floating on its own.

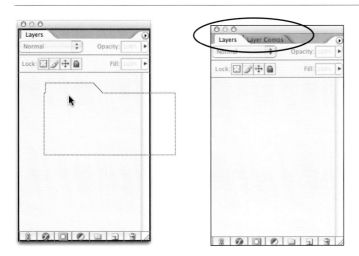

5. Click and drag the **Layer Comps** palette tab onto the **Layers** palette until you see a black line around the perimeter of the **Layers** palette.

*The **Layers** palette and **Layer Comps** palette should now be docked together in a palette group. You will find it useful to create palette groups when you're using just a few features, and you don't want to clutter your workspace with lots of individual palettes.*

6. Leave the palettes as they are so you're ready for the next exercise.

2. [PS/IR] _____ Saving Custom Palette Locations

After you customize the location of your palettes, you may want to save the custom palette configuration so you can use it again. Photoshop CS2 lets you save all of your open palettes, including those in the palette well, exactly where you've left them.

1. If you followed the last exercise, you should have the **Info** palette and **Swatches** palette docked vertically and the **Layers** palette and **Layer Comps** palette docked together in a palette group. If not, go back and complete Exercise 1.

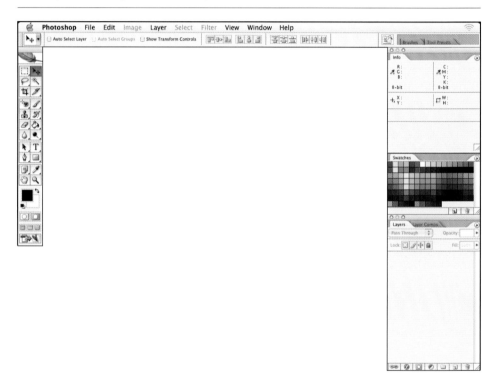

2. Move the **Info** palette and **Swatches** palette and the **Layers** palette and **Layer Comps** palette so they appear as shown in the illustration above. Close any other open palettes by clicking the **close** button in the upper-left corner of the palette (Mac) or the upper-right corner of the palette (Windows).

3. Choose **Window > Workspace > Save Workspace**.

4. In the **Save Workspace** dialog box, type **Custom Workspace** in the **Name** field. Turn on the **Palette Locations** check box, but leave the **Keyboard Shortcuts** and **Menus** check boxes turned off. (You'll learn about customizing keyboard shortcuts and menus later in this chapter.) Click **Save**.

5. Change things around as much as you like—open other palettes, reposition palettes, dock palettes into different palette groups, and so on.

6. Choose **Window > Workspace > Custom Workspace**. Your workspace will immediately return to the saved configuration. Very cool!

TIP | Returning Palettes to Default Settings

After you have reorganized your palettes, you will often want to return them to the way they were organized when you first opened Photoshop CS2 or ImageReady CS2.

In Photoshop CS2, choose **Window > Workspace > Default Workspace**.

In ImageReady CS2, choose **Window > Workspace > Default Palette Locations**.

Keyboard Shortcuts

Photoshop CS2 and ImageReady CS2 have keyboard shortcuts assigned to many common commands. The following two charts provide keyboard shortcuts to commonly used tools when designing Web graphics in Photoshop CS2 and ImageReady CS2.

Photoshop CS2 Shortcut Keys	
Command	Shortcut Key
Eyedropper tool	I
Hand tool	H
Move tool	V
Slice tool and Slice Select tool	K
Switch Background and Foreground Colors	X
Type tool	T
Zoom tool	Z

ImageReady CS2 Shortcut Keys	
Tool/Command	Shortcut Key
Slice tool	K
Slice Select tool	O
Toggle Slice Visibility	Q
Rectangle, Circle, and Polygon Image Map tools	P
Image Map Selection tool	J
Toggle Image Map Visibility	A
Preview Optimized Image	Y
Preview in Browser	Cmd+Option+P (Mac), Ctrl+Alt+P (Windows)

3. [PS]_____Customizing Keyboard Shortcuts

Photoshop CS2 lets you modify the default keyboard shortcuts or create your own custom sets of keyboard shortcuts. You can create custom keyboard shortcuts for menu items, tools, and palette commands. You can also save and print a complete list of the keyboard shortcuts you created.

1. Choose **Edit > Keyboard Shortcuts**.

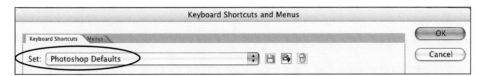

*Notice the current keyboard shortcut set is **Photoshop Defaults**. To avoid overwriting the default set, you'll create your own new set based on the current keyboard shortcuts before making any changes.*

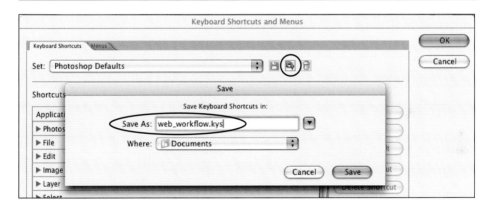

2. Click the **Create New Set** button. In the **Save** dialog box, name your keyboard shortcut set **web_workflow.kys** and keep the default save location. Click **Save**.

*Notice the current set is now **web_workflow**. Now you can begin to make changes without overwriting the default keyboard shortcuts.*

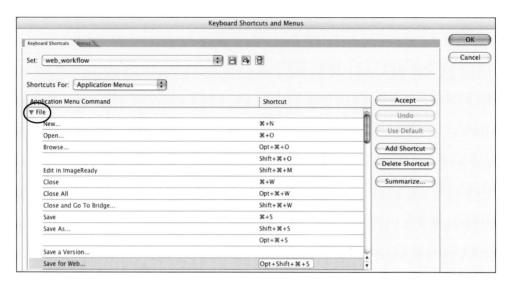

3. In the **Shortcuts For** pop-up menu, choose **Application Menus**. In the **Application Menu Command** list, click the arrow next to **File** to expand the contents of the **File** menu. Scroll down until you see **Save for Web**.

*One of the commands you're going to use frequently is **File > Save for Web**. By default, this command is assigned to **Option+Shift+Cmd+S** (Mac) or **Alt+Shift+Ctrl+S** (Windows), which are complicated shortcuts to use and difficult to remember. You're going to change them to something simpler.*

4. In the **Application Menu Command** list, click **Save for Web** to select it. Now you can edit the keyboard shortcut for this command.

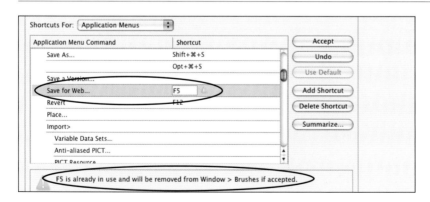

5. Press the **F5** key. You'll see a warning message at the bottom of the **Keyboard Shortcuts and Menus** dialog box indicating the **F5** key is currently used for **Window > Brushes**, which hides and displays the **Brushes** palette.

*Because most of the available keyboard shortcuts are already being used by other commands in Photoshop CS2, you'll have to make some compromises about which keyboard shortcuts to keep and which keyboard shortcuts you can live without. In this case, F5 launches the **Brushes** palette. Since you won't be using the **Brushes** palette very often, you can reassign the F5 keyboard shortcut to the **Save for Web** command. Keep in mind this change will only affect the keyboard shortcuts in the **web_workflow** set. You can always return to the default keyboard shortcuts if you want to undo your changes.*

6. Click **Accept** to assign **F5** to the **File > Save for Web** command.

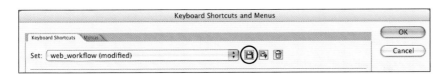

7. Click the **Save** button beside the **Set** pop-up menu to save the changes to the **web_workflow** keyboard shortcut set and click **OK** to close the **Keyboard Shortcuts and Menus** dialog box.

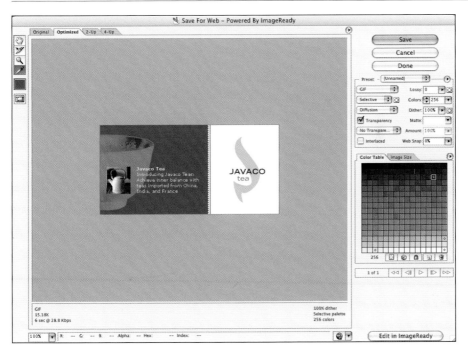

8. To test the new **Save for Web** keyboard shortcut, open **javaco_tea.psd** from the **chap_02** folder you copied to your **Desktop**. Press **F5**.

*The **Save for Web** dialog box opens using the customized keyboard shortcut you created.*

9. Click **Cancel** to close the **Save for Web** dialog box. You'll learn how to use the **Save for Web** feature in Chapter 7, "*Optimizing Images.*"

TIP | Saving and Printing Keyboard Shortcut Sets

After you customize the keyboard shortcuts for menus, palette menus, and tools, you may want to save and print a comprehensive list of keyboard shortcuts for easy reference. Photoshop CS2 summarizes the data from keyboard shortcut sets into an HTML file you can save and print.

To save and print a keyboard shortcut set, choose **Edit > Keyboard Shortcuts**. In the **Keyboard Shortcuts and Menus** dialog box, choose the keyboard shortcut set you want to save or print from the **Set** pop-up menu. Click **Summarize**. Type the filename, and specify the location where you want to save the file. Click **Save**.

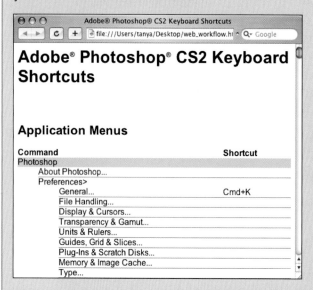

Photoshop CS2 will automatically launch your default Web browser and display a complete list of keyboard shortcuts. You can print this keyboard shortcut list by choosing **File > Print** in your Web browser.

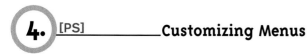

4. [PS] _____Customizing Menus

Photoshop CS2 takes customizing the interface one step further by letting you customize the contents of the application menus and palette menus. Not only can you hide commands you don't use, you can also add color to a menu command to make it more visible and easier to access.

1. Before you get started, take a look at the contents of the **Filter** menu and the **View** menu. In this exercise, you'll customize the contents of these menus. When you're finished, choose **Edit > Menus** to open the **Keyboard Shortcuts and Menus** dialog box.

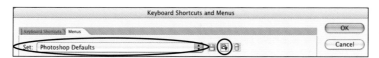

Like the keyboard shortcuts, the current menu set is set to **Photoshop Defaults**. To avoid overwriting the default set, you'll create your own new set based on the current menus before making any changes.

2. Click the **Create New Set** button. In the **Save** dialog box, name your menu set **web_workflow.mnu**, and keep the default save location. Click **Save**.

_Notice the current set is now **web_workflow**. Now you can begin to make changes without overwriting the default menus._

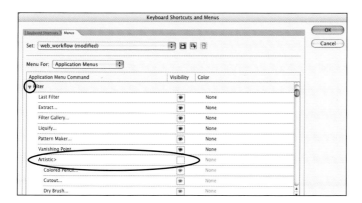

3. In the **Menu For** pop-up menu, choose **Application Menus**. Scroll down until you can see the **Filter** menu. Click the arrow next to the **Filter** menu so you can see the contents of the **Filter** menu. Click the **Eye** icon to turn off the visibility of the **Artistic** menu item.

Notice the visibility of the indented commands below **Artistic** turn off also. Because these items are fly-out menus, when you turn off the visibility of the main menu item, you also turn off the visibility of the options in the fly-out.

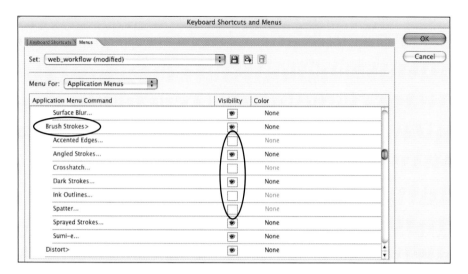

4. Scroll down until you can see **Brush Strokes**. Turn off the visibility of the following filters inside the **Brush Strokes** fly-out menu: **Accented Edges**, **Crosshatch**, **Ink Outlines**, and **Splatter**.

5. Scroll down until you can see the **View** menu. Click the arrow next to the **View** menu so you can see the contents of the **View** menu. Scroll down until you can see **Smart Guides** and **Slices** in the **Show >** fly-out menu.

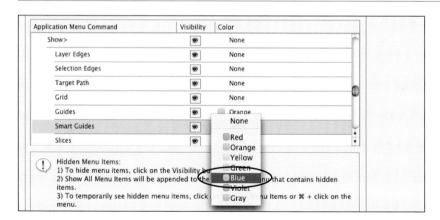

6. Click the word **None** in the **Color** column of the **Smart Guides** row. Choose **Orange** from the **Color** pop-up menu. Click the word **None** in the **Color** column of the **Slices** row and choose **Blue** from the **Color** pop-up menu.

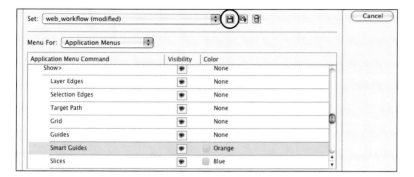

7. Click **Save** to save the changes you made to the **web_workflow** menu set and click **OK** to close the dialog box.

8. To test the changes you made to the **Filter** menu and **View** menu, open **javaco_tea.psd** from the **chap_02** folder you copied to your **Desktop**. Choose **Filter**.

*Notice the **Artistic** menu item and the contents of its fly-out menu no longer appear in the **Filter** menu.*

9. Choose **Filter > Brush Strokes**.

*Notice the **Accented Edges**, **Crosshatch**, **Ink Outlines**, and **Splatter** menu items no longer appear in the fly-out menu.*

10. Choose **View > Show**.

*Notice the **Smart Guides** menu command is highlighted in orange and the **Slices** menu command is highlighted in blue.*

Customizing and highlighting menu commands makes it quicker and easier to access the menu commands you need most when you're working in Photoshop CS2.

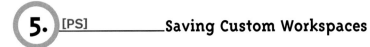

5. [PS] _____Saving Custom Workspaces

In Exercise 2, you learned how to save custom palette configurations. New to Photoshop CS2, you can save entire workspaces, including palette locations, keyboard shortcuts, and menu commands—all in a single step!

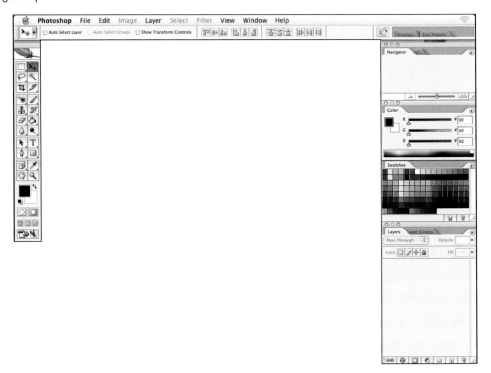

1. Customize your palette configuration so it matches the illustration above. **Note:** If you're not sure how to customize your palettes, refer to Exercise 1.

2. Choose **Edit > Keyboard Shortcuts**. In the **Set** pop-up menu, choose **web_workflow**. **Note:** If you don't have **web_workflow** in your list, go back and complete Exercise 3.

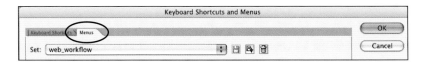

3. In the **Keyboard Shortcuts and Menus** dialog box, click the **Menus** tab. Choose **web_workflow** from the **Set** pop-up menu. **Note:** If you don't have **web_workflow** in your list, go back and complete Exercise 4.

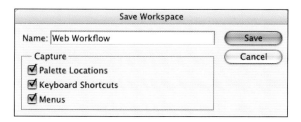

4. Choose **Window > Workspace > Save Workspace**. In the **Save Workspace** dialog box, type **Web Workflow** in the **Name** field. Turn on the **Palette Locations**, **Keyboard Shortcuts**, and **Menus** check boxes. Click **Save**.

5. Change your palette locations—turn on new palettes, add or remove palettes from the palette well, and reposition palettes into new palette groups.

6. Choose **Edit > Keyboard Shortcuts**. Choose **Photoshop Defaults** from the **Set** pop-up menu. In the **Keyboard Shortcuts and Menus** dialog box, click the **Menus** tab. Choose **Photoshop Defaults** from the **Set** pop-up menu. Click **OK**.

Notice the menu commands no longer reflect the changes you made in Exercises 3 and 4.

7. Choose **Window > Workspaces > Web Workflow**.

*Notice the palettes returned to the saved configuration. Check the contents of the **File** menu, the **Filter** menu, and the **View** menu and notice they reflect the changes you made in the **web_workflow** keyboard shortcut set and the **web_workflow** menu set. As you can see from this exercise, saving palette locations, keyboard shortcuts, and menus in a single step makes saving entire custom workspaces quick and easy!*

MOVIE | custom_workspaces.mov

To learn more advanced techniques about customizing palettes, keyboard shortcuts, and menus, check out **custom_workspaces.mov** in the **movies** folder on the **PCS2 HOT CD-ROM**.

Congrats! You just finished the first chapter, and you now have an understanding of the main interface elements in Photoshop CS2 and ImageReady CS2. In the next chapter, you'll learn how to organize your assets using Adobe Bridge—a new addition to Photoshop CS2 and the Adobe Creative Suite 2!

3

Organizing Assets

| Viewing and Organizing Assets |
| Rating and Labeling Assets |
| Keywording and Searching |

chap_03

PCS2Web HOT CD-ROM

Keeping your image assets organized is an important part of the Web design process. In previous versions of Photoshop, you used the File Browser to organize your assets. New in both the standalone version of Photoshop CS2 and the Adobe Creative Suite 2 is Adobe Bridge, which provides excellent tools to help you keep track of all your files. The benefit of having Bridge as a separate application (unlike the File Browser), is that you can organize images created natively in Photoshop CS2, or artwork created in any other Adobe Creative Suite 2 application, including Illustrator CS2, GoLive CS2, and InDesign CS2.

In this chapter, you'll learn the basics of how to use Bridge, including how to view, organize, flag, and rate assets; how to assign keywords; how to search for images; and how to purchase Adobe stock photos directly from the Bridge interface. Although these tasks may not seem directly related to the Web design process, you'll observe the benefits of organizing your assets in such a rich, visual environment.

Interface Overview

If you used recent versions of Photoshop, you'll notice the interface in Bridge resembles the File Browser. If you've never used the File Browser, you'll find it easy to use the rich, visual interface in Bridge because it's organized in a logical way. Here's an overview of the Bridge interface:

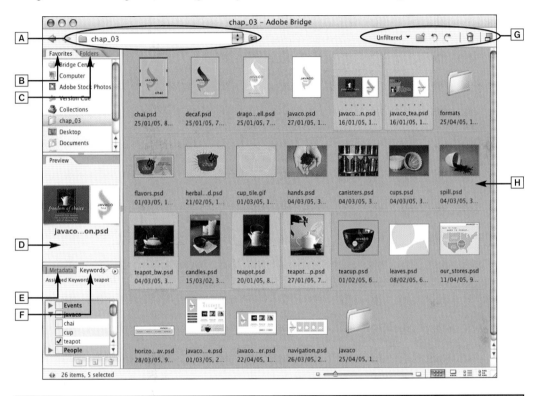

Bridge Interface Components

	Component	Description
A	Look In menu	Lists the folders on your computer in a hierarchical structure. It also lists folders in your Favorites list and Recent Files list.
B	Favorites panel	Provides quick access to folders and files you work with on a regular basis.
C	Folders panel	Lets you navigate through the folder structure on your hard drive to locate the files you need.

continues on next page

Bridge Interface Components *continued*

	Component	Description
D	Preview panel	Lets you preview the image you currently have selected in the content area. If your image is a multipage document, you'll see navigation buttons, which let you navigate between the pages.
E	Metadata panel	Displays the metadata information for the currently selected file in the content area.
F	Keywords panel	Lets you create and assign keywords to images. It also shows which keywords you have applied to the currently selected image(s).
G	Shortcut buttons	Lets you perform common tasks, such as filtering, rotating, and deleting images.
H	Content area	Lets you view the contents of a folder in a visual interface. You can customize the content area by increasing and decreasing the thumbnails and choosing from Thumbnails view, Filmstrip view, Details view, and Versions and Alternates view.

I. [BRIDGE]_____Viewing and Organizing Assets

In this exercise, you'll explore some of the basic features of Bridge, such as locating files and folders, adding folders to the Favorites list, changing thumbnail view and size, viewing different file formats, and reordering, renaming, and moving assets.

1. In Photoshop CS2, choose **File > Browse** to open Bridge.

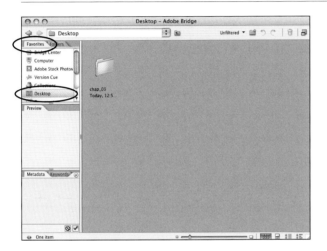

2. Click the **Favorites** panel tab. Click **Desktop**.

*In the content area, you'll see a folder called **chap_03** (as well as any other files and folders you have on your **Desktop**). Since you'll be using the **chap_03** folder quite a bit in this chapter, you'll add it to the **Favorites** list in the **Favorites** panel so you can access it easily at all times.*

3. Click and drag **chap_03** onto the **Favorites** panel. When you see the **+** sign, release your mouse, and **chap_03** will automatically be listed in the **Favorites** panel.

*Note: If you want to reposition a folder inside the **Favorites** panel, simply click and drag above, below, or between entries in the **Favorites** panel. When you release your mouse, it will automatically be repositioned.*

4. In the **Favorites** panel, click **chap_03**.

Notice the contents of the content area update automatically to show you the contents of the
chap_03 *folder.*

5. In the **Favorites** panel, click **Desktop**. In the content area, double-click the **chap_03** folder.

Double-clicking a folder in the content area is another way to view the contents of the folder. Next,
you'll learn how to change the size and format of the thumbnails in the content area.

6. At the bottom of the content area, move the **Thumbnail Size** slider toward the right to increase the
size of the thumbnail preview. Move the **Thumbnail Size** slider toward the left to decrease the size of
the thumbnail preview.

As you can see, you can view the thumbnails in just about any size. You'll find this helpful because some folders will have a lot of images, and some folders will have just a few. Being able to resize the thumbnails with such a simple control makes it easy to view the entire contents of a folder or to help you view the fine details of a file.

7. Choose **Window > Workspace > Reset to Default Workspace** to return your thumbnails to the default size.

*Next, you'll experiment with different ways to view thumbnails in the content area. **Note:** You can increase and decrease the size of thumbnails in any of the views described in the next few steps.*

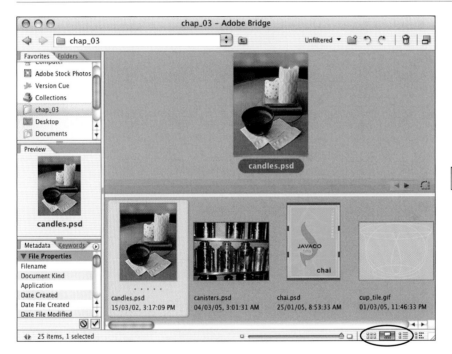

Filmstrip view

8. In the lower-right corner of the Bridge window, click the **Filmstrip View** button.

*In Filmstrip view, you can see a larger version of the currently selected file (in this case **candles.psd**). You can use the scroll bar to browse the other images in the folder.*

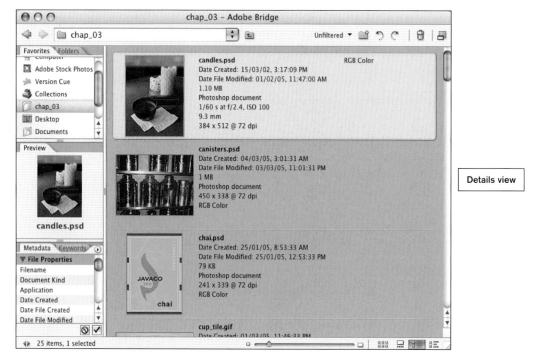

Details view

9. In the lower-right corner of the Bridge window, click the **Details View** button. When you've finished, click the **Thumbnails View** button.

Details view lets you see a preview of the images in the folder and provides information about the file, such as filename, color space, date created, date modified, file size, format, camera settings (for photographs), image size, and resolution. As you can see, Bridge provides a unique, visual interface to preview your assets. You'll find this helpful when you start to amass tens, hundreds, and thousands of files.

*As you may have noticed, the contents of the **chap_03** folder are mostly Photoshop files (with the exception of one lowly GIF). What if you work with other file formats? Follow the next few steps, and you'll see how powerful Bridge is!*

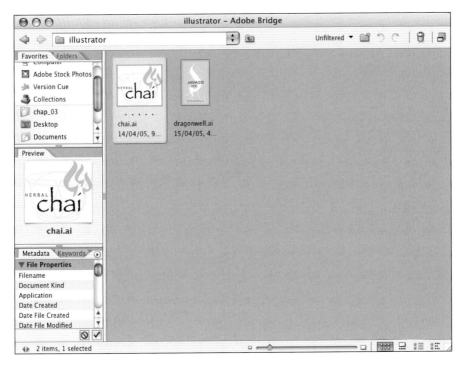

10. With **chap_03** still selected in the **Favorites** panel, in the content area double-click the **formats** folder. Double-click the **Illustrator** folder. Click **chai.ai** to select it.

*As you can see, the Illustrator folder contains two files—**chai.ai** and **dragonwell.ai**. When you click an Illustrator file, you can see a preview in the content area whether you have Illustrator CS2 installed or not. Bridge lets you preview images created in any Adobe Creative Suite 2 program regardless of whether you have the associated program installed on your computer. Pretty cool, huh?*

11. Continue to look through the contents of the other folders in the **formats** folder—**acrobat**, **indesign**, and **other**—to view additional formats supported by Bridge. When you've finished, double-click the **acrobat** folder to open it in the content area.

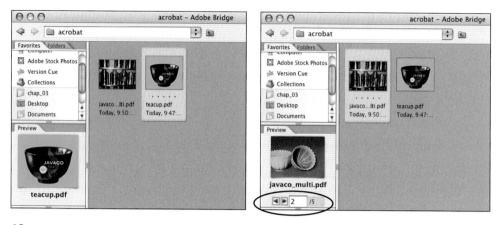

12. In the **acrobat** folder, click **teacup.pdf** to select it. Take a look at the content area. This is a single page PDF. Click **javaco_multi.pdf**.

*Take a look at the content area. As you can see, the **javaco_multi.pdf** file contains more than one page. Not only does Bridge tell you how many pages the document contains (in this case, five), it also gives you **Forward** and **Back** buttons to navigate through each page. How helpful is that?*

13. In the **Favorites** panel, click **chap_03** to go back to the original folder you bookmarked using the **Favorites** feature.

Next, you'll take a look at different ways to organize your images, including reordering, renaming, and moving. By default, images display in the content area in alphabetical order. You may decide you'd like to organize them differently. For example, you may want all photographs together, or you may want similar-looking images together. You'll learn how to reorder images in Bridge in the next few steps.

14. Click **chai.psd** to select it. Click and drag to the left until you see a dark blue line on the left side of the **candles.psd** file. When you release your mouse, **chai.psd** will be positioned on the left side of **candles.psd**.

It can be helpful to reorder images in Bridge in ways that make sense to you visually. At the operating system level and in many programs, you are limited to organizing by filename, date, name (alphabetically), or file type. In Bridge, you can organize files by custom order, which can be quite liberating and useful!

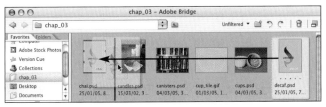 

15. Click **decaf.psd** to select it. Click and drag to the left until you see a dark blue line between **chai.psd** and **candles.psd**. When you release your mouse, **decaf.psd** will be positioned between **chai.psd** and **candles.psd**.

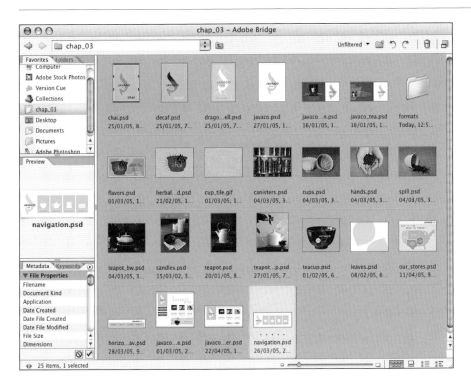

16. Using the techniques you learned in Steps 14 and 15, reposition the images in the **chap_03** folder to match the illustration shown here.

The beauty of reorganizing your images this way is that they will stay in this order until you choose to reorganize them. Therefore, you don't have to reorganize them each time you open the folder.

In addition to moving images around within the same folder, you can move or copy images into different folders. Plus, you can create folders directly in Bridge. You'll learn how in the next few steps.

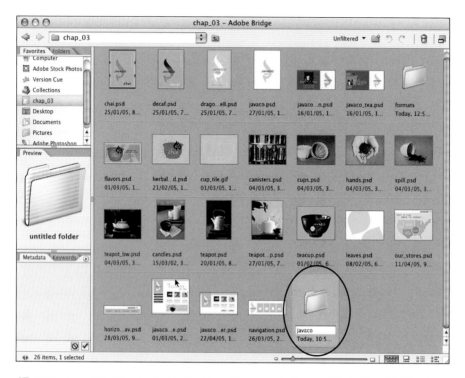

17. With **chap_03** still selected in the **Favorites** panel, choose **File > New Folder**. When you create the new folder, it will automatically appear as the last item in the content area with a bounding box around the folder name. Type **javaco**, and press **Return** (Mac) or **Enter** (Windows).

Note: In order to view all the thumbnails, I increased the size of the Bridge window by clicking and dragging the resize handle in the lower-right corner of the window.

*Tip: If you want to rename a folder, click the folder name once. When the bounding box appears, type a folder name, and press **Return** (Mac) or **Enter** (Windows). You can use the same technique if you want to rename files in Bridge.*

Next, you'll learn how to move files into the folder you just created.

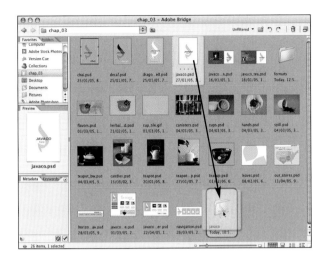

18. Click the **javaco.psd** file to select it. Click and drag it onto the **javaco** folder you created in the last step. When you see the outline around the folder, release your mouse. **javaco.psd** will automatically be moved into the **javaco** folder.

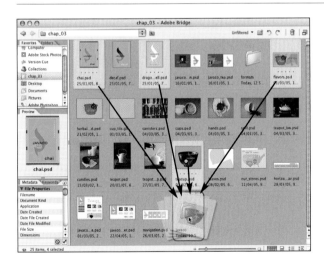

19. Click and **chai.psd** file to select it. Hold down the **Cmd** (Mac) or **Ctrl** (Windows) key and click **dragonwell.psd**, **flavors.psd**, and **teacup.psd**. The **Cmd** (Mac) or **Ctrl** (Windows) key lets you multiple-select images that are not next to each other. With the four images selected, click and drag them onto the **javaco** folder. When you see the outline around the folder, release your mouse. The images will automatically be moved into the **javaco** folder.

As you can see, you can move one image or a series of images into another folder.

20. Double-click the **javaco** folder to open it.

*As you can see, the files you moved in Steps 19 and 20 are now located inside the **javaco** folder. What if you want to copy files rather than move them? You'll learn how in the next few steps.*

21. Click **chai.psd** to select it. Hold down the **Option** (Mac) or **Ctrl** (Windows) key and click and drag **chai.psd** onto the **chap_03** folder in the **Favorites** panel.

*Wondering why you can still see **chai.psd** in the **javaco** folder? This time you copied the file—by using the **Option** (Mac) or **Ctrl** (Windows) key—rather than moving it. Now, you have a copy of **chai.psd** in both the **javaco** folder and the **chap_03** folder.*

22. Click the **dragonwell.psd** file to select it. Hold down the **Shift** key and click the **teacup.psd** file to multiple-select the images in-between. By using the **Shift** key, you can select multiple images that are right next to each other. Hold down the **Option** (Mac) or **Ctrl** (Windows) key and click and drag the files onto the **chap_03** folder in the **Favorites** panel.

23. Click the **chap_03** folder in the **Favorites** panel.

*As you can see, the files you copied in Steps 21 and 22 are now part of the **chap_03** folder and the **javaco** folder. Next, you'll learn how to delete assets from Bridge.*

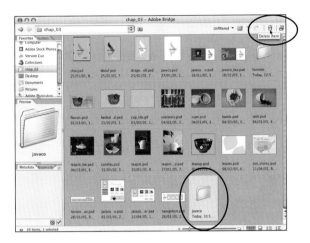

24. Click the **javaco** folder to select it. In the upper-right corner of the Bridge window, click the **Delete Item** button. A warning message will appear, asking if you want to move the **javaco** folder to the **Trash** (Mac) or **Recycle Bin** (Windows). Click **OK**.

The javaco folder will disappear automatically!

25. With **chap_03** selected in the **Favorites** panel, leave Bridge open for the next exercise.

TIP | Rotating Images

When you import images from scanners or digital cameras, they may be rotated incorrectly. You can fix the rotation of an image easily in Bridge without having to edit the image in Photoshop CS2.

Click the image you want to rotate. In the upper-right corner of the Bridge window, click the **Rotate 90° Counterclockwise** or **Rotate 90° Clockwise** button.

Alternately, you can choose one of the following options from the **Edit** menu: **Rotate 180°, Rotate 90° Clockwise, Rotate 90° Counterclockwise.**

2. [BRIDGE] _____Rating and Labeling Assets

In the last exercise, you learned how to organize your images in Bridge by reordering, moving, and copying assets. Another way you can organize your assets is by rating and labeling images, which you'll learn about in this chapter. Rating and labeling provides two benefits: it provides a visual cue so you can quickly identify files; and you can filter or view images based on the rating and labels.

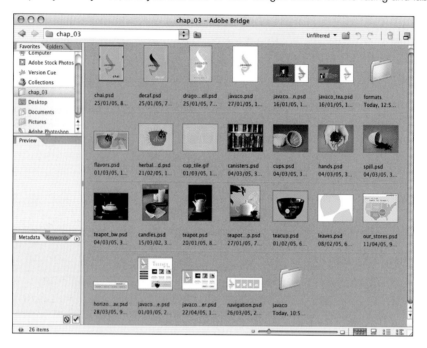

1. If you followed the last exercise, **chap_03** should be selected in the **Favorites** panel. If it's not, in the **Favorites** panel click **chap_03**. (If you haven't added it to the **Favorites** panel, go back and complete Step 3 in Exercise 1.) Make sure the order of the images matches the illustration here. If it doesn't, use the techniques you learned in Exercise 1 to reorder the images.

If you used previous versions of Photoshop, you may be familiar with the flagging feature in the File Browser. To replace flagging, Bridge offers labeling, which provides more functionality than the flagging feature. First you'll learn how to rate your images, which lets you assign a rating of 1, 2, 3, 4, or 5 stars to your images. You'll find this helpful because you can rate your images, then filter your images based on the rating you applied. As a result, you can choose to see all the best (or worst!) images at the same time. I often use this feature with digital photographs because it helps me identify the great shots and the "duds." Likewise, when I'm designing Web graphics, I can easily identify the most compelling designs in order to filter out the weaker ones.

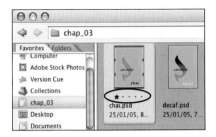

2. Click **chai.psd** to select it. Choose **Label > ***. A warning message will appear, indicating labels and ratings are stored in XMP metadata. Click **OK** to acknowledge the warning.

*Notice **chai.psd** now has a single star under the thumbnail, indicating the 1-star rating you applied.*

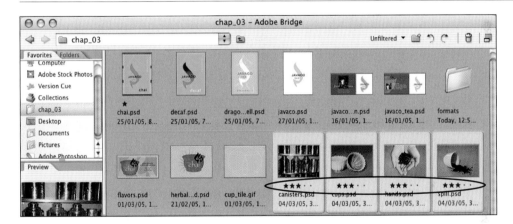

3. Click **canisters.psd** to select it. Hold down the **Shift** key and click **spill.psd** to multiple-select the images in-between. Choose **Label > *****. Click **OK** to acknowledge the warning message.

Notice the four images you selected each have three stars, indicating the 3-star rating you applied.

4. Click **candles.psd** to select it. Hold down the **Shift** key and click **teacup.psd** to multiple-select the images in-between. Choose **Label > ******. Click **OK** to acknowledge the warning message.

Notice the four images you selected each have four stars, indicating the 4-star rating you applied.

5. Click **horizontal.nav.psd** to select it. Hold down the **Shift** key and click **navigation.psd** to multiple-select the images in-between. Choose **Label** > *****. Click **OK** to acknowledge the warning message.

Notice the four images you selected each have five stars, indicating the 5-star rating you applied.

6. Click **decaf.psd** to select it. Hold down the **Cmd** (Mac) or **Ctrl** (Windows) key and click each of the following images: **javaco.psd, javaco_tea_coupon.psd, javaco_tea.psd, flavors.psd, herbal_chai_tiled_background.psd, cup_tile.gif, leaves.psd,** and **our_stores.psd**. Choose **Label** > **. Click **OK** to acknowledge the warning message.

Notice the images you selected each have two stars, indicating the 2-star rating you applied.

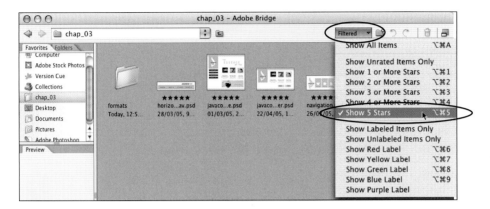

7. Choose **Show 5 Stars** from the **Filter** pop-up menu.

Notice the only images you see in the content area are the four images you rated with the 5-star rating.

8. Experiment with the other options in the **Filter** pop-up menu. When you've finished, choose **Show All Items**.

Notice all the images are organized based on their rating from lowest to highest.

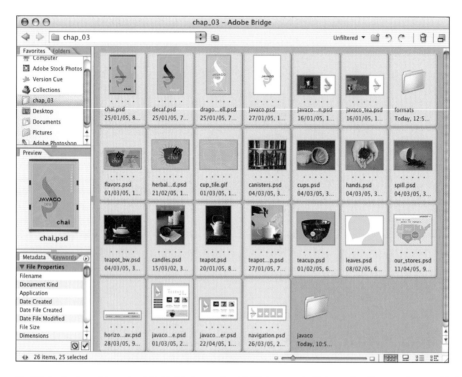

9. Click **chai.psd** to select it. Hold down the **Shift** key and click **navigation.psd** to multiple-select the images in-between. Choose **Label > No Rating**. Click **OK** to acknowledge the warning message.

Notice the images no longer have stars, indicating they no longer have ratings. Next, you'll learn how to label your images.

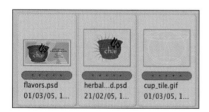

10. Click **flavors.psd** to select it. Hold down the **Shift** key and click **cup_tile.gif** to select it. Choose **Label > Red**. Click **OK** to acknowledge the warning message.

Notice the three images have a red pill-shaped label below the thumbnails. Labeling images is another way to easily identify and filter your images.

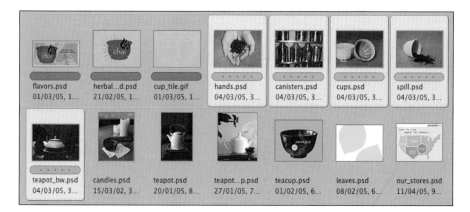

11. Click **hands.psd** to select it. Hold down the **Shift** key and click **teapot_bw.psd** to multiple-select the images in-between. Choose **Label > Green**. Click **OK** to acknowledge the warning.

Notice the five images have a green pill-shaped label below the thumbnails.

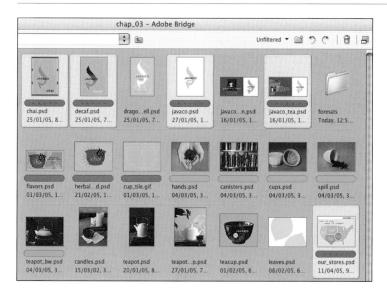

12. Click **chai.psd** to select it. Hold down the **Cmd** (Mac) or **Ctrl** (Windows) key and click to multiple-select the following images: **decaf.psd**, **javaco.psd**, **javaco_tea.psd**, and **our_stores.psd**. Choose **Label > Purple**. Click **OK** to acknowledge the warning.

Notice the images have a purple pill-shaped label below the thumbnails. Next, you'll filter the images using the labels.

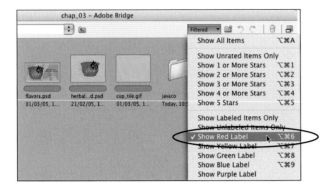

13. Choose **Show Red Label** from the **Filter** pop-up menu.

Notice the only images you see in the content area are the three images you labeled in red.

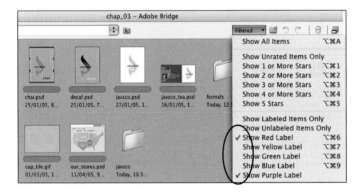

14. Choose **Show Purple Label** from the **Filter** pop-up menu.

Notice you can see both the images you labeled in purple and the images you labeled in red?
*Wondering why you see both? Open the **Filter** pop-up menu, and you'll understand. As you can see,*
*both **Show Red Label** and **Show Purple Label** have a checkmark beside them. If you want to view*
*only the images with a purple label, you must choose **Show Red Label** to turn it off. The interface is*
a bit confusing in this area, but if you can remember to look at the checkmarks, you'll be golden!

15. Choose **Show All Items** from the **Filter** pop-up menu. Click **chai.psd** to select it. Hold down the
Shift key and click **navigation.psd** to multiple-select the images in-between. Chose **Label > No Label**
to remove the **red**, **green**, and **purple** labels. Click **OK** to acknowledge the warning message.

As you can see, the rating and labeling features in Bridge is yet another way to help you keep your
files organized.

16. With **chap_03** selected in the **Favorites** panel, leave Bridge open for the next exercise.

3. [BRIDGE] _____Keywording and Searching

Another way you can keep your assets organized is by assigning keywords. Keywords are search phrases you define to describe your images. You can then use these keywords to search for and locate your images. Here's an exercise to show you how.

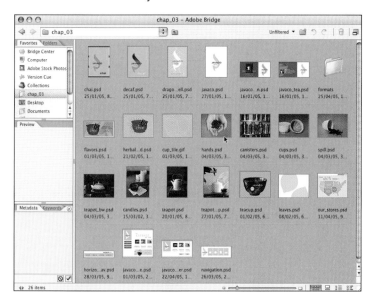

1. If you followed the last exercise, **chap_03** should be selected in the **Favorites** panel. If it's not, click **chap_03** in the **Favorites** panel. (If you haven't added it to the **Favorites** panel, go back and complete Step 3 in Exercise 1.) Make sure the order of the images matches the illustration here. If it doesn't, use the techniques you learned in Exercise 1 to reorder the images.

2. Click the **Keywords** panel tab.

Notice the list of keyword sets and the series of keywords inside the keyword sets. If any of the keyword sets are expanded, click the arrow to the left of the keyword set name to collapse them.

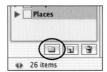

3. At the bottom of the **Keywords** panel, click the **New Keyword Set** button. Name the keyword set **javaco**, and press **Return** (Mac) or **Enter** (Windows).

4. Click the **javaco** keyword set to select it, and at the bottom of the **Keywords** panel click the **New Keyword** button. Name the keyword **teapot**, and press **Return** (Mac) or **Enter** (Windows).

5. Click the **javaco** keyword set to select it. Click the **New Keyword** button, name the keyword **cup**, and press **Return** (Mac) or **Enter** (Windows).

6. Click the **javaco** keyword set to select it. Click the **New Keyword** button, name the keyword **chai**, and press **Return** (Mac) or **Enter** (Windows).

*You should now have three keywords organized alphabetically in the **javaco** keyword set—chai, cup, and **teapot**. Next, you'll assign keywords to images.*

7. Click **chai.psd** to select it. Turn on the **chai** keyword.

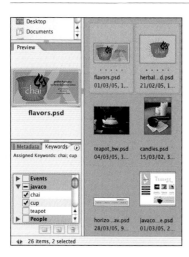

8. Click **flavors.psd** to select it. Hold down the **Shift** key and click **herbal_chai_tiled_background.psd** to select it. Turn on the **chai** and **cup** keywords. When you turn on each keyword, you'll see a warning message, which indicates you have selected multiple files and all files in the selection will be affected. Click **Yes**.

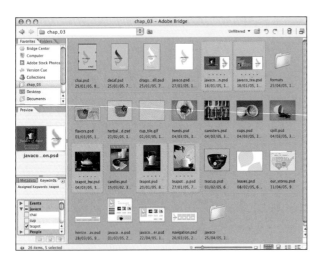

9. Click **teapot_bw.psd** to select it. Hold down the **Cmd** (Mac) or **Ctrl** (Windows) key and click to multiple-select each of the following files: **teapot.psd**, **teapot_teacup.psd**, **javaco_tea_coupon.psd**, and **javaco_tea.psd**. Turn on the **teapot** keyword. Click **Yes** to acknowledge the warning.

10. Click the **cup_tile.gif** file to select it. Hold down the **Cmd** (Mac) or **Ctrl** (Windows) key and click to multiple-select each of the following files: **cups.psd**, **spill.psd**, **candles.psd**, **teapot_teacup.psd**, and **teacup.psd**. Turn on the **cup** keyword. Click **Yes** to acknowledge the warning. A second warning message will appear, indicating the metadata of some of the selected images cannot be changed. Click **Yes** to continue.

As you saw from the second warning message, the **cup** *keyword could not be applied to at least one of the images. In the next steps, you'll figure out which one and why.*

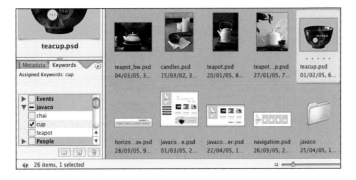

11. Click **teacup.psd** to select it. Take a look at the **Keywords** panel.

As you can see, the **cup** *keyword is turned on. Obviously, this is not the image that caused the error message in the last step.*

12. Click to select the **teapot_teacup.psd, candles.psd, spill.psd,** and **cups.psd** files, taking a look at the **Keywords** panel with each selection.

As you can see, these images did not cause the error message you saw in Step 10.

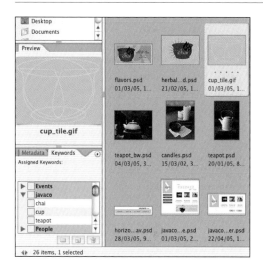

13. Click **cup_tile.gif** to select it. Take a look at the **Keywords** panel.

*Notice **cup_tile.gif** does not have any keywords associated with it. The GIF file format is one of the formats generated from Photoshop CS2 that cannot store metadata, which is what Bridge uses to store keywords. You can, however, apply keywords to many file formats, including Photoshop files, Illustrator files, InDesign files, GoLive files, PDFs, JPEGs, TIFFs, and EPS files. Now that you've applied keywords to your images, it's time to search using the keywords.*

14. In the **Favorites** panel, click **Desktop**. Choose **Edit > Find**.

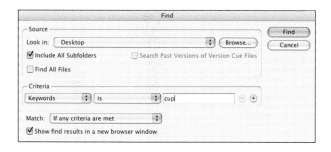

15. In the **Find** dialog box, choose **Desktop** from the **Look in** pop-up menu. Turn on the **Include All Subfolders** option. Match the **Criteria** settings to the ones shown in the illustration here. Turn on the **Show find results in a new browser window** option. Click **Find**.

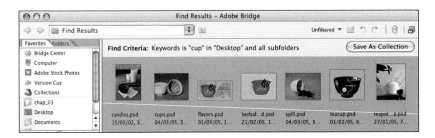

*Notice a new Bridge window opens, and it contains all the images with the keyword **cup**.*

16. Choose **Edit > Find**. The settings should be the same as you specified in Step 15. Replace the word **cup** with the word **chai**, and click **Find**.

*Notice a new Bridge window opens, and it contains all the images with the keyword **chai**.*

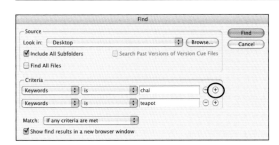

17. Choose **Edit > Find**. The settings should be the same as you specified in Step 16. Click the **Add** (+) button to add a new **Criteria** field. Match the settings to the ones shown in the illustration here.

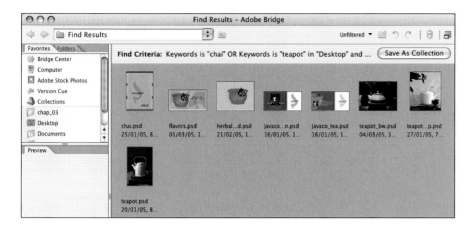

*Notice a new Bridge window opens, and it contains all the images with the keywords **chai** and **teapot**.*

As you can see from this exercise, assigning keywords and searching using keywords as the criteria can be a very powerful feature. As you grow as a designer, so will the number of files on your computer. If you take the time to keep them organized, you'll make your life a lot easier.

18. Close Bridge and return to Photoshop CS2 for the next chapter.

MOVIE | stock_photos.mov

When you're designing Web graphics, you'll often want to use photographs to illustrate a message or evoke a feeling about your Web site. If you don't have the time or technology to take your own photographs, you'll often rely on stock photography. Bridge offers an easy way to search for and purchase from over 230,000 royalty-free images from some of the leading stock photography agencies, such as Photodisc, Comstock Images, Digital Vision, Imageshop, and Amana. To learn how to use the **Adobe Stock Photos** feature in Bridge, check out **stock_photos.mov** in the **movies** folder on the **PCS2Web HOT CD-ROM**.

You've finished another chapter! Next, you'll learn about choosing and using color to create Web graphics.

4

Working with Color

| Color Profiles and the Web |
| Color Considerations for Windows and Mac Users |
| The Decline of Web-Safe Color | Choosing Colors |
| Creating and Saving Custom Swatches |
| Recoloring Layered Images | Copying Color as HTML |

chap_04

PCS2Web HOT CD-ROM

Photoshop CS2 and ImageReady CS2 offer great tools for working with color. In this chapter, you'll learn tips for choosing, editing, and changing colors. You'll explore the Color Picker dialog box, the Colors palette, and the Swatches palette, then recolor images with the colors you choose.

You'll find less emphasis on Web-safe color in this chapter than you might expect from lynda.com books. Today, there's less reason to use to a Web-safe palette, because 8-bit (256-color) computer display systems are practically obsolete. You'll read about the decline of Web-safe color in this chapter, but you'll also discover how to access Web-safe colors when you need them. Along the way, you'll determine how to limit the Color Picker dialog box to Web-safe colors, load a special lynda.com swatch of Web-safe colors, create your own custom color swatches, and copy color values as HTML.

Color Management and the Web

Have you ever looked at the same image on two computers and noticed the colors look different? This very common problem results because there is no calibration standard for computer displays.

In the print world, designers use ICC (International **C**olor **C**onsortium) profiles to make sure the colors onscreen look the same as when they're printed. ICC profiles are embedded into the image file format and provide additional information about the color characteristics of the image. This color information stays with the file so any device can display or print the file accurately.

Unfortunately, ICC profiles are of no value when designing Web graphics. First, embedding ICC profiles increases the image size, which negatively impacts how quickly graphics load. In some cases, a color profile can be upwards of 750 KB, which may be larger than an optimized Web graphic. Second, most Web browsers can't read color profiles. As a result, any efforts you make to keep colors consistent using ICC profiles will be lost as soon as your graphics hit the Web.

Color Management Considerations for Windows Users

In an effort to standardize how colors appear onscreen, Microsoft and Hewlett-Packard developed a color space called sRGB. The goal of sRGB is to produce a reliable and repeatable method for describing color that can be understood by computer monitors and that picks up one calibration based on an average monitor.

Photoshop CS2 offers a preset in the Color Settings dialog box, which uses sRGB as the default working space and will convert any RGB image you open to use sRGB. Therefore, you can rest assured that you'll view all graphics you create for the Web using sRGB. Here's how you can access the preset:

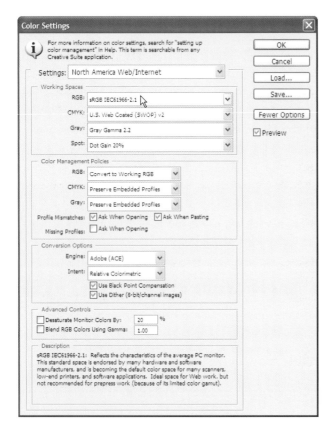

Choose **Edit > Color Settings**. In the **Color Settings** dialog box, choose **North America Web/Internet**. Notice **RGB Working Space** is set to **sRGB** and **RGB Color Management Policies** is set to **Convert to Working RGB**.

Before you begin designing Web graphics, there is one more thing you need to set up—**Proof Colors**. By default, **Proof Colors** is turned on and set to **Working CMYK**, which can negatively impact how your colors appear onscreen.

To change the default **Proof Colors** setup, make sure you do not have any documents open in Photoshop CS2. Choose **View > Proof Setup > Windows RGB** to specify **Windows RGB** as the default **Proof Colors** setup. To make sure **Proof Colors** is turned on, open a file in Photoshop CS2 and take a look at the contents of the **View** menu. You'll know **Proof Colors** is turned on if you see a checkmark beside it in the **View** menu. If it's not, choose **View > Proof Colors**.

The settings described here apply to a Windows setup. Unfortunately, there are a few more factors to consider if you're using a Mac, or if you think your viewers will be using Macs to view your Web site. At the moment, sRGB is a color workspace that is supported natively on Windows, and only in certain applications, such as Photoshop CS2, on the Mac.

Windows Gamma Settings vs. Mac Gamma Settings

sRGB calls for a standard gamma setting of 2.2. What is gamma, you might ask? The gamma affects the appearance of your computer screen by defining a midpoint for gray. Gamma affects the grays, or values between white and black. Windows computers use a 2.2 gamma setting; Macs use a 1.8 gamma setting. As a result, colors appear darker on Windows than they do on Macs. In Photoshop CS2 and ImageReady CS2, there are ways to preview how an image will look on each platform. Here's how:

If you're using Photoshop CS2 and ImageReady CS2 on Windows, open an image in Photoshop CS2 or ImageReady CS2. In Photoshop CS2, to preview how the image will appear on a Mac, choose **View > Proof Setup** and choose **Macintosh RGB**. In Image Ready CS2, choose **View > Preview > Standard Macintosh Color**. To make sure **Proof Colors** is turned on, take a look a the contents of the **View** menu. If there is a checkmark beside **Proof Colors**, it's turned on. If it's not turned on, choose **View > Proof Colors**.

If you're using Photoshop CS2 and ImageReady CS2 on a Mac, open an image in Photoshop CS2 or ImageReady CS2. In Photoshop CS2, to preview how the image will appear on Windows, choose **View > Proof Setup > Windows RGB**. In ImageReady CS2, choose **View > Preview > Standard Windows Color**.

Color Management Considerations for Mac Users

If you're using a Mac, you need to consider a few things about your color settings before you begin designing Web graphics.

If you use the **North America Web/Internet** preset in the **Color Settings** dialog box, Photoshop CS2 will use the sRGB working space, which has a gamma of 2.2. On a Mac, this is can be a problem because colors will appear different in Photoshop CS2 than in most other Mac applications that don't support sRGB, including ImageReady CS2, Macromedia Dreamweaver, and most Web browsers. This can be frustrating when you're designing Web graphics on a Mac because your colors will constantly look different, depending on which application you use.

If you're using a Mac, you should still use the **North American Web/Internet** preset in the **Color Settings** dialog box but use **Proof Colors** (Photoshop CS2) or **Preview** (ImageReady CS2) if you want to simulate how your images will appear in other programs and Web browsers on a Mac.

With no document open in Photoshop CS2, choose **View > Proof Setup > Monitor RGB** to make it the default **Proof Colors** setup. To make sure **Proof Colors** is turned on, take a look at the contents of the **View** menu. If there is a checkmark beside **Proof Colors**, it's turned on. If it's not turned on, choose **View > Proof Colors**.

With no document open in ImageReady CS2, choose **View > Preview > Uncompensated Colors** to make it the default **Preview** setup.

TIP | Adjusting Gamma Settings on a Mac

If you think your Web site will have a larger Windows audience, you may want to change your Mac OS X gamma setting to 2.2 so you can accurately see how the colors will appear on Windows in all applications. This change may save you from potential unanticipated revisions to lighten up your graphics. Keep in mind that changing your gamma settings will affect all applications, not just Photoshop CS2.

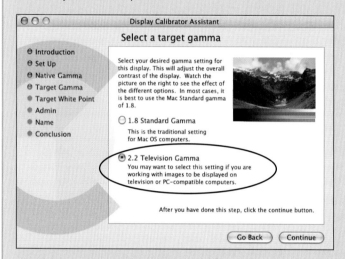

To change your gamma settings, use the calibration utilities built into Mac OS X. Open the **System Preferences** dialog box, and choose **Displays**. Click the **Color** button, then click the **Calibrate** button. Click **Continue** to navigate to the **Select a target gamma** screen. Select **2.2 Television Gamma**. Click **Continue** until you reach the **Give the profile a name screen**. Type a name for your profile. Click **Continue**.

Remember, changing your gamma to match Windows affects all applications, including Photoshop CS2, ImageReady CS2, other graphics applications, HTML editors, and Web browsers.

TIP | Finding Additional Color Management Help

As you can see, color management is a complex topic! Photoshop CS2 ships with additional documentation about color management. For more information, refer to the Color Management topic in the Photoshop CS2 online Help.

The Decline of Web-Safe Color

The concept of Web-safe color was introduced when the Web first gained popularity in the mid-1990s. At that time, the majority of computers were far less capable than they are today. These old computers had 8-bit video cards that could only display 256 colors. Most graphics professionals owned computers with 24-bit video cards that could display millions of colors but cost a lot more money than the average 8-bit consumer computer. For this reason, Web designers with 24-bit video cards produced colors that could not be accurately portrayed on more common computers with 8-bit video cards. As a result, the Web-safe palette was born. It was first published and described in Lynda Weinman's book, *Designing Web Graphics* (1996).

The Web-safe palette contains only 216 colors. However, the 216 colors are special because these colors can be accurately displayed on computers with 8-bit video cards. The term *Web-safe color* refers to the use of these special 216 colors. Other terms, such as the *Web palette*, *browser-safe palette*, *216-color palette*, *Netscape palette*, or *6 × 6 × 6 color cube*, all refer to the same 216 colors.

You should limit your color choices to the Web-safe color palette if you think your Web site will be viewed on computers with 8-bit video cards. Just a few short years ago, almost all computers had 8-bit video cards. When Web design first emerged as a design medium, designers needed to understand Web-safe color and how to create Web graphics in this limited palette. This was no picnic because the browser-safe palette is not very visually exciting—it contains mostly highly saturated colors of medium value and not many light or dark colors, nor many muted or tinted tones.

Good news! In most cases, it is now safe to design Web graphics without the Web-safe palette. Today, very few users have computers with 8-bit video cards, and most users can see any color you design with. If you're unsure about when to use the Web-safe palette, the answer depends on your audience and client. If you're designing Web sites for alternative online publishing devices, such as cell phones, PDAs, or Internet appliances, you may still need to use a Web-safe palette. Most of those devices currently display only 8-bit color, and some display only 1-bit (black-and-white) color.

Some companies still feel it's a badge of Web design honor to work with Web-safe colors, so you might want to know how to use them. Keep in mind there's no harm in using the Web-safe palette—it simply limits your choices to 216 colors. There's no right or wrong about using Web-safe colors as long as you're able to combine them in pleasing and effective ways. As you'll learn in this chapter, the Web-safe palette is built into the color picking tools in Photoshop CS2 and ImageReady CS2, so it's easy to create or recolor a Web graphic in Web-safe colors.

What Happens on an 8-Bit System If You Don't Use Web-Safe Colors?

It's useful to know what your Web graphics will look like if you don't design with Web-safe colors, and your Web site is viewed on a computer with an 8-bit video card. Two problems will occur.

First, the colors you set in the HTML code, such as the colors of page backgrounds, text, and links, will shift in the 8-bit viewer's Web browser. Unpredictable color shifts can cause text or links to be unreadable against a like-colored background.

Graphic viewed in 24-bit color

Same graphic viewed in 8-bit color

Close-up in 24-bit color

Close-up in 8-bit color

The second problem involves color. If you create flat artwork, such as illustrations or cartoons, with non-Web-safe colors, these colors will appear dithered (made up of tiny dots) when the image is viewed on a computer with an 8-bit video card. The unwanted dithering is the result of the viewer's 8-bit video card trying to simulate colors it can't display. The previous illustrations demonstrate what dithering looks like, which shows why you'll want to use Web-safe colors in your flat art Web graphics if you think you may have viewers with 8-bit video cards. However, the opposite is true for photographic content. If you're preparing photographs for the Web, never force them to Web-safe colors. When an 8-bit browser displays photographic images, it converts them to 8-bit on-the-fly and does a better job than if you'd converted them yourself.

In the next few exercises, you'll learn how to use the color picking tools Photoshop CS2 and ImageReady CS2 offer and how to select Web-safe colors when you need them. You'll also learn how to pull it all together with quick and easy ways to recolor layered images.

Choosing Color in Photoshop CS2 and ImageReady CS2

There are three tools for choosing color in Photoshop CS2 and ImageReady CS2: the Color Picker dialog box, the Color palette, and the Swatches palette. Here's an overview of all three:

Photoshop CS2 and ImageReady CS2 Color Tools

Option	Description
Color Picker dialog box 	The **Color Picker** dialog box is the most visual and comprehensive tool for choosing color. You can access it by clicking the **foreground** or **background** colors in the **Toolbox** or by clicking any color swatch inside a dialog box or on the **Options** bar. You'll learn how to use the **Color Picker** dialog box in Exercise 1.
Color palette 	The **Color** palette is an easy way to choose color if you know the exact RGB, HSB, CMYK, or Lab values you wish to use because it provides a useful interface for typing the value and for previewing the color. You can access the **Color** palette by choosing **Window > Color**. See the sidebar at the end of Exercise 1 to learn how to use the **Color** palette.
Swatches palette 	The **Swatches** palette is an excellent way to save colors you wish to use in more than one image. Instead of remembering color values or choosing the colors again from scratch, you can save custom swatches to use in future projects. You can access the **Swatches** palette by choosing **Window > Swatches**. You'll learn how to use the **Swatches** palette in Exercise 3.
Eyedropper tool 	The **Eyedropper** tool lets you sample color from an existing image. If you have an image that uses colors you like, you can use the **Eyedropper** tool to sample the color so you can use the color in your projects. You can access the **Eyedropper** tool by selecting it in the **Toolbox** or by pressing **I**, which is the keyboard shortcut. You'll learn how to use the **Eyedropper** tool in Exercise 3.

I. [PS/IR] Choosing Colors from the Color Picker

In this exercise, you'll learn how to choose color, including Web-safe colors, using the Color Picker dialog box.

1. Click the **Foreground Color** in the **Toolbox** to open the **Color Picker** dialog box.

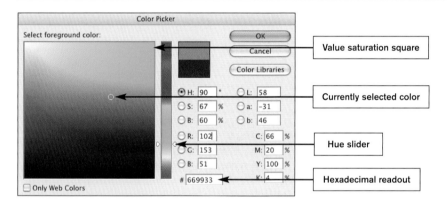

2. Adjust the **Hue** slider and use the circle in the value saturation square to adjust the currently selected color.

Notice the hexadecimal readout at the bottom of the ***Color Picker*** *dialog box. If you move the arrows up the vertical* ***Hue*** *slider, you'll see these readout numbers and the colors on the screen change.*

3. Click the **H, S, B** (Hue, Saturation, Brightness); **R, G, B** (red, green blue); or **L** (lightness), **a** (a-axis: green to magenta), **b** (b-axis: blue to yellow) radio buttons, continue to adjust to **Hue** slider, and watch the value saturation square change.

H, S, and B stand for hue, saturation, and brightness. The ***Color Picker*** *dialog box in the previous screen shot is set to view by hue. All the different radio buttons offer different ways of seeing and picking colors. You may find these choices help you quickly find colors that fit together.*

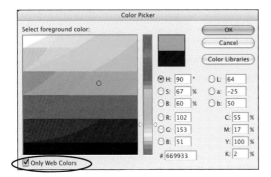

4. Turn on the **Only Web Colors** option.

Notice the value saturation square changes, and you are limited to only a few colors. By turning on **Only Web Colors***, you are limiting yourself to the Web-safe color palette described earlier in this chapter. Using this option will ensure you always choose a Web-safe color.*

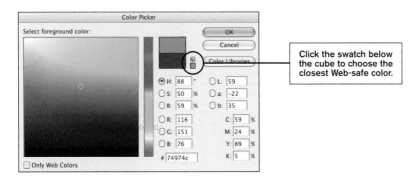

Click the swatch below the cube to choose the closest Web-safe color.

5. Turn off the **Only Web Colors** option. Move the circle inside the value saturation square until you see a small cube with a square swatch to the right of the color preview. The cube alerts you when you've selected a non-Web-safe color. Click the small swatch below the cube.

The selection jumps to the closest Web-safe color, and the cube disappears.

6. In the **Color Picker** dialog box, click **OK**.

Notice the color you chose now appears as the **Foreground Color** *in the* **Toolbox***.*

NOTE | ImageReady CS2 and Photoshop CS2 Color Picker Differences

ImageReady CS2 has a Color Picker dialog box almost identical to the one in Photoshop CS2. The Color Picker dialog box in ImageReady CS2 lacks some print-oriented features, such as feedback about Lab color, CMYK color, and out-of-print-gamut warnings. Photoshop CS2 can be used to design print or Web graphics; ImageReady CS2 is intended specifically for designing Web graphics.

TIP | Choosing Colors from the Color Palette

In addition to choosing colors from the **Color Picker** dialog box, you can choose colors from the **Color** palette in Photoshop CS2 and ImageReady CS2. You may find it easier to choose colors from the **Color** palette because you can leave it open at all times instead of reopening and closing the **Color Picker** dialog box. To choose colors from the **Color** palette, first make sure the **Color** palette is open. If it's not, choose **Window > Color**.

Adjust the sliders, or type a value into the **Color** palette. You can choose to have different sliders appear in the **Color** palette, including **RGB** sliders, **HSB** sliders, **CMYK** sliders, **Lab** sliders, and **Web Color** sliders by choosing the appropriate slider from the **Color** palette menu.

Choose **Web Color Sliders** from the **Color** palette menu.

When you use the Web Color sliders, the colors automatically snap to Web-safe colors at the tick marks. If you want to override the Web Color sliders, hold down the **Option** key (Mac) or **Alt** key (Windows). As soon as you choose a color outside the Web-safe color range, the alert cube appears to the left of the sliders. You can choose the closest Web-safe color by clicking the swatch below the cube, just as you did in the Color Picker dialog box.

Note: In Photoshop CS2, you must choose Web Color sliders to view the alert cube. Because ImageReady CS2 is designed specifically for creating Web graphics, the alert cube is available for all sliders.

2. [PS/IR] Choosing Color with the Swatches Palette

Another way to choose color in Photoshop CS2 and ImageReady CS2 is to use the Swatches palette. Photoshop CS2 and ImageReady CS2 ship with a number of prebuilt swatches, including swatches based on Web-safe colors. In addition, you can load swatches created and saved by other Photoshop CS2 and ImageReady CS2 users.

1. Make sure the **Swatches** palette is visible. If it's not, choose **Window > Swatches**.

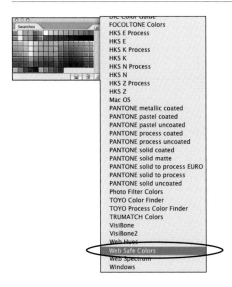

2. Open the **Swatches** palette menu. Notice there are three Web swatches—**Web Hues**, **Web Safe Colors**, and **Web Spectrum**. All three swatches contain the 216 Web-safe colors. The only difference is how the swatches are organized.

3. Choose **Web Safe Colors** from the **Swatches** palette menu.

4. Click **OK** to replace the current swatches in the **Swatches** palette with the contents of the **Web Safe Colors** swatches.

*Note: If you click **Append** instead of **OK**, the contents of the **Web Safe Colors** swatches are automatically added to the current swatches in the **Swatches** palette.*

*The **Swatches** palette automatically updates with the **Web Safe Colors** swatches. Increase the size of the **Swatches** palette so it displays all the colors by dragging the resize handle in the bottom-right corner of the palette. You can choose any color in the **Swatches** palette by clicking it. When you click a color in the **Swatches** palette, the **Foreground Color** in the **Toolbox** automatically changes to reflect your choice.*

*Next, you'll learn how to load the **lynda.com** swatches from the **PSCS2Web HOT CD-ROM**.*

Lynda Weinman and Bruce Heavin wrote a book together in 1997 called Coloring Web Graphics, *which is now out of print. Bruce developed a series of Web swatches for that book, which he organized aesthetically to make it easier to choose Web-safe colors. One of these swatches is included inside the **chap_04** folder of the **PSCS2Web HOT CD-ROM** for you to load and use.*

5. Choose **Replace Swatches** from the **Swatches** palette menu.

Note: *If you choose **Replace Swatches** from the **Swatches** palette menu, you will replace the current swatches with the swatches you're loading. If you choose **Load Swatches**, you will append the current swatches with the colors of the swatches you're loading*

6. Navigate to the **chap_04** folder you copied to your **Desktop** from the **PSCS2Web HOT CD-ROM** and choose **color.aco**. Click **Load** (or **Open** in ImageReady CS2).

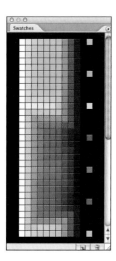

7. Expand the **Swatches** palette window using the resize handle in the bottom-right corner of the palette. Then, use the scroll bar to view the swatches. The swatches are organized by hue (up and down), by value (right to left), and saturation (up and down).

Note: *Many of the colors are repeated to present an array of colors organized to make choosing color easy. Seeing all the hues together is nice. If you want to pick a red, for example, you can view the choices easily. Seeing all the dark colors and/or colors of equal saturation together is also helpful.*

8. Choose **Reset Swatches** from the **Swatches** palette menu. Click **OK** to replace the **lynda.com** swatches with the default swatches.

3. [PS] _____Creating and Saving Custom Swatches

When you're designing Web graphics, you'll often want to use a custom color scheme—either one you create for a project or one a client provides for you—and limiting the Swatches palette to contain only those colors can be helpful. In this exercise, you'll learn how to create custom swatches two ways—by selecting colors from existing swatches and by sampling colors from an image by using the Eyedropper tool.

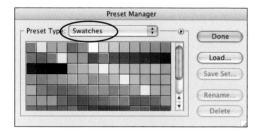

1. Choose **Edit > Preset Manager**. In the **Preset Manager** window, choose **Swatches** from the **Preset Type** pop-up menu.

*The **Preset Manager** in Photoshop CS2 lets you organize content libraries, such as swatches, as well as other application presets, such as brushes, gradients, styles, and patterns. In this exercise, you'll only learn about swatches. For more information about customizing other content libraries, refer to the Photoshop CS2 online Help.*

2. Choose **Web Hues** from the **Preset Manager** menu. Click **OK** to replace the current swatches with the **Web Hues** swatches.

*This will replace the currently loaded swatches in the **Preset Manager** (and in the **Swatches** palette) with swatches of Web-safe colors organized by hue.*

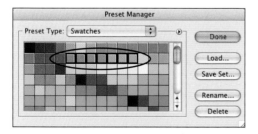

3. Choose a few colors by holding down the **Cmd** (Mac) or **Ctrl** (Windows) key and clicking the colors you want to be part of your new custom swatches.

4. Click **Save Set**. In the **Save** dialog box, type the name **Custom Web Colors.aco** in the **Save As** field (Mac) or **Save in** field (Windows). Be sure to include the **.aco** extension because it will identify the file as Photoshop CS2 swatches. Navigate to the **Color Swatches** folder in the **Presets** folder in the Photoshop CS2 application folder. Click **Save**.

*By saving the **Custom Web Colors.aco** file in the **Presets\Color Swatches** folder, you'll see the swatches in the **Swatches** palette menu the next time you launch Photoshop CS2.*

5. In the **Preset Manager**, click **Done**.

6. Close and relaunch Photoshop CS2.

*You have to close and reopen Photoshop CS2 in order to see the new swatches listed in the **Swatches** palette menu.*

7. Choose **Custom Web Colors** from the **Swatches** palette menu. Click **OK** to replace the current swatch with the **Custom Web Colors** swatch, which will now open up in the **Swatches** palette.

Next, you'll make custom swatches from the colors in an existing image.

8. Open **javaco_tea.psd** from the **chap_04** folder you copied to your **Desktop**.

9. Choose **Preset Manager** from the **Swatches** palette menu.

*The **Preset Manager** opens with your **Custom Web Colors**.*

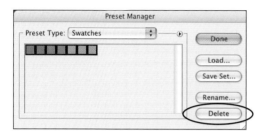

10. Press **Cmd+A** (Mac) or **Ctrl+A** (Windows) to select all the **Custom Web Colors**. In the **Preset Manager** dialog box, click **Delete** to delete all the colors. Click **Done** to close the **Preset Manager**.

*The **Swatches** palette should now appear empty, leaving you to add custom swatches from scratch.*

11. In the **Toolbox**, select the **Eyedropper** tool.

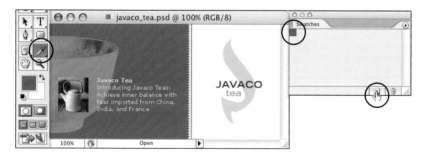

12. With the **Eyedropper** tool selected, click a color in the open image, then at the bottom of the **Swatches** palette click the **New Color** button.

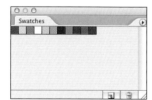

*This will add the color you selected in the image to the **Swatches** palette. Repeat this step until you have all the colors you want in the **Swatches** palette.*

13. Choose **Save Swatches** from the **Swatches** palette menu. Navigate to the **Color Swatches** folder in the **Presets** folder in the Photoshop CS2 application folder, and name the swatches **javaco_tea.aco.** Click **Save.**

*The next time you launch Photoshop CS2, the **javaco_tea.aco** swatches you just created will appear in the list of swatches in the **Swatches** palette menu.*

14. Close the image. You don't need to save your changes.

TIP | Saving Swatches to Use in Other Adobe Creative Suite 2 Programs

Photoshop CS2 has a new option for saving swatches—**Save Swatches for Exchange.** This option lets you save swatches created in Photoshop CS2 and use the swatches in other Adobe Creative Suite 2 programs, including Illustrator CS2 and InDesign CS2. Likewise, Illustrator CS2 and InDesign CS2 also have the Save Swatches for Exchange option, which lets you create and save custom swatches in those programs and use the saved swatches in Photoshop CS2.

Here's how to use the Save Swatches for Exchange option in Photoshop CS2:

Choose **Save Swatches for Exchange** from the **Swatches** palette menu.

In the **Save** dialog box, give the **Swatches** a name but be sure to keep the **.ase** extension. The **.ase** extension is what allows Illustrator CS2 and InDesign CS2 to understand the information contained in the file and open the contents as swatches.

4. [PS/IR] _____ Recoloring Layered Images

Now that you've learned how to choose colors in different ways, how do you make images using those colors? You could brush or paint with any color at any time. You could also use fill tools. This next exercise focuses on how to recolor an existing image. It gives you a chance to work with the Lock Transparent Pixels feature, which lets you easily recolor layered images.

1. Choose **Reset Swatches** from the **Swatches** palette menu. When asked if you want to replace the current color swatches with the default colors, click **OK**.

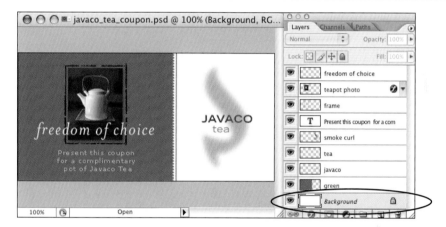

2. Open **javaco_tea_coupon.psd** from the **chap_04** folder you copied to your **Desktop**. Make sure the **Layers** palette is visible. If it's not, choose **Window > Layers**.

Have a look at the contents of the **Layers** palette. This image is composed of multiple layers. It's helpful to set up your files with separate layers like this and give the layers meaningful names so you can work with each layer individually, as we will do in this exercise. If you're wondering what layers are all about, not to worry, Chapter 5, "Working with Layers," will teach you everything you need to know about layers.

3. At the bottom of the **Layers** palette, click the **Background** layer to select it.

Right now the image is colored using shades of greens. To change the color scheme to shades of red (or any other color choices you'd prefer), you'll be working with one layer at a time, starting with the **Background** layer.

4. Choose a **light beige** from the **Swatches** palette, or use the **Eyedropper** tool to sample **light beige** from the photograph inside the image.

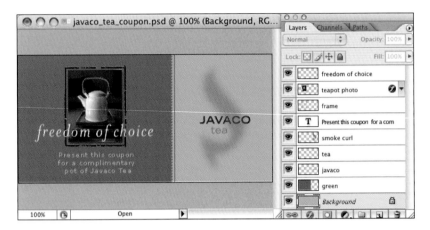

5. To fill the **Background** layer with the color you chose, press **Option+Delete** (Mac) or **Alt+Backspace** or **Alt+Delete** (Windows).

*This is a fantastic shortcut for filling a layer with a color because it is faster than using the **Edit > Fill** menu command or the **Paint Bucket** tool.*

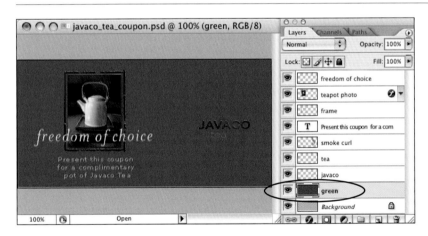

6. Click the **green** layer in the **Layers** palette to select it. Choose a dark red from the **Swatches** palette, or use the **Eyedropper** tool to sample **dark red** from the photograph inside the image. Press **Option+Delete** (Mac) or **Alt+Backspace** or **Alt+Delete** (Windows).

Notice the entire layer is now filled with dark red. In the following steps, you'll learn a valuable trick to recolor just the green area and not the entire layer.

7. Press **Cmd+Z** (Mac) or **Ctrl+Z** (Windows) to undo the dark red fill.

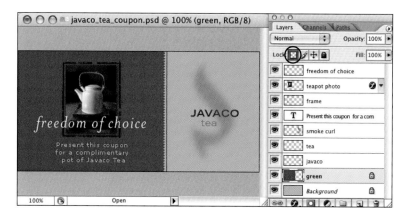

8. In the **Layers** palette, click the **Lock Transparent Pixels** button. Press **Option+Delete** (Mac) or **Alt+Backspace** or **Alt+Delete** (Windows).

Lock Transparent Pixels protects the transparent areas of the layer. When you fill the layer with a new color, Photoshop CS2 fills only the areas of the layer that contains colored pixels, and it preserves the transparent areas. I can't tell you how many students I've watched try to use the Magic Wand or other selection tools to select shapes on layers in order to fill them. The technique you learned here works much better because it's easier, it fills only areas of the layer with colored pixels, and it doesn't leave rough edges on color fills.

9. Click the **javaco** layer to select it, and click the **Lock Transparent Pixels** button. Using the same **dark red**, fill the **javaco** layer by pressing **Option+Delete** (Mac) or **Alt+Backspace** or **Alt+Delete** (Windows).

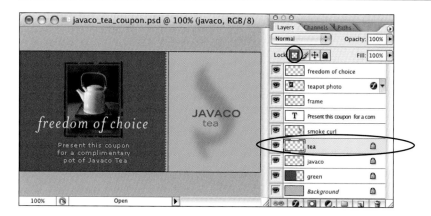

10. Choose a **medium red** from the **Swatches** palette, or use the **Eyedropper** tool to sample color from the photograph. Click the **tea** layer in the **Layers** palette, and click the **Lock Transparent Pixels** button. Press **Option+Delete** (Mac) or **Alt+Backspace** or **Alt+Delete** (Windows).

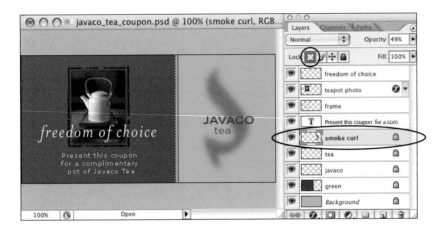

11. Choose a **dark red** from the **Swatches** palette, or sample **dark red** from the image using the **Eyedropper** tool. Click the **smoke curl** layer to select it, and click the **Lock Transparent Pixels** button. Press **Option+Delete** (Mac) or **Alt+Backspace** or **Alt+Delete** (Windows).

*This step is particularly cool. Notice the smoke curl is slightly blurry. The **Lock Transparent Pixels** maintains the blurry quality of the smoke curl while recoloring it with the dark red.*

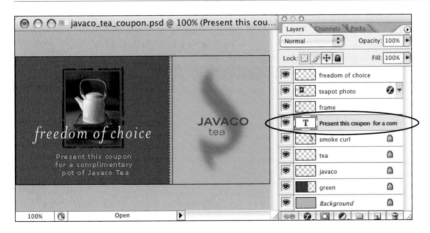

12. Choose a **light beige** from the **Swatches** palette, or sample **light beige** from the image using the **Eyedropper** tool. Click the **Type** layer (the layer with the **T** icon) to select it. Press **Option+Delete** (Mac) or **Alt+Backspace** or **Alt+Delete** (Windows).

*Notice you did not have to turn on the **Lock Transparent Pixels** option—in fact, you can't because it's dimmed. This is the default behavior for an editable type layer—it automatically preserves the transparent areas when you fill the layer.*

13. Choose a **dark red** from the **Swatches** palette, or sample **dark red** from the image using the **Eyedropper** tool. Click the **frame** layer to select it, and click the **Lock Transparent Pixels** button. Press **Option+Delete** (Mac) or **Alt+Backspace** or **Alt+Delete** (Windows).

*Like the **smoke curl** layer, the **frame** layer has a wide variation in the transparent versus nontransparent areas. The **Lock Transparent Pixels** option maintains this variation beautifully!*

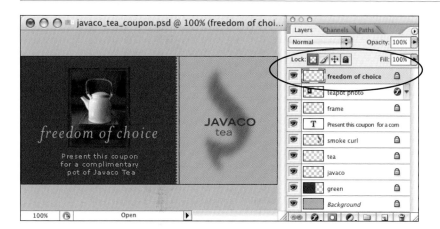

14. Choose a **light beige** color from the **Swatches** palette, or sample **light beige** from the image using the **Eyedropper** tool. Click the **freedom of choice** layer to select it, and click the **Lock Transparent Pixels** button. Press **Option+Delete** (Mac) or **Alt+Backspace** or **Alt+Delete** (Windows).

Now all the layers in your image should be recolored from shades of green to shades of beige and red.

15. Close the file. You don't need to save your changes.

The skills covered in this exercise will help you recolor layered images as you design Web graphics in Photoshop CS2.

5. [PS] _____Copying Color as HTML

This exercise will be of value to you if you're used to programming your own HTML code or working with an HTML editor. If you don't work with HTML, feel free to skip this exercise! If you're making an image in Photoshop CS2 or ImageReady CS2 and want to capture a color from that image to place inside your HTML code so you can color a background, link, or other element in HTML to match the image, you can use the **Copy Color as HTML** feature.

When you specify color in HTML code, you must use values from the hexadecimal numbering system, which uses letters and numbers to identify colors. You don't have to worry about knowing any more than that when you're working with Photoshop CS2 and ImageReady CS2—they take care of the math for you.

The **Copy Color as HTML** feature converts any RGB (red, green, blue) color value to a string of hexadecimal digits. This command also puts the hexadecimal color value into your computer's clipboard so you can paste it as text into other applications—a handy feature if you're writing HTML from scratch and want to place a color value into your code.

1. In Photoshop CS2, open **javaco_tea.psd** from the **chap_04** folder you copied to your **Desktop**.

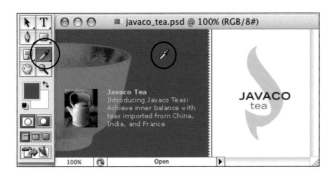

2. Select the **Eyedropper** tool from the **Toolbox**, then click a color in the background of the image.

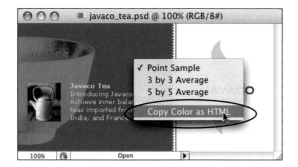

3. Ctrl+click (Mac) or **right-click** (Windows) and choose **Copy Color as HTML** from the shortcut menu.

*If you're working in ImageReady CS2, first click on a color in the document with the **Eyedropper** tool, then **Ctrl+click** (Mac) or **right-click** (Windows) anywhere in the document and choose **Copy Foreground Color as HTML**.*

Note: *The **Eyedropper** tool must be selected for this to work in Photoshop CS2 or ImageReady CS2.*

4. Open a text editor, such as TextEdit (Mac) or Notepad (Windows), or an HTML editor, such as Adobe GoLive or Macromedia Dreamweaver, and choose **Edit > Paste** or press **Cmd+V** (Mac) or **Ctrl+V** (Windows). When you paste the color into a text editor or HTML editor, it will look like this: **color="#336666"**.

5. Close both files without saving.

Now you know how easy it is to choose color in Photoshop CS2 and ImageReady CS2 and how to apply your color choices quickly and efficiently to a layered image. These programs make choosing and using color fun and creative by offering the best color-picking tools around.

In the next chapter, "Working with Layers," you'll learn the benefits of working with layers when you design Web graphics.

5

Working with Layers

| Creating and Renaming Layers |
| Reordering, Flipping, and Moving Layers |
| Adjusting Blending Mode, Fill, and Opacity |
| Moving and Aligning Layers | Using Layer Groups and Comps |
| Using Adjustment Layers | Using Layer Styles |

chap_05

PCS2Web HOT CD-ROM

Understanding layers is one of the most important cornerstones in mastering Photoshop CS2. When you use layers, you separate elements in your images so they can be edited individually. With layers, you can isolate image areas and apply special effects, or change the location, color, or opacity without affecting the contents of the other layers. Photoshop CS2 offers many ways to organize your layers, including layer groups and layer comps, which you'll learn about in detail in this chapter.

Throughout the exercises in this chapter you'll learn the new, object-based interface, which lets you use the Cmd (Mac), Ctrl (Windows), and Shift keys to select, move, and group multiple layers at the same time. You'll also learn about another useful new feature in Photoshop CS2–Smart Guides–which automatically appear when you're moving the contents of layers to help you achieve proper alignment and placement.

Layers are powerful, yet complex, and offer maximum flexibility to experiment and make changes when you're designing Web graphics. Once you complete the exercises in this chapter, you'll be comfortable with most layering tasks.

What Are Layers?

When **layers** were introduced to Photoshop in 1996, they revolutionized the way designers created, edited, and saved their work. Prior to layers, pixels in an image had to be deleted or canceled out if other pixels were placed on top of them. This changed when layers came along.

Separating areas of an image into layers allows you to have stacks and stacks of images on individual layers that can be changed or moved without altering the pixels in the image areas above or below. As long as you don't "flatten" your layers, each layer remains independent of the others so you can make infinite changes.

Although layers were originally introduced to Photoshop to help designers edit specific areas of images, they have grown more powerful with each new version. Now, layers not only isolate areas or elements of an image, but they can contain layer masks, patterns, gradients, solid fills, and vector shapes. Plus, you can use layer groups to organize your layers or use layer comps to save different configurations of visibility, position, and blending all within the same file! These concepts might seem a bit abstract now, but the following exercises will make them come to life for you.

I. [PS/IR] _____Creating and Renaming Layers

The exercises in this chapter are intended to help you understand how layers work and the benefit of using them in your designs. In this first exercise, you'll learn about layer visibility, how to create layers, how to delete layers, and how to rename layers.

1. Open **teapot.psd** from the **chap_05** folder you copied to your **Desktop**. Make sure the **Layers** palette is visible. If not, choose **Window > Layers**.

*Have a look at the contents of the **Layers** palette. Notice that each element of the image is on a separate layer. Also notice that each layer, except **Layer 2**, has an **Eye** icon beside the layer thumbnail. The **Eye** icon indicates that the visibility of the layer is turned on.*

2. Click the **Eye** icon beside the **Layer 2** thumbnail to toggle on and off the visibility of **Layer 2**.

Notice how the composition changes when Layer 2 is turned on—an orange lantern appears behind the leaves. Experiment with the visibility of the other layers by toggling the Eye icons. When you've finished, leave the visibility of all layers turned on, including Layer 2.

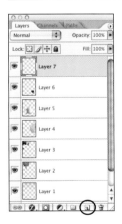

3. In the **Layers** palette, click **Layer 6** to select it. Click the **New Layer** button at the bottom of the **Layers** palette.

Notice that a new, empty layer, called Layer 7, was created above Layer 6. When you create a new layer, it is automatically created above the currently selected layer in the Layers palette.

4. With **Layer 7** selected in the **Layers** palette, select the **Eyedropper** tool from the **Toolbox** and sample color from the beige pattern in the fan.

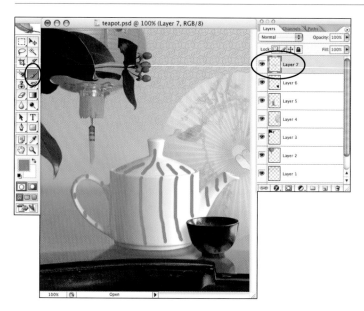

5. With **Layer 7** still selected in the **Layers** palette, select the **Brush** tool from the **Toolbox** and draw some stripes onto the teapot.

Creating the stripes on a separate layer means you can turn off the visibility, or move or delete the layer, without affecting the layers below.

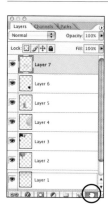 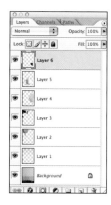

6. Click and drag **Layer 7** onto the **Trash** button at the bottom of the **Layers** palette. When you release your mouse, **Layer 7** will be deleted, and the rest of the composition will be unaffected by the changes you made.

2. [PS/IR] _____Reordering, Flipping, and Moving Layers

In the last exercise, you learned how to adjust the layer visibility to alter a composition. In this exercise, you'll learn more complex techniques for altering a composition, including how to reorder layers in the Layers palette, how to copy layers from other documents, and how to move layers.

1. If you followed the last exercise, you should have **teapot.psd** open. If not, go back and complete Exercise 1. Make sure the **Layers** palette is visible. If not, choose **Window > Layers**.

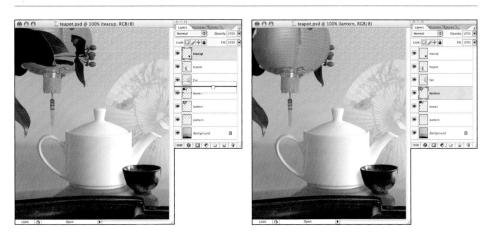

2. Take a look at the stacking order of the layers in the **Layers** palette. Click and drag the **lantern** layer above the **leaves** layer.

Notice how changing the order of the layers in the **Layers** *palette affects the composition. Before you moved the layer, the lantern appeared behind the leaves. Now, the lantern appears in front of the leaves.*

3. Click and drag the **teacup** layer below the **teapot** layer.

*Just like with the last step, changing the stacking order of the layers in the **Layers** palette affects the composition. The teacup now appears behind the teapot.*

4. Click the **Background** layer to select it. Try to click and drag to reposition it elsewhere in the **Layers** palette.

*Did you notice that you cannot move the **Background** layer? A **Background** layer, which is generated automatically when you create a new document with a nontransparent background, has different properties than a layer. You can't move it unless you convert it to a layer, which you'll do in the next step.*

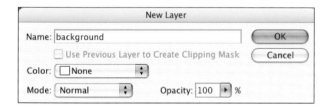

5. Double-click the **Background** layer to open the **New Layer** dialog box. Type **background** in the **Name** field and click **OK**.

*Notice that the lock icon disappeared and the layer name is no longer in italics. Now, you can click and drag to reposition the layer anywhere in the **Layers** palette.*

*In Step 2, you moved the **lantern** layer above the **leaves** layer, which altered the composition. After making that change, you can barely see the leaves, which make the composition look unbalanced. It might look better if the **lantern** layer was repositioned above the fan. In the next step, you'll do just that!*

6. In the **Layers** palette, click the **lantern** layer to select it. Select the **Move** tool from the **Toolbox**. Click and drag the **lantern** to the upper-right corner of the composition, as shown in the illustration here.

*With the lantern in the upper-right corner of the composition, the fan is blocking it from view. In the next step, you'll adjust the order of the layers in the **Layers** palette to make the lantern a prominent focal point in the image.*

7. In the **Layers** palette, click and drag the **lantern** layer above the **fan** layer.

The upper-left corner of the lantern has an unattractive edge

Now, the lantern appears in the foreground of the image, and it has a stronger focal point. Unfortunately, this new position reveals an unattractive edge on the left side of the lantern. Not to worry, you'll fix that in the next step.

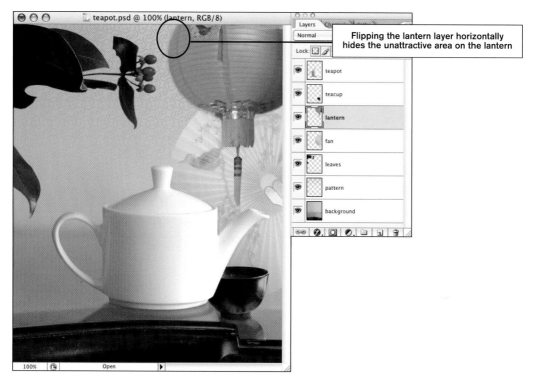

8. With the **lantern** layer selected in the **Layers** palette, choose **Edit > Transform > Flip Horizontal**. In the **Toolbox**, select the **Move** tool and reposition the **lantern** layer (if necessary).

*By flipping the **lantern** layer horizontally, the unattractive edge on the left side of the lantern is no longer visible. It's still part of the layer, but now it's on the right. By positioning the layer in the upper-right corner, you can't see it because it is outside the viewable document area. One of the benefits of working with layers is that their contents don't always have to be inside the viewable document area.*

9. Leave **teapot.psd** open for the next exercise.

3. [PS/IR] ———— Adjusting Blending Mode, Fill, and Opacity

In this exercise, you'll learn how to copy a layer from another file, and you'll learn how to use blending modes to change the appearance of layers without making any permanent changes to the contents of the layers. You'll also learn how to adjust layer opacity and fill.

1. If you followed the last exercise, you should have **teapot.psd** open. If not, go back and complete Exercises 1 and 2. Make sure the **Layers** palette is visible. If not, choose **Window > Layers**.

2. Leave **teapot.psd** open, choose **File > Open**, and open **javaco.psd** from the **chap_05** folder you copied to your **Desktop**.

Drag the javaco layer from javaco.psd onto the teapot in teapot.psd

3. Click the **teapot.psd** image to make it the active image. In the **Layers** palette, click the **teapot** layer to select it. Click the **javaco.psd** image to make it the active image. Click and drag the **javaco** layer onto the **teapot.psd** image.

*The contents of the **javaco** layer now appear in the **teapot.psd** file above the **teapot** layer. If the **javaco** layer is not positioned above the **teapot** layer in the **Layers** palette, click and drag to reposition it above the **teapot** layer, as shown in the illustration here.*

4. With the **javaco** layer selected in the **Layers** palette, select the **Move** tool from the **Toolbox**. Click and drag the **javaco** logo to reposition it onto the center of the teapot.

As it is, the logo looks like a flat logo sitting on top of the teapot, rather than part of the teapot, which is the desired effect. In the next step, you'll change the blending mode to make the logo look like it's printed onto the teapot.

5. With the **javaco** layer selected in the **Layers** palette, choose **Color Burn** from the **Blending Mode** pop-up menu.

Notice how the logo blends with the shadows and highlights of the teapot, which makes it look less like a flat logo on top of a three-dimensional object.

Blending modes control the way the color and tone of the pixels on a selected layer interact with pixels on the layers below. The Color Burn blending mode uses the color and tone in the layer below (in this case the teapot) and uses that information to blend the selected layer (in this case the javaco logo). As a result, the selected layer takes on tones, shadows, and highlights of the layer below.

Although the logo on the teapot looks better than it did before you changed the blending mode, you can still make some adjustments to make the logo appear more like it's printed onto the teapot.

6. With the **javaco** layer selected, decrease the opacity of the **javaco** layer to **95** using the **Opacity** slider in the upper-right corner of the **Layers** palette. Decrease the **fill** of the **javaco** layer to **85%** using the **Fill** slider, which is below the **Opacity** slider in the upper-right corner of the **Layers** palette.

*Adjusting the opacity and fill of the selected layer (in this case the javaco logo), more of the layer below (in this case the teapot) shows through. In this case, reducing the opacity and fill of the **javaco** layer make the logo appear as if it is monogrammed or painted onto the teapot because it naturally reflects the shadows and highlights of the teapot.*

7. Experiment with the different blending modes, opacity, and fill of the **javaco** layer (and other layers, if you like!) to see what other interesting effects you can produce. The more your experiment with layers, the more you'll understand them.

8. Close **teapot.psd** and **javaco.psd**. You don't need to save your changes.

4. [PS/IR] _____Moving and Aligning Layers

In the past two exercises, you used the Move tool to reposition a layer. What if you want to move more than one layer? Or, what if you want to move layers so they are perfectly aligned? When you design Web sites, you'll want to make sure all the elements on your page are carefully aligned so your Web site looks properly balanced. In this exercise, you'll learn how to move and align layers. You'll also learn how to use Smart Guides—a new feature in Photoshop CS2—to align layers.

1. Open **javaco_buttons.psd** from the **chap_05** folder you copied to your **Desktop**. Make sure the **Layers** palette is visible. If not, choose **Window > Layers**.

The file is made up of a number of layers—each layer is a different element of the javaco tea Web page. The elements are scattered all over the page. In this exercise, you'll move and align the elements into proper position.

2. In the **Layers** palette, click the **top bar** layer to select it. In the **Toolbox**, select the **Move** tool. Click and drag to reposition the green bar at the top of the image.

Notice it's a bit tricky to determine how to get the layer perfectly centered.

3. Press **Cmd+Z** (Mac) or **Ctrl+Z** (Windows) to undo the move you made in the last step. Choose **View > Show > Smart Guides**.

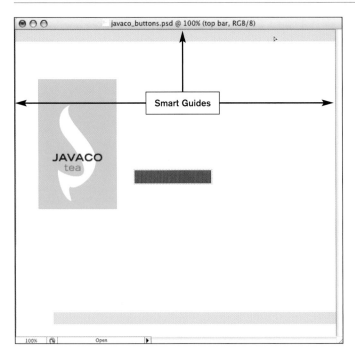

4. With the **top bar** layer selected in the **Layers** palette and the **Move** tool selected in the **Toolbox**, click and drag to position the green bar at the top of the image.

Notice as you click and drag, pink guidelines automatically appear to show you when the layer is aligned. When you see pink guide lines at the sides of the image, as shown in the illustration that follows, you'll know the layer is perfectly centered.

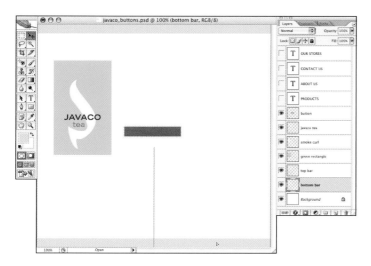

5. Click the **bottom bar** layer from the **Layers** palette. With the **Move** tool selected in the **Toolbox**, click and drag to reposition the **bottom bar** layer at the bottom of the image. Just like in the last step, when you see the pink guidelines at the sides of the image, you'll know the layer is perfectly aligned.

Next, you'll reposition the javaco tea logo and the green rectangle. Because the logo and the smoke curl are perfectly positioned onto the green rectangle, it's important to move all three layers together.

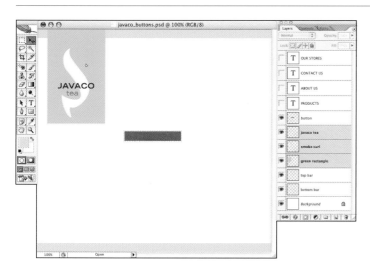

6. In the **Layers** palette, click the **green rectangle** layer to select it. Hold down the **Cmd** (Mac) or **Ctrl** (Windows) key and click the **smoke curl** and **javaco tea** layers to multiple-select all three layers. With the **Move** tool selected in the **Toolbox**, click and drag to move all three layers at the same time.

Multiple-selecting layers allows you to move all three layers at the same time.

TIP | Multiple-Selecting Layers

Multiple-selecting layers is a new feature in Photoshop CS2. It provides an easy way to perform commands on more than one layer at the same time. You can multiple-select layers two ways in Photoshop CS2:

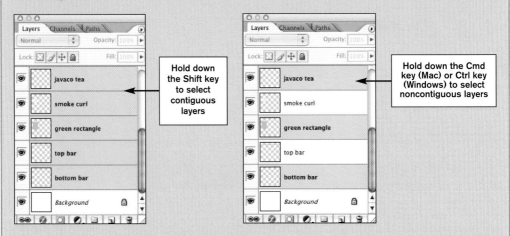

Hold down the Shift key to select contiguous layers

Hold down the Cmd key (Mac) or Ctrl key (Windows) to select noncontiguous layers

To multiple-select contiguous layers (layers next to each other in the **Layers** palette), click the first layer you want to select, hold down the **Shift** key, and click the last layer you want to select. You'll automatically multiple-select the layers in-between.

To multiple-select noncontiguous layers (layers not side-by-side in the **Layers** palette) click the first layer you want to select, hold down the **Cmd** key (Mac) or **Ctrl** key (Windows), and click the other layer(s) you want to select.

7. In the **Layers** palette, click the **button** layer. Choose **Duplicate Layer** from the **Layers** palette menu.

8. In the **Duplicate Layer** dialog box, type **button 2** in the **As** field and click **OK**.

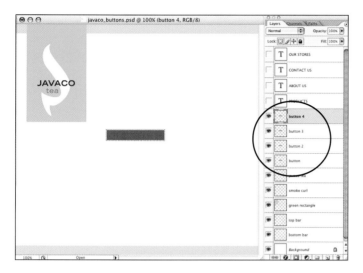

9. Repeat Steps 7 and 8 twice to create two more buttons. Name the buttons **button 3** and **button 4**, as shown in the illustration here.

*Wondering why you can't see the three buttons you created in the document window? When you duplicate layers, they automatically copy in the same location. Right now, they are stacked on top of each other. In the next step, you'll move the buttons with the **Move** tool so you can see all four.*

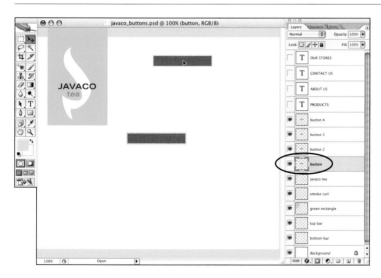

10. In the **Layers** palette, click the **button** layer. With the **Move** tool selected in the **Toolbox**, click and drag to reposition the button inside the document window. Don't concern yourself with the **Smart Guides**—just reposition the button anywhere inside the document window.

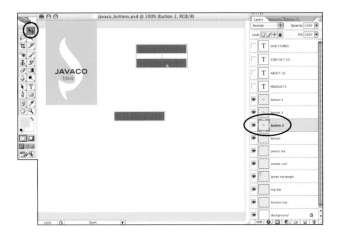

11. In the **Layers** palette, click the **button 2** layer. With the **Move** tool selected in the **Toolbox**, click and drag to reposition the button. This time, use the **Smart Guides** to align the buttons vertically, as shown in the illustration here.

As you reposition the button, you'll see vertical and horizontal guides. At this time, just concern your-self with the vertical guides to make sure your buttons are aligned vertically.

12. In the **Layers** palette, click the **button 3** layer. With the **Move** tool selected in the **Toolbox**, click and drag to reposition the button. Again, use the **Smart Guides** to align the buttons.

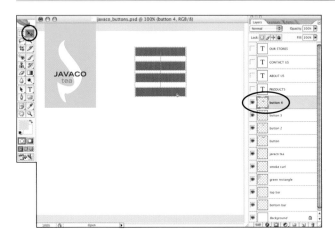

13. In the **Layers** palette, click the **button 4** layer. With the **Move** tool selected in the **Toolbox**, click and drag to reposition the button. Again, use the **Smart Guides** to align the buttons.

Now you have all four buttons aligned vertically. However, the distribution (the spacing between the buttons) is inconsistent. Not to worry, you'll fix the distribution in the next steps.

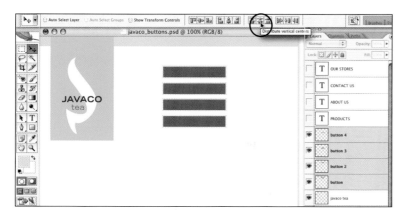

14. In the **Layers** palette, click the **button** layer to select it. Hold down the **Shift** key and click the **button 4** layer to multiple-select the layers in-between. Click the **Distribute Vertical Centers** button on the **Options** bar.

The buttons are now distributed evenly.

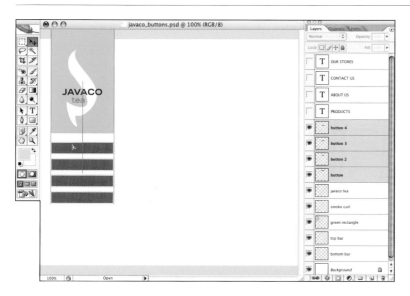

15. With the **button**, **button 2**, **button 3**, and **button 4** layers selected in the **Layers** palette and the **Move** tool selected in the **Toolbox**, click and drag to reposition the layers below the **green rectangle** layer. Use the **Smart Guides** to make sure the layers are vertically aligned.

Next, you'll center text on the buttons.

16. Turn on the visibility of the **PRODUCTS**, **ABOUT US**, **CONTACT US**, and **OUR STORES** layers.

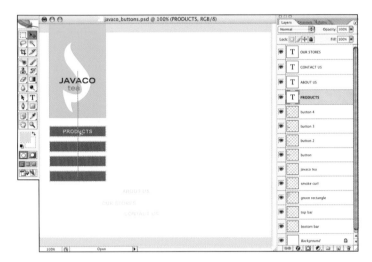

17. In the **Layers** palette, click the **PRODUCTS** layer to select it. With the **Move** tool selected in the **Toolbox**, position it onto the first button. Use the **Smart Guides** to align the text to the button, as shown in the illustration here.

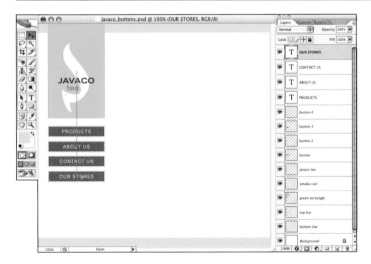

18. In the **Layers** palette, click the **ABOUT US** layer to select it. With the **Move** tool selected in the **Toolbox**, position it onto the second button using the **Smart Guides** to align the text to the button. Repeat the same process for the **CONTACT US** and **OUR STORES** layers, as shown in the illustration here.

As you can see from this exercise, moving, aligning, and distributing is just another great benefit of working with layers. When you're designing Web graphics—specifically Web buttons or entire Web interfaces—it's critical to have all the elements perfectly aligned and spaced.

19. Close **javaco_buttons.psd**. You don't need to save your changes.

TIP | Linking Layers

Another useful technique when you're working with layers is linking. Sometimes you'll have two or more layers you want to keep together and move at the same time. In such a case, multiple-selecting the layers each time can be tedious. Linking layers ensures when you move one layer, the layers linked to it move at the same time. Here's how linking works:

1. In the **Layers** palette, multiple-select the layers you want to link.

2. At the bottom of the **Layers** palette, click the **Link** button. Notice each of the linked layers now has a lock icon, indicating it is linked.

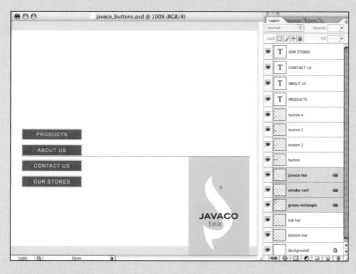

3. Select the **Move** tool from the **Toolbox**. Click and drag. Notice the layers you linked all move at the same time.

5. [PS]_____Using Layer Groups

As you begin to develop more complex images and compositions, keeping your layers organized becomes increasingly important. One way to organize your layers is to place them into a **layer group**. A layer group is a group of layers stored inside a folder in the Layers palette. Layer groups keep your layers organized if you have lots of layers in an image. In addition to the organizational benefit, layer groups also let you make changes to multiple layers at the same time, including visibility, opacity, position, alignment, and blending mode. Note: In ImageReady CS2, layer groups are called **layer sets**.

1. Open **javaco_home.psd** from the **chap_05** folder you copied to your **Desktop**. Make sure the **Layers** palette is visible. If not, choose **Window > Layers**.

*Take a moment to look at the contents of the **Layers** palette—turn on and off the visibility of different layers so you can see how the individual elements make up the composition. This file has a lot of layers. In fact, the file contains so many layers, you can't view them without scrolling through the **Layers** palette. Having a file with this many layers can be confusing and difficult to manage. However, keeping all the individual layers is important so you can retain the flexibility you learned about earlier in this chapter. The best way to organize a file, such as this one, is to use layer groups.*

2. Scroll all the way to the bottom of the **Layers** palette. Toggle on the visibility of the **white back-ground**, **bottom bar**, **top bar**, **green rectangle**, **smoke curl**, and **javaco tea** layers. Make sure you leave the layer visibility turned on when you've finished.

As you can see, these layers make up the background elements of the javaco tea home page, and they could logically be organized into a layer group.

3. In the **Layers** palette, click the **white background** layer to select it. Hold down the **Shift** key and click the **javaco tea** layer to multiple-select all six layers. Press **Cmd+G** (Mac) or **Ctrl+G** (Windows).

*The **white background**, **bottom bar**, **top bar**, **green rectangle**, **smoke curl**, and **javaco tea** layers are now contained inside a layer group called **Group 1**. Just like with layers, you can rename layer groups so they have descriptive and meaningful names.*

4. In the **Layers** palette, double-click the **Group 1** layer group. A bounding box will appear around the layer name. Type **background elements** and press **Return** (Mac) or **Enter** (Windows). When you've finished, click the arrow beside the **background elements** layer group to close the layer group.

As you can see, you've already decreased the size of the layer stack just by creating one layer group!

*Using the keyboard shortcut **Cmd+G** (Mac) or **Ctrl+G** (Windows) is only one way you can create layer groups. You'll learn other techniques in the following steps.*

5. In the **Layers** palette, toggle on the visibility of the **products button, about us button, our stores button, contact us button, PRODUCTS, ABOUT US, OUR STORES,** and **CONTACT US** layers. As you can see, these layers make up the navigation buttons for the javaco tea home page.

6. In the **Layers** palette, click the **CONTACT US** layer to select it. Click the **New Layer Group** button at the bottom of the **Layers** palette to create a new, empty layer group above the **CONTACT US** layer.

7. In the **Layers** palette, click the **CONTACT US** layer to select it. Hold down the **Shift** key and click the **products button** to multiple-select the layers in-between. Click and drag the selected layers into the **Group 1** layer group.

8. Double-click the **Group 1** layer group. When the bounding box appears, rename the layer group to **buttons** and press **Return** (Mac) or **Enter** (Windows). Click the arrow beside the **buttons** layer group to close the layer group.

9. In the **Layers** palette, toggle on the visibility of the **banner background**, **flavor of the month**, and **banner cup** layers. These layers make up the contents of the flavor of the month banner at the bottom of the page.

 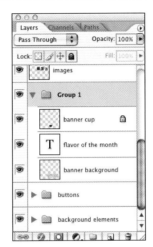

10. In the **Layers** palette, click the **banner background** layer to select it. Hold down the **Shift** key and click the **banner cup** layer to multiple-select the layers in-between. Drag the selected layers onto the **New Layer Group** button at the bottom of the **Layers** palette.

*When you release the mouse, you'll notice a new layer group, **Group 1**, was automatically created in the **Layers** palette, and the layers you selected in the last step are automatically grouped inside the layer group.*

11. Double-click the **Group 1** layer group. When the bounding box appears, type **banner** and press **Return** (Mac) or **Enter** (Windows) to rename the layer group. Click the arrow beside the **banner** layer group to close the contents of the layer group.

12. In the **Layers** palette, toggle the visibility of the **the**, **essence**, and **of tea** layers. These layers make up the contents of the *The Essence of Tea* tagline at the top of the javaco tea home page.

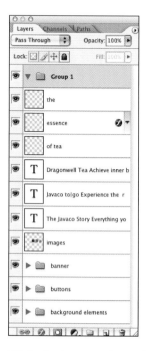

13. In the **Layers** palette, click the **the** layer to select it. Click the **New Layer Group** button at the bottom of the **Layers** palette to create a new, empty layer group.

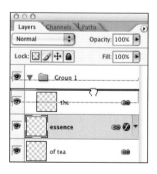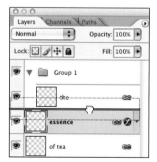

14. Click and drag the **the** layer into the **Group 1** layer group, then drag the **essence** layer into the **Group 1** layer group.

*Notice you can drag the **essence** layer onto the **Group 1** layer group, between the **Group 1** layer group and the **of tea** layer, or below the **of tea** layer. Where you position the layer as you drag it into the layer group will depend on where it is positioned in the layer stack inside the layer group. Experiment with these different options. When you've finished, make sure the **essence** layer is positioned above the **of tea** layer inside the **Group 1** layer group.*

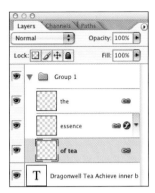

15. Click the **of tea** layer to select it. Click and drag it inside the **Group 1** layer group so it is positioned below the **essence** layer.

16. Double-click the **Group 1** layer group. When the bounding box appears, type **tagline** and press **Return** (Mac) or **Enter** (Windows) to rename the layer group. Click the arrow beside the **tagline** layer group to close the layer group.

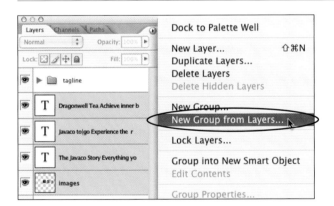

17. You should now have four layers in the **Layers** palette that are not contained in a layer group. Click the **images** layer to select it. Hold down the **Shift** key and click the **Dragonwell Tea Achieve...** layer to multiple-select the layers in-between. Choose **New Group from Layers** from the **Layers** palette menu to group the selected layers into a layer group.

*Note: There are two options for creating layer groups in the **Layers** palette menu: **New Group** creates a new, empty layer group; **New Group from Layers** creates a new layer group with the currently selected layers in the **Layers** palette.*

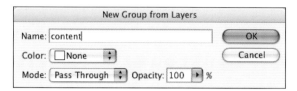

18. Type **content** in the **Name** field of the **New Group from Layers** dialog box. Click **OK**. Click the arrow beside the **content** layer group to close the layer group.

Take a look at the Layers palette. What was once an overwhelming number of layers is now organized into six layer groups. Layer groups offer more than just an organizational benefit. Layer groups also allow you to execute commands, including moving and changing opacity, over all the layers contained inside a layer group.

19. In the **Layers** palette, click the **buttons** layer group to select it. Select the **Move** tool from the **Toolbox**. Click and drag the buttons around onscreen.

Notice all four buttons, including the text, move all together.

20. Press **Cmd+Z** (Mac) or **Ctrl+Z** (Windows) to undo the move you made in the last step.

21. With the **buttons** layer group still selected in the **Layers** palette, decrease the opacity to **50%**.

*Notice the opacity changes on all the layers inside the **buttons** layer group.*

22. Press **Cmd+Z** (Mac) or **Ctrl+Z** (Windows) to undo the opacity change you made in the last step.

As you can see from this exercise, layer groups are an excellent way to keep your layers organized. They offer a quick way to perform the same command, such as moving or changing layer opacity, on more than one layer.

23. Close **javaco_home.psd**. You don't need to save your changes.

TIP | Nesting Layer Groups

Photoshop CS2 lets you nest layer groups up to a maximum of five levels. Nesting layer groups makes keeping your layers organized even easier. For example, if you are designing a Web page, you can create a layer group for the entire page, then create nested layer groups for different elements on the page such as the one shown in the illustration below. Since Web pages are made up of several elements, which are typically contained in separate layers, this is an excellent way for you to keep your layers organized. Further, nesting layer groups allows you to move and make changes to more than one layer group at the same time.

To create nested layer groups, click a layer inside a layer group to select it and click the **New Layer Group** button at the bottom of the **Layers** palette. A new layer group will be created inside the layer group you selected. You can also manually drag a layer group into another layer group to create a nested layer group, or you can drag layers into nested layer groups.

NOTE | ImageReady CS2 Layer Sets

In the last exercise, you used Photoshop CS2 to organize your layers into layer groups. ImageReady CS2 offers similar functionality with the layer sets feature. Unfortunately, it doesn't offer as many options for creating layer sets as Photoshop CS2 offers for creating layer groups. Here's how you can create layer sets in ImageReady CS2:

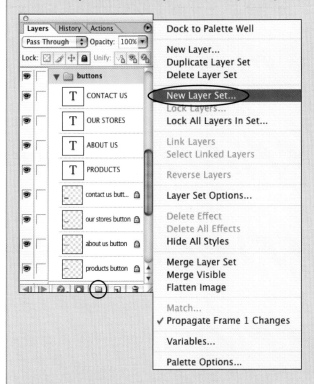

Click the **Layer Set** icon at the bottom of the **Layers** palette, or choose **New Layer Set** from the **Layers** palette menu. The new layer set will automatically appear above the currently selected layer in the **Layers** palette.

6. [PS/IR]_____Using Layer Comps

Layer comps let you save different configurations of layer visibility, position, and appearance all within the same file. This makes it easy to work with different variations of an image without having to save multiple versions of a file. For example, if you're creating a composition for a client, and you want to show different options, you can save a series of layer comps with the different variations in the same Photoshop CS2 file.

1. Open **teapot_comps.psd** from the **chap_05** folder you copied to your **Desktop**. Make sure the **Layers** and **Layer Comps** palettes are visible, as shown in the illustration here. If not, choose **Window > Layers** and **Window > Layer Comps**. **Note:** By default the **Layer Comps** palette is docked in the palette well. Click the **Layer Comps** tab and drag it out of the palette well, below the **Layers** palette.

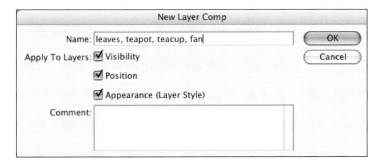

2. In the **Layer Comps** palette, click the **New Layer Comp** button. In the **New Layer Comp** dialog box, type **leaves, teapot, teacup, fan** in the **Name** field. Turn on the **Visibility**, **Position**, and **Appearance (Layer Style)** options, and click **OK**.

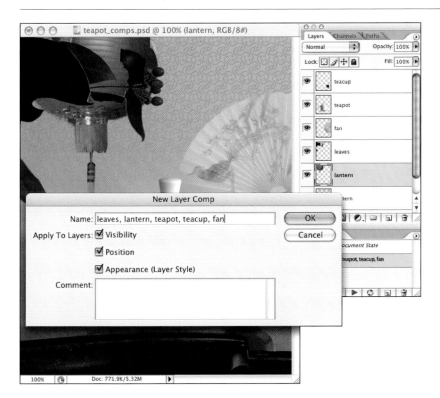

3. In the **Layers** palette, turn on the visibility of the **lantern** layer. In the **Layer Comps** palette, click the **New Layer Comp** button. In the **New Layer Comp** dialog box, type **leaves, lantern, teapot, teacup, fan** in the **Name** field. Make sure the **Visibility**, **Position**, and **Appearance (Layer Style)** options are turned on, and click **OK**.

4. Toggle between the two layer comps in the **Layer Comps** palette. Be sure to click in the square beside the layer comp name to show the two layer comps you created.

Notice the layer comps remember the visibility of the layers in the Layers palette as they were when you saved the layer comps.

5. In the **Layers** palette, turn off the visibility of the **fan** layer. Click the **lantern** layer to select it. Select the **Move** tool from the **Toolbox** and move the **lantern** layer over to the upper-right corner of the image window.

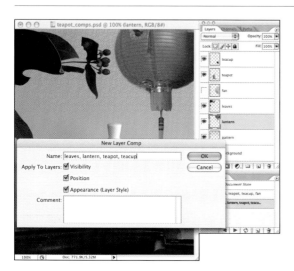

6. In the **Layer Comps** palette, click the **New Layer Comp** button. In the **New Layer Comp** dialog box, type **leaves, lantern, teapot, teacup** in the **Name** field. Make sure the **Visibility**, **Position**, and **Appearance** options are turned on and click **OK**.

7. Toggle between the three layer comps in the **Layer Comps** palette.

*Notice the layer comps remember the visibility and position of the layers in the **Layers** palette when you saved the layer comps.*

8. In the **Layers** palette, turn off the visibility of the **lantern** layer. In the **Layer Comps** palette, click the **New Layer Comp** button. In the **New Layer Comp** dialog box, type **leaves, teapot, teacup**. Make sure the **Visibility**, **Position**, and **Appearance (Layer Style)** options are turned on and click **OK**.

9. In the **Layers** palette, turn off the visibility of the **pattern** layer. In the **Layer Comps** palette, click the **leaves, teapot, teacup** layer comp to select it. At the bottom of the **Layers Comps** palette, click the **Update Layer Comp** button.

10. Toggle between the four layer comps in the **Layer Comps** palette.

*Notice the change you made to the visibility of the pattern layer affects only the **leaves, teapot, teacup** layer comp because it is the only one you updated.*

11. In the **Layers** palette, turn on the visibility of the **fan** layer. At the bottom of the **Layers** palette, choose **Color Overlay** from the **Layer Styles** pop-up menu.

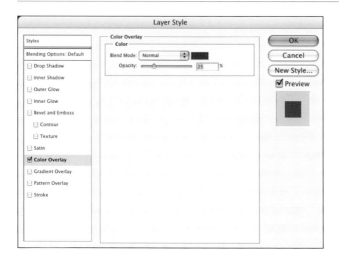

12. In the **Layer Style** dialog box, click the **Color Overlay** box to open the **Color Picker** dialog box. Choose a **dark green**, and click **OK** to close the **Color Picker** dialog box. Decrease the **Opacity** to **25%**, as shown in the illustration here, and click **OK** to close the **Layer Style** dialog box.

13. In the **Layer Comps** palette, click the **New Layer Comp** button. In the **New Layer Comp** dialog box, type **leaves, teapot, teacup, fan with overlay** in the **Name** field. Make sure the **Position, Visibility,** and **Appearance (Layer Style)** options are turned on. Click **OK**.

14. Toggle between the different layer comps in the **Layer Comps** palette. Notice the color overlay layer style you applied to the **fan** layer is only present in the **leaves, teapot, teacup, fan with overlay** layer comp.

As you can see, layer comps are an excellent way to save different configurations of a layered image in the same file. Experimenting with the visibility, position, and appearance of different combinations of layers will help you achieve the best possible composition.

15. Close **teapot_comps.psd**. You don't need to save your changes.

MOVIE | layer_comps.mov

To learn more about layer comps—specifically how you can use layer comps to save different pages of a Web site in the same Photoshop CS2 file—check out **layer_comps.mov** in the **movies** folder on the **PCS2Web HOT CD-ROM**.

7. [PS] Using Adjustment Layers

Adjustment layers let you make tonal and color changes without permanently modifying the image. When you use an adjustment layer, the changes you make are contained on a separate layer, and they affect all the layers below. If you change your mind about the changes you make to an image using adjustment layers, you can modify or delete those changes. Using adjustment layers is a great way to change contrast, hue, or color balance levels in an image. **Note:** You cannot create adjustment layers in ImageReady CS2, but ImageReady CS2 will recognize adjustment layers created in Photoshop CS2.

1. Open **candles.psd** from the **chap_05** folder you copied to your **Desktop**.

2. In the **Layers** palette, with the **candles** layer selected, choose **Hue/Saturation** from the **Create new fill or adjustment layer** pop-up menu.

*Notice the **Hue/Saturation** dialog box opens automatically. This dialog box has the same controls as the one you'd see if you chose **Image > Adjustments > Hue/Saturation**. Making hue and saturation changes with an adjustment layer offers more flexibility because you don't harm the original image in the process. Nondestructive editing is always best because it allows you the flexibility to experiment without making permanent changes to your image. You never know when you might need that original image again!*

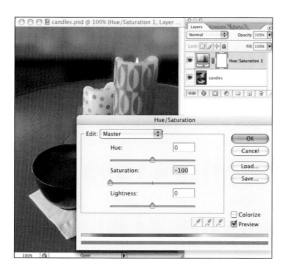

3. Reduce the **Saturation** to the lowest setting, and click **OK**.

Notice the image looks like a black-and-white image. Reducing the saturation in an image removes the appearance of color. However, because the image is still an RGB image, the color information still exists in the file. This is a great technique for converting color images to black-and-white because you can get back to the original color information when you need it.

4. Choose **Brightness/Contrast** from the **Create new fill or adjustment layer** pop-up menu. Increase the **Contrast** slider slightly, as shown in the illustration here. Click **OK**.

When you reduced the saturation, the image looked a bit washed out. Increasing the contrast helps define the blacks and whites in the image.

5. Choose **Color Balance** from the **Create new fill or adjustment layer** pop-up menu.

In Step 3, you reduced the saturation to produce a black-and-white image. Because reducing the saturation did not convert the image to black-and-white, color information still exists in this file. You'll use the Color Balance adjustment layer to add color back into this image.

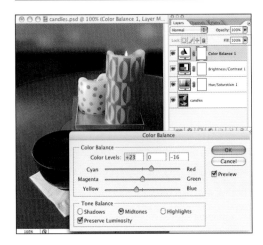

6. Move the **Cyan/Red** slider closer to **Red**. As you can see, you're slowly adding color back into the image. Move the **Yellow/Blue** slider closer to **Yellow**.

Now, instead of having a black-and-white image, you have a sepia-colored image.

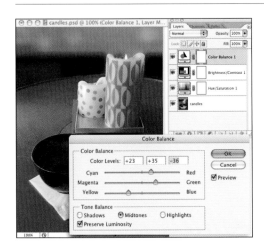

7. Move the **Magenta/Green** slider closer to **Green**, and move the **Yellow/Blue** slider closer to **Yellow** to change the tones in the image to shades of white, green, and black. Click **OK**.

Notice the contents of the Layers palette. Each adjustment layer you applied is its own separate layer.

8. Toggle the visibility of the adjustment layers you created and notice how the image changes with different combinations of layer visibility. When you turn off the visibility of all three adjustment layers, notice your original image is still intact. The changes you made in this exercise have not affected your image.

As you can see from this exercise, adjustment layers offer a nondestructive way to make tonal and color changes without permanently altering the pixels in the original image.

9. Close **candles.psd**. You don't need to save your changes.

8. [PS/IR]_____Using Layer Styles

Layer styles let you apply shadows, glows, bevels, textures, patterns, gradients, colors, and stroked outlines to layers. You'll find layer styles useful when you're creating Web graphics because you'll often want to apply drop shadows and glows to images and buttons. Layer styles are nondestructive—when you apply a layer style to a layer, the contents of the layer are not affected by the change. As a result, you can edit or delete the layer style at any time without affecting the original contents of the layer.

1. Open **javaco_pics.psd** from the **chap_05** folder you copied to your **Desktop**. Make sure the **Layers** and **Styles** palettes are visible. If not, choose **Window > Layers** and **Window > Styles**.

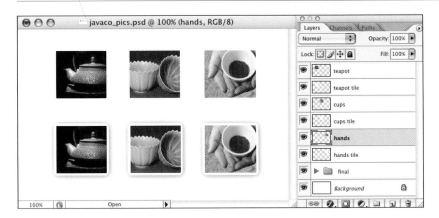

2. Toggle the visibility of the **final** layer group. Click the arrow beside the **final** layer group to take a look at contents of the **final** layer group in the **Layers** palette. When you've finished, close the **final** layer group, and turn off the visibility.

*Notice the white tiles behind the images in the **final** layer group have a drop shadow. Without the drop shadow, the tile behind the images isn't visible because it's the same color as the background. The drop shadow gives the image and the tile the effect of a white border around the image.*

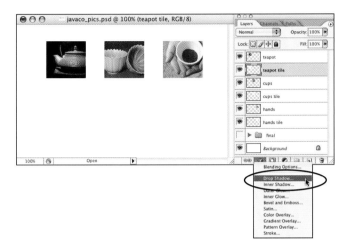

3. In the **Layers** palette, click the **teapot tile** layer to select it. Choose **Drop Shadow** from the **Layer Style** pop-up menu at the bottom of the **Layers** palette.

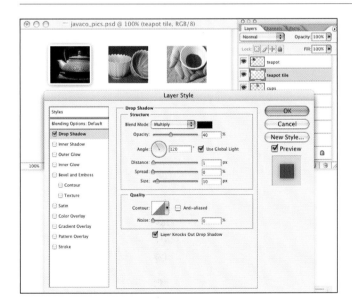

4. In the **Layer Style** dialog box, experiment with the different settings. Make sure the **Preview** option is checked so you can preview the drop shadow as you make changes in the **Layer Style** dialog box. When you've finished experimenting, match the settings in the **Layer Style** dialog box to the ones shown in the illustration here. Click **OK**.

Now you should see a drop shadow behind the white tile around the teapot image. Next, you'll apply the same settings to the other two images using two different methods.

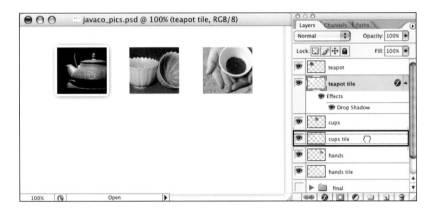

5. In the **Layers** palette, hold down the **Option** (Mac) or **Alt** (Windows) key and click and drag the **Drop Shadow** layer style onto the **cups tile** layer. Make sure you see a black box around the perimeter of the **cups tile** layer before you release the mouse.

*Notice the same layer style you created in the last step has been applied to the **cups tile** layer. Copying layer styles from one layer to another is an easy way to avoid setting the same properties in the **Layer Style** dialog box over and over. What if you want to use the properties you created in another document? In that case, you can save the layer style, which you'll learn in the next step.*

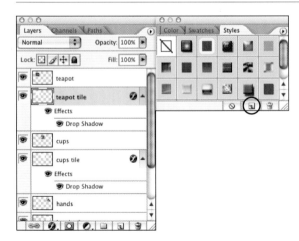

6. In the **Layers** palette, click the **teapot tile** layer to select it. In the **Styles** palette, click the **New Style** button.

7. In the **New Style** dialog box, type **tile drop shadow** in the **Name** field, and make sure the **Include Layer Effects** option is turned on. Click **OK**.

Now you can apply the saved layer style to any layer in any image.

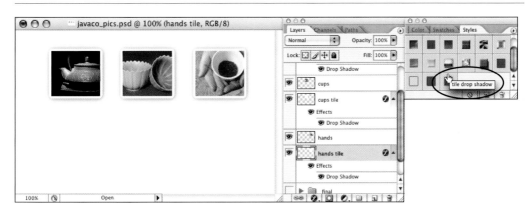

8. Click the **hands tile** layer to select it. In the **Styles** palette, click the **tile drop shadow** layer to apply the layer style you saved to the **hands tile** layer.

9. Toggle the visibility of the layer styles you created.

Notice the contents of the original image remain the same. Layer styles offer a nondestructive way to add interesting effects, such as drop shadows, to your images. You'll find yourself using layer styles a lot as you design Web graphics, and you'll use the skills you learned in this exercise in upcoming chapters.

10. Close **javaco_pics.psd**. You don't need to save your changes.

Photoshop CS2 and ImageReady CS2 Layer Styles

Photoshop CS2 and ImageReady CS2 have a number of different layer styles, which you'll use often when you're designing Web graphics. Here's a handy chart to show you the different styles:

Photoshop CS2 and ImageReady CS2 Layer Styles		
Layer Style	Functionality	Example
Drop Shadow	Adds a shadow behind the edges of a layer.	
Inner Shadow	Adds a shadow inside the edges of a layer, which makes the layer appear recessed.	
Outer Glow	Adds a glow to the outside edges of a layer.	
Inner Glow	Adds a glow to the inside edges of a layer.	
Bevel and Emboss	Adds a beveled edge or embossed edge to the edges of a layer, which makes the layer appear three-dimensional.	
Satin	Adds shading to the inside of a layer, which results in a satiny appearance.	
Color Overlay	Fills the layer with solid color. Because you can change the opacity, you can have the contents of the layer appear through the solid color.	
Gradient Overlay	Fills the layer with a gradient.	
Pattern Overlay	Fills the layer with a pattern.	
Stroke	Outlines the layer with a color, gradient, or pattern.	

MOVIE | clipping_masks.mov

Have you ever seen type that contains a photographic image inside the letters?

You can achieve that effect by using clipping masks in Photoshop CS2. To learn more about clipping masks, check out **clipping_masks.mov** in the **movies** folder on the **PCS2Web HOT CD-ROM**.

You've just finished a long chapter. Now that you've seen how powerful layers can be, put them to work, and boost your creativity and productivity as you create Web graphics in Photoshop CS2 and ImageReady CS2.

Next, you'll learn all about type!

6

Creating Type

| Creating Character Type | Creating Paragraph Type |
| Checking Spelling | Finding and Replacing Type |

chap_06

PCS2Web HOT CD-ROM

Working with type on the Web can be frustrating because HTML affords very little typographic control. Many Web designers avoid the limitations of HTML type by embedding text in GIF or JPEG files. Photoshop CS2 and ImageReady CS2 offer incredible tools for creating, formatting, and editing type, making it easy to create typographic imagery for the Web.

Photoshop CS2 and ImageReady CS2 offer two methods for creating type—character type and paragraph type. You'll learn about both in this chapter. You'll also learn to edit type using the spell-checking and find-and-replace features. Plus, you'll check out the new WYSIWYG (What You See Is What You Get) font menu in Photoshop CS2.

Vector-Based Type

Photoshop CS2 and ImageReady CS2 let you enter vector-based type directly into the document window. Vector-based type is defined mathematically rather than by pixels. As a result, type layers remain editable, which means you can scale, rotate, skew, or warp type without degrading its appearance.

Character Type vs. Paragraph Type

In Photoshop CS2 and ImageReady CS2, you can create character type and paragraph type.

Character type is best suited for short strings of type as short as a few characters or words, or as long as a few lines.

Paragraph type is best suited for longer sections of type, specifically type spanning more than one paragraph. Before you get started with the hands-on exercises, take a minute to familiarize yourself with the controls on the Type Options bar, the Character palette, and the Paragraph palette. It's important to understand these controls—you'll be using them in the exercises that follow.

The Type Options Bar

The Type Options bar is available when the Type tool is selected in the Toolbox. The Type Options bar provides a quick way to access some of the commonly used type formatting controls. The following illustration and chart describe each control.

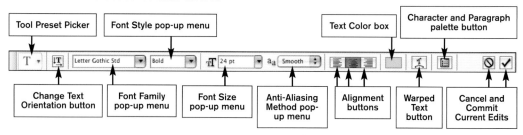

Type Options Bar Controls	
Feature	**Function**
Tool Preset Picker	Provides access to create and select tool presets
Change Text Orientation button	Toggles between the Horizontal Type tool and the Vertical Type tool
Font Family pop-up menu	Changes the font
Font Style pop-up menu	Changes the font style
Font Size pop-up menu	Changes the font size
Anti-Aliasing Method pop-up menu	Changes the anti-aliasing method, such as smooth or crisp
Alignment buttons (Left, Center, Right)	Aligns text to the left, center, or right
Font Color box	Opens the Color Picker dialog box, which lets you choose a font color
Warped Text button	Opens the Warp Text dialog box, which lets you warp your text in different ways, such as Arc, Flag, Twist, and so on
Character and Paragraph palette button	Toggles the Character and Paragraph palettes on and off
Cancel Current Edits button	Cancels edits and returns type to the last state
Commit Current Edits button	Commits edits when you've finished formatting type

The Character Palette

You can access the **Character** palette by choosing **Window > Character** or by clicking the toggle **Character and Paragraph** palette button on the **Type Options** bar. The Character palette provides access to all the formatting controls for character type. Some of the controls in the Character palette are the same as the ones you saw on the Type Options bar; others are only available in the Character palette. The following illustration and chart describe each control.

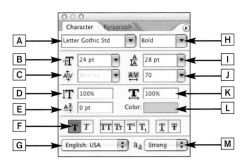

Character Palette Controls		
Feature		**Function**
A	Font Family pop-up menu	Changes the font
B	Font Size pop-up menu	Changes the font size
C	Kerning pop-up menu	Adjusts the spacing between characters
D	Vertical Scale field	Distorts type by scaling it on a vertical axis
E	Baseline field	Adjusts the baseline of type to create subscript or superscript
F	Faux Style Buttons	Applies faux styles to fonts that don't have bold or italic styles; from left to right: Faux Bold, Faux Italic, All Caps, Small Caps, Superscript, Subscript, Underline, Strikethrough
G	Language pop-up menu	Changes the dictionary referenced by the spell checker
H	Font Style pop-up menu	Changes the font style, such as bold or italic
I	Leading pop-up menu	Adjusts the amount of space between lines of type
J	Tracking pop-up menu	Adjusts the amount of space equally between selected characters in a word or paragraph

continues on next page

Character Palette Controls *continued*	
Feature	**Function**
K **Horizontal Scale field**	Distorts type by scaling it on a horizontal axis
L **Font Color box**	Changes the color of a selected character, word, or line of type
M **Anti-Aliasing Method pop-up menu**	Blends and smoothes edges

The Paragraph Palette

You can access the **Paragraph** palette by choosing **Window > Paragraph** or by clicking the toggle **Character and Paragraph** palette button on the **Type Options** bar. The Paragraph palette provides access to all the formatting controls for paragraph type. Some of the controls in the Paragraph palette are the same as the ones you saw on the Type Options bar; others are only available in the Paragraph palette. The following illustration and chart describe each control.

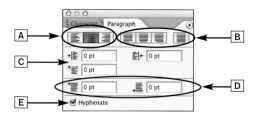

Paragraph Palette Controls	
Feature	**Function**
A **Alignment buttons (Left, Center, Right)**	Aligns paragraph type to the left, center, or right
B **Justification buttons (Last Left, Last Centered, Last Right, Justify All)**	Justifies paragraph type
C **Indent fields (Indent Left Margin, Indent Right Margin, Indent First Line**	Indents paragraph type
D **Spacing fields (Before Paragraph, After Paragraph)**	Adds space between paragraphs
E **Hyphenate check box**	Determines if words can be hyphenated over a line break

I. [PS/IR] Creating Character Type

In this exercise, you'll learn how to create and format character type using different controls on the Options bar and in the Character palette.

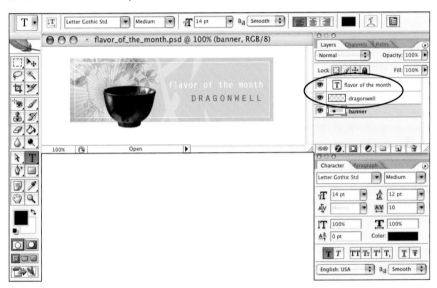

1. Open **flavor_of_the_month.psd** from the **chap_06** folder you copied to your **Desktop**. Make sure the **Layers** palette and the **Character** palette are visible. If not, choose **Window > Layers** and **Window > Character**.

In the Layers palette, you'll see a layer with a T icon, which means it is an editable, vector-based type layer. There is another layer, labeled dragonwell, which contains type but has no T icon. The dragonwell type was originally created as a type layer, but it was rasterized, which means the type was converted to pixels. You'll learn how and why to rasterize type layers later in this chapter.

Note: The type in flavor_of_the_month.psd uses the Letter Gothic Standard font. If you don't have Letter Gothic installed on your computer, an error message will appear when you open the file, indicating you don't have the proper font(s) installed. Click OK to open the file. Double-click the T icon of the type layer in the Layers palette. A warning message will appear asking if you want to substitute the missing fonts. Click OK.

2. In the **Layers** palette, click the **flavor of the month** layer to select it. Hold down the **Shift** key and click the **dragonwell** layer to multiple-select both layers. Click and drag the layers onto the **Trash** icon at the bottom of the **Layers** palette to delete the layers. You'll learn how to re-create them in the next few steps.

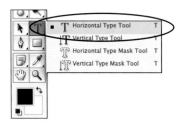

3. In the **Toolbox**, select the **Horizontal Type** tool. The **Options** bar automatically changes to display the type controls.

4. On the **Options** bar, choose **Letter Gothic Std** (or any other font you'd like to use if you don't own the Letter Gothic font) from the **Font Family** pop-up menu, choose **Medium** from the **Font Style** pop-up menu, and choose **14 pt** from the **Font Size** pop-up menu to set the font settings for the type you're about to create.

*Notice the new WYSIWYG (What You See Is What You Get) **Font Family** pop-up menu–it offers a preview of the font beside the font family name. This new feature in Photoshop CS2 is really helpful because you can see what the font looks like before you choose it!*

Note: *Depending on which font you selected in the **Font Family** pop-up menu, you may not have **Medium** as an option in the **Font Style** pop-up menu. Each font has a different selection of styles available. If the font you chose in Step 4 doesn't have **Medium** as a style, choose a different style from the **Font Style** pop-up menu and continue with the exercise.*

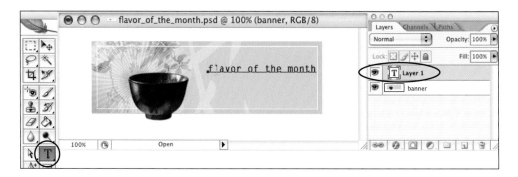

5. Click inside the document window and type the words **flavor of the month**.

*In the **Layers** palette, Photoshop CS2 automatically creates a separate layer for the new type.*

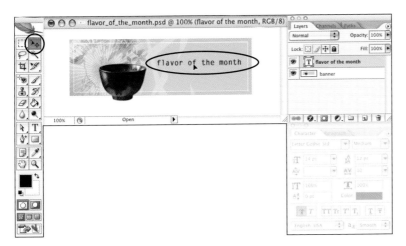

6. Select the **Move** tool from the **Toolbox**. Click and drag inside the document window to position the type layer you just created, as shown in the illustration here.

7. With the **flavor of the month** layer selected in the **Layers** palette, select the **Horizontal Type** tool from the **Toolbox**. Click the **Font Color** box on the **Options** bar to open the **Color Picker** dialog box. Choose **white** (or a color of your choice) and click **OK**.

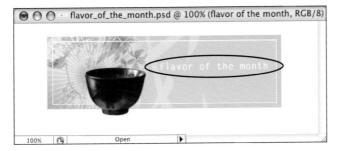

The flavor of the month type layer should now be white (or whatever color you chose in the Color Picker dialog box). You can also change the color of selected type on a type layer. You'll learn how in the next step.

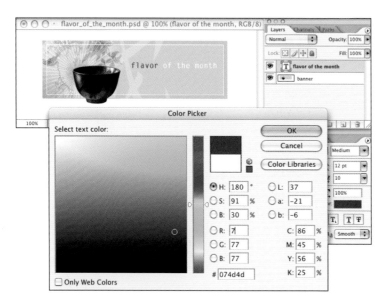

8. With the **Horizontal Type** tool selected in the **Toolbox**, click and drag your cursor across the word **flavor**. Click the **Font Color** box on the **Options** bar to open the **Color Picker** dialog box. Choose a **dark turquoise** and click **OK**.

*Note: Even though you have the type selected, when you open the **Color Picker** dialog box, you can't see the highlight. Photoshop CS2 automatically hides the highlight when the **Color Picker** dialog box is open so you can accurately preview the color before you make your final color selection.*

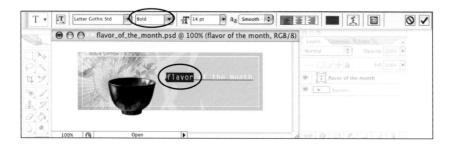

9. With the word **flavor** still highlighted, choose **Bold** from the **Font Style** pop-up menu.

*Note: Depending on which font you selected in the **Font Family** pop-up menu in Step 4, you may not have **Bold** as an option in the **Font Style** pop-up menu. Each font has a different selection of styles available. If the font you chose in Step 4 doesn't have **Bold** as a style, choose a different style from the **Font Style** pop-up menu and continue with the exercise.*

10. On the **Options** bar, click the **Commit Current Edits** button (the checkmark) to accept the changes you made to the selected type.

*You have to accept or cancel type edits and move out of the type editing mode before you can per-form other operations in Photoshop CS2. There are other ways to commit type edits other than click-ing the **Commit Current Edits** button on the **Options** bar, including clicking another layer in the **Layers** palette and choosing a different tool in the **Toolbox**. If you want to cancel type edits, click the **Cancel Current Edits** button on the **Options** bar.*

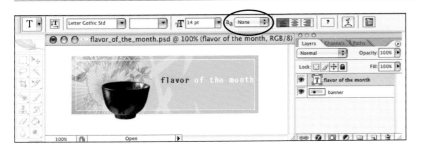

11. With the **Horizontal Type** tool selected in the **Toolbox**, and the **flavor of the month** layer selected in the **Layers** palette, choose **None** from the **Anti-Aliasing Method** pop-up menu.

Notice that the edges of the type now appear jagged.

12. Choose **Smooth** from the **Anti-Aliasing Method** pop-up menu.

Tip: *Use **None** and **Sharp** if your type is smaller than 14 pt. Use **Crisp**, **Strong**, or **Smooth** if your type is 14 pt or larger.*

NOTE | What Is Anti-Aliasing?

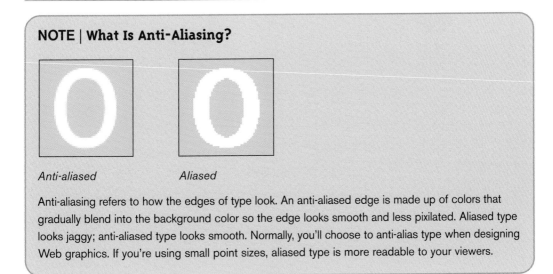

Anti-aliased   *Aliased*

Anti-aliasing refers to how the edges of type look. An anti-aliased edge is made up of colors that gradually blend into the background color so the edge looks smooth and less pixilated. Aliased type looks jaggy; anti-aliased type looks smooth. Normally, you'll choose to anti-alias type when designing Web graphics. If you're using small point sizes, aliased type is more readable to your viewers.

*Now that you've learned how to format character type using the **Options** bar, it's time to learn some of the more advanced formatting options in the **Character** palette.*

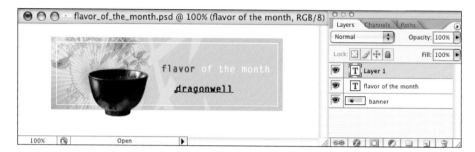

13. With the **Horizontal Type** tool selected in the **Toolbox**, click inside the document window, and type the word **dragonwell**.

*Notice as soon as you clicked inside the document window, a new type layer was automatically created in the **Layers** palette.*

14. In the **Layers** palette, double-click the **T** icon of the **dragonwell** type layer.

This is a handy shortcut for highlighting the contents of a type layer.

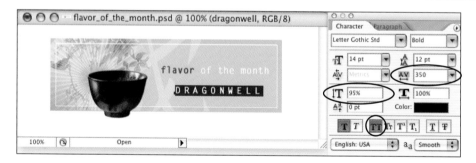

15. In the **Character** palette, click the **All Caps** button to change the type from all lowercase to all uppercase characters.

16. In the **Character** palette, type **95** in the **Vertical Scale** field to decrease the height of the type without affecting the point size.

17. In the **Character** palette, type **350** in the **Tracking** field to increase the spacing between the letters.

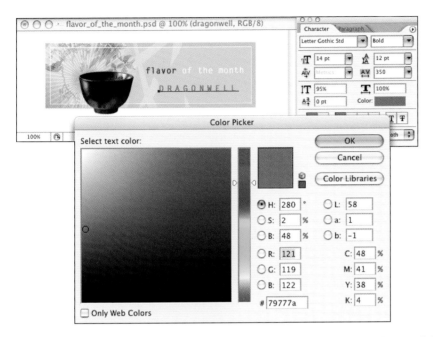

18. In the **Character** palette, click the **Font Color** box to open the **Color Picker** dialog box. Choose a grey-purple color and click **OK**.

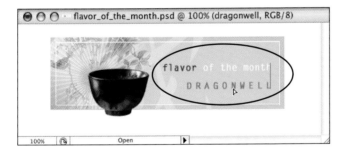

19. In the **Toolbox**, select the **Move** tool and reposition the type on screen. Use the **Smart Guides** (**View > Show > Smart Guides**) to vertically align the **flavor of the month** and the **DRAGONWELL** type, as shown in the illustration here.

*As you can see, the **Character** palette offers more advanced controls for formatting type. Experiment with the other options in the **Character** palette. The more you experiment with the controls, the more you'll understand how they work.*

20. Close **flavor_of_the_month.psd**. You don't need to save your changes.

TIP | Rasterizing Type

Working with vector-based type in Photoshop CS2 and ImageReady CS2 gives you the flexibility to edit your type without degrading the quality of the type with each edit. In some situations, you may want to convert vector-based type layers to pixel-based layers. For example, you may want to apply filters, distort type, or apply brush strokes using the Brush tool. Or, you may want to share a file with someone who doesn't own the font you've chosen. In these cases, you'll want to rasterize type layers. Here's how:

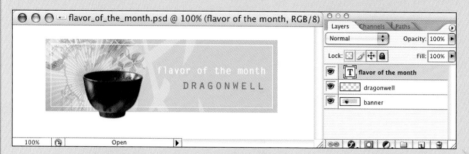

With the type layer you want to rasterize selected in the **Layers** palette, choose **Layer > Rasterize > Type**.

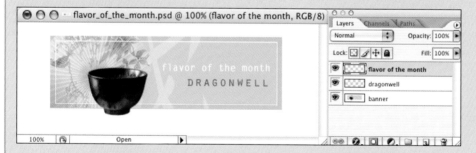

The vector-based type layer will be automatically converted to a regular layer.

Before you rasterize type layers, give careful consideration to whether you will ever need to edit or modify the type again (chances are you will!). If so, choose **Duplicate Layer** from the **Layers** palette menu and turn off the visibility of the duplicate layer. By creating a duplicate layer, you still have an editable type layer should you ever need it again.

2. [PS/IR] Creating Paragraph Type

Paragraph type is defined by a bounding box and is intended for creating, formatting, and editing type with one or more paragraphs. It allows you to rotate, scale, or skew an entire paragraph of type at once. You can also reshape paragraph type, controlling how it flows, aligns, justifies, and indents inside its bounding box. In this exercise, you'll use the controls in the Paragraph palette to format paragraph type.

1. Open **javaco_contact.psd** from the **chap_06** folder you copied to your **Desktop**. Make sure the **Layers** palette and **Paragraph** palette are visible. If not, choose **Window > Layers** and **Window > Paragraph**.

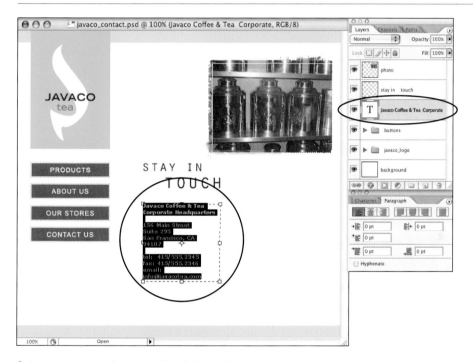

2. In the **Layers** palette, double-click the **T** icon of the type layer.

Just like with character type, the type is automatically highlighted. The highlighted type in this layer is paragraph type, which is defined by the bounding box.

3. Click and drag the resize handles around the perimeter of the bounding box.

The flow of the paragraph type automatically adjusts as you resize the bounding box. **Note:** *If you see a cross in the bottom-right corner of the bounding box, it means the box is too small to contain the type.*

4. Hold down the **Cmd** (Mac) or **Ctrl** (Windows) key and click and drag the corner of the bounding box.

The type automatically increases and decreases in size, and it positions itself inside the bounding box, depending on the size of the bounding box.

5. Position your cursor outside the bounding box until you see the **rotate** cursor appear. Click and drag to rotate the type inside the bounding box.

6. In the **Toolbox**, click the **Move** tool. Click and drag the type to reposition it onscreen.

Now that you have an understanding of how paragraph type works in Photoshop CS2, it's time to learn how to create and edit paragraph type from scratch.

7. With the type layer selected in the **Layers** palette, click the **Trash** icon to delete the type layer.

STAY IN
TOUCH

8. With the **Horizontal Type** tool selected in the **Toolbox**, choose **Verdana** from the **Font Family** pop-up menu, **Regular** from the **Font Style** pop-up menu, and **10 pt** from the **Font Size** pop-up menu. Click and drag inside the document window to create a new bounding box.

Javaco Coffee & Tea
Corporate Headquarters

156 Main Street
Suite 295
San Francisco, CA
94107

tel: 415/555.2345
fax: 415/555.2346
email:
info@javacotea.com

9. Click inside the bounding box and type the following:

Javaco Coffee & Tea Corporate Headquarters

156 Main Street
Suite 295
San Francisco, CA
94107

tel: 415/555.2345
fax: 415/555.2346
email:
info@javacotea.com

When you've finished typing, click the **Commit Current Edits** button on the **Options** bar to commit your changes.

10. Using the techniques you learned earlier in this exercise, resize and reposition the bounding box as necessary to match the illustration shown here.

11. With the **Horizontal Type** tool selected in the **Toolbox**, click and drag to highlight the words **Javaco Coffee & Tea Corporate Headquarters**. On the **Options** bar, click the **Font Color** box to open the **Color Picker** dialog box. Choose a **grey-purple** color and click **OK**. Choose **Bold** from the **Font Style** pop-up menu on the **Options** bar. Click and drag to highlight the remainder of the type. On the **Options** bar, click the **Font Color** box to open the **Color Picker** dialog box. Choose a **lime green** color and click **OK**.

12. In the **Layers** palette, double-click the **T** icon to highlight the paragraph type. Experiment with the **Alignment** controls in the **Paragraph** palette.

When you're adding large amounts of type to Web pages, as in this example, it's usually best to align your type to the left side. However, there will be times when you need to center, right-align, and justify your paragraph type, so it's important to understand what these options are all about.

13. With the **Horizontal Type** tool selected in the **Toolbox**, highlight the address. Experiment with the **Indent** controls in the **Paragraph** palette.

Again, for an example such as this, it's best not to indent the paragraph type. However, you never know when you will need to indent one or more lines of paragraph type.

14. With the address still highlighted, experiment with the spacing controls on the **Paragraph** palette.

These options are very handy, as sometimes you'll want to evenly increase the amount of spacing between lines of type. Remember, readability is the most important aspect of type on the Web. Sometimes, increasing the spacing between lines of type can make the type easier to read.

15. When you've finished experimenting with the options on the **Paragraph** palette, close **javaco_contact.psd**. You don't need to save your changes.

TIP | Simulating HTML Type with System Layout

When you're mocking up a Web page, you can use the **System Layout** option to simulate the appearance of HTML type.

Javaco Coffee & Tea Corporate Headquarters 156 Main Street Suite 295 San Francisco, CA 94107 tel: 415/555.2345 fax: 415/555.2346 email: info@javacotea.com	Javaco Coffee & Tea Corporate Headquarters 156 Main Street Suite 295 San Francisco, CA 94107 tel: 415/555.2345 fax: 415/555.2346 email: info@javacotea.com

Default 12 pt type   *12 pt type with the System Layout option turned on, simulating HTML type*

In the **Layers** palette, select the type layer you want to simulate as HTML. Choose **System Layout** from the **Character** palette menu.

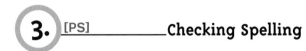

3. [PS]_____Checking Spelling

In this exercise, you'll learn how to check the spelling of the contents of type layers.

1. Open **coupon.psd** from the **chap_06** folder you copied to your **Desktop**.

2. Choose **Edit > Check Spelling**.

*The **Check Spelling** dialog box opens automatically. By default, Photoshop CS2 checks spelling on all the type layers. If you want to limit spell checking to the selected layer, turn off **Check All Layers** at the bottom of the dialog box.*

3. The spell checker identifies **complamentary** as a misspelled word, offers a preferred spelling, and suggests other spellings. Click to select the word **complimentary** in the **Suggestions** area of the **Check Spelling** dialog box. Click **Change**.

Complamentary is automatically changed to complimentary.

4. The spell checker identifies **Javaco** because it is not in the English–USA dictionary that ships with Photoshop CS2. Click **Ignore** to leave **Javaco** spelled as it is. Alternately, you can click **Add** to add **Javaco** to the active dictionary so it won't be identified as misspelled again.

*Photoshop CS2 ships with dictionaries in various languages. You can change the spell checker's active dictionary by choosing a language from the **Language** pop-up menu at the bottom of the **Character** palette.*

5. Click **OK** to acknowledge the completion of the spell checking and to close the **Check Spelling** dialog box.

6. Close **coupon.psd**. You don't need to save your changes.

4. [PS] _____Finding and Replacing Type

Photoshop CS2 offers a find-and-replace feature, which is helpful if you want to change all the instances of a word in the same file. Here's a short exercise to show you how it works.

1. Open **javaco_home.psd** from the **chap_06** folder you copied to your **Desktop**.

2. Choose **Edit > Find and Replace Text** to open the **Find And Replace Text** dialog box.

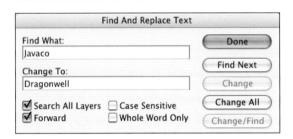

3. In the **Find What** field, type **Javaco**. In the **Change To** field, type **Dragonwell**. Click **Find Next**.

4. Click **Change/Find** to find the next instance of the word **Javaco**. Click **Change/Find** again to find the next instance of the word **Javaco**.

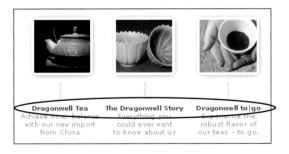

5. A warning dialog box appears, indicating there are no more instances of the word **Javaco**, but three replacements were made. Click **OK**.

6. Close **javaco_home.psd**. You don't need to save your changes.

MOVIE | warping_type.mov

With warping, you can distort type to create interesting shapes, such as an arc, twist, or wave, while maintaining type as vector-based objects. To learn more about warping type, check out **warping_type.mov** in the **movies** folder on the **PCS2Web HOT CD-ROM**.

MOVIE | type_on_a_path.mov

Another way to create interesting shapes is to place type on a path. Like with warping, you can use type on a path to create interesting effects, while maintaining the type as vector-based objects. To learn more about creating type on a path, check out **type_on_a_path.mov** in the **movies** folder on the **PCS2Web HOT CD-ROM**.

You've mastered how to create, format, and edit type in Photoshop CS2 and ImageReady CS2! Next, you'll learn how to optimize images for the Web—an important skill for every Web designer.

7

Optimizing Images

| Optimizing JPEGs |

| Selective JPEG Optimization with Alpha Channels |

| Optimizing GIFs | Choosing the Right Color Reduction Palette |

| Reducing Colors | Locking Colors | Selective GIF Optimization |

| Previewing Images in a Web Browser |

| Optimizing GIFs and JPEGs in ImageReady CS2 |

chap_07

PCS2Web HOT CD-ROM

Anyone who has ever used the Web has likely been frustrated by slow-loading Web sites. It's the first design medium where the file size of the graphics translates into how fast someone can view them. Making small Web graphics is an art and a science. Fortunately, Photoshop CS2 and ImageReady CS2 provide the ideal tools to help you master this craft.

Prepare for a long chapter because optimization is a complex subject that both Photoshop CS2 and ImageReady CS 2 handle in great detail. If terms such as *dither*, *adaptive palettes*, *bit depth*, *JPEG*, and *GIF* are unfamiliar to you, they won't be for long. If you're a pro at optimizing Web graphics, you'll be impressed by the superb optimization capabilities in Photoshop CS2 and ImageReady CS2.

What Affects Speed on the Web?

Unfortunately, just making your file sizes small in Photoshop CS2 or ImageReady CS2 does not guarantee fast Web site performance. Here are some other factors that slow down Web sites:

- **Connection speed:** If the connection speed of a Web server is slow, your Web site will be slow.

- **Routing problems:** If router problems exist, your Web site will be slow.

- **Traffic:** If you are using a large Internet service provider, such as AOL, EarthLink, or GeoCities, your Web site may slow down during heavy usage hours due to a high volume of Web traffic. If you're using a small, local Internet service provider, your Web site may be slow because the Internet service provider does not have resources to handle the heaviest traffic periods.

Solutions? Make sure you host your Web site from a fast connection or hire a hosting company who guarantees a fast connection. If you have a serious business site, get a dedicated hosting service instead of a large, consumer-based Web service.

If the Web is slow because of router problems, it affects everyone. Such is life. Control the things you can (like file size). The only predictable thing about the Web is that it won't always perform in a predictable manner.

Understanding Web File Formats

There are only a small number of graphic file formats you can use when optimizing Web graphics. The most popular formats are **JPEG** and **GIF**.

GIF stands for **Graphic** Interchange Format; JPEG stands for Joint **Photographic** Experts Group. The words *graphic* and *photographic* are intentionally bolded here to indicate what each file format handles best. It isn't that GIF is better than JPEG, or vice versa. Each compression scheme is best suited for a certain type of image:

- GIFs are best for flat or simple graphic images with solid areas of color, such as logos, illustrations, cartoons, line art, and so on.

- JPEGs are best for continuous-tone images, such as photographs, glows, gradients, drop shadows, and so on.

Some images don't fall into either category because they are hybrids of line art and continuous-tone graphics. In these cases, you have to experiment with GIF and JPEG to see which gives you the smallest file size and the best image quality.

Transparency and Animation

Whether a graphic contains flat color or continuous tones is not the sole deciding factor for choosing the best file format. The GIF and SWF formats can do a couple of things the JPEG format cannot, such as transparency and animation. If you're looking for specific information about saving files as transparent GIFs, animated GIFs, or animated SWFs, you can refer to Chapter 10, "*Creating Transparent Graphics*," Chapter 11, "*Creating Animated GIFs*," or Chapter 19, "*Integrating with Macromedia Flash*." In the meantime, here's a brief explanation of these terms because their capabilities may factor into your optimization strategy.

Transparency and Animation Terms	
Term	**Description**
Transparency	All digital image files are rectangular. The shape of your Photoshop CS2 document window is always square or rectangular. Even if an image inside is not in that shape, the file itself is defined by rectangular boundaries. What if you have a circular button design you intended to be viewed on a colored or patterned background? In such a case, you use transparent pixels to mask out parts of the image, leaving a shape that appears circular in a Web browser. If you want to use transparent images on the Web, you can choose one of two file formats: GIF or SWF.
GIF transparency	The GIF file format supports 1-bit masking, which means the image can be turned off in specified areas, making it possible to create irregularly shaped graphics. Because the file format supports only 1-bit transparency, there are no degrees of opacity except on or off (visibility or no visibility for each pixel). For more information, check out Chapter 10, "*Creating Transparent Graphics*."
Macromedia Flash transparency	Like the GIF format, SWF also supports masking, but of much higher quality. SWF supports 32-bit masking, whereas GIF supports 1-bit masking. The process for exporting SWF files with transparency is identical to exporting SWF files without transparency, which you'll learn about in Chapter 19, "*Integrating with Macromedia Flash*."
Animation	Animations are a series of still images (called frames) that appear in motion. When you work with animations, you can control how fast and how many times the animation plays. Photoshop CS2 lets you save animations as animated GIFs; ImageReady CS2 lets you save animations in two different formats: animated GIFs and SWF.

continues on next page

Transparency and Animation Terms *continued*	
Term	**Description**
GIF animation	A single GIF file can contain multiple images and display them in a slideshow fashion. GIF files containing multiple images are called animated GIFs. For more information on how the GIF file format supports animation, check out Chapter 11, "*Creating Animated GIFs.*"
Macromedia Flash animation	With Macromedia Flash (SWF) files, you can create more complex animations than with animated GIFs. Although you can't take advantage of all the features of Macromedia Flash in ImageReady CS2, exporting files as SWF is a huge benefit. Once you've exported files as SWF, you can open and edit the files directly in Macromedia Flash. For more information, check out Chapter 19, "*Integrating with Macromedia Flash.*"

Lossy or Lossless?

There are two categories of file compression: lossy and lossless. **Lossy** file compression reduces file size by discarding visual information. **Lossless** file compression reduces file size without throwing away visual information. JPEG is a lossy compression method. Traditionally, GIF was a lossless method, but in Photoshop CS2 and ImageReady CS2, you can add lossiness to GIF compression to reduce file size.

WARNING | Don't Recompress a Compressed Image

Recompressing a JPEG or a lossy GIF can erode the image quality because you throw away visual information each time you apply lossy compression. The result can be visible, unwanted compression artifacts, which cause the image to look distressed. If you need to make a change to an image that's already been compressed as a JPEG or lossy GIF, find the original, uncompressed version of the image, make your changes, and compress the file as a fresh JPEG or lossy GIF to maintain the image's quality. This is one reason you should always save the original PSD (**P**hoto**S**hop **D**ocument) files you create in Photoshop CS2 or ImageReady CS2.

How Can You Make Small JPEGs?

Before you start optimizing JPEGs for the Web, you need to understand what types of images work best with the JPEG format and what can help make JPEGs smaller without compromising image quality. Here is a handy chart to help you understand these considerations. You'll practice these techniques in the upcoming exercises.

JPEG Compression	
What to Do	**Why Do It**
Start with an image with tonal qualities, such as a photograph, continuous-tone graphic, or an image with effects, such as glows and drop shadows.	The JPEG file format looks for the type of data it is best at compressing: areas with low contrast, subtle variation, and slight tonal shifts. It can't compress areas of solid color effectively, and it doesn't work well for flat, graphic-style artwork.
Add blur.	The JPEG format compresses blurry images effectively. Adding a little blur to a JPEG can decrease its file size.
Add more JPEG compression.	The more JPEG compression you add, the smaller the file size. Too much JPEG compression can cause unwanted compression artifacts. It's your job to find the balance between making the file small and making it look good.
Decrease the saturation.	The JPEG format has an easier time compressing images with low color saturation than images with highly saturated colors. Decreasing saturation usually results in a smaller-sized JPEG.
Decrease the contrast.	The JPEG format favors low-contrast images. Decreasing the contrast in an image usually results in a smaller-sized JPEG.
Use an alpha channel.	Compressing different areas in a single image with two different levels of JPEG compression sometimes lowers the overall file size. The two areas are delineated by an alpha channel. You'll learn how to do this later in the chapter.

JPEG Optimization Options

In the upcoming exercises, you'll use the Save For Web dialog box in Photoshop CS2 to optimize images as JPEGs. When you open the Save For Web dialog box, you'll see lots of options for JPEG optimization. Here's a quick reference guide to help you understand the different settings. You'll try out the majority of these settings in the exercises that follow. Although the diagram shows the options in the Photoshop CS2 Save For Web dialog box, you can find identical options in the Optimize palette in ImageReady CS2.

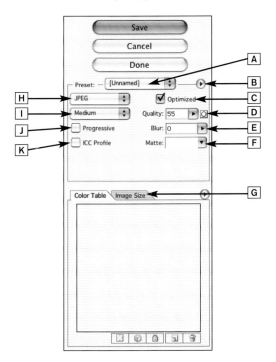

JPEG Options		
A	Preset pop-up menu	Choose from preset compression values, including settings that ship with Photoshop CS2 and your own custom settings.
B	Optimize menu	Save and load custom settings for the Preset pop-up menu (A).
C	Optimized check box	Turn on the Optimized setting, which will make the smallest possible JPEG images.

continues on next page

JPEG Options *continued*		
D	Quality slider	Set the compression quality. You can manually type the value or use the slider and drag to the desired value. Click the alpha channel button beside the Quality pop-up menu to access the Modify Quality Setting dialog box, where you can use alpha channels to modify the quality in different parts of the image.
E	Blur slider	Choose a blur value. JPEGs compress better when they are slightly blurry than when they are sharp images. You can manually type in the value or use the slider and drag to the desired value.
F	Matte pop-up menu	Set a matte color to replace the transparency when an image is saved as a JPEG. This is important when you begin with an image that is against a transparent background. You'll learn more about this option in Chapter 10, "*Creating Transparent Graphics.*"
G	Image Size tab	Change the physical dimensions of an image by adjusting the pixel or percent values.
H	File Format pop-up menu	Apply JPEG, GIF, or PNG compression to an image.
I	Compression Quality pop-up menu	Choose a preset quality value for a JPEG image. You can use one of the presets or enter values into the Quality setting (D).
J	Progressive check box	Turn on the Progressive setting. Remember, JPEGs, like interlaced GIFs, appear chunky and come into focus as they download.
K	ICC Profile check box	Turn on ICC (International Color Consortium) profiles. ICC profiles work with some printing devices, but not with Web browsers. They add file size to a compressed image. Therefore, I don't recommend using them for Web images at present. However, there might come a day when browsers recognize ICC profiles.

Now that you understand the options available for JPEG optimization, and you understand some of the considerations you need to make during the optimization process, let's put that knowledge to work on a few practical exercises.

I. [PS] _____Optimizing JPEGs

This exercise walks you through the process of optimizing and saving a JPEG. It introduces you to the Save For Web dialog box in Photoshop CS2, which gives you control over so many options that, once you master its nuances, you'll be able to make the smallest Web graphics possible.

1. Open **candles.psd** from the **chap_07** folder you copied to your **Desktop**.

2. Choose **File > Save For Web**.

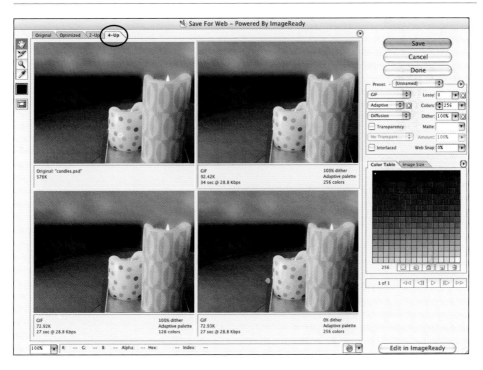

3. In the **Save For Web** dialog box, click the **4-Up** tab. In this tab, you can use the multiple previews to compare different compression settings.

Notice the upper-left tab has the term Original *in it? This lets you compare the original, uncompressed image to the other previews, which show how the image looks with different combinations of compression settings.*

*If you have already used the **Save For Web** dialog box, your settings may default to different settings than you see here because Photoshop CS2 remembers the last settings you used. If that's the case, don't worry; you'll learn what settings to input in the following steps.*

4. Click the upper-right image preview to select it. You'll see a blue border around the preview, which indicates that it is the active preview.

By making it the active preview, the changes you make to the compression settings affect this preview.

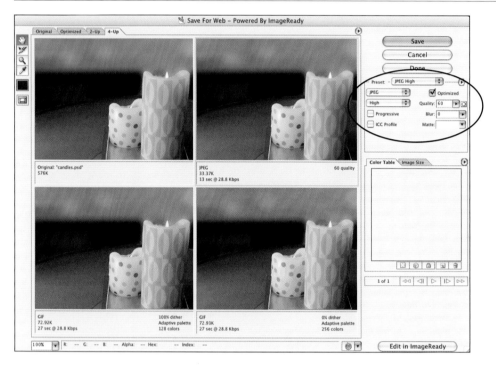

5. Choose **JPEG** from the **File Format** pop-up menu. Choose **High** from the **Compression Quality** pop-up menu (which automatically sets the **Quality** of the selected preview to **60**).

Notice the JPEG is better looking than any of the other GIF previews? This illustrates how continuous-tone images, such as photographs, always compress better as JPEGs than as GIFs.

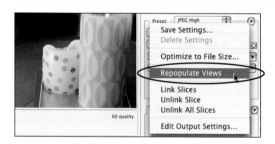

6. Choose **Repopulate Views** from the **Optimize** menu. This changes the other two previews in the bottom frames to the same file format as the selected preview (JPEG in this case).

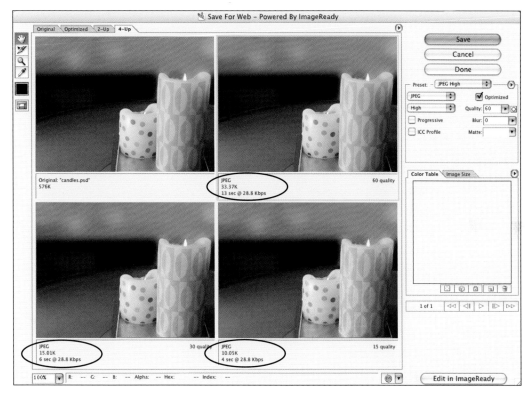

Notice the readout below each preview? It tells you the JPEG quality and file size of each preview. Photoshop CS2 estimates how long this graphic will take to load over a slow connection. **Note:** This is a theoretical estimate of speed; it may not be accurate due to other factors, such as server speed. Your readouts may also have different numbers than those cited in this example because Photoshop CS2 remembers the compression levels from the last time you used the **Save For Web** dialog box with JPEG settings.

Judging from the relative image quality and file sizes of all the previews in this example, it looks like the best choice for the JPEG compression quality is between **60** and **30**. The higher the compression quality, the larger the file size will be. The lower the quality setting, the more artifacts you'll see. With every image you optimize, you'll have to balance quality with image size.

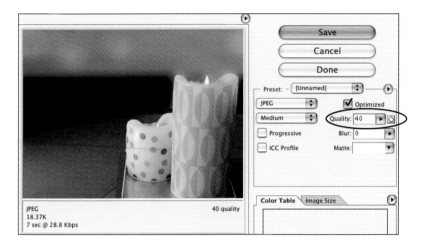

7. With the upper-right preview selected, set the **Quality** slider to **40**. **Note:** You must release the slider for the results of the new setting to take effect.

You can see quite a few artifacts around the flame in the candle, which means you need to adjust the **Quality** *slider higher than* **40** *but lower than* **60**. *Because the flame around the candle is a focal point in the image, you want to make sure there are as few artifacts as possible in that area because viewers will naturally be drawn to that point.*

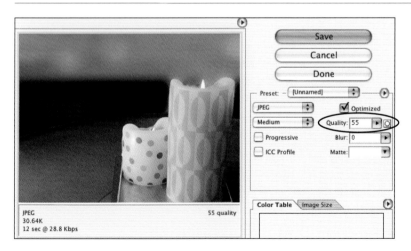

8. Increase the **Quality** slider to **55**. The artifacts around the flame disappear, but the file size is still a bit big.

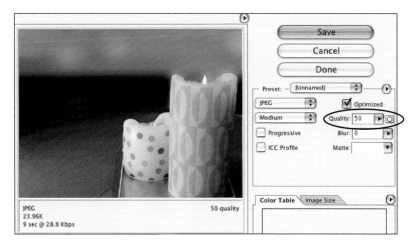

9. Decrease the **Quality** slider to **50**.

By decreasing the Quality slider to 50, you still can't see any artifacts around the flame, and the file size is a bit smaller than when the Quality slider was set to 55. As mentioned before, the trick with optimization is to find the best quality with the smallest size.

If you remember from earlier in the chapter, one way to help reduce the size of JPEGs is to apply a slight blur. In the next step, you'll do just that!

10. Using the **Blur** slider, increase the blur to **0.5**.

Notice that the file size dropped, but the quality of the image is now very blurry. Just like with the Quality setting, you want to find the best quality image with the lowest file size. In this case, applying a blur of 0.5 negatively affected the quality of the image.

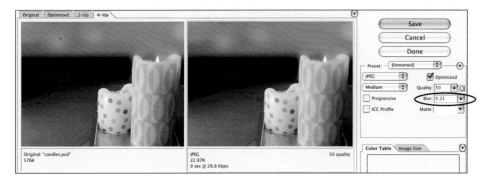

11. Using the **Blur** slider, reduce the blur to **0.21**.

This blur setting reduced the file size slightly but didn't compromise the crispness of the image. Although it may not seem like a huge savings in file size, keep in mind that every little bit helps!

Until now, we've only looked at the top half of the image because that's all we can see in the preview window. You need to look at the effect of the settings over the entire image, not just part of it, because the compression settings can negatively affect an area of the image you may not expect.

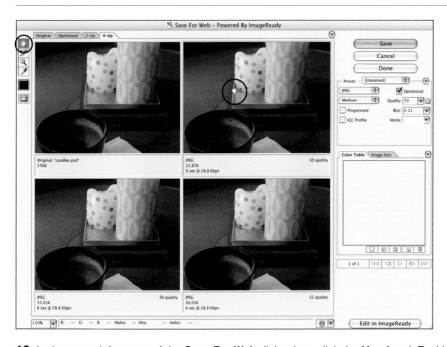

12. In the upper-left corner of the **Save For Web** dialog box, click the **Hand** tool. Position your cursor inside the upper-right preview. Click and drag to reposition in the image inside the preview area, making sure the settings you specified don't cause any unwanted artifacts in other areas of the image.

13. When you are satisfied with the optimization settings, click **Save** to open the **Save Optimized As** dialog box.

Photoshop CS2 automatically adds a .jpg file extension to the filename for you. It also generates a filename based on the name of the original image, which you can change easily if you want to.

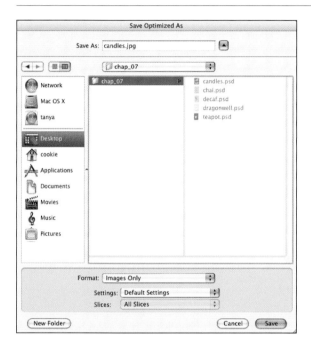

14. Navigate to the **chap_07** folder you copied to your **Desktop**, choose **Images Only** from the **Format** pop-up menu, and click **Save**. For more information about the options in the **Format** pop-up menu, refer to the sidebar at the end of this exercise.

*Notice that the original, uncompressed **candles.psd** file remains open in Photoshop CS2. You haven't altered the original image. When you use the **Save For Web** dialog box, Photoshop CS2 saves an optimized copy of the file and does not modify the original file. This is a huge benefit because oftentimes you'll need your original image—either to make some adjustments or to use it for another project.*

15. Close the original **candles.psd** image without saving.

TIP | Saving Images and HTML, Images Only, and HTML Only

When you save optimized images in Photoshop CS2 and ImageReady CS2, you have three format options—**Images and HTML**, **Images Only**, and **HTML Only**. You need to understand what each of these options means and when to use them.

Web pages require two things: images in a proper optimized format, and HTML code to make the images and other elements on the page work inside a Web browser. When you save optimized images in Photoshop CS2 or ImageReady CS2, you can choose to save the images and the HTML code, just the images, or just the HTML code. If you want to save the entire page so it will work in a Web browser, use the **Images and HTML** option. If you're just creating and saving images so you can add them to an HTML file in an HTML editor, use the **Images Only** option. If you just want to save the HTML code, use the **HTML Only** option.

This may seem like a confusing concept now, but as you work through some of the more complex exercises in this book, you'll see the advantage to saving HTML code directly from Photoshop CS2 and ImageReady CS2.

2. [PS] _____Selective JPEG Optimization with Alpha Channels

When you're optimizing photographs, you need to make sure the focal point—the object or area in the composition that draws the eye of the viewer—is crisp and with as few compression artifacts as possible. In order to keep your file size down, sometimes you'll want the compression quality to be higher in those focal areas than in the rest of the image. In such a case, you can use an alpha channel, which is a type of mask, to specify different compression settings for the masked area than the rest of the image. This selective optimization technique helps reduce the overall file size of a JPEG.

1. Open **teapot.psd** from the **chap_07** folder you copied to your **Desktop**.

Notice the contents of this image are on two layers—the green background is on one layer and the teapot, tray, books, and table are on a separate layer. In this image, the teapot, tray, and books are the focal point. As a result, you want to make sure those objects have the highest compression quality possible and, to keep file size down, you can compromise the compression quality of the background.

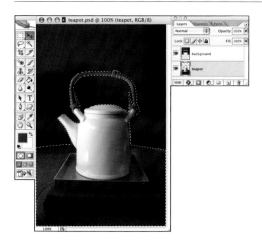

2. Hold down the **Cmd** (Mac) or **Ctrl** (Windows) key and, in the **Layers** palette, click the **teapot** layer thumbnail. The cursor will change to a hand with a rectangle, and a selection marquee will appear around the contents of the **teapot** layer.

*This is my favorite shortcut for creating a perfect selection around the contents of a layer. It's much better than using the **Magic Wand** tool or any of the other selection tools in Photoshop CS2 because it always gives you a perfect selection. Any time you have a layer with content and transparency, this is the best method for making a selection. However, if you are working with an image that does not have transparent layers, you can use any of the selection tools in Photoshop CS2 to create a selection and then use the optimization technique taught in this exercise.*

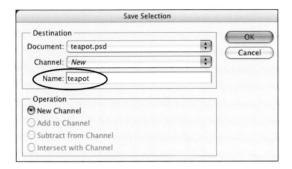

3. Choose **Select > Save Selection** to open the **Save Selection** dialog box. In the **Name** field, type **teapot**, and click **OK**.

See how easy it is to turn an ordinary selection into an alpha channel?

4. Press **Cmd+D** (Mac) or **Ctrl+D** (Windows) to deselect the contents of the **teapot** layer.

*If you want to see the alpha channel you just created, click the **Channels** palette tab, which is next to the **Layers** palette. In the **Channels** palette, click the **teapot** alpha channel to display the grayscale mask in the document window. When you're done viewing the mask, click the **RGB** channel in the **Channels** palette, and return to the **Layers** palette. This step is optional. You do not have to view the alpha channel for it to work; it's simply a suggestion if you've never worked with alpha channels before.*

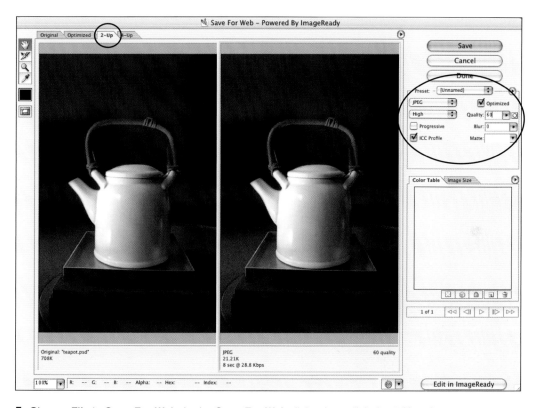

5. Choose **File** > **Save For Web**. In the **Save For Web** dialog box, click the **2-Up** tab so you can see the entire image in the preview area. Choose **JPEG** from the **File Format** pop-up menu. Set the **Quality** slider as low as possible but without noticeable artifacts on the most important areas of the image—the teapot, tray, and books.

*Tip: Try setting the **Quality** slider to **60**. With the entire image compressed at 60%, the file size is approximately **21.21 K.***

6. Click the **alpha channel** button (to the right of the **Quality** slider) to open the **Modify Quality Setting** dialog box. In the **Channel** pop-up menu, choose **teapot**.

*Notice the black-and-white preview of your alpha channel and the two sliders in the **Quality** area. The white slider (on the right) sets the quality for the content inside the white area of the alpha channel (the teapot, the tray, the books, and the table). The black slider sets the level of quality for the content in the black area of the alpha channel (the background of the image).*

7. Leave the **white** slider set to **60%**. In the preview image, notice the artifacts around the spout and lid of the teapot (shown in the previous illustration). This area is covered by the black area of the alpha channel.

8. Increase the **Black** slider to **42%** to eliminate the artifacts. Click **OK**.

*With the white and black sliders set to their defaults, **60%** and **0%** respectively, the overall size of the file (reported at the bottom left of the preview window) is less than it was when you had the **Quality** of the entire image set to **60**, back in Step 5. As you move the black slider to the right, increasing the quality of the image covered by the black part of the alpha channel to **42**, the file size increases slightly, but it's still less than when the **Quality** of the entire image was set to **60**.*

In this example, applying relatively high compression (low quality) to the black areas of the alpha channel, without sacrificing the higher quality necessary for the more important areas in the white areas of the alpha channel, resulted in a small reduction in overall file size. The file size savings you can achieve with this technique varies from image to image and alpha channel to alpha channel. In most cases, it's worth experimenting with this technique to see if you can lower file size while applying optimal compression to different areas of an image.

---

9. Click **Save**. In the **Save Optimized As** dialog box, navigate to the **chap_07** folder you copied to your **Desktop**, choose **Images Only** from the **Format** pop-up menu, and click **Save**.

---

10. Close **teapot.psd**. You don't need to save your changes.

Now that you've mastered JPEG optimization, it's time to move on to GIF optimization. Before you start the exercises, take some time to review the information about how to make small GIFs and understand the GIF optimization options offered in the Photoshop CS2 and ImageReady CS2.

How Can You Make Small GIFs?

The principles for making a small GIF are almost opposite to those for making a small JPEG. The GIF file format works best on areas of solid color—and that's why it's best for line art, logos, illustrations, and cartoons.

GIF Compression	
What to Do	**Why Do It**
Start with an image with large areas of solid color.	The GIF file format looks for patterns in artwork, such as large runs of a single color in a horizontal, vertical, or diagonal direction. **Note:** Areas of color change cause increased file sizes.
Reduce the number of colors.	Reducing the number of colors in a GIF image reduces the file size. At some point during the color reduction process, the image won't look right, and that's when you'll have to go back and add in more colors. The objective is to find a balance between the image looking good but containing the fewest number of colors.
Reduce the amount of dithering.	Dithering adds different-colored pixels in close proximity to each other to simulate secondary colors or smooth gradations of color. A dithered image often looks noisy or has scattered pixels. Some images must contain dithering to look good, but it's best to use the least amount of dithering possible to keep the image size small.
Add lossy compression.	Adding a small amount of lossy compression to a GIF will often reduce its file size.
Add an alpha channel.	Use an alpha channel to weight the choice of colors and the amount of dither applied to different areas of a GIF during compression. You can also apply these techniques to a type or vector layer. You'll see how this works when you learn about weighted GIF optimization in an upcoming exercise.

NOTE | Recompressing GIFs

Compression artifacts are not an issue with GIFs (as long as they don't use lossy compression, which you'll learn about later in this chapter) as they are with JPEGs. You can recompress a GIF with no ill compression effects, though it's sometimes preferable to begin with a clean original PSD, PICT, or BMP than to recompress an already compressed GIF. For example, if you recompressed a GIF that had been set to eight colors, you wouldn't be able to introduce any more colors even if you wanted to. You would have more latitude with your choices if, instead, you compressed a GIF from the original source image.

GIF Optimization Options

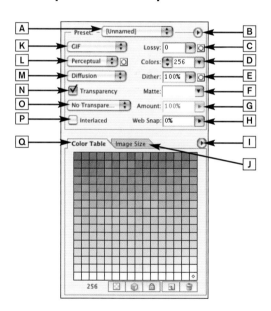

	GIF Options	
A	Preset pop-up menu	Choose from preset compression values, including settings that ship with Photoshop CS2 and your own custom settings.
B	Optimize menu	Save and load custom settings for the Preset menu (A).

continues on next page

GIF Options *continued*		
C	Lossy slider	Add lossy compression to your GIF images. Small values of lossy compression can decrease the file size of a GIF. This works best on continuous-tone GIF files such as photographs. The alpha channel button to the right of the Lossy pop-up menu allows access to the Modify Lossiness Setting dialog box, where you can use alpha channels to vary lossy compression in different parts of the image.
D	Colors pop-up menu	Reduce the number of colors in a GIF image to decrease file size. The trick is to find the perfect combination of the fewest colors for the best-looking image.
E	Dither slider	Choose the amount of dither. Adding dither to a GIF always increases file size, but it is sometimes necessary for the image color to look best. The alpha channel button next to the slider allows access to the Modify Dither dialog box, where you can use alpha channels to vary the amount of dither in different parts of an image.
F	Matte pop-up menu	Change the matte color of an image with transparent areas to blend the image into a Web page background. You'll get a chance to do this in Chapter 10, "*Creating Transparent Graphics.*"
G	Transparency Dither Amount slider	Set the amount of dither to partially transparent pixels on the edges of a transparent GIF. Transparency dither sometimes helps blend an image with a patterned Web page background.
H	Web Snap slider	Set a threshold to quickly "snap" non-Web-safe colors to Web-safe colors. I recommend changing colors to Web-safe colors individually instead of using the Web Snap slider so you can maintain control over which colors shift.
I	Color Palette menu	Sort the colors in your color palette, load and save color palettes, and create new colors in your color palette.
J	Image Size tab	Change the physical dimensions of an image by adjusting the pixel or percent values.

continues on next page

	GIF Options *continued*	
K	**File Format pop-up menu**	Apply JPEG, GIF, or PNG compression to an image.
L	**Color Reduction Palette pop-up menu**	Choose the best color palette to compress your GIF images. The Adobe engineers give you a lot of options for using different palettes to best compress your GIF images. You'll try them out in several upcoming exercises. The alpha channel button next to the Color Reduction Palette pop-up menu allows access to the Modify Color Reduction dialog box, where you can use alpha channels to influence the palette applied to different parts of an image.
M	**Dither Algorithm pop-up menu**	Choose different dither options. *Dither algorithm* is just a fancy way of saying there are a few types of dithering options. You'll try them out in this chapter.
N	**Transparency check box**	Turn on Transparency to make transparent GIF images. You might find the check box is dimmed, which likely means your image doesn't contain any transparent areas. You'll learn all about how to make perfect transparent GIFs in Chapter 10, "*Creating Transparent Graphics.*"
O	**Transparency Dither Algorithm pop-up menu**	Choose which type of dithering to apply to partially transparent edges of a transparent GIF to help blend it with a Web page background. You'll try out this technique in Chapter 10, "*Creating Transparent Graphics.*"
P	**Interlaced check box**	Turn on Interlaced to create interlaced GIFs. Interlaced images will look chunky until they finish downloading. Interlaced GIFs work on all Web browsers, so you don't have to worry about compatibility issues. I suggest you don't use interlacing on images with text because it can be frustrating to wait for an image to appear in focus when you have to read it. If you're ever going to use interlacing, it might be on graphics that contain no text; but the truth is I never use interlacing because I don't like the way it looks. To each his or her own!
Q	**Color Table tab**	View the colors being assigned to a GIF image. You'll explore this feature later in the chapter.

3. [PS] _____Optimizing GIFs

Optimizing images as GIFs is more complex than optimizing images as JPEGs because there are so many GIF settings that affect file size. The next few exercises will show you the key settings for optimizing GIFs, including techniques for lowering the number of colors, adjusting dither options, and choosing a color reduction palette.

1. Open **dragonwell.psd** from the **chap_07** folder you copied to your **Desktop**. Choose **File > Save For Web**.

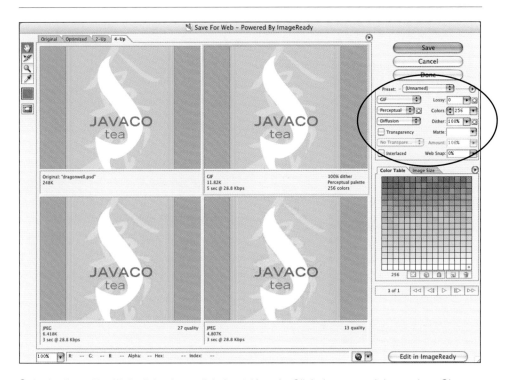

2. In the **Save For Web** dialog box, click the **4-Up** tab. Click the upper-right preview. Choose **GIF** from the **File Format** pop-up menu. Change the settings on the right side of the **Save For Web** dialog box to match those in the illustration here (**GIF, Perceptual, Diffusion, Lossy: 0, Colors: 256, Dither: 100%**).

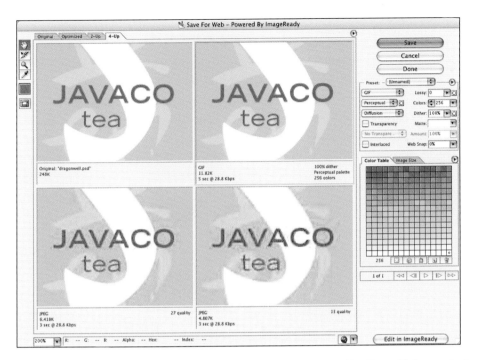

3. In the **Save For Web** dialog box, select the **Zoom** tool from the **Toolbox**. Click once in the upper-right preview to change the magnification in all the views to **200%**. Next, choose the **Hand** tool. Click and drag inside any of the preview panes to match the position of the image to the illustration here.

Notice the two JPEG previews on the bottom contain artifacts, but the upper-right GIF preview looks more like the original image. As you can see from this example, flat graphics are best optimized as GIFs, not JPEGs.

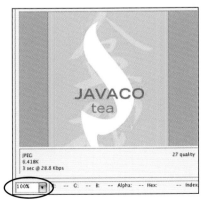

4. Choose **100%** from the **Zoom Level** pop-up menu to return all the previews to normal size.

5. Click the lower-left **JPEG** preview, then click back on the **GIF** preview on the top right, keeping your eye on the settings in the **Save For Web** dialog box. As you switch from **JPEG** to **GIF**, notice the optimization settings in the context-sensitive window change, and more options are available for GIF than for JPEG.

*Notice when a preview is set to GIF, the **Color Table** is visible. The GIF file format supports a maximum of 256 colors. All the colors in the original image have been converted or mapped to a limited palette of colors, which you'll learn to select in an upcoming exercise. The **Color Table** displays the colors in the currently selected palette to which this GIF preview is mapped. The JPEG format supports millions of colors, so a JPEG doesn't need to map to a limited palette.*

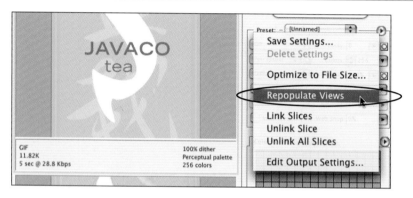

6. Click the upper-right preview. Choose **Repopulate Views** from the **Optimize** menu. This changes all the views to the same format as the selected preview—in this case GIF.

7. Leave **dragonwell.psd** open in the **Save For Web** dialog box for the next exercise.

*Note: If you click **Cancel**, the **Save For Web** dialog box will not remember these settings. If you have to take a break and can't leave the dialog box open, click **Done** to save the settings so they appear the next time you open any image in the **Save For Web** dialog box.*

[PS] _____Choosing the Right Color Reduction Palette

The color reduction palette settings for the GIF file format are the most difficult controls to understand. This exercise is designed to shed some light on these mysterious settings and help you through the hardest part of optimizing GIFs.

1. The image **dragonwell.psd** should be open in the **Save For Web** dialog box from the previous exercise. If it's not, go back and complete Exercise 3. Click the **2-Up** tab.

You'll see the original image on the left and a single preview on the right.

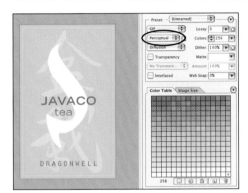

Perceptual

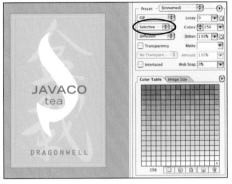

Selective

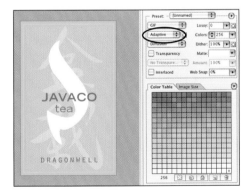

Adaptive

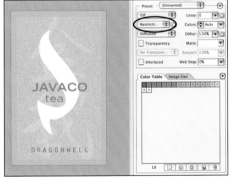

Restrictive (Web)

2. With the preview on the right selected, choose **Perceptual**, then **Selective**, then **Adaptive**, and then **Restrictive (Web)** from the **Color Reduction Palette** pop-up menu to see how these settings affect the file size and appearance of the selected preview.

Notice the Color Table, file size, and image appearance are almost identical when the **Color Reduction Palette** pop-up menu is set to **Perceptual**, **Selective**, or **Adaptive**. These three color palettes are derived from the colors in the image, each by means of a slightly different algorithm. The **Restrictive (Web)** palette has fewer colors, and it doesn't look very good. The **Restrictive (Web)** palette is independent of the colors in an image and tries to force the colors in an image to a set palette. For this reason, I almost always use the **Adaptive**, **Perceptual**, or **Selective** palette instead of the **Restrictive (Web)** palette when optimizing GIFs.

So, when should you use the **Perceptive**, **Selective**, or **Adaptive** color reduction palettes? To choose between them, apply each of the three palettes to an image preview, as you did here. Choose the palette with the smallest file size but whose color and appearance are as close to the original image as possible. Every image will look better with a different color reduction palette (you need to experiment with the different color reduction palettes so you can decide which one produces the best result).

The only time to use the **Restrictive (Web)** palette is if you need a quick-and-dirty way to convert an image with non-Web-safe colors to one with Web-safe colors. As mentioned before, the **Restrictive (Web)** palette has no relationship to the original image, which typically affects your optimized image negatively. If you do have to convert to Web-safe colors, do so selectively using the technique at the end of this exercise.

---

3. Once you've looked at these palette choices, choose **Perceptual** from the **Color Reduction Palette** pop-up menu, choose **Diffusion** from the **Dither Algorithm** pop-up menu, set the **Dither** slider to **100%**, and choose **256** from the **Colors** pop-up menu. There's nothing magical about these particular settings—they're just settings you should return to so your settings match those in the rest of the GIF optimization exercises.

---

4. Leave the **Save For Web** dialog box open and move to the next exercise. If you have to quit Photoshop CS2 now and start the next exercise later, click **Done**, which will save your settings for the next time you open the **Save For Web** dialog box.

NOTE | Changing Selected Colors in a Palette to Web-Safe Colors

If you must convert a non-Web-safe image to a Web-safe one, change only those colors that fill large, solid-color areas of your image to eliminate the most noticeable dithering in an 8-bit Web browser, while keeping the GIF as true as possible to the colors in the original image. Avoid the **Restrictive (Web)** color reduction palette or the **Snap to Web** slider because both are wholesale solutions and don't let you control which colors will be changed to Web-safe colors. Instead, do the following:

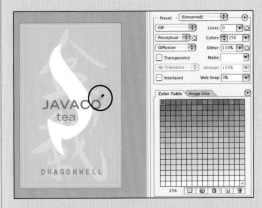

In the **Save For Web** dialog box, select the **Eyedropper** tool from the **Toolbox**. Click the color in the image preview you want to change. The corresponding color swatch will become highlighted in the **Color Table**.

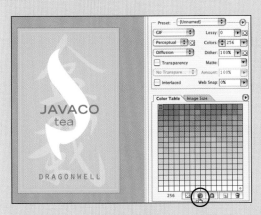

At the bottom of the **Color Table**, click the **Shift to Web-Safe Color** icon (the cube). This shifts the color in the image preview to the nearest Web-safe color from the color reduction palette you chose (in this case **Perceptual**).

continues on next page

NOTE | Changing Selected Colors in a Palette to Web-Safe Colors *continued*

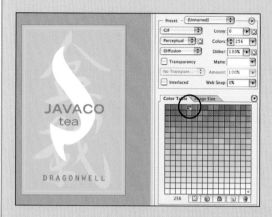

The color swatch in the Color Table now contains two small icons. The diamond indicates the swatch is a Web-safe color, and the square indicates the swatch is locked. The lock means this color will be retained in the Color Table even if you reduce the number of colors in the image. You'll learn how the lock works in Exercise 6.

If you don't like the Web-safe color that was chosen for you, and you want to change to a different color, double-click the highlighted color swatch in the **Color Table** to open the **Color Picker** dialog box, which will let you choose a different Web-safe color.

5. [PS] Reducing Colors

Minimizing the number of colors in a GIF is the most significant thing you can do to reduce GIF file size. Your goal is to reduce the number of colors until you arrive at the fewest colors necessary to keep the image looking good.

1. The file **dragonwell.psd** should still be open in the **Save For Web** window from the last exercise. Make sure the upper-right preview is selected and the optimization settings for the preview are the same as they were at the end of the last exercise (**GIF**, **Perceptual**, **Colors: 256**, **Diffusion**, **Dither: 100%**).

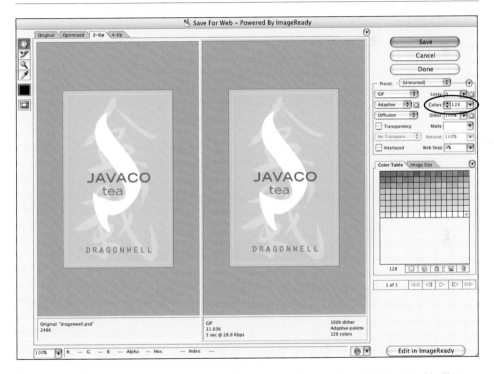

2. Using the **Colors** pop-up menu, change the number of colors from **256** to **128**. You'll see the file size get smaller right away. Compare this preview to the original, and you'll see the preview still looks great. Try smaller values until the image stops looking good.

*The image looks best at 32 colors, which results in a file size of about **7.3 K**. Reducing the colors to 16 makes edges of the text look too rough for my taste. That said, it's still possible to reduce this file size slightly by adjusting the dither.*

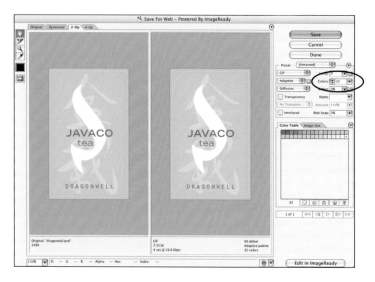

3. With the number of colors set to 32, move the **Dither** slider to **0%**.

*Notice the file size is now slightly smaller—about **7.1 K**. Different types of images realize different amounts of file savings with the dithering set to zero, but lowering or omitting dither almost always results in some file savings.*

4. Click **Save** to open the **Save Optimized As** dialog box. Navigate to the **chap_07** folder you copied to your **Desktop**. Click **Save** to save the **dragonwell.gif**.

5. Close **dragonwell.psd**. You don't need to save your changes.

NOTE | What Is Dither?

When you limit the number of colors available in the Color Table, you might make it impossible to reproduce some of the colors from the original image. Photoshop CS2 takes two colors in the Color Table and places small dots of each color next to one another to try to simulate the original color. Photoshop CS2 offers three patterns of dither dots—diffusion, pattern, and noise—which differ mainly in the way the dither dots are arranged. You can apply any of these dither patterns to an image preview by choosing one from the Dither Algorithm pop-up menu. The diffusion dither regulates the amount of dither applied by using the Dither slider, as you did in this exercise.

In most cases, your best bet is to avoid dither, because it adds to the file size and makes the image appear dotted. However, if your image has a large area of gradient, glow, or shadow, adding dither can sometimes improve its appearance. Try each of the dither patterns and the Dither slider to see if changing the dither improves the appearance of the image without increasing the file size significantly.

6. [PS] _____Locking Colors

Photoshop CS2 and ImageReady CS2 let you influence which colors are included in a GIF, even when you greatly reduce the number of colors in the Color Table.

1. Open **chai.psd** from the **chap_07** folder you copied to your **Desktop**. Choose **File > Save For Web**.

2. Click the **2-Up** tab and change the settings to **GIF**, **Perceptual**, **Diffusion**, **Lossy: 0**, **Colors: 32**, and **Dither: 0%**.

You may already see these settings because they are the same settings you used at the end of the last exercise.

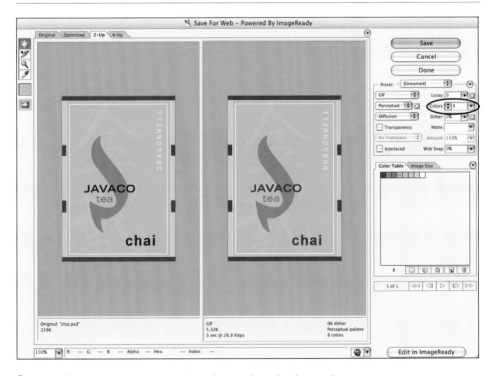

3. In the **Colors** pop-up menu, reduce the number of colors to **8**.

Notice this causes some of the central colors to change in the preview, specifically the dark blue in the words Javaco and chai. Some unanticipated colors changed in the preview because Photoshop CS2 decided which colors to throw away without your input.

4. In the **Colors** pop-up menu, return the number of colors to **32**.

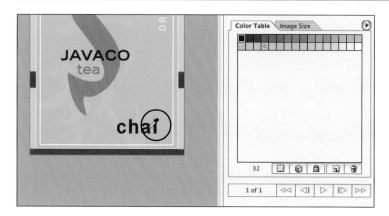

5. Using the **Eyedropper** tool, click the blue color in the word **chai**. Its corresponding color swatch in the **Color Table** will be highlighted.

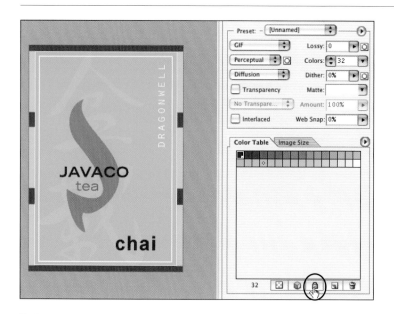

6. At the bottom of the **Color Table**, click the **Lock** button to lock the color.

After you lock the color, a small, white square will appear in the lower-right corner of the color swatch.

7. Go through the image with the **Eyedropper** tool and lock all the colors you want to preserve.

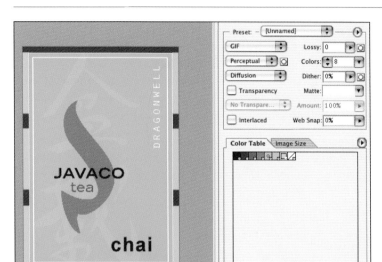

8. After you have all the colors locked, reduce the **Colors** to **8**.

This time, all the important colors in the image were preserved because you locked them in the **Color Table**.

9. Close **chai.psd**. You don't need to save your changes.

[PS]　　　　　　　　**Selective GIF Optimization with Alpha Channels**

Earlier, you learned how to selectively optimize parts of a JPEG using alpha channels. You can also apply selective optimization to GIF files using alpha channels, which you can use to control color reduction, dither, and lossy compression. The purpose of selective GIF optimization is to apply different levels of compression to two different parts of an image. The objective is to protect important areas of an image from degradation by giving them higher quality while giving the other parts inferior quality. This reduces file size and lets the important part of the image look as good as possible.

Photoshop CS2 can automatically create an alpha channel from type layers or vector-based shape layers in your image. This exercise will show you how to create an automatic alpha channel from a shape layer and a type layer, and how you can selectively optimize color reduction, dither, and the amount of lossy compression.

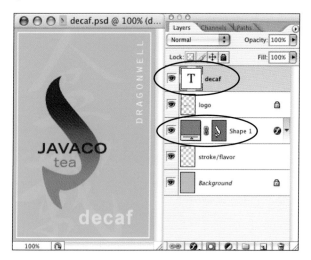

1. Open **decaf.psd** from the **chap_07** folder you copied to your **Desktop**.

*In the **Layers** palette, notice the file has a vector-based shape layer, which contains the javaco smoke curl. Also notice the color of the shape fades from dark blue to green. Because of this fade, you'll need to optimize the shape at a higher quality than the rest of the image.*

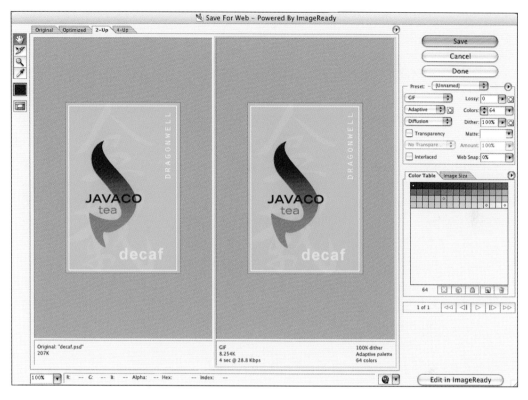

2. Choose **File > Save For Web**. Click the **2-Up** tab and choose **GIF** from the **File Format** pop-up menu. Match the rest of the settings to the ones you see in the illustration here (**Adaptive**, **Diffusion**, **Dither: 100%**, and **64** colors).

Even with 64 colors, the fade from blue to green doesn't look as smooth as the original.

Note: *In Exercise 4, you learned the importance of experimenting with different color reduction palettes to produce the best-looking image. This image is a prime example. Notice I specified* **Adaptive** *for this image. Try* **Perceptual** *and* **Selective***, and you'll see* **Adaptive** *produces the best-quality image.*

3. Click the **alpha channel** button next to the **Color Reduction Palette** pop-up menu to open the **Modify Color Reduction** dialog box.

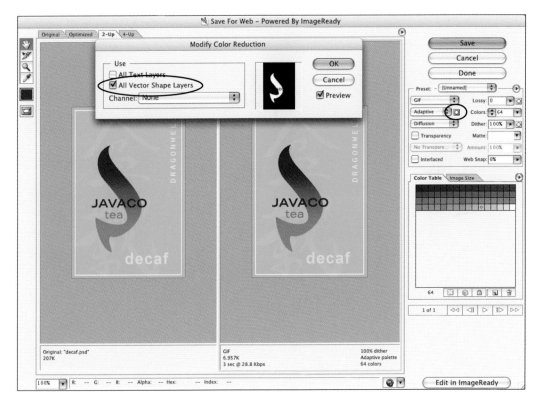

4. Turn on the **All Vector Shape Layers** option.

*Notice the colors in the **Color Table** change to different shades of blue and green. The **Color Table** is now weighted toward the blue and green colors in the shape layer, rather than uniformly represent-ing all the colors in the image. Unfortunately, the word **decaf** now looks jagged—the weighting of the colors in favor of the shape have negatively impacted the type. Not to worry, you'll fix this in the next step!*

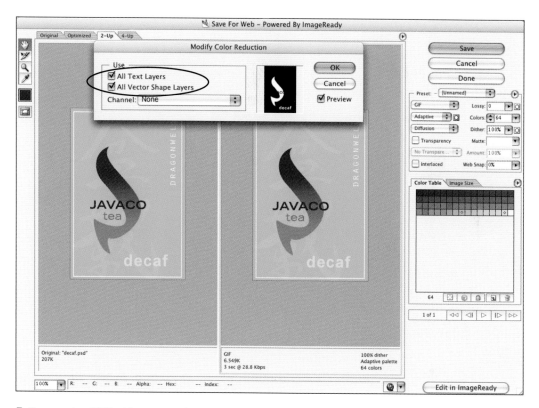

5. Turn on the **All Text Layers** option.

*Notice the colors in the **Color Table** changed again—this time with a few more shades of yellow, which improves the quality of the word **decaf** but still maintains the quality of the shape.*

6. In the **Modify Color Reduction** dialog box, click **OK**.

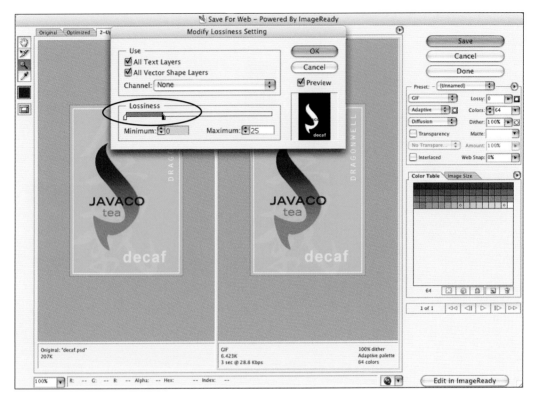

7. Click the **alpha channel** button next to the **Lossy** slider to open the **Modify Lossiness Setting** dialog box. Turn on the **All Text Layers** and **All Vector Shape Layers** options.

8. Adjust the **white** and **black Lossiness** sliders to adjust the amount of lossy compression to the shape and type than to the rest of the image. Leave the **white** slider at **0** and move the **black** slider to the left until the background looks good to you (try **25**). Click **OK**.

*The **white** slider controls the amount of lossiness applied to the shape and type (the white area of the alpha channel). The **black** slider controls the amount of lossiness applied to the rest of the image (the black area of the alpha channel).*

9. Click the **alpha channel** button next to the **Dither** slider to open the **Modify Dither Setting** dialog box. Turn on the **All Text Layers** and **All Vector Shape Layers** options.

You could use the sliders to apply different amounts of dither to the shape and type than to the rest of the image. However, there's no reason to do that in this case because no area of the image stands to benefit from dithering. In fact, applying dithering to the shape makes it look worse, not better.

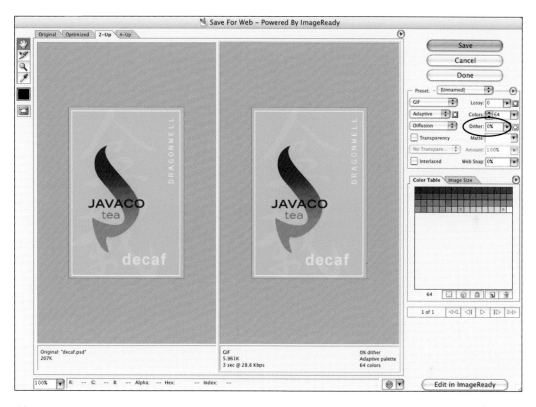

10. In the **Modify Dither Setting** dialog box, click **Cancel**. Set the **Dither** slider to **0%**.

---

11. In the **Save For Web** dialog box, click **Save** to open the **Save Optimized As** dialog box. Navigate to the **chap_07** folder you copied to your **Desktop**. Click **Save** to save **decaf.gif** in the **chap_07** folder.

*Using the techniques in this exercise, you decreased the size of the original **decaf.psd** file from **207 K** to **5.96 K**.*

---

12. Close **decaf.psd**. You don't need to save your changes.

8. [PS] _____ Previewing Images in a Web Browser

When you're optimizing images, you'll often want to see how they look in a Web browser. Here's a short exercise to show you how.

1. Open **dragonwell.psd** from the **chap_07** folder you copied to your **Desktop**.

2. Choose **File > Save For Web**.

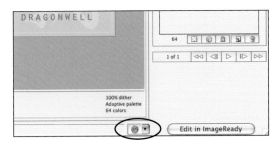

3. In the **Save For Web** dialog box, click the **Preview in Default Browser** button. The image will automatically open up in your default Web browser.

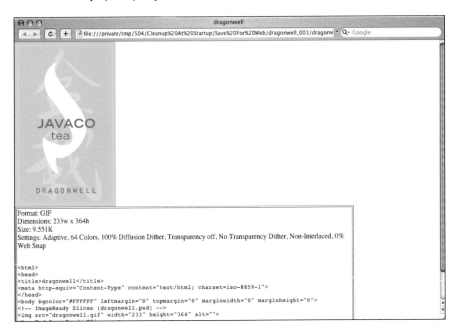

Note: My computer is set up to use Safari as the default Web browser. Your computer may be set up to use a different default Web browser.

4. Close the Web browser and return to the **Save For Web** dialog box.

When you're designing Web graphics, you need to see how the images appear in more than one Web browser because there is no guarantee your viewers will all use the same Web browser. Therefore, you should preview your images in something other than your default Web browser.

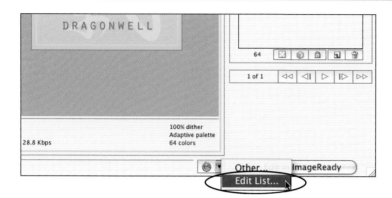

5. Click the **Preview in Default Browser** pop-up menu and choose **Edit List**.

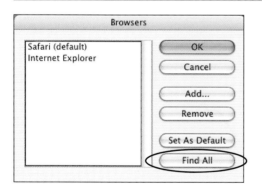

6. In the **Browsers** dialog box, click **Find All**.

*Photoshop CS2 automatically searches for all the Web browsers on your computer and lists them in the **Browsers** dialog box.*

*If you'd like to remove a Web browser, select it from the list and click **Remove**. If the Web browser you want to use is not listed, click **Add** and locate the Web browser you want to use.*

7. In the **Browsers** dialog box, click **OK** when you're satisfied with the list of Web browsers.

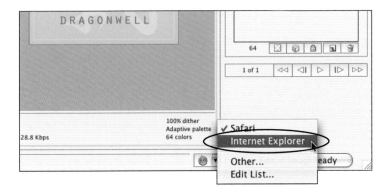

8. Click the **Preview in Default Browser** pop-up menu. You'll see the Web browsers you specified in the previous two steps.

*The Web browser with the checkmark beside it is the default. Anytime you click the **Preview in Default Browser** button, your images will open in that Web browser. If you want to open the image in a different Web browser, simply choose it from the **Preview in Default Browser** pop-up menu.*

9. In the **Save For Web** dialog box, click **Cancel**. Close **dragonwell.psd**. You don't need to save your changes.

Optimizing Images in Photoshop CS2 vs. ImageReady CS2

Photoshop CS2 and ImageReady CS2 offer identical options for optimizing images for the Web. The only difference between the two programs is the interface.

As you've seen in the preceding exercises, Photoshop CS2 has a Save For Web dialog box, which contains the tools, preview options, and optimization options you need to optimize Web graphics. You probably noticed the title bar of the dialog box says *Powered By ImageReady*. Because the Save For Web dialog box is powered by ImageReady CS2, the optimization options in Photoshop CS2 are identical to the ones in ImageReady CS2.

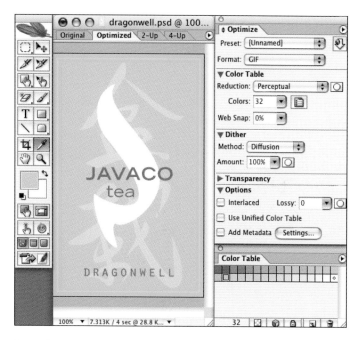

ImageReady CS2 has an Optimize palette and a Color Table palette that provide all the options required to optimize Web graphics. The Original, Optimized, 2-Up, and 4-Up tabs you saw in the Save For Web dialog box are part of the document window in ImageReady CS2. Likewise, the tools you saw in the Toolbox in the Save For Web dialog box are part of the ImageReady CS2 Toolbox. Because ImageReady CS2 is designed specifically for creating Web graphics, these tools are more readily accessible in ImageReady CS2 than they are in Photoshop CS2, so you can easily make changes to your images during the optimization process.

So, which application is best to use for optimizing Web graphics? Because both programs have the same options (they are both powered by ImageReady CS2), it makes no difference from a technical perspective. You'll be able to achieve the same results with either program. However, as you develop a workflow for designing Web graphics, you'll likely begin to favor the interface in one of the two programs. My advice is if you're using Photoshop CS2, optimize your images in Photoshop CS2; if you're using ImageReady CS2, optimize your images in ImageReady CS2. Once you're familiar with both interfaces, decide for yourself which one suits your workflow best.

Since all the exercises in this chapter have shown how to optimize images in Photoshop CS2, here are a couple of exercises to show you how to optimize images in ImageReady CS2.

9. [IR] _____Optimizing JPEGs in ImageReady CS2

So far in this chapter, you have optimized images exclusively in Photoshop CS2. In this exercise, you'll learn how to optimize images in ImageReady CS2. The options are the same—the only difference is the interface.

1. Open **candles.psd** from the **chap_07** folder you copied to your **Desktop**. Make sure the **Optimize** palette is visible. If it's not, choose **Window > Optimize**.

2. In the **Document** window, click the **2-Up** tab. Click the preview on the right side. If you need to, select the **Hand** tool from the **Toolbox** and click and drag inside the preview to reposition the image.

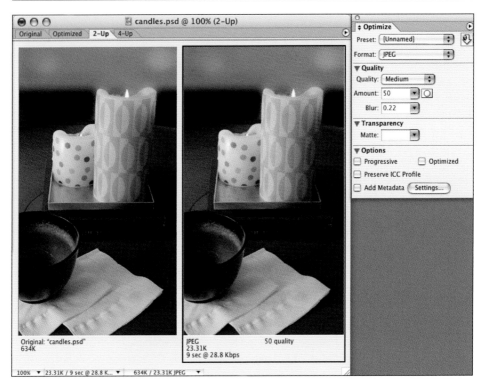

3. Using the optimization techniques you learned in Exercise 1, adjust the settings in the **Optimize** palette to produce the smallest file size and the best quality image.

4. When you're happy with the settings, choose **File > Save Optimized As**.

*Note: You need to choose **Save Optimized As**, not **Save As** (which will not let you save an optimized image–it only lets you save using the PSD file format). The **Save Optimized As** option will let you save the image using the settings you specified in the **Optimize** palette.*

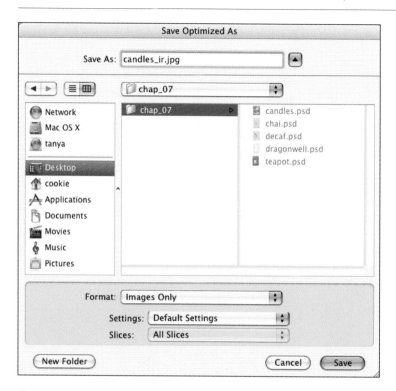

5. In the **Save Optimized As** dialog box, navigate to the **chap_07** folder you copied to your **Desktop**. In the **Save As** field, name the file **candles_ir.jpg**. Choose **Images Only** from the **Format** pop-up menu. Click **Save**.

As you can see, once you've mastered optimizing images in Photoshop CS2, it's a snap to optimize images in ImageReady CS2. In the next exercise, you'll learn how to optimize GIFs in ImageReady CS2.

TIP | Previewing Images in ImageReady CS2

In Exercise 8, you learned how to preview images in a Web browser using the **Save For Web** dialog box in Photoshop CS2. You can also preview images in a Web browser from ImageReady CS2. Here's how:

On the ImageReady CS2 **Toolbox**, click the **Preview in Default Browser** button. The image will automatically open up in your default Web browser. (On my computer, the default Web browser is Safari; on your computer, the default Web browser may be different.)

If you have more than one Web browser installed on your computer, you'll notice a small arrow in the lower-right corner of the **Preview in Default Browser** button. If you click and hold, you'll see a list of the Web browsers installed on your computer. If you want to choose a Web browser other than the default, you can choose it here.

[IR] _____Optimizing GIFs in ImageReady CS2

In this exercise, you'll take the GIF optimization knowledge you acquired earlier in this chapter and apply it to ImageReady CS2.

1. Open **dragonwell.psd** from the **chap_07** folder you copied to your **Desktop**. Make sure the **Optimize** palette and **Color Table** palette are visible. If they're not, choose **Window > Optimize** and **Window > Color Table**.

2. In the image window, click the **2-Up** tab. Click the preview on the right side.

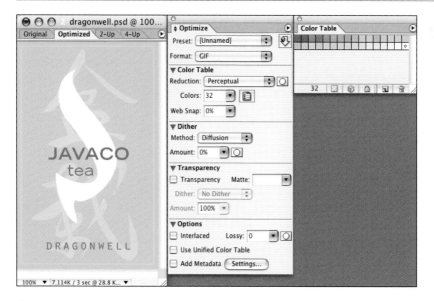

3. Using the optimization techniques you learned in Exercises 3, 4, 5, and 6, adjust the settings in the **Optimize** palette and **Color Table** palette to produce the best quality image with the smallest file size.

4. Choose **File > Save Optimized As**. In the **Save Optimized As** dialog box, navigate to the **chap_07** folder you copied to your **Desktop**. In the **Save As** field, name the file **dragonwell_ir.gif**. Choose **Images Only** from the **Format** pop-up menu. Click **Save**.

5. Close **dragonwell.psd**. You don't need to save your changes.

Congratulate yourself for learning so much in this chapter! Knowing how to optimize images is one of the most valuable skills a Web designer can have, and it is well worth the time and effort you put into the exercises in this chapter.

8

Creating Web Backgrounds

| Defining and Previewing Background Images |
| Optimizing and Saving Background Images |
| Creating Symmetrical Background Images |
| Creating Seamless Backgrounds from Photographs |
| Creating Full-Screen Backgrounds | Using Directional Tiles |

chap_08

PCS2Web HOT CD-ROM

Designing for HTML is challenging because standard HTML is capable of displaying only two layers—a background layer and a foreground layer. In most graphics applications, including Photoshop CS2, ImageReady CS2, Adobe Illustrator, and Macromedia FreeHand, you can work with an unlimited number of layers. Because HTML restricts you to only two layers, knowing how to create a variety of appearances for the background layer is very important. This chapter will show you techniques for creating background images for Web pages.

One way to get around the two-layer limitation of HTML is to use style sheets instead of standard HTML. However, this book is about designing Web graphics, not about writing code or using a Web page editor, so this chapter focuses on the challenges of, and solutions for, making effective background images that work with standard HTML.

There are two core issues to think about when you're making a background image: the speed at which it will load, which you learned about in Chapter 7, "*Optimizing Images*," and its appearance, which you'll learn about in this chapter.

What Is a Background Image?

Background images appear on the background layer of a Web page. Background images are made up of a series of tiles that repeat to make up an entire background image. By default, background images repeat to fill the size of the active Web browser window. You can restrict the default repeat of background images by using **C**ascading **S**tyle **S**heets (CSS), but that is a programming topic outside the scope of this book. The number of times a background tile repeats depends on the size of the original image and the size of the active Web browser window. As a result, background images often appear differently on different monitors. The challenge in designing background images is to prepare a graphic that can look different from monitor to monitor and still look good. Not an easy task! Fortunately, this chapter offers a number of solutions to help you design effective Web backgrounds.

Regardless of how many times a background tile repeats in a Web browser window, it downloads only once to the viewer's computer. Each time the tile appears on a Web page it is recalled from the cache in the viewer's computer, rather than being downloaded again and again. As a designer, you can get a lot of mileage from a background tile. If you create a tile with a small file size, you can fill an entire Web browser window in very little time.

HTML allows you to use a single background image and multiple foreground images. As a result, you can put other images on top of a background layer. If you want an illustration, a photograph, text, or any other image to float on top of a background image, you must identify the background image as an HTML background, which you'll learn to do in this chapter.

What differentiates background images from regular images in HTML code is the **BODY** tag. Understanding HTML for a tiled background is simple. Here's an example of the HTML required to create a tiled background from a simple image (**small.jpg** in this case):

```
<html>
<body background="small.jpg">
</body>
</html>
```

NOTE | Vocabulary: Background Tile and Tiling

In this chapter, you'll run into the terms *tiling* and *background tile*. *Tiling* refers to the horizontal and vertical repetition of an HTML background image in a Web browser when the image is smaller than the Web browser window. *Background tile* is used interchangeably with the term *background image* to mean a GIF or JPEG that repeats in an HTML background.

TIP | Design Tips for Readability

When you're creating background images, pay attention to your color choices. Try to use either all dark colors or all light colors. If you combine darks and lights in a single background image, your background might look great on its own, but your viewers may have problems reading the type.

Light background   *Dark background*

If you're wondering how to choose colors for backgrounds in relation to foreground type, here are some basic guidelines:

- If you're using a light background, use dark type.

- If you're using a dark background, use light type.

- Avoid using a medium value for a background image, because neither light nor dark type will read well on top of it.

- In a background image, avoid using contrasting values, which make type very difficult to read.

About Background Image Sizes

You can use graphics of any dimension for background images. The size of a background tile determines the number of times it repeats inside a Web browser window.

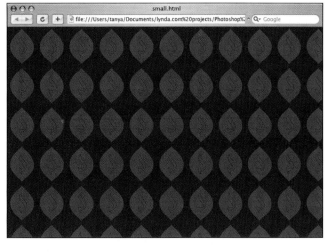

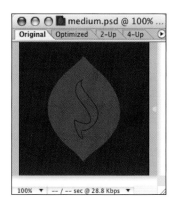

Small   *Result in Web browser*

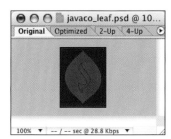

Medium   *Result in Web browser*

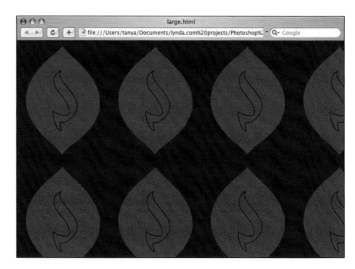

Large   *Result in Web browser*

As you can see in these examples, a background tile with larger dimensions repeats less often than a smaller background tile. For example, a background tile measuring 40 × 40 pixels will repeat 192 times (16 times across and 12 times down) in a 640 × 480 Web browser window. A background tile measuring 320 × 240 pixels will repeat four times (two times across and two times down) in a 640 × 480 Web browser window. You can also create extra-large background images so they repeat only once in a standard-size Web browser window. Before you decide which size to make the background tile, you need to decide what kind of effect you want to create.

Enlarging the dimensions of a background tile will increase its file size. A 50 K background tile will increase the size of your Web page by 50 KB, which will increase the time it takes to load. A rough formula for determining load time is as follows: 1 K equals 1 second. Although this formula isn't scientifically accurate, it's what many designers use as a rough guideline when designing Web graphics. Therefore, it's just as important to practice good optimization skills when creating background images as it is with other types of images.

I. [IR] Defining and Previewing Background Images

ImageReady CS2 lets you define any image as a background image by using options in the Output Settings dialog box. In this exercise, you'll learn how to define background images and preview the images in your default Web browser.

1. Open **javaco_leaf.psd** from the **chap_08** folder you copied to your **Desktop**. In the **Toolbox**, click the **Preview in Default Browser** button.

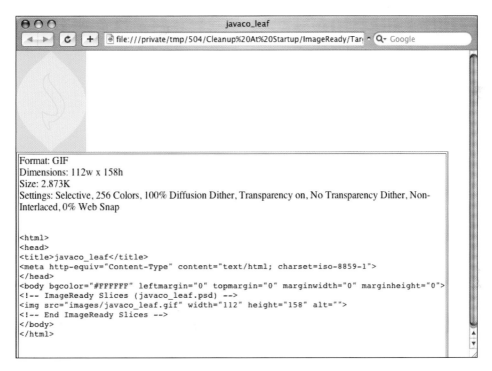

ImageReady CS2 currently views this image as a foreground image, which is the reason you see the image appear only once in the upper-left corner of the Web browser window. In order for ImageReady CS2 to display the image as a tiled background, you must define the image as a background, which you'll do in the next steps.

2. Choose **File > Output Settings > Background** to open the **Output Settings** dialog box.

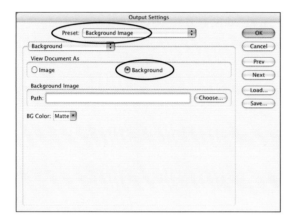

3. In the **Output Settings** dialog box, choose **Background Image** from the **Preset** pop-up menu. Select the **View Document As: Background** option to identify the image as an HTML background. Click **OK**.

4. In the **Toolbox**, click the **Preview in Default Browser** button to open your default Web browser.

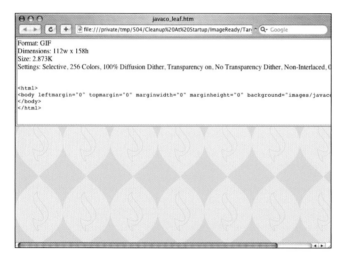

Now you can see the image as a tiled background. Notice the preview includes a white text box containing information about how the image was optimized and the HTML code required to define the image as a background. When you choose to preview images in a Web browser, you always see this information. If you save the image and the required HTML code, which you'll learn how to do in the next exercise, then open the saved HTML file, you won't see this information.

5. Return to ImageReady CS2. Leave **javaco_leaf.psd** open for the next exercise.

2. [IR] _____Optimizing and Saving Background Images

In order for a background image to work properly in a Web browser, you must do two things:

• Save the image as an optimized JPEG or GIF.

• Save the HTML code that tells the Web browser the image is a background tile.

Fortunately, in ImageReady CS2 this process is easy—you can save both the image and the required HTML code in a single step. Alternately, you could save the optimized image without HTML, open the image in an HTML editor, and write the required HTML code from scratch to specify the image as a background tile. In this exercise, you'll learn how to optimize and save background tiles.

1. If you followed the last exercise, **javaco_leaf.psd** should be open in ImageReady CS2. If it's not, go back and complete Exercise 1. Make sure the **Optimize** palette is visible. If it's not, choose **Window > Optimize**.

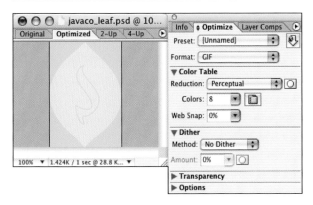

2. In the document window, click the **Optimized** tab. Using the GIF optimization techniques you learned in Chapter 7, "*Optimizing Images*," create the smallest GIF with the best image quality.

3. Choose **File > Save Optimized As**.

4. In the **Save Optimized As** dialog box, browse to the **chap_08** folder you copied to your **Desktop**. Click the **New Folder** button to create a new folder inside the **chap_08** folder. Name the folder **javaco_leaf_background**. Choose **HTML and Images** from the **Format** pop-up menu. Click **Save**.

*Note: You can also define images as background images from the **Save Optimized As** dialog box by choosing **Background Image** from the **Settings** pop-up menu.*

*Because you defined the image as a background image in the last exercise in the **Output Settings** dialog box, ImageReady CS2 automatically knows the image is a background image (even though **Custom** is selected in the **Settings** pop-up menu). If you know you want to save an image as a background image, specifying **Background Image** in the **Save Optimized As** dialog box will save you an extra step.*

NOTE | Saving HTML from ImageReady CS2

Some designers do not use the HTML file that ImageReady CS2 generates for background images because they prefer to use an HTML editor, such as Adobe GoLive or Macromedia Dreamweaver, to assemble Web pages. Using a dedicated HTML editor allows more precise control over place-ment of foreground images on top of the background. Whether you use ImageReady CS2 or an HTML editor to create HTML is up to you. Remember, saving an image and the HTML from ImageReady CS2 is a great way to view the background image without the white preview text readout and eliminates the need to use another application during the design process.

5. Browse to the **javaco_leaf_background** folder inside the **chap_08** folder on your **Desktop**.

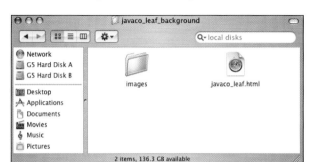

*Notice a folder called **images**, which contains an image called **javaco_leaf.gif** and a file called **javaco_leaf.html** (which contains the **<body background>** tag that identifies the GIF as a background image). Because you defined the image as a background image in the last exercise, ImageReady CS2 automatically saved the required HTML code when you saved the file.*

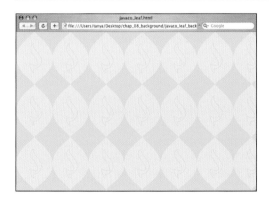

6. Double-click **javaco_leaf.html** to open the file in your default Web browser.

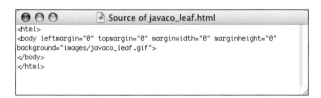

7. Choose **View > View Source** (Safari) or **View > Source** (Internet Explorer) to view the HTML code ImageReady CS2 generated.

8. Return to ImageReady CS2 and close the file.

TIP | Defining and Saving Background Images from Photoshop CS2

So far in this chapter, you've used ImageReady CS2 to define and save background images. You can also define and save background images from Photoshop CS2—it's just a bit more tedious, which is the reason I prefer to use ImageReady CS2 for this task.

In the **Save For Web** dialog box, choose **Edit Output Settings** from the **Optimize** menu. In the **Output Settings** dialog box, choose **Background** from the pop-up menu. Choose **View Document As: Background**. Click **OK**.

If you want to preview the background image, click the **Preview in Default Browser** button at the bottom of the **Save For Web** dialog box.

If you want to save the background image, in the **Save For Web** dialog box click **Save** to open the **Save Optimized As** dialog box. Like in ImageReady CS2, you can save both the background image and the required HTML code by choosing **HTML and Images** from the **Format** pop-up menu.

3. [PS/IR]   Creating Symmetrical Background Images

The background images you created in the last two exercises produced patterns with linear repetitions. In this exercise, you'll learn how to use the Offset filter in ImageReady CS2 to create the illusion of a seamless (nonrepeating) background image. For this exercise, you'll use ImageReady CS2, but the Offset filter works the same way in Photoshop CS2.

1. Open **javaco_leaf_small.psd** from the **chap_08** folder you copied to your **Desktop**.

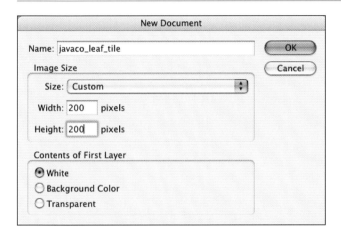

2. Choose **File > New**. In the **New Document** dialog box, type **javaco_leaf_tile** in the **Name** field, **200** in the **Width** field, and **200** in the **Height** field. In the **Contents of First Layer** section, select **White**. Click **OK**.

You need to make the canvas larger than the graphic you plan to use for the seamless tile. The relationship between the tile size you're creating and the size of the graphic determines the spacing of the graphic on the background tile. In this case, the javaco leaf graphic is 50×50 pixels, so a 200×200–pixel file should do the trick.

3. Click inside the document window of the **javaco_leaf_small.psd** image to make it the active document. Press **Cmd+A** (Mac) or **Ctrl+A** (Windows) to select the entire image.

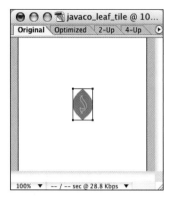

4. Press **Cmd+C** (Mac) or **Ctrl+C** (Windows) to copy the graphic to the clipboard. Click inside the document window of the new image, **javaco_leaf_tile.psd**, to make it the active document. Press **Cmd+V** (Mac) or **Ctrl+V** (Windows) to paste the graphic into the new document.

*The javaco leaf appears in the center of the image. When you paste an element into a document, ImageReady CS2 centers it automatically. With the graphic in place, you're ready to start creating a seamless tile by using the **Offset** filter.*

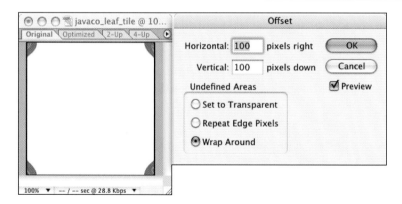

5. Choose Filter > Other > Offset. In the **Offset** dialog box, type **100** in the **Horizontal** field and **100** in the **Vertical** field. In the **Undefined Areas** section, select **Wrap Around**. Click **OK**.

*Because you're making a symmetrical repeating tile, you want to keep the **Horizontal** and **Vertical** settings the same. The graphic should look like it's split into four quarters, which are positioned at the four corners of the tile, as shown in the illustration here.*

6. Press **Cmd+V** (Mac) or **Ctrl+V** (Windows) to paste another copy of the javaco leaf into the center of the image.

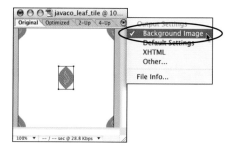

7. Choose **Background Image** from the document window menu.

This achieves the same result as specifying a background image by using the Output Settings dialog box—it's a great shortcut!

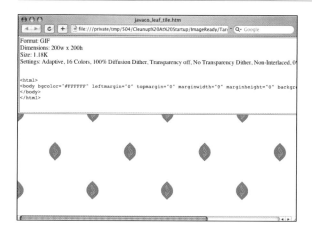

8. In the **Toolbox**, click the **Preview in Default Browser** button.

Notice the javaco leaf image is spaced evenly over the background. Each repeat of the graphic is an equal distance from the others because you started with a square image, pasted the graphics into the square, and set the Horizontal and Vertical offset values to 100.

9. Return to ImageReady CS2, and save **javaco_leaf_tile.psd** in the **chap_08** folder on your **Desktop**.

MOVIE | offset_filter.mov

In the last exercise, you learned to create symmetrical backgrounds by using the Offset filter. To learn more about the Offset filter, including how to create nonsymmetrical backgrounds, check out **offset_filter.mov** in the **movies** folder on the **PCS2Web HOT CD-ROM**.

4. [IR] _____**Creating Seamless Backgrounds from Photographs**

In the last exercise, you created a seamless background image using flat, graphical elements. What if you want to create a background using a photograph? With the Tile Maker filter in ImageReady CS2, you can create perfect, seamless backgrounds from photographs because it blends the edges of a photograph, which creates a convincing seamless pattern. Consider this technique if you're looking for ways to incorporate photographic backgrounds into your Web pages, but you want to keep the file size down. The Tile Maker filter works best on abstract photographs because they are least likely to show easily discernible, repeating patterns.

1. Open **tea_leaves.psd** from the **chap_08** folder you copied to your **Desktop**. Make sure the **Layers** palette and **Optimize** palette are visible. If they're not, choose **Window > Layers** and **Window > Optimize**.

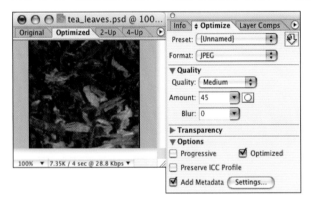

2. In the document window, click the **Optimized** tab. Using the JPEG optimization techniques you learned in Chapter 7, "_Optimizing Images_," optimize the image using the controls in the **Optimize** palette.

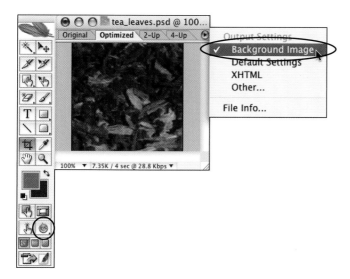

3. Choose **Background Image** from the document window menu. In the **Toolbox**, click the **Preview in Default Browser** button.

*Notice the obvious repeats in the pattern from the edges and seams of the source image. The **Tile Maker** filter will transform the image into a seamless pattern in a snap!*

4. Return to ImageReady CS2. With the **tea leaves** layer selected in the **Layers** palette, choose **Filter > Other > Tile Maker**.

5. In the **Tile Maker** dialog box, select **Blend Edges**, type **10** in the **Width** field, and turn on the **Resize Tile to Fill Image** option. Click **OK**.

*The illustration here shows how the image will look after you apply the **Tile Maker** filter. You can see it's a little magnified.*

*Tip: Selecting the **Kaleidoscope Tile** option in the **Tile Maker** dialog box can give you some beautiful abstract effects. You might want to experiment with it later.*

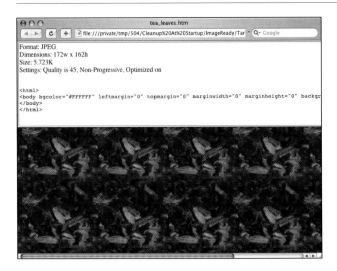

6. In the **Toolbox**, click the **Preview in Default Browser** button.

Notice the background appears softer, and the edge blending has hidden the sharp edges where the tea leaves run off the background tile. Although this image is attractive and has no visible seams, it contains too much contrast to work effectively as a background image. Next, you'll modify its brightness and hue so it works more effectively as a background image.

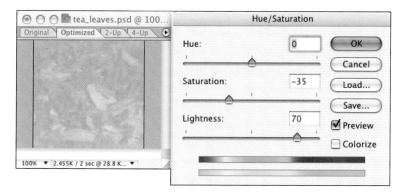

7. Return to ImageReady CS2. Choose **Image > Adjustments > Hue/Saturation**. In the **Hue/Saturation** dialog box, adjust the settings until you're satisfied with the result. In this example, I significantly increased the **Lightness** and slightly decreased the **Saturation**. As a result, the image appears faded with lighter colors, making the background image more subtle and decreasing the file size when optimized. When you've finished, click **OK**.

8. In the **Toolbox**, click the **Preview in Default Browser** button.

The background image is now much lighter, which will make type or images placed on top easier to read and view.

9. Close the file. You don't need to save your changes.

5. [PS/IR]_____Creating Full-Screen Backgrounds

Using a full-screen graphic as a background image can produce an impressive effect. If it's optimized properly, you can create a full-screen graphic background that loads quickly. The key to creating fast-loading background images is to limit your colors and use large areas of flat color.

The challenge in designing full-screen graphic backgrounds is considering the different screen resolutions your viewers will be using when they view your Web site, and creating background images that look good at each resolution. If you design a background image at 800 × 600, and your Web page is viewed at 1024 × 768, the Web browser will automatically repeat (or tile) the background image to fill the entire browser window, which probably won't look good.

Before you begin designing background images, consider the highest screen resolution your viewers will be using. Then, use this same size to design your background images. From there, you can rework your image to make it look good at lower resolutions.

This exercise will show you a helpful technique for viewing background images at different resolutions.

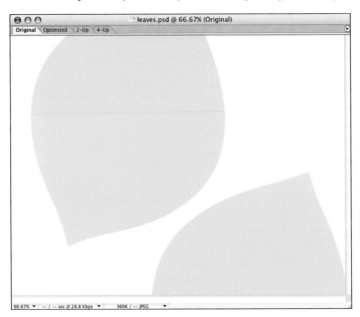

1. Open **leaves.psd** from the **chap_08** folder you copied to your **Desktop**.

It's a big file—1024 × 768 pixels—but when optimized as a GIF with four colors, its file size is less than 11 K. Images with large areas of solid colors optimize unbelievably well. You don't have to worry too much about download speed, but you do need to worry about how the image will look at different resolutions.

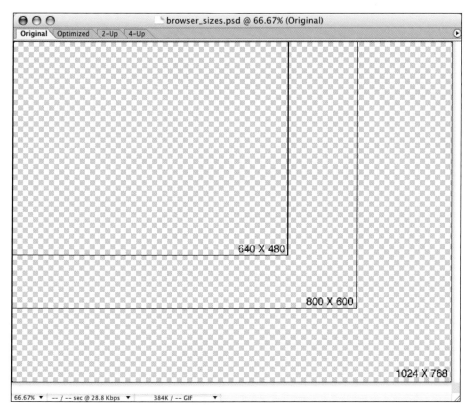

2. Open **browser_sizes.psd** from the **chap_08** folder you copied to your **Desktop**.

You can use this file to help you see how full-screen backgrounds look with different screen resolutions. For example, viewers with their screen resolutions set to 640×480 pixels will see only a portion of the background image and any foreground elements you place on top of it that fit within the box marked 640×480. Sound a bit confusing? Follow the next few steps, and you'll understand.

3. Select the **Move** tool from the **Toolbox**. In the **browser_sizes.psd** file, click the **screen resolutions** layer in the **Layers** palette to select it.

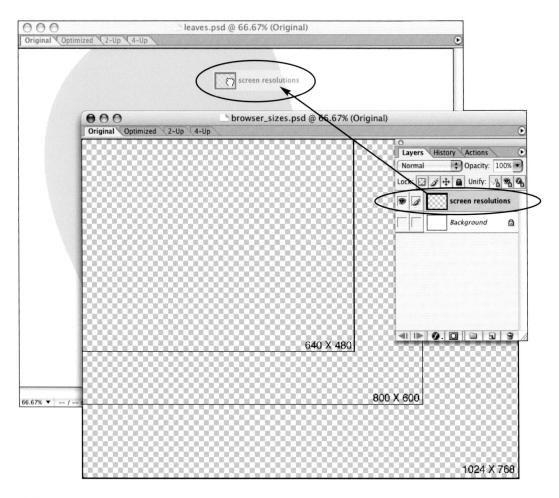

4. Drag and drop the **screen resolutions** layer from the **Layers** palette in the **browser_sizes.psd** file anywhere inside the **leaves.psd** document window.

*When you drag and drop the layer, you'll see the **screen resolutions** layer appear in the **Layers** palette of the **leaves.psd** file. Make sure the **screen resolutions** layer is at the top of the layer stack. If it's not, click and drag it to the top.*

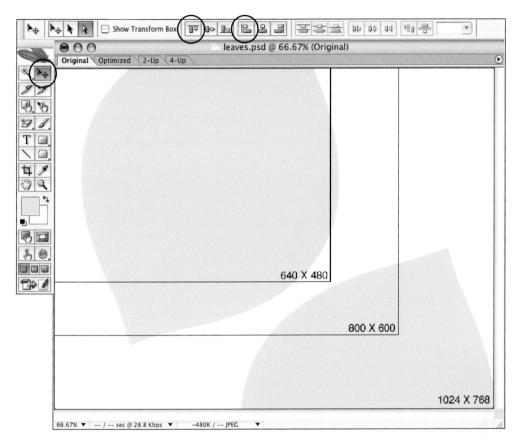

5. In the **Layers** palette, click the **screen resolutions** layer to select it. Using the **Move** tool and the arrow keys on your keyboard, align the upper-left corners of the **screen resolutions** layer and the **Background** layer. Since these are large images, you might want to zoom in to fine-tune the alignment. Alternately, you can use the alignment buttons on the **Options** bar to align the screen resolution layer. Try clicking the **Align layer top edges** and **Align layer left edges** buttons.

Now you can see how the background image will appear at 640×480, 800×600, and 1024×768. Using an overlay like this one will save you the time-consuming task of previewing the image at different resolutions while you're designing the background image.

6. Close both files. You don't need to save your changes.

This exercise showed you how to give careful consideration to resolution when designing full-screen graphic backgrounds. The overlay provided helps you visualize how a background will look at different resolutions. Feel free to use this overlay when you're designing your own large background images.

6. [IR] _____Using Directional Tiles

A wonderful trick that's widely used in Web design is to make directional tiles—graphics that are short and wide or narrow and tall so they can expand to full-screen images when repeated as background images. You can create the illusion of a large, full-screen graphic background with a tiny tile. Because the original image is so small, you get maximum effect for minimal download time.

In this exercise, you'll work with a small file to create a vertically striped background image. You'll use ImageReady CS2, but it works similarly in Photoshop CS2.

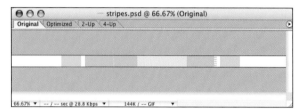

1. Open **stripes.psd** from the **chap_08** folder you copied to your **Desktop**.

2. Choose **Background Image** from the document window menu.

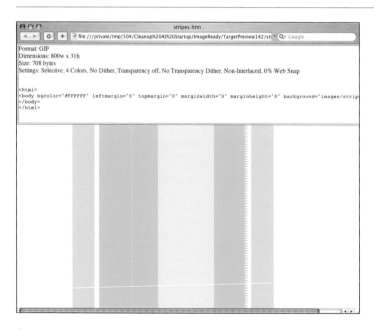

3. In the **Toolbox**, click the **Preview in Default Browser** button.

Notice the effect of the short, wide tile—a background image composed of vertical stripes.

4. Return to ImageReady CS2. Choose **Image > Rotate Canvas > 90°CW** to rotate the image 90 degrees clockwise.

CW stands for clockwise, which means it rotates the image to the right. CCW stands for counterclockwise, which means it rotates the image to the left.

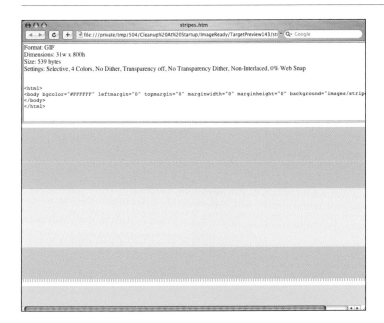

5. In the **Toolbox**, click the **Preview in Default Browser** button.

Notice the effect of the tall, narrow tile—a background image composed of horizontal stripes.

You should now have an idea of how directional tiles work. Try filling the image with a different color scheme or select and fill a new area to create a new stripe. Now that you know how images repeat inside Web browsers, the sky's the limit!

6. Save and close the file.

You've finished another chapter! With the techniques you've learned here, you can design unique, yet functional, background images for any Web page! In the next chapter, you'll learn techniques for optimizing transparent graphics.

9

Designing Navigation

| Planning Effective Navigation |
| Creating a Horizontal Navigation Bar | Creating Elliptical Buttons |
| Editing Multiple Buttons with Smart Objects |
| Creating Pill-Shaped and Three-Dimensional Buttons |
| Creating Tabbed Navigation Bars |
| Creating Navigation Bars with Icons |

chap_09

PCS2Web HOT CD-ROM

Designing an effective navigation system for a Web site is one of the most important aspects of Web design. Without a proper navigation system, your viewers won't find the information they need. If they can't find the information they need, they probably won't return.

Fortunately, Photoshop CS2 offers excellent tools, including the shape tools, type tools, and layer styles feature, to help you design effective and creative navigation systems, such as buttons and navigation bars. In this chapter, you'll also learn about the new Smart Objects feature in Photoshop CS2, which you can use to update the contents of multiple objects at the same time—it's a dream when you're designing buttons.

In this chapter, you'll learn exclusively about designing navigational elements, such as navigation bars and buttons. In Chapter 12, "*Slicing*," you'll learn how to slice and how to link to URLs. In Chapter 13, "*Creating Rollovers*," you'll learn how to make navigational elements interactive by adding over, down, and remote states.

Planning Effective Navigation

When you design a navigation system, you should answer the following questions for your audience:

- Where am I?

- What's here?

- Where else can I go?

- How do I go forward?

- How do I get back?

In this chapter, you'll learn how to design different navigation systems, including different types of Web buttons and navigation bars that help address these questions.

Shape Tools, Type Tools, and Layer Styles

The shape tools and type tools in Photoshop CS2 and ImageReady CS2 are vector-based, not pixel-based. You can use the shape tools to make buttons and navigation bars with crisp edges that remain scalable and editable in a layered Photoshop CS2 file. Likewise, you can add scalable and editable type to your buttons and navigation bars with the type tools. Drawing with the shape tools automatically creates a special kind of layer (just like the type tools do). In this chapter, you'll learn how to use the shape tools and type tools to create different types of navigation.

Photoshop CS2 and ImageReady CS2 define shapes as individual objects. Therefore, you can select, edit, and move shapes individually. Shapes are defined by smooth outlines called paths, which can be modified after shapes have been drawn. Shapes have a number of attributes, such as fill color and style, which you can change at any time using the controls on the Options bar. Because shapes are vector-based, you can resize them without degrading the quality of the image or making the edges fuzzy.

Keep in mind, when you save images in a file format other than the native Photoshop CS2 file format (PSD), shape layers and type layers are automatically rasterized (converted to pixels), and you lose the vector properties. Remember, you should always save copies of your layered images in the native Photoshop CS2 file format in case you need to make changes to the images later.

Layer styles, which you learned about in Chapter 5, "*Working with Layers*," offer a nondestructive way to add special effects, such as a drop shadow or bevel, to Web buttons and navigation bars. Applying a layer style does not affect the contents of the original layer—the effect exists as its own separate layer, which you can edit or delete. The beauty of applying layer styles to shape or type layers is that they remain vector-based, which means you can edit them at any time.

Comparing Bitmap Images and Vector Graphics

When you design a navigation system, you'll use the shape tools, which are vector-based features in Photoshop CS2 and ImageReady CS2. Before you begin the exercises, take a minute to understand the differences between *bitmap* and *vector*.

Bitmap images are made up of a series of pixels with each pixel assigned a specific color and location. Vector graphics are defined by mathematical instructions. For example, a bitmap circle is composed of pixels arranged in a circular shape on an invisible grid. A vector circle is composed of mathematical instructions, such as *radius=100*. You may have worked with vector drawing programs, such as Adobe Illustrator, CorelDRAW, Macromedia FreeHand, or Macromedia Flash.

This behind-the-scenes explanation helps you understand the differences between the terms *bitmap* and *vector*. But you're probably wondering how and when you should use a bitmap image instead of a vector graphic. Here's a chart to help you understand:

Bitmap Images vs. Vector Graphics		
	Bitmap Images	**Vector Graphics**
When to use	Best for continuous tone images, such as photographs, glows, soft edges, and blurs	Best for flat, graphical content, such as shapes, type, and objects that require sharp edges
How to create	By using the painting tools or fill commands, or by scanning images (from a digital camera, for example)	By using the shape tools, pen tools, or type tools
How to edit	By modifying individual pixels	By manipulating the anchor points with the Direct Selection tool

I. [PS/IR]_____Creating a Horizontal Navigation Bar

Navigation bars are one of the simplest and most effective forms of navigation. In this exercise, you'll use the shape and type tools to create a horizontal navigation bar.

1. Open **horizontal_nav_bar.psd** from the **chap_09** folder you copied to your **Desktop**. Make sure the **Layers** palette is visible.

2. In the **Toolbox**, click the **Default Foreground and Background Color** button to return the **Foreground Color** to black and the **Background Color** to white. Select the **Rectangle** tool from the **Toolbox**.

3. On the **Options** bar, click the **Shape Layers** and the **Create a New Shape Layer** buttons.

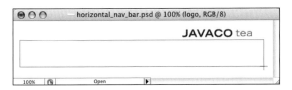

4. Position your cursor inside the document window. Click and drag to create a rectangle, as shown in the illustration here. Don't concern yourself with the position of the rectangle, just the size and shape. You'll fix the position of the shape later in this exercise.

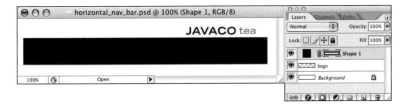

*When you release your mouse to create the shape, take a look at the contents of the **Layers** palette. Three components make up the **Shape 1** layer—a fill layer, a vector mask, and a link.*

TIP | Understanding Shape Layers

When you draw a shape with one of the shape tools, a shape layer is automatically created in the Layers palette. Shape layers are made up of three components: a fill layer, a vector mask, and a link. Here are descriptions of each:

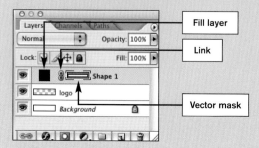

- **Fill layer:** Fill layers contain information about the fill color and fill style. By default, fill layers are solid color fills, and they pick up the foreground color in the Toolbox. You can change the solid color fill to a gradient fill or pattern fill. The left icon on a shape layer represents the fill layer.

- **Vector mask:** Vector masks are black-and-white images that hide and reveal the contents of fill layers. Vector masks contain a path, which is an outline of the shape. They mask (or hide) any part of the fill layer that appears outside the path. Paths are vector-based, which gives them smooth edges and allows them to be resized without degrading the quality of the shape. The right icon on a shape layer represents the vector mask.

- **Link:** By default, fill layers and vector masks are linked so you can move and edit them together. There may be times when you want to move the fill layer independent of the vector mask. For example, if a fill layer contains a pattern, you may want to unlink the vector mask so you can reposition the fill layer and see a different part of the pattern inside the shape. The Link icon is located between the fill layer icon and the vector mask icon on a shape layer.

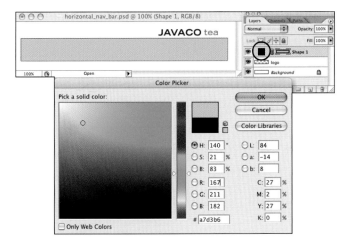

5. On the **Layers** palette, double-click the **fill layer** icon of the **Shape 1** layer to open the **Color Picker** dialog box. Choose a **turquoise green**, and click **OK** to accept the color choice and close the **Color Picker** dialog box.

Notice as you choose different colors in the Color Picker dialog box, the shape in the document window updates automatically to show you the color choice.

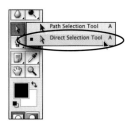

6. Select the **Direct Selection** tool (the white arrow) from the **Toolbox**.

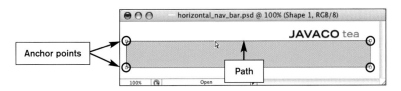

7. Click anywhere on the path around the perimeter of the rectangle. You'll know you've successfully selected the path when you see anchor points at the corners of the rectangle, as shown in the illustration here.

Because the rectangle is a vector-based object, you can use these anchor points to resize and reshape the rectangle while keeping the crisp edges.

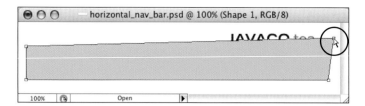

8. Click the anchor point in the upper-right corner of the rectangle. You'll know the anchor point is selected when it is solid gray. Click and drag the anchor point toward the upper-right corner of the document window to reshape the rectangle.

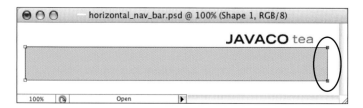

9. Press **Cmd+Z** (Mac) or **Ctrl+Z** (Windows) to return the shape to the original rectangle. The upper-right anchor point should still be selected. Hold down the **Shift** key, and click the lower-right anchor point. Both the upper-right and lower-right anchor points should now be selected.

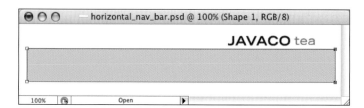

10. Click and drag the anchor points toward the right side of the document window to increase the size of the rectangle. To keep the rectangle straight, begin dragging then hold down the **Shift** key as you click and drag.

*As you can see, the **Direct Selection** tool lets you resize and reshape vector-based objects without affecting the quality of the edges.*

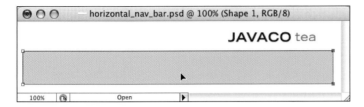

11. Select the **Move** tool from the **Toolbox**. Click and drag to reposition the rectangle inside the document window, centering the rectangle horizontally and leaving more space between the javaco tea logo and the top of the rectangle.

*Just like on any other layer, you can use the **Move** tool to reposition a shape layer anywhere inside the document window.*

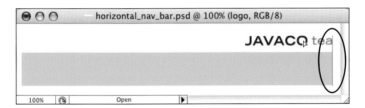

12. In the **Layers** palette, click the **logo** layer to select it. Using the **Smart Guides** (**View > Show > Smart Guides**), click and drag to right-align the logo and the rectangle, as shown in the illustration here.

13. In the **Layers** palette, click the **Shape 1** layer to select it. Double-click the **Shape 1** layer name. When the bounding box appears, rename the layer **nav bar**, and press **Return** (Mac) or **Enter** (Windows).

You can rename shape layers by double-clicking the layer name. As with any other layered project file, you need to give your layers descriptive names so you can easily identify the contents of each layer.

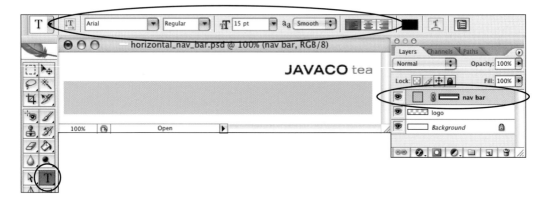

14. With the **nav bar** layer selected in the **Layers** palette, select the **Horizontal Type** tool from the **Toolbox**. On the **Options** bar, choose **Arial** from the **Font Family** pop-up menu, **Regular** from the **Font Style** pop-up menu, **15 pt** from the **Font Size** pop-up menu, and **Smooth** from the **Anti-Aliasing** pop-up menu, and click the **Left Align** button.

*Note: If you don't see 15 pt in the **Font Size** pop-up menu, type **15** in the **Font Size** pop-up menu.*

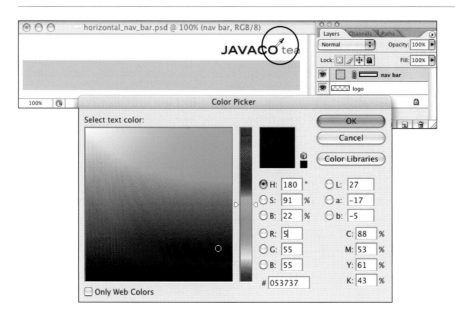

15. On the **Options** bar, click the **Font Color** box to open the **Color Picker** dialog box. Position your cursor over the word **javaco** in the document window. When you move your cursor outside the **Color Picker** dialog box, it automatically changes to the **Eyedropper** cursor. Click to sample the dark blue color from the word **javaco**. In the **Color Picker** dialog box, click **OK**.

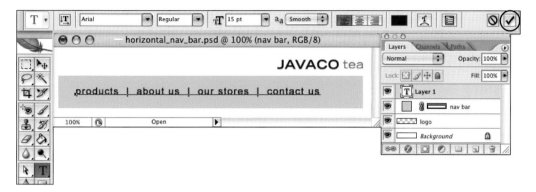

16. Click anywhere inside the document window and begin typing the type labels, as shown in the illustration here. When you've finished, on the **Options** bar, click the **Commit Current Edits** button.

Note: Use the pipe character, which is shared with the backslash key on your keyboard, to create the dividing lines between the words. Leave two spaces between the beginning and ending of each word and the dividing line.

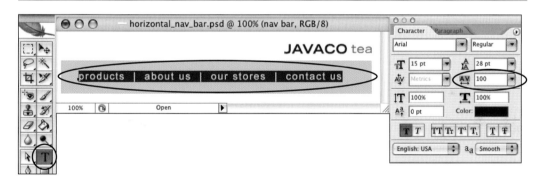

17. Double-click the **T** icon of the type layer you created in the last steps to highlight the type. Choose **Window > Character** to turn on the **Character** palette. Set the **Tracking** to **100**. When you've finished, on the **Options** bar, click the **Commit Current Edits** button.

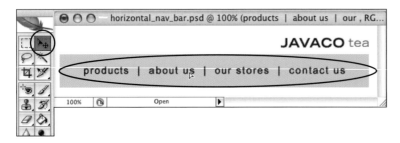

18. Select the **Move** tool from the **Toolbox**. Click and drag to position the type inside the rectangle. Use the **Smart Guides** to help align the type layer with the rectangle.

Tip: You can also use the alignment techniques you learned in Chapter 5, "Working with Layers," to align the text to the rectangle.

Although the navigation bar looks good as it is, the dividing lines between the words are too dominant. Creating an appropriate focal point is important, so in this case, the words should have a stronger presence than the dividing lines. To achieve this effect, you'll change the color of the dividing lines in the next step.

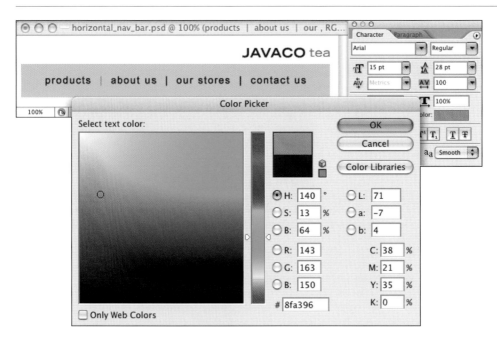

19. Select the **Horizontal Type** tool from the **Toolbox**, and click and drag to select the first dividing line. Click the **Font Color** box on the **Character** palette to open the **Color Picker** dialog box. Choose a light gray, make note of the **RGB** values (R=143, G=163, B=150), and click **OK**.

20. Click and drag to select the second dividing line. In the **Character** palette, click the **Font Color** box to open the **Color Picker** dialog box. Type the **RGB** values you chose in the last step (**R=143, G=163, B=150**). Click **OK**. Repeat this step for the third dividing line.

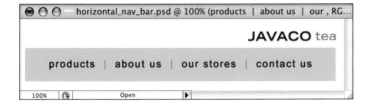

With the color changes you made to the dividing lines, the words now appear stronger and are the clear focal point on the navigation bar.

21. Save your changes, and close the file.

Wondering how to slice the navigation bar, how to assign URLs, and how to create rollovers? Chapter 12, "Slicing," and Chapter 13, "Creating Rollovers," will address these questions.

2. [PS/IR] _____Creating Elliptical Buttons

Another useful and popular form of Web site navigation is buttons. In the next few exercises, you'll use the shape tools, type tools, and layer styles feature to create a variety of different-shaped buttons. In this exercise, you'll learn how to create elliptical buttons with a soft, inner glow and a crisp outline.

1. Open **elliptical_button.psd** from the **chap_09** folder you copied to your **Desktop**. Make sure the **Layers** palette is visible. If it's not, choose **Window > Layers**.

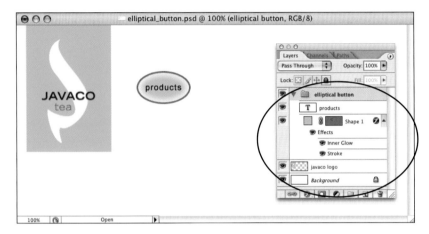

Take a look at the contents of the **elliptical button** layer group so you can see how the elliptical button in this image was created. As you can see, the button contains a shape layer and two layer styles—**Inner Glow** and **Stroke**.

2. Drag and drop the **elliptical button** layer group onto the **Trash** icon, which is at the bottom of the **Layers** palette.

3. Select the **Ellipse** tool from the **Toolbox**.

4. Click and drag to create a small ellipse inside the document window, as shown in the illustration here.

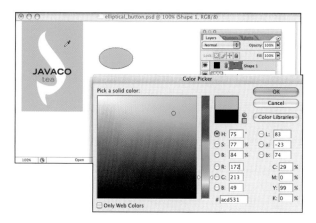

5. In the **Layers** palette, double-click the **Fill Layer** icon of the **Shape 1** layer to open the **Color Picker** dialog box. Position your cursor over the lime green rectangle and click to sample the color. The ellipse will automatically change from black to lime green. Click **OK** to close the **Color Picker** dialog box.

6. At the bottom of the **Layers** palette, choose **Stroke** from the **Layer Style** pop-up menu.

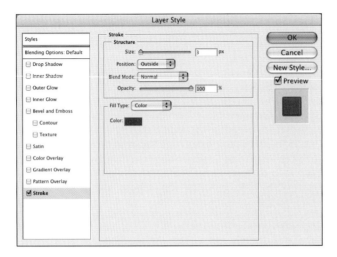

7. Experiment with the different settings in the **Structure** section of the **Layer Style** dialog box. Make sure you turn on the **Preview** option so you can see how the changes affect the image. When you've finished experimenting, match the settings to the ones shown in the illustration here.

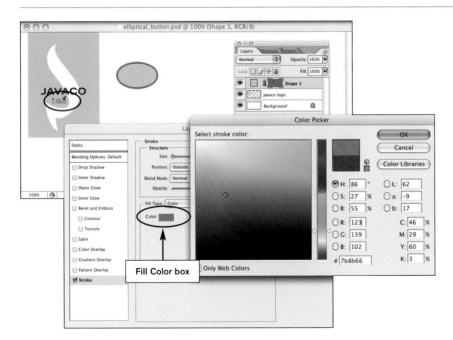

8. Click the **Fill Color** box in the **Layer Style** dialog box to open the **Color Picker** dialog box. Position your cursor over the word **tea** and click to sample the color. The stroke should automatically change from red to gray. Click **OK** to close the **Color Picker** dialog box.

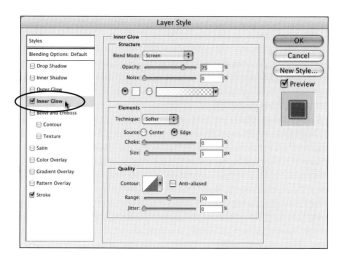

9. In the **Layer Style** dialog box, click the **Inner Glow** option.

*Note: You must click the words **Inner Glow** in order for the contents of the **Layer Style** palette to change to the **Inner Glow** options.*

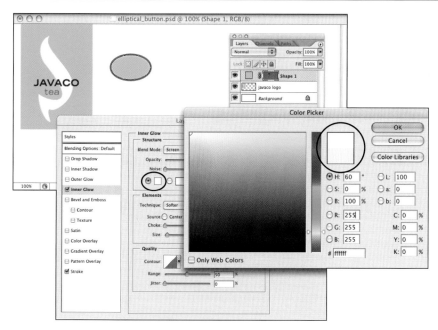

10. Click the **Inner Glow Color** box to open the **Color Picker** dialog box. Choose **white**, and click **OK**.

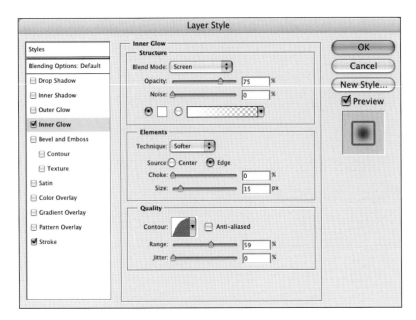

11. Experiment with the **Inner Glow** options. Make sure you turn on the **Preview** option so you can see how the changes affect the image. When you've finished, match the settings to the ones shown in the illustration here. Click **OK** to close the **Layer Style** dialog box.

12. In the **Layers** palette, click the **arrow** next to the **Layer Style** icon to show the layer styles you applied to the ellipse. Toggle the visibility (the **Eye** icons) of the layer styles so you can see how they change the ellipse's appearance.

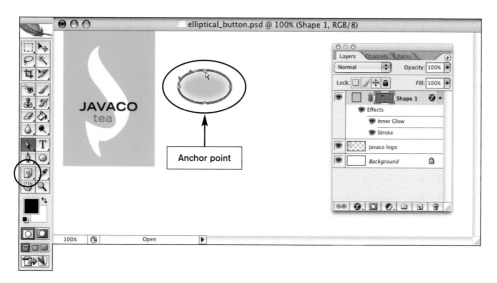

13. With the **Shape 1** layer selected in the **Layers** palette, select the **Direct Selection** tool (the white arrow) from the **Toolbox**. Click to select the path around the perimeter of the ellipse. You'll know the path is selected when you see the anchor points.

14. Click and drag the anchor point on the right side to reshape the ellipse.

Notice the layer styles automatically adjust as you reshape the ellipse. The beauty of using layer styles is that they do not affect vector-based objects, such as shapes. As a result, you can reshape and resize vector-based shapes and still keep the crisp edges. Plus, the layer styles update automatically!

15. Press **Cmd+Z** (Mac) or **Ctrl+Z** (Windows) to undo the change you made in the last step.

16. Select the **Horizontal Type** tool from the **Toolbox**. Choose **Arial** from the **Font Family** pop-up menu, **Regular** from the **Font Style** pop-up menu, **15 pt** from the **Font Size** pop-up menu, and **Smooth** from the **Anti-Aliasing** pop-up menu.

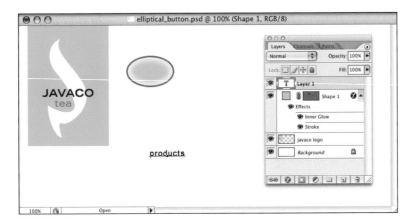

17. Position your cursor inside the document window, and type the word **products**.

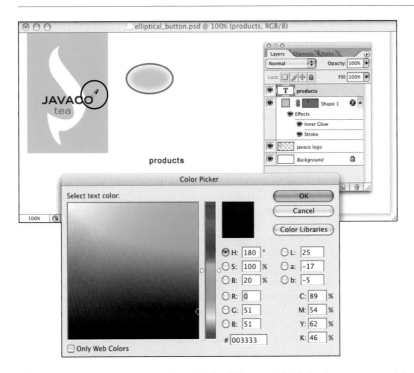

18. In the **Layers** palette, double-click the **T** icon to highlight the contents of the type layer you created in the last step. Click the **Font Color** box to open the **Color Picker** dialog box. Position your cursor over the word **javaco** and click to sample color. Click **OK** to close the **Color Picker** dialog box.

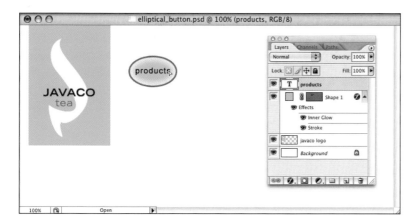

19. Select the **Move** tool from the **Toolbox**. Click and drag to reposition the type inside the button. Use the **Smart Guides** (**View > Show > Smart Guides**) to help center the type inside the button.

As you can see, using the shape tools, type tools, and layer style feature is an excellent way to create unique and interesting Web buttons.

---

20. Double-click the **Shape 1** layer name. When the bounding box appears, rename the layer **products button** and press **Return** (Mac) or **Enter** (Windows).

---

21. Leave **elliptical_button.psd** open for the next exercise.

 MOVIE | rectangular_buttons.mov

In the last exercise, you learned how to create elliptical-shaped buttons. To learn how to create rectangular buttons, as shown in the illustration here, check out **rectangular_buttons.mov** in the **movies** folder on the **PCS2Web HOT CD-ROM**.

3. [PS] _____Editing Multiple Buttons with Smart Objects

Once you create one button, you can use the new Smart Objects feature in Photoshop CS2 to create additional buttons with the same properties. The benefit of using Smart Objects, versus just duplicating the layer(s), is that each time you update one Smart Object, all other Smart Objects update, too. As a result, you can make changes to one button and update all the others at the same time! As you'll see from this exercise, Smart Objects are a fabulous new addition to Photoshop CS2.

1. If you followed the last exercise, you should have **elliptical_button.psd** open. If not, go back and complete **Exercise 2**. Make sure the **Layers** palette is visible. If it's not, choose **Window > Layers**.

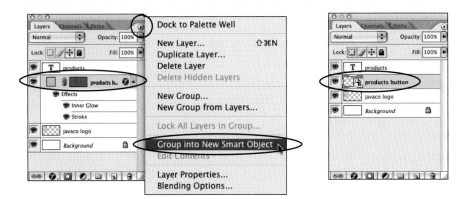

2. In the **Layers** palette, click the **products button** layer to select it. Choose **Group into New Smart Object** from the **Layers** palette menu.

*The contents of the **products button** layer, including the shape layer and the layer styles, should now be contained in a single **Smart Object**, as shown in the illustration here. Although it looks like the layer has been flattened and the shape layer and layer styles have been lost, when you edit the **Smart Object**, you'll have access to the information again. You'll learn how later in this exercise.*

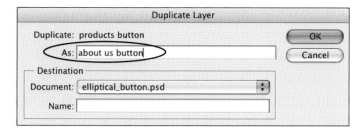

3. With the **products button** layer selected in the **Layers** palette, choose **Duplicate Layer** from the **Layers** palette menu. In the **Duplicate Layer** dialog box, type **about us button** in the **As** field, and click **OK**.

4. With the **products button** layer selected in the **Layers** palette, choose **Duplicate Layer** from the **Layers** palette menu. In the **Duplicate Layer** dialog box, type **our stores button** in the **As** field, and click **OK**.

5. With the **products button** layer selected in the **Layers** palette, choose **Duplicate Layer** from the **Layers** palette menu. In the **Duplicate Layer** dialog box, type **contact us button**, and click **OK**.

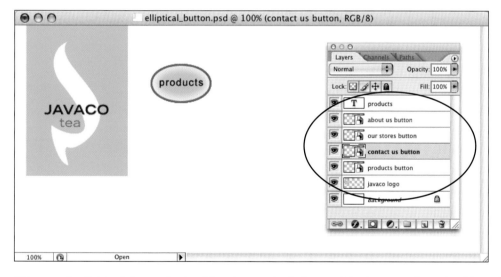

*When you've finished, the contents of the document window and the **Layers** palette should match what you see in the illustration shown here. Because you duplicated the layers, they are positioned on top of each other. You'll reposition the layers in the next step.*

6. In the **Layers** palette, click and drag the layers to match the stacking order shown here.

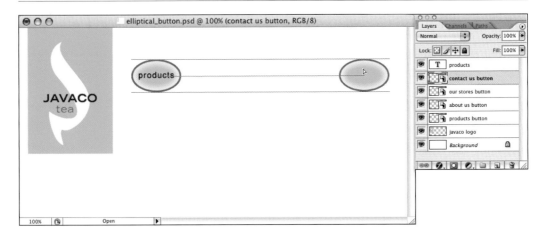

7. With the **contact us button** layer selected in the **Layers** palette, click and drag to reposition the button, as shown in the illustration here. Use the **Smart Guides** (**View > Show > Smart Guides**) to align the buttons horizontally. Because you duplicated the layers, you also duplicated their position, which means they are stacked on top of each other in the document window.

8. In the **Layers** palette, click the **our stores button** layer to select it. Click and drag to reposition the button next to the **contact us button** layer. Use the **Smart Guides** to align the buttons horizontally.

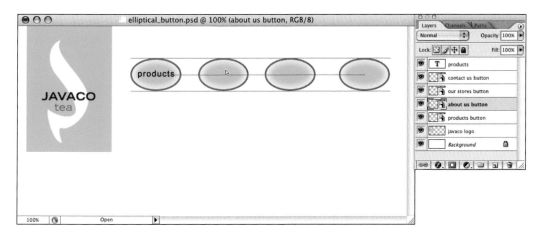

9. In the **Layers** palette, click the **about us button** layer to select it. Click and drag to reposition the button next to the **our stores button**. Use the **Smart Guides** to align the buttons horizontally.

10. In the **Layers** palette, click the **products button** layer to select it. Hold down the **Shift** key and click the **contact us button** layer to multiple-select the layers in-between, as shown in the illustration here.

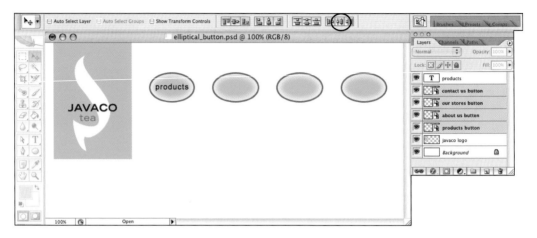

11. On the **Options** bar, click the **Distribute Horizontal Centers** button to evenly space the buttons.

*Now that you've created the buttons as **Smart Objects**, it's time to see the benefit of using **Smart Objects** to make changes to all the buttons at the same time.*

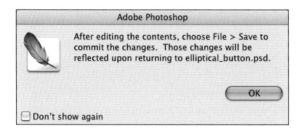

12. Double-click the **products button** layer. A warning message will appear. Click **OK**.

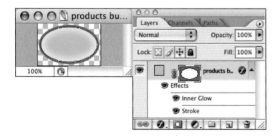

*The button automatically opens in a separate document window. Have a look at the contents of the **Layers** palette. The properties of the shape layer and layer styles you created in the last exercise have been accurately maintained. As a result, you can adjust the vector-based shape while keeping the crisp edges. You can also edit the layer styles.*

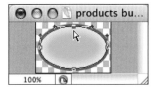

13. Select the **Direct Selection** tool (the white arrow) from the **Toolbox**. Click the path inside the shape so you see the anchor points, as shown in the illustration here.

14. Reshape the ellipse using the anchor points and the reshape handles.

15. In the **Layers** palette, double-click the **Stroke** layer style to open the **Layer Style** dialog box.

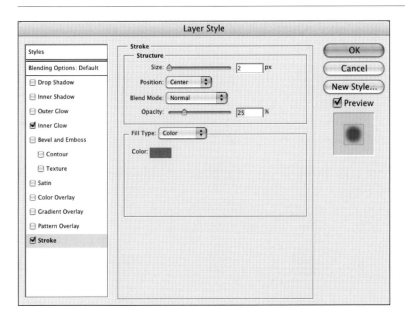

16. Adjust the **Stroke** properties—decrease the **Size**, change the **Position** from **Outside** to **Center**, and decrease the **Opacity**.

17. In the **Styles** section of the **Layer Style** dialog box, click the **Inner Glow** layer style.

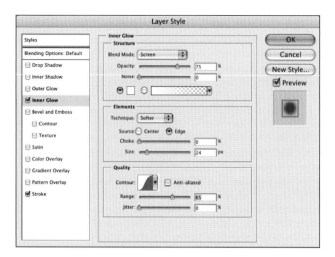

18. Adjust the **Inner Glow** properties—increase the **Size**, change the **Contour**, and increase the **Range**. When you've finished, click **OK** to close the **Layer Style** dialog box.

19. Choose **File > Save** to save your changes. Choose **File > Close** to close the **Smart Object**.

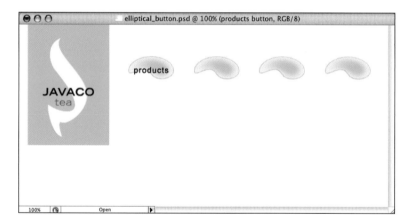

*As soon as you close the **products button Smart Object**, all four buttons update automatically with the changes you made. As you can see, **Smart Objects** are a great new feature in Photoshop CS2. When you're designing buttons, which must share the same properties for consistency, updating all four buttons at the same time is a huge time-saver! And, since **Smart Objects** maintain the original vector-based shape and layer style properties, it's easy to make changes to buttons while keeping the crisp edges.*

20. In the **Layers** palette, click the **products** type layer to select it. Select the **Move** tool from the **Toolbox**. Reposition the type inside the newly shaped button.

21. With the **products** type layer still selected in the **Layers** palette, choose **Duplicate Layer**. In the **Duplicate Layer** dialog box, type **about us**, and click **OK**.

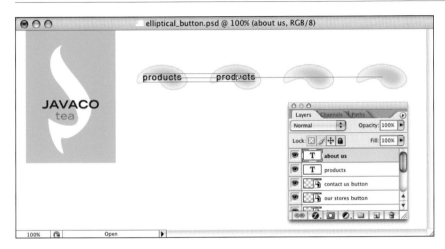

22. Select the **Move** tool from the **Toolbox**. With the **about us** layer selected in the **Layers** palette, click and drag to reposition the type onto the **about us** button. Use the **Smart Guides** to help position the type onto the button.

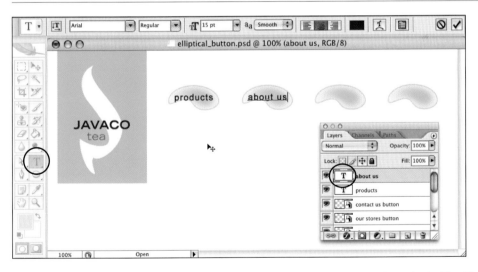

23. Double-click the **T** icon of the **about us** type layer to highlight the word **products**. The **Horizontal Type** tool will automatically be selected in the **Toolbox**. Type **about us**, and on the **Options** bar, click the **Commit Current Edits** button.

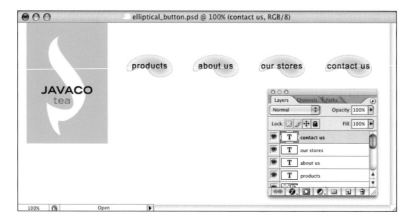

24. Repeat steps 21, 22, and 23 to create labels for the other two buttons—**our stores** and **contact us**—as shown in the illustration here.

*Because the type is different for each button label, you can't group the type layers into a **Smart Object** and change the properties as you did with the shape layers. Fortunately, you can update the properties of more than one type layer by multiple-selecting type layers in the **Layers** palette. Multiple-selecting layers is also a new feature in Photoshop CS2.*

25. In the **Layers** palette, click the **contact us** type layer to select it. Hold down the **Shift** key, and click the **products** layer to multiple-select the layers in-between.

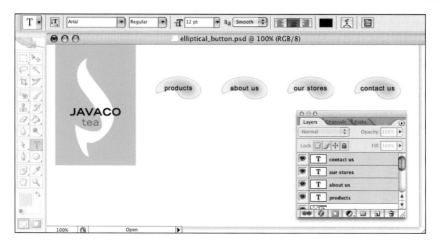

26. Select the **Horizontal Type** tool from the **Toolbox**. Choose **12 pt** from the **Font Size** pop-up menu.

Notice the font size updates in all four type layers.

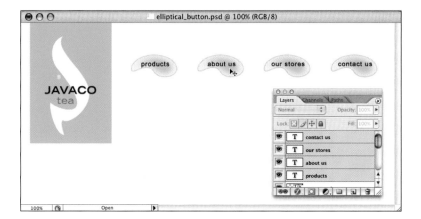

27. Select the **Move** tool from the **Toolbox**. Click and drag to reposition the type inside the buttons.

As you can see, by multiple-selecting type layers, you can edit and reposition more than one type layer at the same time. When you're working with type labels for buttons, which typically share the same properties, updating all the type layers at the same time is a huge time-saver!

28. Save your changes and close the file.

4. [PS/IR] _____Creating Pill-Shaped Buttons

In this exercise, you'll learn how to use the Rounded Rectangle tool in Photoshop CS2 to create rounded, pill-shaped buttons. You'll also learn some advanced shape editing techniques, including how to subtract from a shape.

1. Open **next_back.psd** from the **chap_09** folder you copied to your **Desktop**. Make sure the **Layers** palette is visible. If it's not, choose **Window > Layers**.

Notice each button has a rounded pill shape on one end and a rectangular shape on the other end. In this exercise, you'll learn how to achieve this effect using the shape tools.

2. Close the **next back buttons** layer group, and drag it onto the **Trash** icon at the bottom of the **Layers** palette.

3. Select the **Eyedropper** tool from the **Toolbox**. Click inside the green rectangle behind the **javaco tea** logo to sample color. Select the **Rounded Rectangle** tool from the **Toolbox**.

*You'll use the bright green you selected with the **Eyedropper** tool to create a rounded rectangle.*

4. On the **Options** bar, click the **Shape Layers** button and the **Create a New Shape Layer** button. Type **5 px** in the **Radius** field.

5. Click and drag inside the document window. The shape you created doesn't look like a pill–it still looks like a rounded rectangle.

6. Press **Cmd+Z** (Mac) or **Ctrl+Z** (Windows) to undo the shape you created.

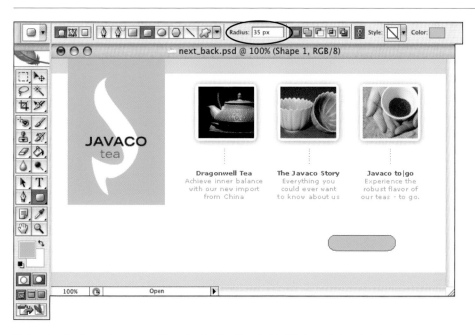

7. On the **Options** bar, type **35 px** in the **Radius** field. Click and drag inside the document window.

As you can see, the radius controls how the corners of the shape appear. The higher the value of the radius, the more rounded the corners.

*Because shapes are made from paths, you can easily edit the paths to create different shapes. In Exercise 2, you used the **Direct Selection** tool to reshape the path to create a different shape. You can also add to and subtract from paths to create different shapes. You'll learn how in the next steps.*

8. On the **Options** bar, click the **Rectangle** tool button and the **Subtract from Shape Area** button.

*Choosing the **Rectangle** tool from the **Options** bar is the same as choosing it from the **Toolbox**. Any time you use a shape tool or a pen tool, you have access to all the shape tools and pen tools on the **Options** bar.*

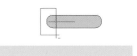

9. Click and drag to create a rectangle, as shown in the illustration here. The purpose of this step is to create a flat edge on the left side of the button.

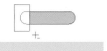

*Notice as you release your mouse, the area you overlapped with the rectangle no longer has any color. Because you subtracted from the shape, the overlapping area is now empty. Also notice there are now two sets of paths—one for the shape you created with the **Rounded Rectangle** tool and one for the rectangle you created in the last step.*

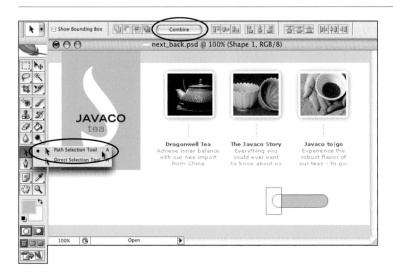

10. Select the **Path Selection** tool (the black arrow) from the **Toolbox**. On the **Options** bar, click the **Combine** button.

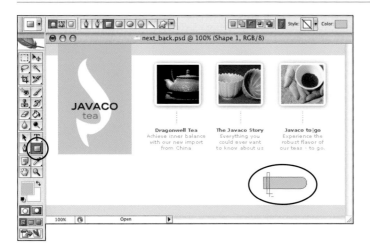

*Clicking the **Combine** button combines the path of the original shape you created with the **Rounded Rectangle** tool and the path from the rectangle you created with the **Rectangle** tool.*

11. Select the **Rectangle** tool from the **Toolbox**. On the **Options** bar, click the **Shape Layers** and **Subtract from Shape Area** buttons. Click and drag to create a narrow rectangle inside the pill shape, as shown in the illustration here.

12. Click the **Path Selection** tool (the black arrow) from the **Toolbox**. Click the narrow rectangle you created in the last step to select it. You'll know it's selected when you see solid-gray editing nodes at the corners, as shown in the illustration here.

13. With the narrow rectangle selected, choose **Edit > Copy** and then **Edit > Paste**.

You won't see a change onscreen with this step because the pasted path is on top of the existing path. When you copy and paste, the pasted path maintains the properties of the original path, including the position.

14. With the **Path Selection** tool still selected in the **Toolbox**, click and drag the pasted path slightly to the right, as shown in the illustration here.

When you release the mouse, you'll notice the new path has the same properties as the original—it also subtracts from the shape.

TIP | Hiding and Showing Paths

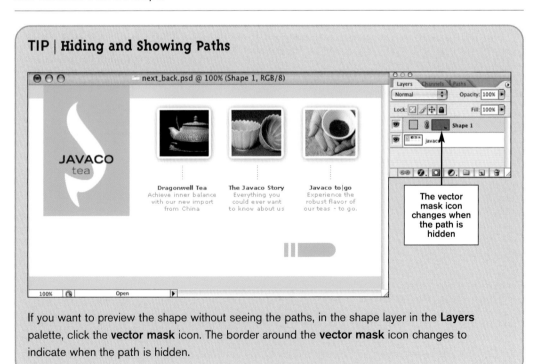

If you want to preview the shape without seeing the paths, in the shape layer in the **Layers** palette, click the **vector mask** icon. The border around the **vector mask** icon changes to indicate when the path is hidden.

15. With the **Path Selection** tool selected in the **Toolbox**, on the **Options** bar, click the **Combine** button.

Now that you've created one button, you can easily create the second button using the new Smart Objects feature in Photoshop CS2. You'll learn how in the next steps.

16. In the **Layers** palette, click the **Shape 1** layer to select it. Choose **Group into New Smart Object** from the **Layers** palette menu. Double-click the **Shape 1** layer name. When the bounding box appears, rename the layer **next**, and press **Return** (Mac) or **Enter** (Windows).

17. Choose **Duplicate Layer** from the **Layers** palette menu. In the **Duplicate Layer** dialog box, type **back** in the **As** field, and click **OK**.

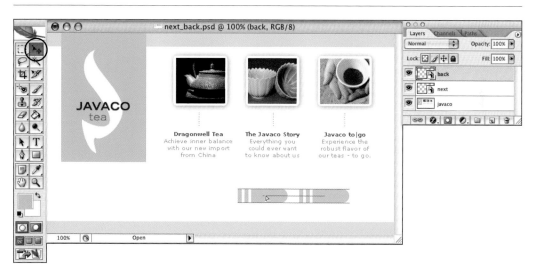

18. In the **Layers** palette, click the **back** layer to select it. Select the **Move** tool from the **Toolbox**. Click and drag to reposition the **back** layer to the left of the **next** layer, as shown in the illustration here. Use the **Smart Guides** (**View > Show > Smart Guides**) to help position the buttons.

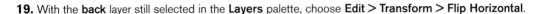

19. With the **back** layer still selected in the **Layers** palette, choose **Edit > Transform > Flip Horizontal**.

*Even though the buttons now mirror each other, they are still based on the same **Smart Object**. As a result, you can make changes to one button and update the other at the same time. You'll learn how in the next steps.*

20. In the **Layers** palette, double-click the **back** layer. Click **OK** to acknowledge the **Smart Object** warning message.

21. Select the **Direct Selection** tool (the white arrow) from the **Toolbox**. Click to select the path around the perimeter of the pill shape. You'll know the path is selected when you can see the anchor points.

22. Click and drag the anchor points to reshape the button. When you've finished, choose **File > Save**. Choose **File > Close** to close the **Smart Object**.

*Notice both buttons updated with the change you made, and they remained a mirror of each other. As you can see, the **Smart Objects** feature in Photoshop CS2 has endless useful possibilities!*

23. Press **Cmd+Z** (Mac) or **Ctrl+Z** (Windows) to undo the change you made to the **Smart Object**.

Although the shapes you created were cool, they weren't very functional next and back buttons.

24. Select the **Horizontal Type** tool from the **Toolbox**. Choose **Arial** from the **Font Family** pop-up menu, **Regular** from the **Font Style** pop-up menu, **15 pt** from the **Font Size** pop-up menu, and **Smooth** from the **Anti-Aliasing** pop-up menu. Click the **Font Color** box to open the **Color Picker** dialog box. Choose a **dark blue**, and click **OK**.

25. Click inside the document window and type **back**. Select the **Move** tool from the **Toolbox**. Click and drag to position the type on the button, as shown in the illustration here.

26. Select the **Horizontal Type** tool from the **Toolbox**. Click inside the document window and type **next**. Select the **Move** tool from the **Toolbox**. Click and drag to position the type on the button, as shown in the illustration here.

27. Save your changes and close the file.

 MOVIE | rounded_buttons.mov

In the last exercise, you learned how to create interesting, pill-shaped next and back buttons using the **Rounded Rectangle** tool and the subtract mode in Photoshop CS2.

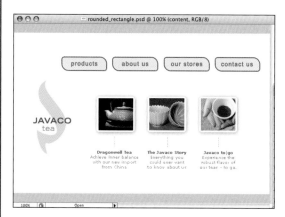

To learn more about the **Rounded Rectangle** tool and to learn how to create the buttons shown in the illustration here, check out **rounded_buttons.mov** in the **movies** folder on the **PCS2Web HOT CD-ROM**.

5. [PS/IR] _____Creating Three-Dimensional Buttons

In the last few exercises, you've learned how to use layer styles to add interesting effects to flat Web buttons. You can also create three-dimensional buttons using the bevel and emboss layer styles in Photoshop CS2. Here's an exercise to show you how.

1. Open **3d_button.psd** from the **chap_09** folder you copied to your **Desktop**. Make sure the **Layers** palette is visible. If it's not, choose **Window > Layers**.

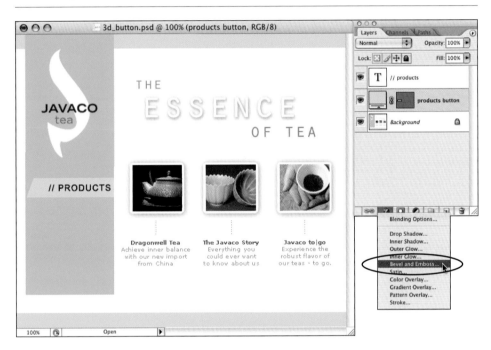

2. In the **Layers** palette, click the **products button** shape layer to select it. Choose **Bevel and Emboss** from the **Layer Styles** pop-up menu.

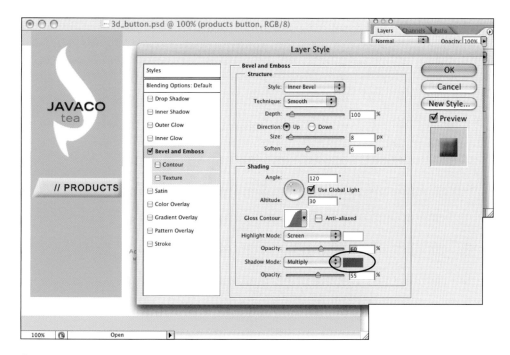

3. In the **Layer Style** dialog box, choose **Inner Bevel** from the **Style** pop-up menu. Experiment with the other settings to see the different effects you can achieve with the **Inner Bevel** style. Make sure the **Preview** option is turned on so you can see how the changes affect the appearance of the button. When you've finished experimenting, match the settings in the **Layer Style** dialog box to the ones shown in the illustration shown here. In the **Layer Style** dialog box, click **OK** to apply the layer style to the button.

*Tip: To change the color of the shadow, as shown here, click the **Shadow Color** box to open the **Color Picker** dialog box. Choose a **dark green**, and click **OK**.*

*As you can see, the **Inner Bevel** layer style adds shadows and highlights to make the button appear three-dimensional. **Inner Bevel** is just one of the bevel and emboss styles. You'll experiment with others in the next steps.*

4. With the **products button** layer selected in the **Layers** palette, choose **Duplicate Layer** from the **Layers** palette menu. In the **Duplicate Layer** dialog box, type **about us button** in the **As** field, and click **OK**.

Notice when you duplicate a layer, the layer style is automatically duplicated as well.

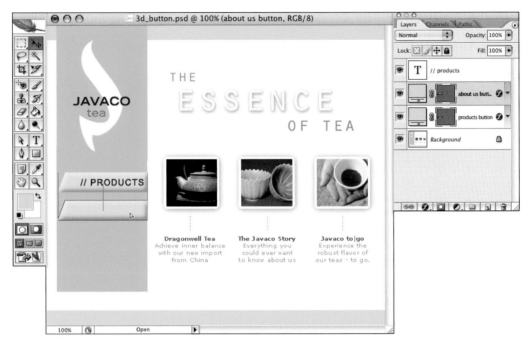

5. Select the **Move** tool from the **Toolbox**. Click and drag to reposition the **about us button** below the **products button,** as shown in the illustration here.

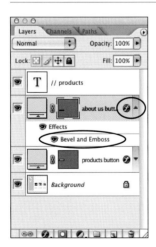

6. In the **about us button** layer, click the arrow next to the **Layer Style** icon so you can see the layer style. Double-click the **Bevel and Emboss** layer style of the **about us button** layer to open the **Layer Style** dialog box.

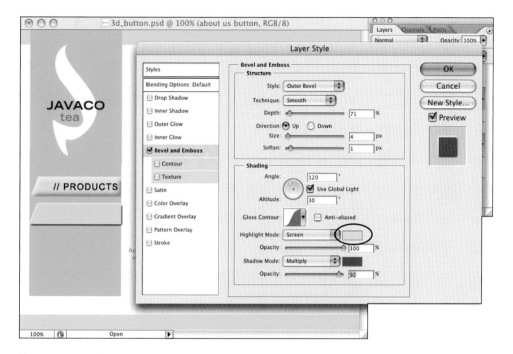

7. In the **Layer Style** dialog box, choose **Outer Bevel** from the **Style** pop-up menu. Experiment with the other settings for the **Outer Bevel** style. When you've finished experimenting, match the settings to the ones shown in the illustration here. In the **Layer Style** dialog box, click **OK** to apply the layer style to the button.

*Tip: To change the color of the highlight, as shown here, click the **Highlight Color** box to open the **Color Picker** dialog box. Choose a **light green**, and click **OK**.*

8. With the **about us button** layer still selected in the **Layers** palette, choose **Duplicate Layer** from the **Layers** palette menu. Type **our stores button** in the **As** field of the **Duplicate Layer** dialog box, and click **OK**.

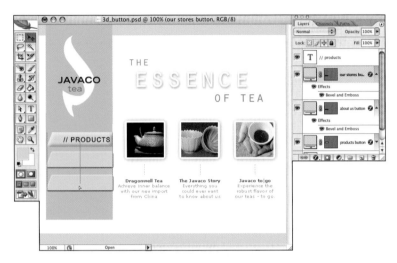

9. Select the **Move** tool from the **Toolbox**. Click and drag to reposition the **our stores button** below the **about us button**, as shown in the illustration here.

10. Double-click the **Bevel and Emboss** layer style of the **about us button** layer to open the **Layer Style** dialog box.

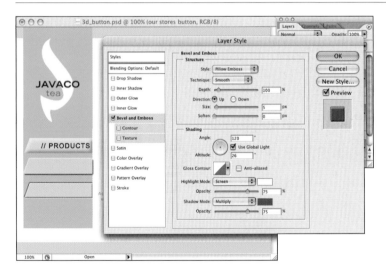

11. In the **Layer Style** dialog box, choose **Pillow Emboss** from the **Style** pop-up menu. Experiment with the other settings for the **Pillow Emboss** style. As you can see, the **Pillow Emboss** style gives a different three-dimensional texture to the button than the **Inner Bevel** and **Outer Bevel** styles. When you've finished experimenting, match the settings to the ones shown in the illustration here. In the **Layer Style** dialog box, click **OK** to apply the layer style to the button.

As you can see, the bevel and emboss layer style can add a variety of interesting three-dimensional textures to your Web buttons. In this exercise, we used a different setting for each button to get an idea of the different effects you can achieve. When you're designing Web buttons for your own Web sites, keep the same appearance for all buttons—a consistent look is always best!

12. Close **3d_button.psd**. You don't need to save your changes.

TIP | Creating an Angled Button

Wondering how to create the angled edge on the button in the last exercise? It's easy! Here's how:

1. Create a simple rectangle with the **Rectangle** tool.

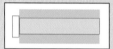

2. On the **Options** bar, click the **Subtract from Shape Area** button. Click and drag to create a small rectangle, flush with the rectangle you created in the last step.

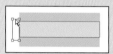

3. Select the **Direct Selection** tool (the white arrow) from the **Toolbox**. Click the path of the small rectangle until you see the anchor points in the four corners.

4. Click and drag the upper-right anchor point to the right to create an angled line.

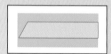

5. Select the **Path Selection** tool (the black arrow) from the **Toolbox**. On the **Options** bar, click the **Combine** button. Voilà! You just created a perfectly angled edge to your button!

6. [PS] _____Creating Tabbed Navigation Bars

Taking its design cue from traditional notebook tabs, tabbed navigation bars are a useful, compact navigation system that has been popularized by well-known Web sites, such as apple.com and amazon.com. In this exercise, you'll learn how to create a tabbed navigation bar. Because spacing alignment is critical to an effective tabbed navigation bar, you'll also learn how to use rulers and guides.

1. Open **tab_nav_bar.psd** from the **chap_09** folder you copied to your **Desktop**.

Before you begin creating the tabbed navigation bar, you must set up some guides to ensure even spacing between the tabs.

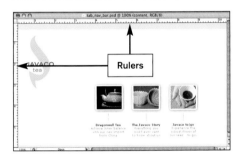

2. Choose **View > Rulers**.

Notice the top and left side of the document window are outlined with a ruler. By default, the rulers are set to inches. When you design Web graphics, you always use pixels as a measurement. Not to worry, you can easily change the rulers to use pixels. You'll learn how in the next step.

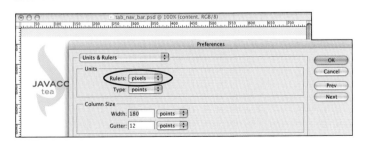

3. Choose **Photoshop > Preferences > Units & Rulers** (Mac) or **Edit > Preferences > Units & Rulers** (Windows). Choose **pixels** from the **Rulers** pop-up menu, and click **OK**.

Notice the rulers update automatically as soon as you choose **pixels** from the **Rulers** pop-up menu. The size of your image depends on the number of pixels between each mark on the ruler. In this image, the markings are positioned at 5-pixel intervals. Next you'll set up guides.

4. Select the **Move** tool from the **Toolbox**. Position your cursor on the **horizontal ruler**, and click and drag.

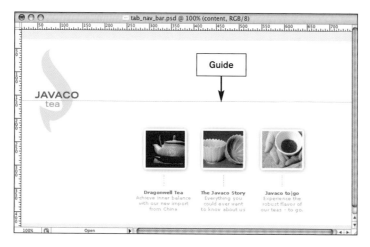

When you release the mouse, you'll see a line across the document window. This line is a nonprinting guide. If you optimize or print the file, you won't see the guide—it's just there to help you with alignment during the design process.

5. Make sure the guide is positioned flush against the top of the letter **t** in the word **tea**, as shown in the illustration above. If it's not, position your cursor over the line. When you see the cursor change to the double arrow, click and drag to reposition the guide.

When you create the tabbed navigation bar, you'll use this guide to align the bottom edges of the tabs.

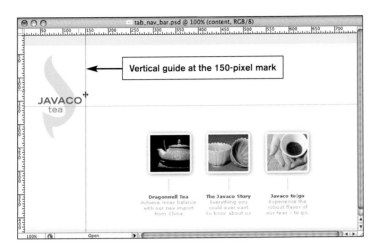

6. With the **Move** tool still selected in the **Toolbox**, position your cursor over the **vertical ruler**. Click and drag to create a vertical guide. Release the mouse when the guide is positioned at the **150-pixel** mark on the **horizontal ruler**, as shown in the illustration here.

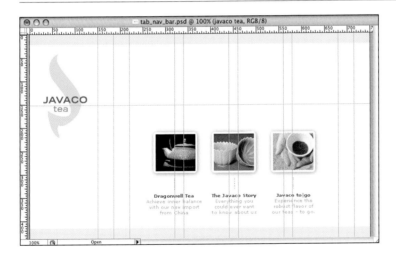

7. Continue to add vertical guides until the guides in your image match the illustration shown here (vertical guides positioned at the **150-, 185-, 220-, 320-, 340-, 440-, 460-, 560-, 580-, 680-,** and **715-pixel** marks).

Wondering about the significance of the positions for these vertical guides? When you're designing tabbed navigation, it's critical to ensure each tab is the same width and each tab is spaced evenly so the navigation bar looks aesthetically pleasing. Once you start drawing the tabs, it will all make sense!

TIP | Changing the Color of Guides

By default, the guides are a turquoise blue.

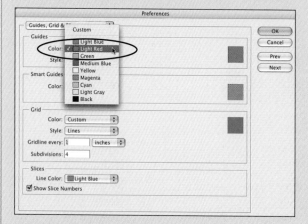

If you want to change the guides to a different color, choose **Photoshop > Preferences > Guides, Grid & Slices** (Mac) or **Edit > Preferences > Guides, Grid & Slices** (Windows). In the **Guides** section of the dialog box, choose a different color from the **Color** pop-up menu.

Now that you have the guides positioned properly, you can use the shape tools to create the tabbed navigation bar.

8. Select the **Line** tool from the **Toolbox**.

9. On the **Options** bar, click the **Shape Layers** and **Create a New Shape Layer** buttons. Type **10 px** in the **Weight** field. The weight determines the thickness of the line. On the **Options** bar, click the **Shape Color** box to open the **Color Picker** dialog box. Choose a **bright blue**, and click **OK**.

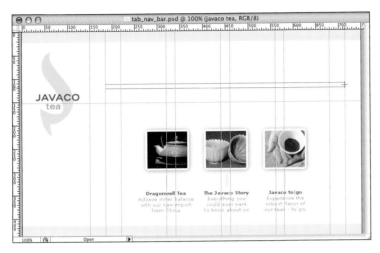

10. Position your cursor over the second vertical guide. Hold down the **Shift** key and click and drag to create a straight line. Make sure the line extends from the second vertical guide to the last vertical guide, as shown in the illustration here. Use the **Smart Guides (View > Show > Smart Guides)** to help you ensure they are aligned flush against the guides. Don't worry about the horizontal position—you'll fix that in the next step.

*Tip: Holding down the **Shift** key while drawing with the **Line** tool constrains the line so you can create a straight line.*

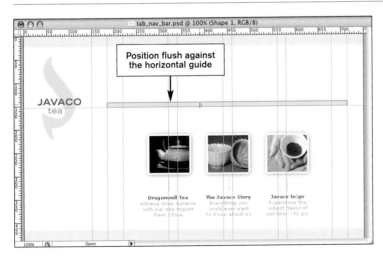

11. Select the **Move** tool from the **Toolbox.** Click and drag (or use the arrow keys on your keyboard) to position the line you created in the last step so the bottom edge is flush against the horizontal guide. Use the **Smart Guides** to help you.

12. Select the **Rounded Rectangle** tool from the **Toolbox**. On the **Options** bar, click the **Shape Layer** button and the **Add to Shape Area** button. You want to add to the shape, rather than create a new shape for the tab. On the **Options** bar, type **15 px** in the **Radius** field. Leave the color in the **Shape Color** box the same so the tabs match the line you created in Step 10.

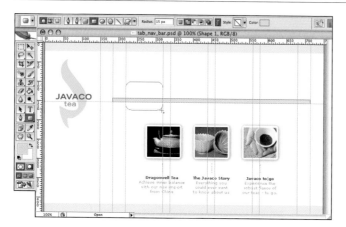

13. Click and drag to create the first tab. Position the tab between the third and fourth vertical guide. When you create the rounded rectangle, make sure the rounded edges are well below the line, as shown in the illustration here.

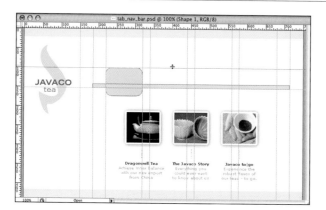

14. Click and drag a new guide from the **horizontal ruler**. Position it at the top of the tab you created in the last step. This guide will help you line up the tabs so they are all the same height.

*Although you could use the **Smart Guides** to ensure the tabs are the same height, you'll find it easier to use a guide because you can line up your cursor where the guides intersect before you begin drawing. This helps make sure the tabs are the same height. When the cursor changes to pink, you know the tab will be positioned flush against the vertical and horizontal guides.*

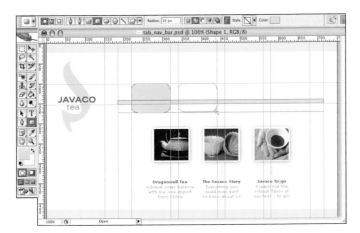

15. With the **Rounded Rectangle** tool still selected in the **Toolbox**, click and drag to create the second tab. Before you begin drawing, make sure the **Add to Shape Area** button is still enabled on the **Options** bar. Position the tab between the fifth and sixth vertical line, and make sure it is aligned horizontally with the first tab.

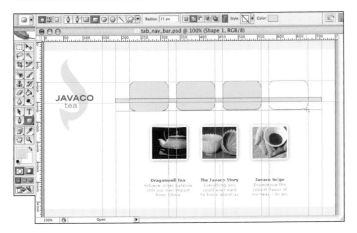

16. Repeat Step 15 to create two more tabs, as shown in the illustration here. Make sure the **Add to Shape Area** button is enabled on the **Options** bar. Use the guides and **Smart Guides** to ensure proper alignment and spacing.

Right now, the navigation bar looks like four rounded rectangles on top of a line. To make this look like a tabbed navigation bar, you need to remove the bottom rounded corners.

17. Select the **Rectangle** tool from the **Toolbox**. On the **Toolbox**, click the **Subtract from Shape Area** button.

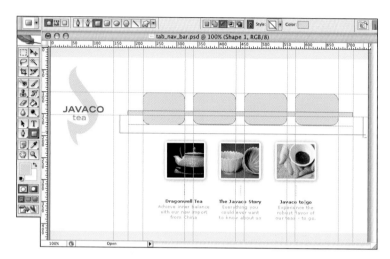

18. Align your cursor against the bottom vertical guide. Click and drag to create a large rectangle. Make sure the rectangle is flush against the bottom vertical guide, and make sure it extends beyond the bottom of the rounded rectangles.

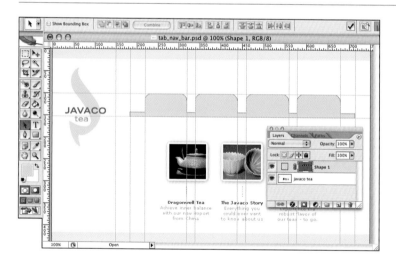

19. Select the **Path Selection** tool (the black arrow) from the **Toolbox**. On the **Options** bar, click the **Combine** button. Press **Cmd+;** (Mac) or **Ctrl+;** (Windows) to turn off the visibility of the guides so you can see the tabbed navigation bar. When you've finished, press **Cmd+;** (Mac) or **Ctrl+;** (Windows) to turn on the visibility of the guides.

You should now have a tabbed navigation bar, which is made up of a single shape layer. Notice the tabs are all the same height, and the spacing between the tabs is identical. As you can see, spending the time to set up guides pays off in the end! Next, you'll add a second color to the tabs.

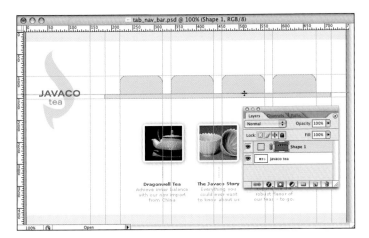

20. Select the **Move** tool from the **Toolbox**. Click and drag a horizontal guide from the ruler. Position it flush against the top of the line, as shown in the illustration here.

Tip: You can drag guides from the rulers when other tools are selected in the **Toolbox.** *However, you cannot reposition the guides once they are positioned unless the* **Move** *tool is selected in the* **Toolbox.**

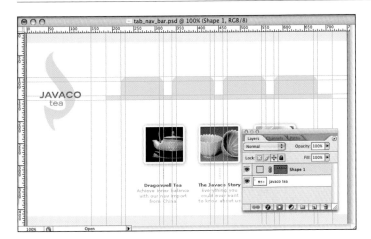

21. Click and drag a second horizontal guide from the ruler. Position it 10 pixels below the uppermost horizontal guide (in my case, at the 110-pixel mark on the **vertical ruler**). Click and drag vertical guides from the ruler. Position the guides at the **230-, 310-, 350-, 430-, 470-, 550-, 590-,** and **670-pixel** marks on the **horizontal ruler**.

22. Select the **Rounded Rectangle** tool from the **Toolbox**. On the **Options** bar, click the **Shape Layers** button and **Create a New Shape Layer** button. Type **15 px** in the **Radius** field. On the **Options** bar, click the **Shape Color** box to open the **Color Picker** dialog box. Choose a **light blue**, and click **OK**.

| 283 |

23. Position your cursor at the intersection of the second horizontal guide and the fourth vertical guide, as shown in the illustration here. Make sure the cursor turns pink so you know it is perfectly aligned with the guides.

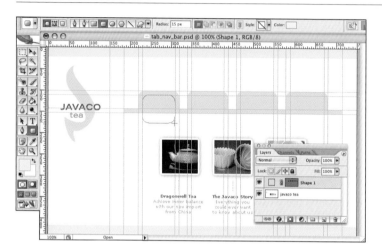

24. Click and drag to create a rounded rectangle inside the tab. Make sure you position the bottom corners of the rounded rectangle well below the bottom line of the tabbed navigation bar, as shown in the illustration here.

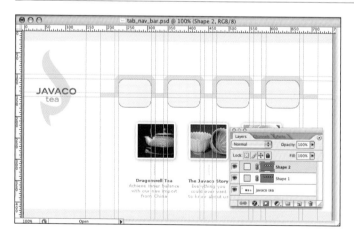

25. On the **Options** bar, click the **Add to Shape Area** button. Repeat Steps 23 and 24 to create rounded rectangles inside the tabs, as shown in the illustration here.

26. Choose the **Rectangle** tool from the **Toolbox**. On the **Options** bar, click the **Subtract from Shape Area** button.

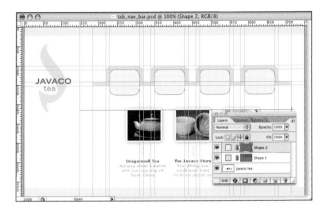

27. Position your cursor at the intersection of the first vertical guide and the third horizontal guide. Click and drag to create a rectangle, as shown in the illustration here.

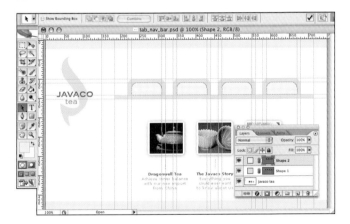

28. Select the **Path Selection** tool (the black arrow) from the **Toolbox**. On the **Options** bar, click the **Combine** button.

29. Press **Cmd+;** (Mac) or **Ctrl+;** (Windows) to view the tabbed navigation bar without the guides.

30. In the **Layers** palette, double-click the **Shape 1** layer. When the bounding box appears, type **outer tabs**, and press **Return** (Mac) or **Enter** (Windows). Double-click the **Shape 2** layer. When the bounding box appears, type **inner tabs**, and press **Return** (Mac) or **Enter** (Windows).

Next, you'll add a drop shadow to the tabbed navigation bar.

31. In the **Layers** palette, click the **outer tabs** layer to select it. Choose **Drop Shadow** from the **Layer Style** pop-up menu.

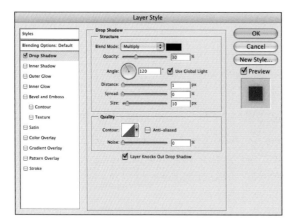

32. In the **Layer Style** dialog box, experiment with the settings for the **Drop Shadow** layer style. When you've finished, match the settings to the ones shown in the illustration here. Click **OK**.

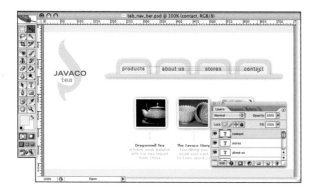

33. Using the techniques you learned in this chapter and in Chapter 6, "*Creating Type*," add labels to the buttons, as shown in the illustration here. Use the **Move** tool and the **Smart Guides** to ensure the labels are positioned and aligned correctly on the tabs.

As you can see, a tabbed navigation bar is a simple, effective navigation system, and Photoshop CS2 provides excellent tools to help you create one quickly and easily.

34. Save and close the file.

 MOVIE | tab_nav_bar.mov

To learn more about creating a tabbed navigation bar, check out **tab_nav_bar.mov** in the **movies** folder on the **PCS2Web HOT CD-ROM**.

7. [PS] _____Creating Navigation Bars with Icons

Combining icons with type can create an interesting and effective navigation system. In this exercise, you'll learn how to use the custom shapes tool to create icons from preset shapes in Photoshop CS2. Plus, you'll learn how to use the pen tools to create your own unique shapes.

1. Open **icon_buttons.psd** from the **chap_09** folder you copied to your **Desktop**.

*In this exercise, you'll add icons above the type labels **products**, **about us**, **shop**, and **contact**. First, you'll add icons using some of the preset custom shapes in Photoshop CS2. Once you've mastered drawing with the **Custom Shape** tool, you'll move on to creating your own custom icons with the pen tools.*

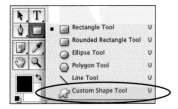

2. Select the **Custom Shape** tool from the **Toolbox**.

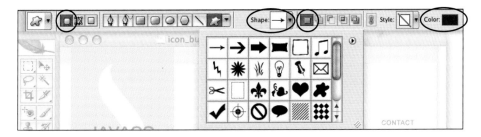

3. On the **Options** bar, click the **Shape Layers** and **Create a New Shape Layer** buttons. On the **Options** bar, click the **Shape Color** box to open the **Color Picker** dialog box. Choose a **dark blue**, and click **OK**. Click to expand the **Shape** pop-up menu. Take a look at the selection of preset shapes.

4. Click the **Shape** pop-up menu. Notice the additional categories of preset shapes in Photoshop CS2. Choose **All**. A warning dialog box will appear, asking if you want to replace the current shapes with the shapes from **All.csh**. Click **Append**.

*You should now have a longer list of shapes in the **Shape** pop-up menu.*

*Note: Clicking **Append** adds the shapes to the **Shape** pop-up menu, keeping the existing shapes intact. Clicking **OK** replaces the current shapes.*

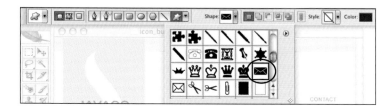

5. Scroll through the list of shapes. Click to select the **black envelope**.

PRODUCTS   ABOUT US   SHOP   CONTACT

6. Position your cursor inside the document window. Click and drag to draw a small envelope, as shown in the illustration here.

PRODUCTS   ABOUT US   SHOP   CONTACT

7. Select the **Move** tool from the **Toolbox**. Click and drag to center the envelope icon over the word **CONTACT**. Use the **Smart Guides** (**View > Show > Smart Guides**) to help you.

PRODUCTS   ABOUT US   SHOP   CONTACT

8. Select the **Custom Shape** tool from the **Toolbox**. On the **Options** bar, click the **Shape Layer** and **Create a New Shape Layer** buttons. Select the **shopping cart** from the **Shape** pop-up menu. Position your cursor inside the document window. Hold down the **Shift** key, and click and drag to create a small shopping cart icon, as shown in the illustration here.

*Holding down the **Shift** key maintains the original proportions of the shopping cart shape.*

9. Select the **Move** tool from the **Toolbox**. Click and drag to position the shopping cart icon. Use the **Smart Guides** to ensure the icon is centered over the word **SHOP** and aligned with the envelope icon.

*Now that you have an understanding of how to create icons with the **Custom Shapes** tool, it's time to take things up a level and learn how to create your own custom shapes. To do this, you'll use the **Pen** tool to trace a shape and then define it as a custom shape, which you can use to create icons for the **products** and **about us** buttons. It sounds complicated, but you'll be surprised how easy it is!*

10. Leave **icon_buttons.psd** open, and open **teapot.psd** from the **chap_09** folder you copied to your **Desktop**.

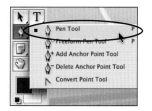

11. Select the **Pen** tool from the **Toolbox**. On the **Options** bar, click the **Shape Layer** and **Create a New Shape Layer** buttons.

12. In the **Layers** palette, click the **Background** layer to select it. Position your cursor at the left corner of the teapot. Click to create an anchor point.

*As soon as you click inside the document window with the **Pen** tool, a shape layer will automatically be created in the **Layers** palette.*

13. Continue to click to add anchor points around the shape of the teapot. When you get all the way around to the first anchor point you created, position your cursor directly over the anchor point. When you see the small circle next to the **Pen** tool cursor, click to close the shape.

*Tip: If you click to add an anchor point but don't like where you've positioned it, press **Cmd+Z** (Mac) or **Ctrl+Z** (Windows) to undo.*

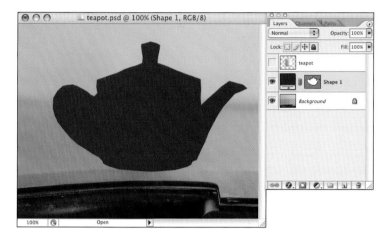

14. In the **Layers** palette, turn off the visibility of the **teapot** layer. As you can see, you've created a shape based on the teapot. Unfortunately, the handle is not well defined. You'll fix that in the next step.

15. Turn on the visibility of the **teapot** layer. In the **Layers** palette, click the **Shape 1** layer to select it. With the **Pen** tool still selected in the **Toolbox**, on the **Options** bar, click the **Subtract from Shape Area** button.

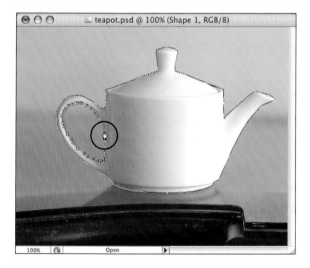

16. Click to add an anchor point on the inside of the handle. Continue to click to add a series of anchor points around the inside of the handle, as shown in the illustration here. When you get all the way around to the first anchor point you created on the inside of the handle, position your cursor over the anchor point. When you see a small circle next to the **Pen** tool cursor, click to close the shape.

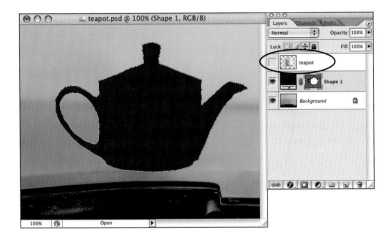

17. Turn off the visibility of the **teapot** layer.

*You just successfully created a vector-based teapot shape using the **Pen** tool! Next, you'll define the teapot as a custom shape so you can draw with the teapot shape in other images.*

18. In the **Layers** palette, click the **Shape 1** layer to select it. Choose **Edit > Define Custom Shape**.

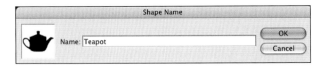

19. In the **Shape Name** dialog box, type **Teapot** in the **Name** field. Click **OK**.

*Notice that the thumbnail preview in the **Shape Name** dialog box is the shape of the teapot.*

20. Close **teapot.psd**. You don't need to save your changes. Return to the **icon_buttons.psd** image.

21. Select the **Custom Shape** tool from the **Toolbox**. On the **Options** bar, click to expand the contents of the **Shape** pop-up menu. Scroll to the bottom where you'll find the **Teapot** custom shape you defined in Step 19. Double-click to select it.

PRODUCTS   ABOUT US   SHOP   CONTACT

22. On the **Options** bar, click the **Shape Layer** and **Create a New Shape Layer** buttons. Position your cursor inside the document window. Hold down the **Shift** key and click and drag to create a small teapot.

23. Select the **Move** tool from the **Toolbox**. Click and drag to reposition the **teapot** icon. Use the **Smart Guides** to ensure that the teapot is centered over the word **PRODUCTS** and aligned with the shopping cart and envelope icons you created and positioned earlier in this exercise.

24. Open **teacup.psd** from the **chap_09** folder you copied to your **Desktop**.

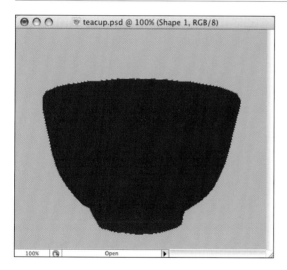

25. Using the techniques you learned in this exercise, use the **Pen** tool to trace the tea cup. When you've finished, choose **Edit > Define Custom Shape**. Type **Tea Cup** in the **Shape Name** dialog box, and click **OK**.

26. When you've finished, close **teacup.psd**, and return to **icon_buttons.psd**. You don't need to save your changes.

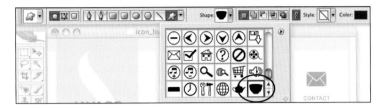

27. Select the **Custom Shape** tool from the **Toolbox**. On the **Options** bar, click to expand the contents of the **Shape** pop-up menu. Scroll to the bottom and click to select the **Tea Cup** custom shape.

PRODUCTS   ABOUT US   SHOP   CONTACT

28. Position your cursor inside the document window. Hold down the **Shift** key and click and drag to create a small tea cup icon.

29. Select the **Move** tool from the **Toolbox**. Click and drag to position the tea cup. Use the **Smart Guides** to ensure the tea cup icon is centered over the words **ABOUT US** and aligned with the teapot, shopping cart, and envelope icons you created in this exercise.

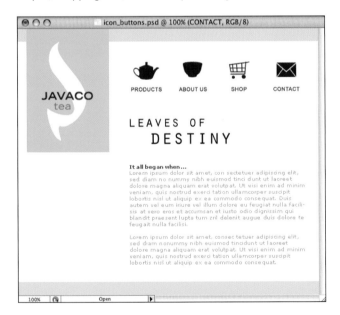

*As you can see, creating your own custom shapes is very easy. You don't have to be a trained artist to create fun, interesting icons—all you need is a photograph and the **Pen** tool!*

30. Save and close **icon_buttons.psd**.

 MOVIE | icon_buttons.mov

To learn more about how to create Web buttons with icons, check out **icon_buttons.mov** in the **movies** folder on the **PCS2Web HOT CD-ROM**.

Congratulate yourself for completing a long, complex chapter. This chapter introduced a number of new concepts, including different types of navigation, as well as the intricacies of working with shape tools, shape layers, and layer styles. In Chapter 12, "Slicing," you'll learn how to slice and how to link to URLs. In Chapter 13, "Creating Rollovers," you'll learn how to make your navigation interactive by applying different rollover states. Next, you'll learn how to optimize transparent graphics.

10

Creating Transparent Graphics

| Creating and Previewing Transparent GIFs |
| Fixing the Edges of Transparent GIFs | Saving Optimized Transparent GIFs |
| Creating Transparent GIFs from Nontransparent Images |
| Simulating Transparency with JPEGs |

chap_10

PCS2Web HOT CD-ROM

By default, all computer-generated graphics are rectangular or square. As a result, most images you see on the Web are rectangular, causing many sites to look similar. Fortunately, you can work around the rectangular limitation by creating transparent GIFs.

Currently, GIF is the only file format in wide use for the Web that supports transparency. Unfortunately, GIF transparency settings are limited and can produce an unwanted halo around graphics. As you'll see in this chapter, both Photoshop CS2 and ImageReady CS2 have excellent tools for countering the inherent transparency problems in the GIF file format.

In this chapter, you'll learn several techniques for creating transparent GIFs. You'll also learn how to simulate transparency with the JPEG format.

Understanding the Limitations of GIF Transparency

In Photoshop CS2 or ImageReady CS2, when you create graphics with soft edges, such as drop shadows, glows, feathered edges, or anti-aliased edges, you're using 8-bit (or 256-level) transparency. This functionality lets the programs display different levels of partially transparent pixels at the edges of graphics. As a result, edges appear smooth with 8-bit transparency, making nonrectangular graphics look natural.

Photoshop CS2 anti-aliased edge   *Photoshop CS2 glow*

Photoshop CS2 and ImageReady CS2 use up to 256 levels of transparency. As a result, anti-aliased edges, glows, and other soft edges appear smooth and natural.

Unfortunately, the GIF file format supports only 1-bit masking instead of the sophisticated 8-bit transparency native to Photoshop CS2 and ImageReady CS2. One-bit masking does not support partially transparent pixels, which means pixels in a GIF are either fully transparent or fully opaque (either on or off). The 1-bit masking limitation causes an unattractive halo (sometimes called a fringe or matte) of colored pixels. Not to worry, you'll learn how to fix this problem in the upcoming exercises in this chapter.

GIF anti-aliased edge   *GIF glow edge*

The GIF file format is limited to 1-bit masking. Notice the halos around the edges of the transparent GIFs in these illustrations when they are displayed against a colored HTML background. In this chapter, you'll learn why this happens and how to fix it.

What Is Anti-Aliasing?

The term *anti-alias* describes the edge of a graphic that blends into a surrounding color. The advantage of anti-aliasing is that it hides the otherwise jagged nature of color transitions in computer-generated graphics. Most graphics programs offer the capability to anti-alias. Photoshop CS2 and ImageReady CS2 include an anti-aliasing option for most of the creation tools, including the selection tools, the Type tool, the shape tools, the brushes, and the erasers.

An anti-aliased edge

An aliased edge

Recognizing Transparent Layers

One way to create transparent GIFs in Photoshop CS2 or ImageReady CS2 is to create your graphic on (or convert it to) a transparent layer. How can you tell if your graphic is using transparent layers? The checkerboard pattern in Photoshop CS2 or ImageReady CS2 is the visual cue that lets you identify transparent pixels.

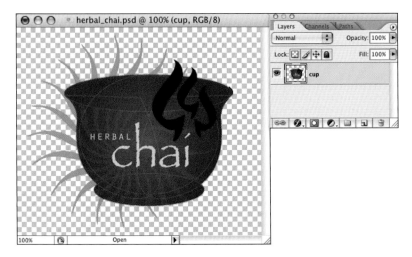

In Photoshop CS2 and ImageReady CS2, the checkerboard pattern in the background of your images means your images are on a transparent layer. If you have other layers turned on that prevent you from seeing the checkerboard background, you must turn them off before you save the image as a transparent GIF.

Understanding GIFs, Masks, and Transparency

This chapter includes references to a number of different terms, such as *GIFs*, *masks*, and *transparency*. Here's a chart to help you understand what the terms mean.

Terminology	
Term	**Definition**
GIF	GIF stands for **G**raphic **I**nterchange **F**ormat. GIFs are one of the two main graphic file formats you can use when optimizing Web graphics. (JPEG is the other.) GIFs are best used for flat or simple graphic images that incorporate solid areas of color, such as logos, illustrations, cartoons, and line art. Because GIFs support transparency (JPEGs do not), GIF is the format to use if you want to include transparent areas in your Web graphics. You can turn on GIF transparency in the Save For Web window in Photoshop CS2 and in the Optimize palette in ImageReady CS2.
Masks	Masks hide the visibility of specific areas of an image. In a transparent GIF, the mask hides the transparent areas. The mask is invisible to the end user.
Transparent	Transparent means you can "see through" pixels to images or layers below. In Photoshop CS2 and ImageReady CS2, transparent areas are defined by a checkerboard background. When you add graphics to a transparent layer in Photoshop CS2 or ImageReady CS2, the program automatically creates an invisible mask called a transparency channel. The transparency channel, or mask, hides and shows transparent areas in an image.
Transparent GIF	Transparent GIFs include an invisible mask that hides and shows transparent areas of the image in a Web browser. As a result, you can create images that have the illusion of being a shape other than a rectangle or a square.

Understanding Offset Problems in Browsers

You might be wondering, why fuss with this transparency stuff? Couldn't you just incorporate the background image into the foreground image and position it over the same background layer? If you're designing a Web site with a flat, single-color background, you can use that technique. Unfortunately, if your background image is made from a pattern or a photograph, your foreground image will not line up correctly with the background image. Due to the constraints of HTML, foreground and background images don't line up in browsers, and as a result, you end up with an unwanted offset, as shown in the following illustration.

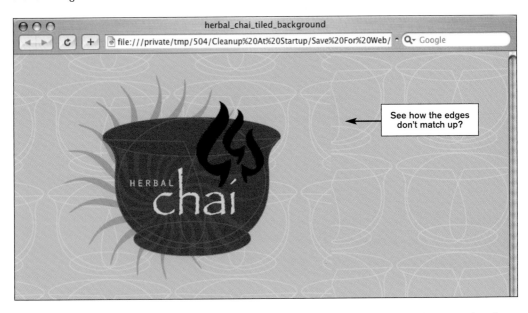

You can't forgo making a foreground GIF transparent because if you just place the foreground and background images together, they won't necessarily line up in browsers. Note the offset in this image.

I. [IR] _____Creating and Previewing Transparent GIFs

In this exercise, you'll learn how to create transparent GIFs and how to preview the results in a Web browser. You can create transparent GIF files in both Photoshop CS2 and ImageReady CS2. For this exercise, you'll use ImageReady CS2 because it's easier to define background and foreground images and preview the results in a Web browser than in Photoshop CS2. Later in this chapter, you'll learn how to achieve the same result in Photoshop CS2.

1. Open **herbal_chai.psd** from the **chap_10** folder you copied to your **Desktop**. Make sure the **Optimize** palette is visible. If it's not, choose **Window > Optimize** and **Window > Color Table**.

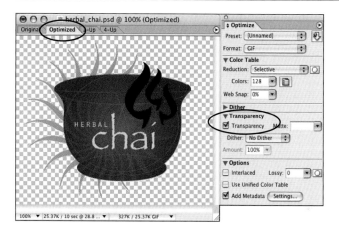

2. In the document window, click the **Optimized** tab. Adjust the settings in the **Optimize** palette to match the ones shown in the illustration here. Make sure you turn on the **Transparency** option—this option defines your image as transparent when you save it as a GIF.

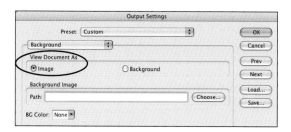

3. Choose **File > Output Settings > Background**. In the **Output Settings** dialog box, select **View Document As: Image**.

This option tells ImageReady CS2 you want to specify the image as a foreground image, not a background image.

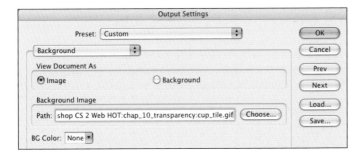

4. In the **Output Settings** dialog box, click the **Choose** button. Navigate to the **chap_10** folder you copied to your **Desktop**. Choose **cup_tile.gif**, and click **Open**. The path to the background image should appear in the **Background Image** section of the **Output Settings** dialog box. Click **OK**.

*This process tells ImageReady CS2 you want **cup_tile.gif** to appear as the background image behind the transparent **herbal_chai.psd** foreground image.*

---

5. In the **Toolbox**, click the **Preview in Default Browser** button.

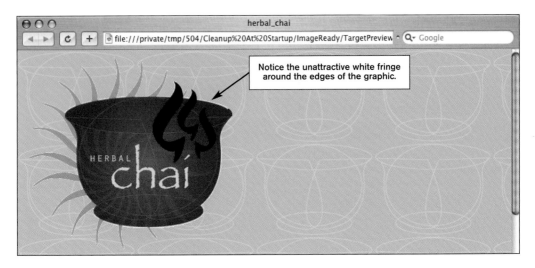

*Your default Web browser will open automatically, and you'll see the transparent **herbal_chai.psd** image on top of the **cup_tile.gif** image.*

*You can see the transparency settings are working, but notice the white fringe or jagginess around the edges of the **herbal_chai.psd** image. In the next exercise, you'll learn how to eliminate that ugly edge to simulate the appearance of a smooth, anti-aliased edge.*

---

6. Return to ImageReady CS2, and leave the file open for the next exercise.

---

2. [IR] _____Fixing the Edges of Transparent GIFs

In the last exercise, you learned how to create a transparent GIF using the transparency controls in the Optimize palette. When you previewed the image over a background, a white fringe or halo appeared around the outside edges of the image. In this exercise, you'll learn how to eliminate the unwanted halo so the edges around the image look crisp and clean.

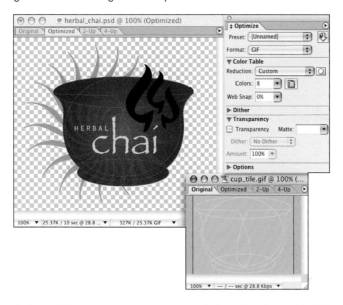

1. If you followed the last exercise, **herbal_chai.psd** should still be open in ImageReady CS2. If it's not, go back and complete Exercise 1. Leave **herbal_chai.psd** open, and open **cup_tile.gif** from the **chap_10** folder you copied to your **Desktop**.

2. Select the **Eyedropper** tool from the **Toolbox**. Click the **beige** background of the **cup_tile.gif** image to sample the color and to change the **Foreground Color**.

3. Close **cup_tile.gif** and return to the **herbal_chai.psd** image. If it's hidden behind other windows on your screen, choose **Window > Documents > herbal_chai.psd**. Click the **Optimized** tab.

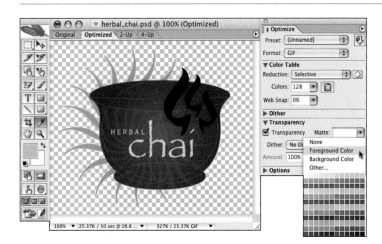

4. In the **Transparency** section of the **Optimize** palette, choose **Foreground Color** from the **Matte** pop-up menu, as shown in the illustration here.

*The color you selected from the background image should now appear in the **Matte** field of the **Transparency** section of the **Optimize** palette.*

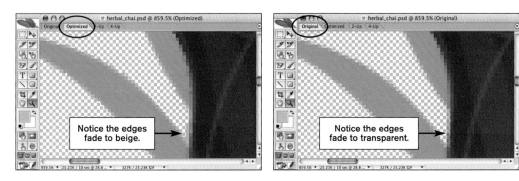

5. Select the **Zoom** tool from the **Toolbox**. Zoom in on the edges of the **herbal_chai.psd** file, and look closely at the edges. You should see the beige under the anti-aliased edge of the graphic. Toggle between the **Optimized** tab and the **Original** tab to see the change you made.

Notice in the original image, the edges fade from opaque to transparent, and in the optimized image, the edges fade to beige. This will help blend the image into the background, and it will eliminate the white fringe.

6. When you've finished observing the changes, in the **Toolbox**, double-click the **Zoom** tool to reset the zoom level to **100%**.

7. In the **Toolbox**, click the **Preview in Default Browser** button.

The background image is still set from the last exercise. In the Web browser, you'll see the ***herbal_chai.psd*** *image as the foreground image and* ***cup_tile.gif*** *as the background image. Unlike the last exercise, you won't see a distracting white halo around the edges of the* ***herbal_chai.psd*** *image. Instead,* ***herbal_chai.psd*** *has a beige matte around the edge that blends in with the background. With a finely patterned background like this, even though the background is busy, the matte color produces a crisp, clean edge.*

8. Return to ImageReady CS2. Leave **herbal_chai.psd** open for the next exercise.

3. [IR] _____Fixing Soft Edges of Transparent GIFs

Changing the matte color to match the color in the background image eliminated the white fringe on a simple, anti-aliased foreground image. What if the edge of your foreground image contains a very soft edge, such as a drop shadow or a glow? As you'll see in this exercise, the matching technique you just learned can camouflage even a soft drop shadow or glow.

1. If you followed the last exercise, **herbal_chai.psd** should still be open in ImageReady CS2. If it's not, go back and complete Exercise 2. In the document window, click the **Original** tab. Make sure the **Layers** palette and **Optimize** palette are visible. If they're not, choose **Window > Layers** and **Window > Optimize**.

*Tip: Switching back to the **Original** tab is important. Otherwise, ImageReady CS2 tries to optimize the graphic as you're editing, which makes the editing process unnecessarily slow. Also, when the **Original** tab is active, you can perform editing tasks, such as using brush, shape, and type tools, which are not available when the **Optimized** tab is active.*

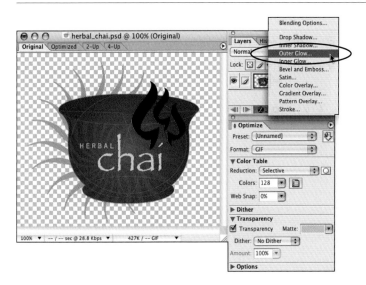

2. In the **Layers** palette, choose **Outer Glow** from the **Layer Style** pop-up menu.

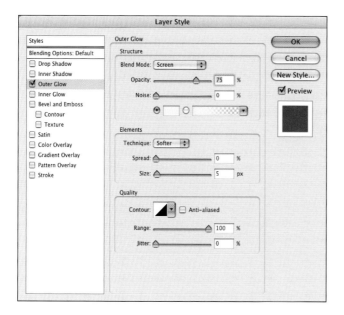

3. Match the settings in the **Layer Style** dialog box to the ones shown in the illustration here.

4. Click the **Optimized** tab. You'll see a beige border around the image, which is a result of the matte color you applied in the last exercise.

Notice you can still see the edges of the outer glow clearly against the matte. Although the image looks strange with this beige matte, it will look just fine against the background image in a Web browser, which you'll get to preview in the next step.

5. In the **Toolbox**, click the **Preview in Default Browser** button.

Notice that the integrity of the outer glow is still intact. If you look closely, you can see small areas of the beige matte where it meets the background image. Regardless, it sure beats having unwanted colored edges around the entire image, and it maintains soft edges of the outer glow.

6. Return to ImageReady CS2. Leave **herbal_chai.psd** open for the next exercise.

4. [IR] **Saving Optimized Transparent GIFs**

In the last few exercises, you learned how to create transparent GIFs. Next you'll learn how to save an optimized transparent GIF with its corresponding background image using the Save Optimized As feature in ImageReady CS2. In Exercise 5, you'll learn how to create and save transparent GIFs in Photoshop CS2.

> **1.** If you followed the last exercise, **herbal_chai.psd** should still be open in ImageReady CS2. If it's not, go back and complete Exercise 3. Make sure the **Optimize** palette is visible. If it's not, choose **Window > Optimize**.

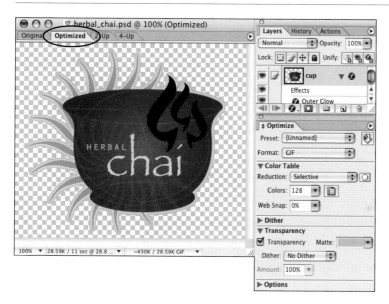

2. In the document window, click the **Optimized** tab. Match the settings in the **Optimize** palette to the illustration shown here.

3. Choose **File > Save Optimized As**. The **Save Optimized As** dialog box opens automatically.

*Notice ImageReady CS2 automatically keeps the filename the same and changes the file extension to the appropriate format. (The file extension is dependent upon the option you choose from the **Format** pop-up menu.)*

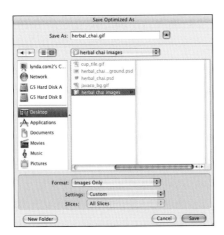

4. In the **Save Optimized As** dialog box, choose **Images Only** from the **Format** pop-up. Navigate to the **chap_10** folder on your **Desktop**. Create a new folder called **herbal_chai_images**. In the **Save Optimized As** dialog box, make sure the **herbal_chai_images** folder is selected. Click **Save**.

*Note: Choosing **Images Only** saves the foreground and background images. If you want to save the required HTML code as well as the images, choose **HTML and Images** from the **Format** pop-up menu. Choosing to save the HTML depends on whether you want to build your Web page using ImageReady CS2 or whether you prefer to build pages using an HTML editor, such as Adobe GoLive or Macromedia Dreamweaver.*

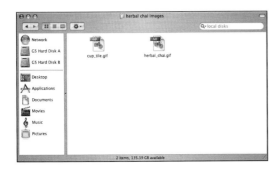

5. Browse to the **herbal_chai_images** folder in the **chap_10** folder on your **Desktop**.

*In the **herbal_chai_images** folder, you'll notice both the foreground image (**herbal_chai.gif**) and the background image (**cup_tile.gif**) saved automatically. One of the benefits of using the **Save Optimized As** feature in ImageReady CS2 is the capability to save both foreground and background images at the same time.*

6. Close **herbal_chai.psd**. You don't need to save your changes.

<u>[PS]</u> **Creating and Saving Transparent GIFs in Photoshop CS2**

In this chapter, you've learned to create, troubleshoot, and save transparent GIFs in ImageReady CS2. There will be times when you'll want to create transparent GIFs in Photoshop CS2 instead of ImageReady CS2. In this exercise, you'll learn how to set a matte color to avoid the white fringe around transparent images and how to save transparent GIFs in Photoshop CS2.

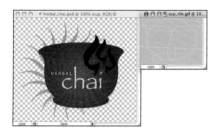

1. In Photoshop CS2, open **herbal_chai.psd** and **cup_tile.gif** from the **chap_10** folder you copied to your **Desktop**.

---

2. Click **cup_tile.gif** to make it the active image. Choose **File > Save For Web**.

First, you'll sample color from cup_tile.gif so you can specify it as the matte color for herbal_chai.psd.

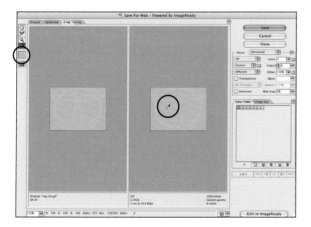

3. Select the **Eyedropper** tool in the **Save For Web Toolbox**. Click the **beige** background of **cup_tile.gif** to sample the color. Click **Done**.

Note: Unlike in ImageReady CS2, you must sample color in the Save For Web dialog box, not in the main Photoshop CS2 application window. This is one of the reasons you'll find it easier to create transparent GIFs in ImageReady CS2 rather than Photoshop CS2.

---

4. Click **herbal_chai.psd** to make it the active image. If it's hidden behind other windows on your screen, choose **Window > Documents > herbal_chai.psd**.

5. Choose **File > Save For Web**.

*Notice the beige you sampled in Step 3 is still the current **Eyedropper** color.*

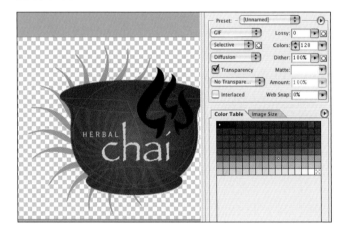

6. Adjust the settings in the **Save For Web** dialog box to match the settings shown in the illustration here.

7. Choose **Eyedropper Color** from the **Matte** pop-up menu.

8. In the **Save For Web** dialog box, choose **Edit Output Settings** from the **Optimize** menu.

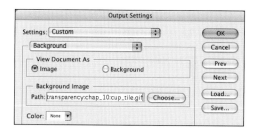

9. In the **Output Settings** dialog box, choose **Background** from the pop-up menu. Select **View Document As: Image**. Click the **Choose** button. Navigate to the **chap_10** folder you copied to your **Desktop**, and choose **cup_tile.gif**. Click **Open**. Click **OK** to close the **Output Settings** dialog box.

*Specifying **cup_tile.gif** in the **Path** field tells Photoshop CS2 you want **herbal_chai.psd** to be viewed as the foreground image and **cup_tile.gif** as the background image.*

10. In the **Save For Web** dialog box, click the **Preview in Default Browser** button to preview the settings before saving.

In the Web browser, you'll see the transparent GIF on top of the background image you specified in the last step.

11. Close the Web browser, and return to return to the **Save For Web** dialog box in Photoshop CS2. Click **Save** to open the **Save Optimized As** dialog box.

12. In the **Save Optimized As** dialog box, navigate to the **chap_10** folder you copied to your **Desktop**. Click the **New Folder** button, and create a folder called **herbal_chai_ps**. Choose **HTML and Images** from the **Format** pop-up menu. Click **Save**.

*If you'd rather create the HTML code in an HTML editor, choose **Images Only** from the **Format** pop-up menu.*

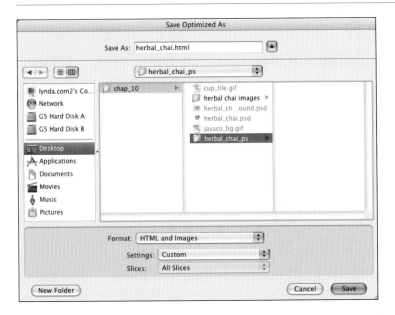

13. Browse to the **herbal_chai_ps** folder in the **chap_10** folder on your **Desktop**. Take a look at the contents of the **herbal_chai_ps** folder. If you'd like, double-click **herbal_chai_ps.html** to view the saved results.

14. Return to Photoshop CS2. Close **herbal_chai.psd**. You don't need to save your changes.

6. [PS] Creating Transparent GIFs from Nontransparent Images

Throughout this chapter, you've worked with **herbal_chai.psd**, which was created in Photoshop CS2 using transparent layers. Because the image contained transparent layers, it was easy to create and save it as a transparent GIF. What if you're working with an image that doesn't have transparent layers, but you want to create a transparent GIF? How would you define which areas of the image you want to be transparent? In this exercise, you'll learn to use the Map Transparency option in Photoshop CS2 to help you define transparent areas.

1. Open **flavors.psd** from the **chap_10** folder you copied to your **Desktop**.

Notice the image has no transparent areas (indicated by a checkerboard pattern).

2. Choose **File > Save For Web**. Choose **GIF** from the **Optimized File Format** pop-up menu, choose **128** from the **Colors** pop-up menu, turn on the **Transparency** option, and watch the results in the preview section of the **Save For Web** window.

Notice nothing happens. Because this file does not have transparent layers, Photoshop CS2 doesn't know which part of the image should be transparent in the optimized GIF. In order to create transparent GIFs, your images must contain transparent layers. In the next few steps, you'll learn how to instruct Photoshop CS2 to convert regular pixels to transparent pixels.

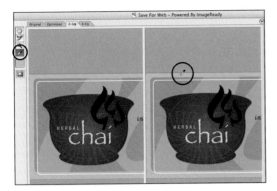

3. Select the **Eyedropper** tool from the **Save For Web Toolbox**. Click in the **light green** around the perimeter of the rounded rectangle.

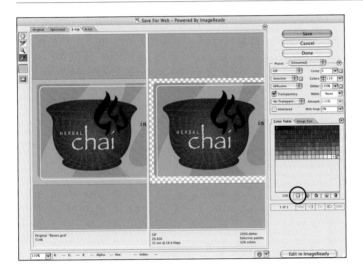

4. At the bottom of the **Color Table**, click the **Map Transparency** button.

*Notice the areas that were previously light green are now a checkerboard pattern, which indicates transparency. Photoshop CS2 converted the color you selected with the **Eyedropper** tool to transparent pixels.*

This feature is very useful when you must work with an image that doesn't have areas of transparency. Once you have converted colored pixels to transparent pixels, you can use the techniques you learned in this chapter to specify a background image, apply a matte color, and save the optimized transparent GIF.

5. In the **Save For Web** dialog box, click **Cancel**. Close the file. You don't need to save your changes.

TIP | Creating Transparent Areas with the Magic Eraser

In the last exercise, you learned how to convert colored pixels to transparent pixels in the Save For Web window. This technique is helpful when you're optimizing an image, and you want to create transparent areas. However, there will be times when you want to convert colored pixels to transparent pixels in the image itself. Fortunately, Photoshop CS2 has a handy feature, the **Magic Eraser** tool, which converts colored pixels to transparent pixels in a snap. Here's how:

1. Select the **Magic Eraser** tool from the **Toolbox**.

2. Click an area of the image you want to convert from colored pixels to transparent pixels. Voilà! The colored pixels are automatically transformed to transparent pixels.

Note: The **Magic Eraser** works best on areas of solid color.

7. [IR] _____Simulating Transparency with JPEGs

In this chapter, you've learned how to optimize images with transparency as GIFs because GIF is currently the only Web file format that supports transparency. As you know from Chapter 7, "*Optimizing Images*," the GIF file format is best for flat or simple graphic images with solid areas of color, such as logos, illustrations, cartoons, and line art. What if you have a continuous tone image, such as a photograph with areas of transparency? You can simulate transparency using the JPEG file format, but there are some limitations. Here's an exercise to help you understand.

Transparent areas

1. Open **teapot.psd** from the **chap_10** folder you copied to your **Desktop**. Make sure the **Layers** palette and **Optimize** palette are visible. If they're not, choose **Window > Layers** and **Window > Optimize**.

Notice the photograph has rounded corners. The negative areas, or the areas beyond the rounded corners, are transparent.

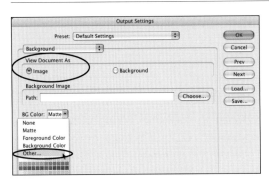

2. Choose **File > Output Settings > Background**. Select **View Document As: Image**. Choose **Other** from the **BG Color** pop-up menu to open the **Color Picker** dialog box.

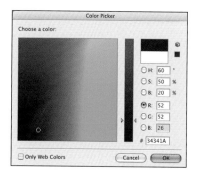

3. In the **Color Picker** dialog box, specify the following **RGB** values: **R=52, G=52**, and **B=26**. Click **OK** to close the **Color Picker** dialog box. In the **Output Settings** dialog box, click **OK**.

*Choosing a color from the **BG Color** pop-up menu will add a solid colored background image to the **teapot.psd** foreground image.*

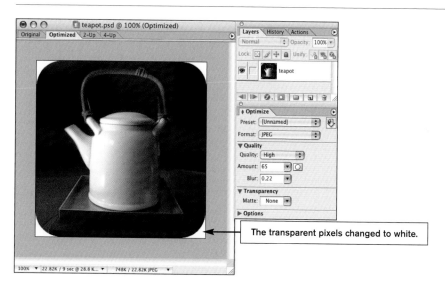

The transparent pixels changed to white.

4. In the document window, click the **Optimized** tab. Match the settings in the **Optimize** palette to the ones shown in the illustration here.

*Did you notice when you switched from the **Original** tab to the **Optimized** tab that the transparent areas changed from transparent to white? Because the JPEG file format does not support transparency, transparent pixels are automatically converted to colored pixels. By default, ImageReady CS2 converts transparent pixels to white.*

5. In the **Toolbox**, click the **Preview in Default Browser** button.

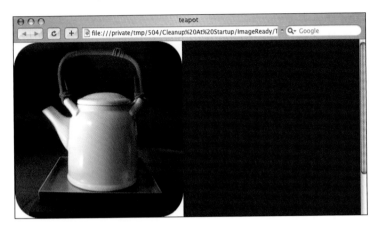

As you can see, the nicely rounded edges don't look so pretty when they are white against a dark green background. Not to worry, you can simulate the appearance of transparency by using a matte color that matches the colored background. You'll learn how in the next steps.

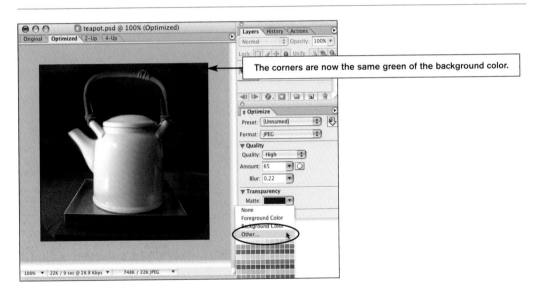

The corners are now the same green of the background color.

6. Close the Web browser and return to ImageReady CS2. In the **Transparency** section of the **Optimize** palette, choose **Other** from the **Matte** pop-up menu. Type the same **RGB** values you specified in Step 3—**R=52, G=52,** and **B=26**.

Notice the corners switched from white to green—the same green you specified for the background color in Step 3.

7. In the **Toolbox**, click the **Preview in Default Browser** button.

Because the transparent pixels are filled with the same color as the background, you get the effect of a transparent image sitting on a colored background.

TIP | JPEG Transparency and Patterned Backgrounds

Because you can only use a solid color to fill transparent pixels during JPEG optimization, simulating transparency using the technique you learned in this exercise is only effective on solid-colored backgrounds.

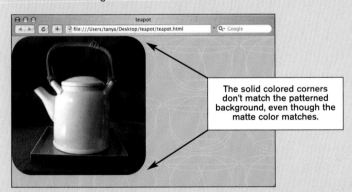

The solid colored corners don't match the patterned background, even though the matte color matches.

If you have a patterned background, the result can be unpleasing because it will be obvious which pixels are solid colored even if you match the matte color to one of the colors in the patterned background.

As a result, you should consider the content you want to use on your Web site—both the foreground and background images—and decide early in the design process if you'd rather have a patterned background or the look of transparent photographic content, such as the one in this exercise.

You've finished another complex chapter! Now you're ready to create transparent GIFs in Photoshop CS2 and ImageReady CS2! Next, you'll learn how to create animated GIFs.

Creating Animated GIFs

| Creating Animations from Layer Visibility | Tweening with Opacity |

| Selecting, Duplicating, and Reversing Frames |

| Tweening with Position and Layer Styles |

| Optimizing and Saving Animated GIFs |

| Optimizing Transparent Animated GIFs |

chap_11

PCS2Web HOT CD-ROM

One of the best things about designing Web graphics is the ability to create animations, which you can't do in print design. If you have a background in printing, it's possible you've never worked with animation before. No need to worry, Photoshop CS2 and ImageReady CS2 are excellent tools to help you create animated Web graphics. If you've created animations before, you'll be surprised how easy it is to create animations in Photoshop CS2 and ImageReady CS2.

Although animations appear to move when you view them on a computer, the movement is simulated from a series of still images. You can save animations from Photoshop CS2 or ImageReady CS2 into two formats—GIF and SWF (Macromedia Flash). The GIF format is popular for Web animation because it doesn't require any plug-ins—all Web browsers can natively read this format. Animated GIFs are also popular because they are backwards-compatible with older Web browsers.

This chapter will focus on creating and saving animated GIFs. In Chapter 19, "*Integrating with Macromedia Flash*," you'll learn how to export animated SWF files. In the past, the animation features were only available in ImageReady. New in this version, Photoshop CS2 now includes the same animation features as ImageReady CS2.

The Animation Palette

When you create animations in either Photoshop CS2 or ImageReady CS2, you'll use the Animation palette to specify different settings. The Animation palette is identical in Photoshop CS2 and ImageReady CS2. Here's an overview of its features:

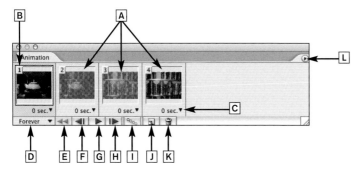

Animation Palette Controls		
A	Frames	Displays a preview of the contents in a frame
B	Frame number	Identifies the frame number
C	Frame Delay pop-up menu	Selects the frame delay time
D	Looping pop-up menu	Selects the looping option (how many times to play the animation)
E	First Frame button	Selects the first frame
F	Previous Frame button	Selects the previous frame
G	Play/Stop button	Plays or stops the animation
H	Next Frame button	Selects the next frame
I	Tween button	Tweens the animation, which tells Photoshop CS2 or ImageReady CS2 to automatically generate frames between frames you specify
J	Duplicate Current Frame button	Duplicates the current frame to make a new frame
K	Delete Selected Frame button	Deletes the currently selected frame
L	Animation palette menu	Provides options for creating and editing animations

Controlling the Timing of Animations

Animation is a time-based medium. The timing of animations is based on how long you want the animation to play and the number of frames. Sometimes slideshow style animation is what you'll want, and other times you'll want to make movement feel faster. The GIF format supports delays between frames and allows timing to change within a single animation file.

Video and film animation are also time-based mediums, with one key difference from animated GIFs: video and film play back at specific frame rates (30 frames per second for video, 24 frames per second for film). Unfortunately, animated GIFs play back at different speeds depending on the computer they're being played on. The slower the processor, the slower the animation will play. Unfortunately, there's no way to predict how quickly (or slowly!) animations will play on different computers. If you can, make sure you preview your animations on a variety of different computers with different processor speeds before you create your final Web pages.

Animation Aesthetics

Animations on a Web page attract more attention than static images on a page. Make sure the subject matter you pick for animations is worthy of more attention than other images on the page. Many Web pages contain so many animations they distract viewers from the content instead of enhancing it. Good uses for animation might include ad banners, movement from certain words so they stand out, diagrams brought to life, slideshows of photographs, or cartoon characters. You'll learn how to create different kinds of animation in this chapter.

The Animated GIF Format

The GIF file format is one of the few Web file formats to support animation. A Web browser treats animated GIFs the same as static GIFs, but an animated GIF displays multiple images (called **frames** in animation terminology) in a sequence (much like a slideshow) instead of a single, static image. Different frames can have different timings, which allows you to speed up and slow down frames in an animation.

Animated GIFs do not require plug-ins to Web browsers, which means they are viewable in all Web browsers (except text-only or 1.0 browsers). The HTML code required to insert animated GIFs on a Web page is no different than the code for a static GIF. You can instruct animated GIFs to repeat (called **looping** in animation lingo), to play only once, or to play a specific number of times. The looping information is stored in the animated GIF, not in the HTML code.

GIF Compression Challenges

The principles for compressing animated GIFs are similar to those for compressing static GIFs. Large areas of solid color compress better than areas with a lot of noise or detail. If you use photographic images in an animated GIF, be sure to add lossy compression, which will make a substantial difference in file savings.

Animated GIFs will always be larger than static GIFs. Photoshop CS2 and ImageReady CS2 have two animation compression features—Bounding Box and Redundant Pixel Removal, which are both enabled by default. These features ensure file size is increased only for those areas that change from one frame to the next. For example, if you have a frame with a photographic background, and the only change in the next frame is the addition of type, the photographic area will be written only once to the file, limiting the total file size. If you change every pixel of an animation, you won't be able to keep the size down using the Bounding Box and Redundant Pixel Removal features.

When you compress an animated GIF, remember the file will stream in, meaning frames will appear before the entire file has finished loading. For this reason, you should divide the file size by the number of frames to figure out the size of each frame. For example, if you have a 100 K animated GIF with 10 frames, each frame is only 10 K.

I. [PS] _____Creating Animations from Layer Visibility

In this exercise, you'll learn how to create animations by turning on and off the visibility of layers in the Layers palette. For this exercise, you'll use Photoshop CS2 but it works similarly in ImageReady CS2.

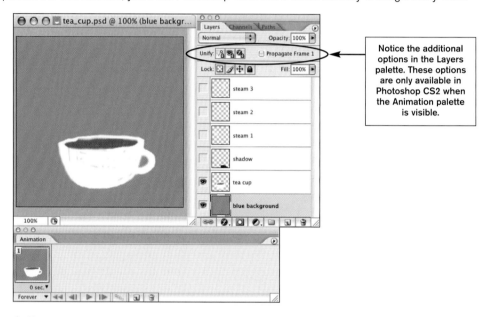

Notice the additional options in the Layers palette. These options are only available in Photoshop CS2 when the Animation palette is visible.

1. Open **tea_cup.psd** from the **chap_11** folder you copied to your **Desktop**. Make sure the **Layers** palette and **Animation** palette are visible. If they're not, choose **Window > Layers** and **Window > Animation**.

*Notice the **Layers** palette has additional options? These options are specific to creating animations and appear only when the **Animation** palette is visible.*

*Notice there is only one frame in the **Animation** palette. To make this file into an animation, you must have at least two frames with differing content. One way to create differing content in the frames is to turn on and off the visibility of different layers in the frames. The layers in this exercise have already been created for you. In the next few steps, you'll create new frames by turning on and off the visibility of layers.*

2. In the **Animation** palette, click **Frame 1** to select it. In the **Layers** palette, make sure the visibility of the **blue background** and **tea cup** layers is turned on.

3. At the bottom of the **Animation** palette, click the **Duplicate Current Frame** button.

*Notice the newly created **Frame 2** is a duplicate of **Frame 1**.*

4. In the **Layers** palette, turn on the visibility of the **steam 2** layer.

*Notice **Frame 2** updates with the change you made to the visibility of the **steam 2** layer.*

5. With **Frame 2** selected in the **Animation** palette, click the **Duplicate Current Frame** button. In the **Layers** palette, turn off the visibility of the **steam 2** layer, and turn on the visibility of the **steam 1** layer.

6. With **Frame 3** selected in the **Animation** palette, click the **Duplicate Current Frame** button. In the **Layers** palette, turn off the visibility of the **steam 1** layer, and turn on the visibility of the **steam 3** layer.

7. In the **Animation** palette, click the **Play** button to view the animation you just created. When you're finished viewing the animation, click the **Stop** button.

*What if you want to turn on the visibility of a new layer and have it turned on in all the frames in the **Animation** palette? Remember the options in the **Layers** palette that appeared when you turned on the **Animation** palette? One of the options—the **Unify Layer Visibility** option—is the answer.*

8. In the **Animation** palette, click **Frame 1** to select it. In the **Layers** palette, turn on the visibility of the **shadow** layer.

*Notice the shadow appears only in **Frame 1**. You could go through and click each frame and manually turn on the visibility for each frame, but that's a time-consuming process—especially if you have a complex animation with tens or hundreds of frames.*

9. In the **Layers** palette, click the **Unify Layer Visibility** button. A warning message will appear asking if you want the visibility in the other frames to match the current visibility. Click **Match**.

*Notice all the frames in the **Animation** palette now have the visibility of the **shadow** layer turned on.*

10. Leave **tea_cup.psd** open for the next exercise.

2. [PS/IR] _____Setting Looping and Speed

In the last exercise, the animation you created played at a rapid pace and repeated (or looped) until you clicked the Stop button. In this exercise, you'll learn how to decrease the speed of the animation and how to change the looping from the Forever setting to a specific number of repeats.

1. If you followed Exercise 1, **tea_cup.psd** should still be open in Photoshop CS2. If it's not, go back and complete Exercise 1. Make sure the **Animation** palette is visible. If it's not, choose **Window > Animation**.

2. At the bottom of the **Animation** palette, click the **Play** button. Let the animation play a few times, and then click the **Stop** button.

*Notice the animation repeats, or loops until you click the **Stop** button. You can control how many times the animation repeats, or loops, easily.*

3. Choose **Once** from the **Looping** pop-up menu. In the **Animation** palette, click the **Play** button.

Unlike the last time you played the animation, this time the animation played once and stopped.

4. Choose **Other** from the **Looping** pop-up menu to open the **Set Loop Count** dialog box. Type **3** in the **Play** field, and click **OK**. In the **Animation** palette, click the **Play** button.

This time, the animation played three times and stopped. As you can see, you have a lot of control over how many times the animation plays. Next, you'll adjust the speed of the animation.

5. Choose **File > Save For Web**. Choose **GIF** from the **File Format** pop-up menu. At the bottom of the **Save For Web** dialog box, click the **Preview in Default Browser** button.

Notice the animation plays much faster in your Web browser than it did in Photoshop CS2. Photoshop CS2 builds the animation as it plays. Web browsers play a prebuilt animated GIF, which makes it play significantly faster. If you were to upload this file to the Web, the speed might be different, due to bandwidth or server speed. Animation playback on the computer is an inexact science because it is dependent on so many factors—processor speed, bandwidth, browsers, and operating systems!

Next, you'll learn how to reduce the speed of an animation by using delay settings.

*Tip: If you're using ImageReady CS2 to create your animations, you can preview the animation in a Web browser by simply clicking the **Preview in Default Browser** button.*

6. Click **Done** to close the **Save For Web** dialog box. In the **Animation** palette, click **Frame 1**. Hold down the **Shift** key, and click **Frame 4** to multiple-select the frames in between.

7. Choose **0.2** seconds from the **Frame Delay** pop-up menu under **Frame 2**.

Notice the frame delay changed for all four frames. Because all four frames were selected, the change to the frame delay was automatically applied to each frame.

8. Choose **File > Save For Web**. At the bottom of the **Save For Web** dialog box, click the **Preview in Default Browser** button.

Notice the animation plays significantly slower.

*Tip: You can change the frame delay for all frames in an animation or for individual frames. To change the frame delay for individual frames, click a frame to select it, and choose a frame delay time from the **Frame Delay** pop-up menu. You can also specify a specific time by choosing **Other** from the **Frame Delay** pop-up menu and typing a value in the **Set Frame Delay** dialog box.*

9. Close the Web browser. In the **Save For Web** dialog box, click **Done**. Close **tea_cup.psd**. You don't need to save your changes.

You'll learn how to optimize and save animated GIFs in Exercise 6.

3. [PS/IR] _____Tweening with Opacity

In the last few exercises, you created animations by turning on and off layer visibility. This technique is helpful if you have a layered file, but there will be times when you want to create animations from a flat image without having to create multiple layers for each frame. In this exercise, you'll learn how to create animations using the Tween feature.

1. Open **white_tea.psd** from the **chap_11** folder you copied to your **Desktop**. Make sure the **Layers** palette and **Animation** palette are visible. If they're not, choose **Window > Layers** and **Window > Animation**.

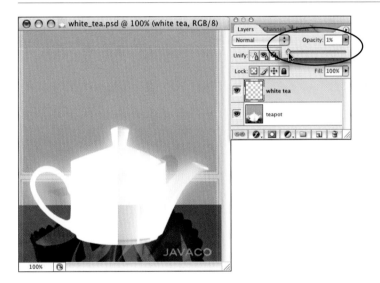

2. In the **Layers** palette, click the **white tea** layer to select it. Reduce the **Opacity** of the **white tea** layer to **1%** using the **Opacity** slider in the **Layers** palette.

Notice the words white tea *are no longer visible.*

3. At the bottom of the **Animation** palette, click the **Duplicate Current Frame** button to create a new frame with the same properties as **Frame 1**.

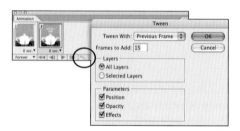

4. With **Frame 2** selected in the **Animation** palette, and the **white tea** layer selected in the **Layers** palette, increase the opacity of the **white tea** layer to **100%** using the **Opacity** slider in the **Layers** palette.

5. At the bottom of the **Animation** palette, click the **Tween** button to open the **Tween** dialog box. Choose **Previous Frame** from the **Tween With** pop-up menu. Type **15** in the **Frames to Add** field. Select the **All Layers** option, and turn on **Position**, **Opacity**, and **Effects**. Click **OK**.

*You should now have 17 frames in the **Animation** palette. Photoshop CS2 automatically created 15 intermediary steps, which will allow the words* white tea *to fade in slowly.*

6. Click **Play** to view the animation. You should see the words *white tea* fade into the image. Click **Stop** when you've finished viewing the animation.

Notice when you play the animation, there is an abrupt change when it repeats. You could change the looping to once, which you learned in the last exercise. Or, you could fade the text out the same way it faded it. You'll learn how in the next exercise.

[PS/IR] **Selecting, Duplicating, and Reversing Frames**

In the last exercise, you created an animation by increasing the opacity from 1% to 100% over the course of 17 frames. What if you want to make the words fade into 100%, hold at 100% for a few seconds, then fade out to 1%? Here's an exercise to show you how:

1. If you followed the last exercise, **white_tea.psd** should still be open in Photoshop CS2. If it's not, go back and complete Exercise 1. Make sure the **Animation** palette is visible. If it's not, choose **Window > Animation**.

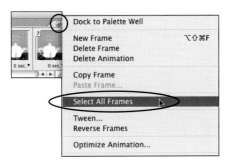

2. Click **Frame 1** in the **Animation** palette to select it. Choose **Select All Frames** from the **Animation** palette menu.

3. With all 17 frames selected, choose **Copy Frames** from the **Animation** palette menu.

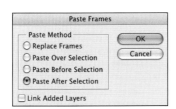

4. Click **Frame 17** to select it, and choose **Paste Frames** from the **Animation** palette menu. In the **Paste Frames** dialog box, choose the **Paste After Selection** option, and click **OK**.

You should now have 34 frames in your animation. Photoshop CS2 created another full set of 17 frames from the original 17 frames in the animation and appended them to the end. As you can see, **Frame 1** *through* **Frame 17** *are the original frames.* **Frame 18** *through* **Frame 34** *are the new frames.*

Tip: Instead of copying and pasting frames, you can also use the **Duplicate Current Frame** *button at the bottom of the* **Animation** *palette.*

5. In the **Animation** palette, **Frame 18** through **Frame 34** (the frames you pasted in the last step) should already be selected. If they're not, click **Frame 18**, hold down the **Shift** key, and click **Frame 34** to multiple-select the frames in-between.

6. Choose **Reverse Frames** from the **Animation** palette menu.

*The order of **Frame 18** to **Frame 34** is reversed. The opacity in **Frame 18** is **100%**, and the opacity in **Frame 34** is **1%**.*

7. Click **Play**. Click **Stop** when you've finished previewing the animation.

Notice that the words white tea *evenly fade in and out. Next, you'll change the timing of **Frame 17** so the animation holds at full opacity before fading out.*

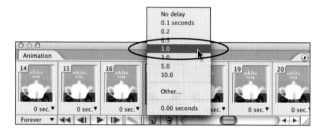

8. In the **Animation** palette, click **Frame 17** to select it. Choose **1.0** from the **Frame Delay** pop-up menu.

9. Click **Frame 1** to select it. Click **Play**. The animation now holds at full opacity then fades out. When you've finished watching the animation, click **Stop**.

Photoshop CS2 allows you to change the timing for all the frames in an animation (which you did in the last exercise) or individual frames (which you did in the last step).

10. Close **white_tea.psd** without saving your changes.

5. [PS/IR] _____Tweening with Position and Layer Styles

So far in this chapter, you've learned how to create animations by turning on and off layer visibility. You've also learned how to create animations that fade in and out by tweening with opacity. There are two other useful techniques when you're creating animations: tweening with position and tweening with layer styles.

1. Open **white_tea.psd** from the **chap_11** folder you copied to your **Desktop**.

2. In the **Layers** palette, click the **white tea** layer to select it. Select the **Move** tool from the **Toolbox**. Click and drag the **white tea** layer to the top of the document window, as shown in the illustration here.

3. At the bottom of the **Animation** palette, click the **Duplicate Current Frame** button.

4. With **Frame 2** selected in the **Animation** palette, the **Move** tool still selected in the **Toolbox**, and the **white tea** layer still selected in the **Layers** palette, click and drag the **white tea** layer to the bottom of the document window, as shown in the illustration here.

Notice **Frame 2** automatically updated to reflect the change you made to the layer position.

5. With the **white tea** layer selected in the **Layers** palette, and **Frame 2** selected in the **Animation** palette, choose **Gradient Overlay** from the **Layer Style** pop-up menu at the bottom of the **Layers** palette.

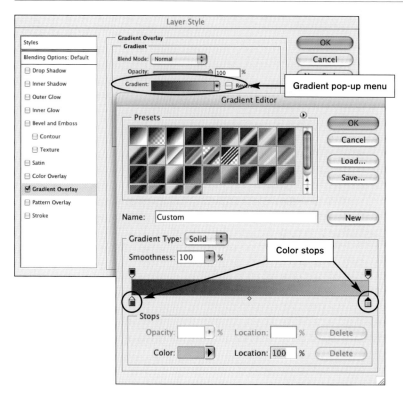

6. Click inside the **Gradient** pop-up menu to open the **Gradient Editor** dialog box. On the left side of the **Gradient** preview, double-click the **color stop** to open the **Color Picker** dialog box. Choose a bright purple, and click **OK**. On the right side of the **Gradient** preview, double-click the **color stop** to open the **Color Picker** dialog box. Choose a light purple, and click **OK**. In the **Gradient Editor** dialog box, click **OK**. In the **Layer Style** dialog box, click **OK**.

*Notice you only applied the **Gradient Overlay** layer style to **Frame 2** in the **Animation** palette. What if you want to apply the layer style to all the frames? You'll learn how in the next step.*

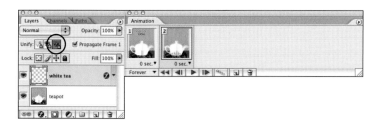

7. In the **Layers** palette, click the **Unify Layer Style** button. When the warning message appears, click **Match**.

*Frame 1 updated with the **Gradient Overlay** layer style you applied in Step 5.*

---

8. Press **Cmd+Z** (Mac) or **Ctrl+Z** (Windows) to undo the **Unify Layer Style**.

---

9. With **Frame 2** selected in the **Animation** palette, at the bottom of the **Animation** palette, click the **Tween** button. In the **Tween** dialog box, make sure **Previous Frame** is selected in the **Tween With** pop-up menu. Type **10** in the **Frames to Add** field. Click **OK**.

*You now have 12 frames in the **Animation** palette.*

10. In the **Animation** palette, click the **Play** button to watch the animation. Click **Stop** when you've finished viewing your handiwork.

Notice the words white tea *move down the page as the gradient slowly fades in. Photoshop CS2 created an animation by tweening the position of the words* white tea *and the visibility of the* **Gradient Overlay** *layer style.*

---

11. Leave **white_tea.psd** open for the next exercise.

---

6. [PS] _____ Optimizing and Saving Animated GIFs

So far in this chapter, you've learned different techniques for creating animations. In this exercise, you'll learn how to optimize animated GIFs for the Web.

1. If you followed the last exercise, **white_tea.psd** should still be open in Photoshop CS2. If it's not, go back and complete Exercise 5.

2. Choose **File > Save For Web**. Click the **2-Up** tab. Choose **GIF** from the **File Format** pop-up menu. Experiment with the other settings using the techniques you learned in Chapter 7, "*Optimizing Images*," until you come up with the best quality image with the smallest file size.

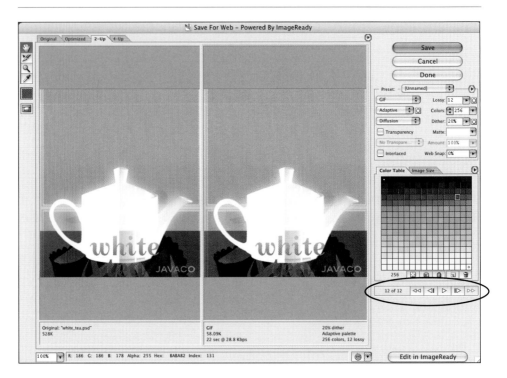

3. In the **Save For Web** dialog box, use the **Previous Frame** and **Next Frame** buttons below the **Color Table** to preview the optimization settings on each frame.

One of the limitations of the GIF file format is that you have to use the same settings for all frames. Make sure you're happy with the optimization settings for each frame before you continue with the next step.

4. When you're happy with the optimization settings, in the **Save For Web** dialog box, click **Save**.

5. In the **Save Optimized As** dialog box, navigate to the **chap_11** folder you copied to your **Desktop**. Click the **New Folder** button. Create a new folder called **white_tea_animation**. Choose **Images Only** from the **Format** pop-up menu. Click **Save**.

*You may wonder why you chose **Images Only** in the **Format** pop-up menu and not **HTML and Images**, which you've done in the last several chapters. Animated GIFs do not require additional HTML code to make them work in a Web browser. You can insert an animated GIF into an HTML editor just like any other GIF. You can even load an animated GIF into a Web browser without creating any HTML code.*

6. Open a Web browser (any one will do!). Choose **File > Open**. Navigate to the **white_tea_anima-tion** folder in the **chap_11** folder you copied to your **Desktop**, and select **white_tea.gif**. Click **Open**.

As you can see, the animated GIF plays in a Web browser without any need for additional HTML code.

7. Return to Photoshop CS2. Close **white_tea.psd**. You don't need to save your changes.

TIP | Optimizing and Saving Animated GIFs in ImageReady CS2

In the last exercise, you learned how to optimize and save animated GIFs in Photoshop CS2. You can also optimize and save animated GIFs in ImageReady CS2.

1. Click the **Optimized** tab in the document window.

2. Specify settings in the **Optimize** palette. Make sure you select each frame in the **Animation** palette to preview the **Optimization** settings on each frame.

3. Choose **File > Save Optimized As**. Choose a location to save the file, and click **Save**.

7. [PS/IR] _____Optimizing Transparent Animated GIFs

In the last few exercises, you've created animated GIFs with solid backgrounds. In this exercise, you'll learn how to create animated GIFs with transparent backgrounds.

1. Open **herbal_chai.psd** from the **chap_11** folder you copied to your **Desktop**. Make sure the **Layers** palette and **Animation** palette are visible. If they're not, choose **Window > Layers** and **Window > Animation**.

2. Take a look at the contents of the **Layers** palette. All of the layers in the **Layers** palette have transparent backgrounds. You can tell layers are transparent by the checkerboard background.

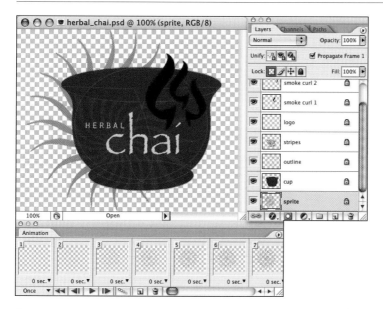

3. Take a look at the contents of the **Animation** palette. Click the **Play** button to play the animation. Like in the **Layers** palette, all of the frames in the **Animation** palette are transparent. Like with layers, you can tell frames are transparent by the checkerboard background.

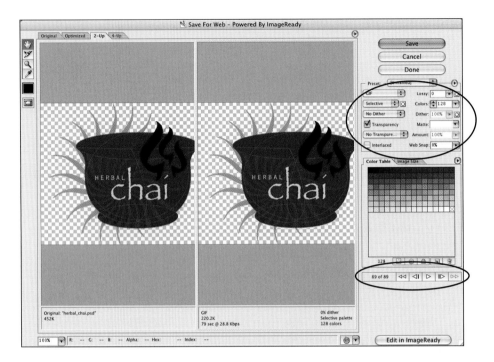

4. Choose **File > Save For Web**. In the **Save For Web** dialog box, turn on the **Transparency** option. Using the techniques you learned in Chapter 7, "*Optimizing Images*," experiment with the other settings until you come up with the best quality image with the smallest file size.

*Make sure you use the **Previous** and **Next Frame** buttons to take a look at the optimization settings on some of the other frames in the animation. As you know from the last exercise, you can only specify one optimization setting for all the frames in an animated GIF.*

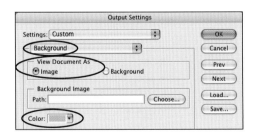

5. Choose **Edit Output Settings** from the **Optimize** menu. In the **Output Settings** dialog box, choose **Background** from the pop-up menu. Select **View Document As: Image** to specify the transparent image as the foreground image. Choose **Other** from the **Color** pop-up menu to open the **Color Picker** dialog box. In the **Color Picker** dialog box, specify the following **RGB** values: **R=195**, **G=195**, and **B=145**. Click **OK** to close the **Color Picker** dialog box. Click **OK** to close the **Output Settings** dialog box.

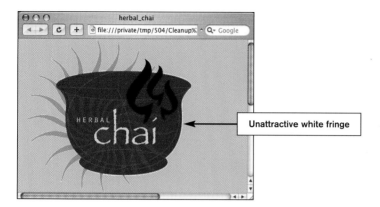

6. At the bottom of the **Save For Web** dialog box, click the **Preview in Default Browser** button.

Just like with any other transparent GIF, if you don't specify a matte color to match the color of your background image, you'll see an annoying white fringe around the outside of the animation when you view it in a Web browser.

7. Close the Web browser and return to the **Save For Web** dialog box. Choose **Other** from the **Matte** pop-up menu to open the **Color Picker** dialog box. In the **Color Picker** dialog box, specify the same **RGB** values you specified for the **Background Color** in Step 5 (**R=195**, **G=195**, and **B=145**).

8. At the bottom of the **Save For Web** dialog box, click the **Preview in Default Browser** button.

Now when you preview the animation, you no longer see the white halo around the transparent animation. For more information about creating transparent GIFs, refer to Chapter 10, "Creating Transparent Graphics." The techniques you learned in Chapter 10 also apply to transparent animated GIFs.

9. Close **herbal_chai.psd**. You don't need to save your changes.

8. [IR] _____Creating an Animated Slideshow

If you have a series of photographs you want to make into a slideshow, you can put the photographs into a folder and import the contents of the folder as separate frames. Once you import the images into ImageReady CS2, you can easily use the tweening feature to create a cross-fading animation.

1. In ImageReady CS2, choose **File > Import > Folder as Frames**. Navigate to the **chap_11** folder on your **Desktop**. Select the **slideshow** folder, and click **Choose**.

2. Make sure the **Layers** palette and **Animation** palette are visible. If they're not, choose **Window > Layers** and **Window > Animation**.

3. Take a look at the contents of the **Layers** palette and the **Animation** palette. The **Animation** palette contains five frames, and the **Layers** palette contains five layers. The contents of each are the five images from the **slideshow** folder.

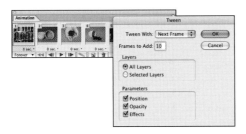

4. Click **Frame 1** in the **Animation** palette to select it. Click the **Tween** button. In the **Tween** dialog box, choose **Next Frame** from the **Tween With** pop-up menu. Type **10** in the **Frames to Add** field. Click **OK**.

5. Click **Frame 12** in the **Animation** palette to select it. Click the **Tween** button. In the **Tween** dialog box, choose **Next Frame** from the **Tween With** pop-up menu. Type **10** in the **Frames to Add** field. Click **OK**.

6. Click **Frame 23** in the **Animation** palette to select it. Click the **Tween** button. In the **Tween** dialog box, choose **Next Frame** from the **Tween With** pop-up menu. Type **10** in the **Frames to Add** field. Click **OK**.

7. Click **Frame 34** in the **Animation** palette to select it. Click the **Tween** button. In the **Tween** dialog box, choose **Next Frame** from the **Tween With** pop-up menu. Type **10** in the **Frames to Add** field. Click **OK**.

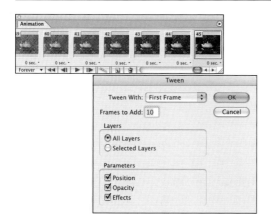

8. Click **Frame 45** in the **Animation** palette to select it. Click the **Tween** button. In the **Tween** dialog box, choose **First Frame** from the **Tween With** pop-up menu. Type **10** in the **Frames to Add** field. Click **OK**.

9. In the **Animation** palette, click the **Play** button. Click **Stop** when you've finished viewing the animation.

The animation is complete. As you can see, it's very easy to create a cross-fading animation in ImageReady CS2. Remember, when you optimize and save the animation, you must save the file as an animated GIF even though the content of the animation is photographic. Be sure to turn on lossy compression to cut down the file size.

10. Save and close the file.

You've finished another chapter! Next, you'll learn all about slicing!

I2

Slicing

| Creating User and Layer-Based Slices |
| Renaming, Optimizing, and Saving Slices |
| Applying Alt Text and Status Bar Messages |
| Assigning URLs to Slices | Using Slice Sets |

chap_12

PCS2Web HOT CD-ROM

Slicing allows you to cut a single image or layout into multiple sections so they can be reassembled in an HTML table. Wondering why you would ever do that? There are two reasons: first, you can optimize different parts of an image with different compression settings and file formats in order to reduce the file size; second, you can use slices to create rollovers or animated sections of a static image. In this chapter, you'll learn the slicing basics. In Chapter 13, "*Creating Rollovers*," you'll apply your knowledge of slicing to create rollovers.

At first glance, slicing looks very simple, but it can be deceptively complex. Although cutting images into slices is easy, managing the resulting images takes practice and an understanding of HTML. In this chapter, you'll learn about different types of slicing, how to create and edit slices, how to optimize and save slices (including the required HTML code), and how to work with slice sets.

About Slices

With slices, you can divide a single large image or layout into a number of smaller sections. The smaller images are then reassembled using an HTML table to look like the original image. When you slice an image, you can apply different optimization settings to each slice, which decreases download time and maintains the highest quality. Here is an example:

The **perfect_harmony.psd** image can be sliced effectively into six sections: the top red section, the three photos on the left, the herbal chai graphic on the right, and the bottom red section. Because the top and bottom slices are made up of single colors, you can optimize these slices as GIFs and set the Color Table to 2 colors, which will make downloading faster. You can optimize the herbal chai section as a GIF but increase the Color Table to 128 colors. You can optimize the photographs as JPEGs and give a different quality setting to each of the three photographs (even though the other three slices are GIFs) because they will optimize better as JPEGs than as GIFs. The result will be higher-quality optimization and faster download time.

When you slice and save images in Photoshop CS2 or ImageReady CS2, the program creates one image for each slice along with the required HTML table code to reassemble the images in their exact formation. The HTML table code allows Web browsers to assemble the images seamlessly and consistently so they look like a single image.

In the following exercises, you'll learn how to use the slicing tools and options in ImageReady CS2. You can slice images in Photoshop CS2, but I find it easier to slice images in ImageReady CS2 because it has a number of additional slicing features. Plus, it's easier to access the slicing options in the Toolbox, Web Content palette, Slice palette, and Optimize palette in ImageReady CS2 rather than the Save For Web dialog box in Photoshop CS2. For these reasons, you'll use ImageReady CS2 exclusively for the exercises in this chapter.

About Slice Types

Before you begin creating slices, you need to understand the four different types of slices, which are represented by four different icons that appear when you slice a document. Here is a chart to explain them:

Slice Types	
User slice	You can create user slices with the Slice tool or from guides or selections. User slices are the most flexible because they offer the following editing capabilities: move, duplicate, combine, divide, resize, delete, arrange, align, and distribute. You can also apply different optimization settings to user slices in the same image.
Layer-based slice	You can create layer-based slices from the contents of a specific layer. If you move or edit the contents of a layer, the layer-based slice will update automatically to reflect the changes. Layer-based slices offer limited editing capabilities. To achieve the flexibility of user slices, you can promote layer-based slices to user slices.
Auto slice	The program creates auto slices automatically when you create or edit user slices or layer-based slices. If you define a single slice in an image, a series of auto slices will automatically be generated to fill up the remainder of the image. If you add to or edit the user or layer-based slices, the auto slices will automatically update. Auto slices offer no editing capabilities. To achieve the flexibility of user slices, you can promote auto slices to user slices.
Sub slice	Sub slices are a form of auto slices that appear automatically when you create three or more overlapping slices. Sub slices are regenerated automatically each time you create, edit, or modify slices in an image. Sub slices offer no editing capabilities. To achieve the flexibility of user slices, you can promote sub slices to user slices.

About Slice Lines, Slice Numbers, Slice Symbols, and Slice Colors

In addition to understanding the slice types in Photoshop CS2 and ImageReady CS2, it's helpful to understand the visual components that identify slices. Each slice you create will have four key visual components: a series of slice lines, a slice number, a slice symbol, and a slice color. Here is a chart to help you understand:

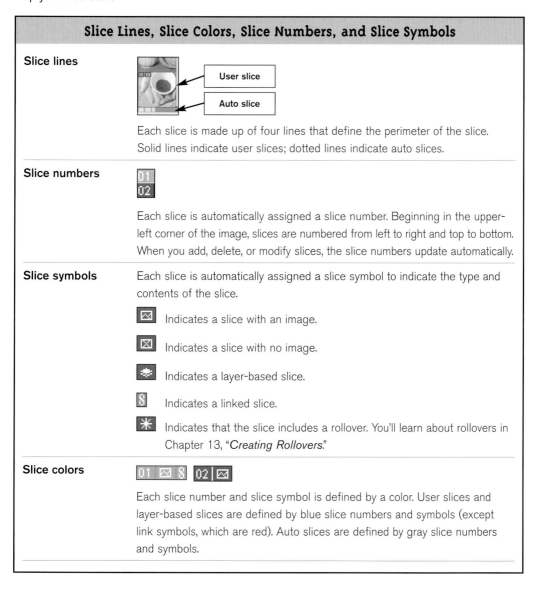

Slice Lines, Slice Colors, Slice Numbers, and Slice Symbols	
Slice lines	Each slice is made up of four lines that define the perimeter of the slice. Solid lines indicate user slices; dotted lines indicate auto slices.
Slice numbers	Each slice is automatically assigned a slice number. Beginning in the upper-left corner of the image, slices are numbered from left to right and top to bottom. When you add, delete, or modify slices, the slice numbers update automatically.
Slice symbols	Each slice is automatically assigned a slice symbol to indicate the type and contents of the slice. Indicates a slice with an image. Indicates a slice with no image. Indicates a layer-based slice. Indicates a linked slice. Indicates that the slice includes a rollover. You'll learn about rollovers in Chapter 13, "*Creating Rollovers.*"
Slice colors	Each slice number and slice symbol is defined by a color. User slices and layer-based slices are defined by blue slice numbers and symbols (except link symbols, which are red). Auto slices are defined by gray slice numbers and symbols.

About the Web Content and Slice Palettes

When you're working with slices in ImageReady CS2, you'll need to access the Web Content and Slice palettes. Here is an overview of the palettes and their roles in the slicing process.

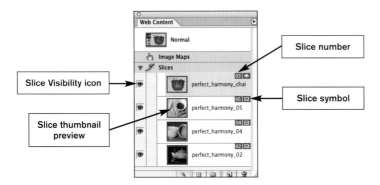

The Web Content palette lets you preview user slices in an image. Similar to the Layers palette, the Web Content palette displays a thumbnail preview of the slice and the slice name, and you can also use it to turn on and off the visibility of a slice. The Web Content palette also displays the slice number, slice symbol, and information about rollovers and image maps (which you'll learn about in later chapters).

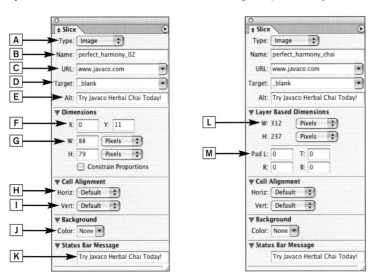

The Slice palette lets you specify slice options, which control how slices and slice data appear in a Web browser. The Slice palette is context-sensitive, and it changes depending on the currently selected slice. The Slice palette is divided into sections: Slice, Dimensions (for user slices), Layer Based Dimensions (for layer-based slices), Cell Alignment, Background, and Status Bar Message. Here's a handy chart to help you understand the controls in the Slice palette:

Slice Palette Controls

A	Type pop-up menu	Choose one of the following slice content types for the currently selected slice: Image, No Image, or Table.
B	Name field	Specify a name for the currently selected slice.
C	URL pop-up menu	Specify a URL you want the currently selected slice to link to.
D	Target pop-up menu	Choose one of the following target types when you specify a URL for the slice: _blank, _self, _parent, or _top.
E	Alt field	Specify the text you want viewers to see when images are turned off in a Web browser.
F	X and Y Coordinates	Specify the left edge (X) and top edge (Y) of a slice.
G	Width and Height fields	Specify the width and height of a slice, in either pixels or percent.
H	Horizontal Cell Alignment pop-up menu	Choose one of the following options: Left, Right, Center, or Default.
I	Vertical Cell Alignment pop-up menu	Choose one of the following options: Top, Baseline, Middle, Bottom, or Default.
J	Background Color pop-up menu	Choose a background color for transparent sections of the slice.
K	Status Bar Message field	Specify the message you want to appear in the status bar of the Web browser when you position your mouse over a slice.
L	Layer Width and Height pop-up menus (available for layer-based slices only)	View or edit size information for the currently selected layer-based slice.
M	Slice Outset fields (available for layer-based slices only)	Specify the slice size for layer-based slices. For example, if your layer-based slice is 100×100 pixels, and you want the slice to be 10 pixels larger than the layer, you can specify 5 pixels in the Left, Right, Top, and Bottom fields, and the slice will increase to 110×110 pixels.

I. [IR] _____Creating User Slices

In this exercise, you'll learn how to use the Slice tool to create user slices, how to identify auto slices, and how to promote auto slices to user slices. You'll also learn how to resize, delete, and hide slice visibility.

1. Open **javaco_stores.psd** from the **chap_12** folder you copied to your **Desktop**. Make sure the **Web Content** palette is visible. If it's not, choose **Window > Web Content**.

The **Web Content** palette displays information about slice, image map, and rollover informa-tion. The **Web Content** palette is one of the reasons I prefer to use ImageReady CS2, rather than Photoshop CS2, to slice images—it provides quick and easy access to slice information. Plus, I can optimize slices in the document window without having to go to the **Save For Web** dialog box.

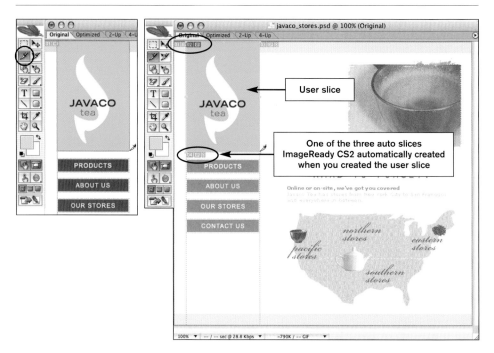

2. Select the **Slice** tool from the **Toolbox**. Click and drag around the **green rectangle** con-taining the Javaco logo (beginning in the upper-left corner and extending to the lower-right corner), as shown in the illustration here.

Take a look at the document window. Notice that the user slice you created has a blue icon. Notice three other slices with gray icons were created automatically. The slice you created is called a user slice because you (the user) defined it. The other slices are called auto slices. ImageReady CS2 automatically creates auto slices for the undefined areas so the entire image is divided into slices. In the document window, notice each slice has a number. Are you wondering why the first slice you created is labeled **Slice 02**? ImageReady CS2 keeps track of all slices, including user, layer-based, auto, and sub slices by assigning a number to each slice. Slices are numbered from left to right and top to bottom starting in the upper-left corner.

Take a look at the **Web Content** palette. Notice only one slice appears in the **Web Content** palette, even though four slices are visible in the document window? The **Web Content** palette shows only user slices and layer-based slices. In this example, only one slice appears in the **Web Content** palette— the user slice you just created with the **Slice** tool. The **Web Content** palette is where you set rollovers and animation options to user slices and layer-based slices, which you'll learn about in future chapters.

TIP | Slice Preferences

ImageReady CS2 lets you snap slices to the edges of other slices. You'll find this helps align slices and avoid overlap. Snapping is turned on by default. If it's not turned on, choose **View > Snap To > Slices**.

3. With the **Slice** tool selected in the **Toolbox**, click and drag to create a slice around the **ABOUT US** button, as shown in the illustration here.

You should now have two user slices and four auto slices. Next, you'll learn to promote the auto slices to user slices. Because user slices offer more flexibility, you'll often want all slices in an image to be user slices. Converting auto slices to user slices is a quick and easy way to create user slices because you don't have to manually select areas of the image with the **Slice** tool.

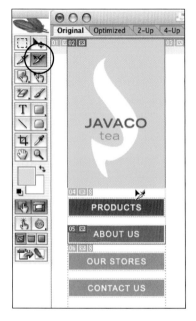

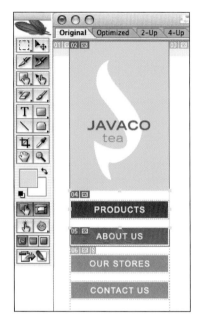

4. Select the **Slice Select** tool from the **Toolbox**. Click anywhere inside the **Slice 04** auto slice to select it. Choose **Slices > Promote to User Slice**.

*Notice the gray slice number and slice symbols are now blue, indicating **Slice 04** is now a user slice. The **Slice 04** auto slice you converted to a user slice doesn't need to be as big as it is—ideally, it should hug the edges of the button, just like the slice you created for the **about us** button. Not to worry, you can easily resize slices. You'll learn how in the next step.*

5. With **Slice 04** selected, position your cursor over the upper-middle node until you see the **resize** cursor, as shown in the illustration here. Click and drag to resize the slice so it is flush against the top edge of the **products** button.

*Notice when you resized the slice, another auto slice, **Slice 05**, was automatically created. **Slice 04** remains an auto slice and fills the space between the **Slice 02** and **Slice 05** user slices.*

6. Position your cursor over the lower-middle node until you see the **resize** cursor appear. Click and drag to resize the slice so it is flush against the bottom edge of the **products** button.

7. Using the techniques you learned in this exercise, create user slices for the remaining two buttons— **our stores** and **contact us**.

*There should now be five user slices in the **javaco_stores.psd** image. Take a look at the **Web Content** palette to see how the slice names, symbols, and thumbnails are displayed. The slice names are created automatically based on the original filename (**javaco_stores.psd**) and the slice number. You can change the name of slices, which you'll learn to do in an upcoming exercise.*

You might be wondering if you can turn off the slices so you can see the image without the interference of slice borders and icons. You'll learn how in the next step.

8. In the **Toolbox**, click the **Toggle Slices Visibility** button, or press the shortcut key (**Q**).

Now you can see the image without the slice lines, numbers, and symbols.

9. In the **Toolbox**, click the **Toggle Slices Visibility** button to turn on the visibility of the slices. Leave **javaco_stores.psd** open for the next exercise.

TIP | Deleting Slices

When you create a user slice or a layer-based slice, you can delete it easily. Here's how:

In the **Toolbox**, select the **Slice Select** tool. Click to select the slice you want to delete. Press the **Delete** (Mac) or **Backspace** (Windows) key, or choose **Slices > Delete Slices**. The slice will disappear. Sometimes, an auto slice will take its place, depending on how the image is sliced.

2. [IR] _____Creating Layer-Based Slices

In this exercise, you'll learn how to create layer-based slices. Layer-based slices are a great way to slice images containing several layers because they create slices the same size as the layer. As a result, you don't have to resize slices to ensure they exactly match the dimensions of the layer. In addition, if you change the contents of a layer or move a layer, the slice updates automatically. This great feature of layer-based slices will save you time from reslicing images if you need to make changes to your Web graphics. You can also move layer-based slices, which you can't do with user slices. Plus, if you decide you want to promote a layer-based slice to a user slice, you can do so easily.

1. If you followed the last exercise, **javaco_stores.psd** should still be open in ImageReady CS2. If it's not, go back and complete Exercise 1. Make sure the **Layers** palette, the **Web Content** palette, and the **Slice** palette are visible. If they're not choose **Window > Layers**, **Window > Web Content**, and **Window > Slice**.

_Notice **javaco_stores.psd** is made up of a number of layers. In the next few steps, you'll create layer-based slices from the layers in this image._

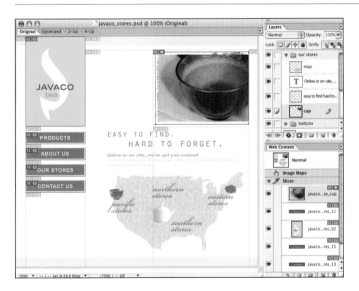

2. In the **Layers** palette, click the arrow next to the **our stores** layer group to expand the contents of the layer group. Click the **cup** layer to select it. Choose **Layer > New Layer Based Slice**.

Notice a layer-based slice, **Slice 05**, was created automatically as well as additional auto slices. Also, the slices you created in the last exercise automatically updated with new slice numbers. The slice symbol indicates **Slice 05** is a layer-based slice.

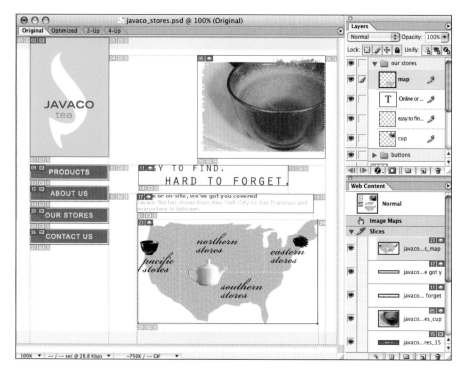

3. Using the technique you learned in the last step, create layer-based slices for each of the following layers in the **our stores** layer group: the **easy to find...** layer, the **type** layer, and the **map** layer.

There are now a total of 28 slices in the image—4 layer-based slices, 5 user slices, and 19 auto slices, which were automatically created to slice the rest of the image. Don't worry if the slice numbers don't match up exactly as shown here. Follow the exercise keeping the slice numbers you have in your image.

Wondering why you'd use layer-based slices instead of user slices? The benefit of using layer-based slices is that if you move or resize layers, the slices update automatically—you don't have to reslice your image!

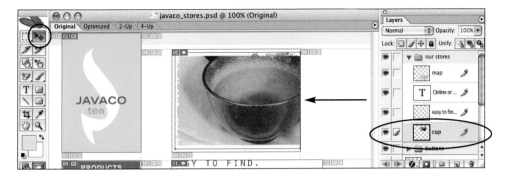

4. In the **Layers** palette, click the **cup** layer. Select the **Move** tool from the **Toolbox**. Click and drag to reposition the **cup** layer, as shown in the illustration here.

*Notice when you release your mouse, the slices update automatically. The **cup** layer remains a layer-based slice, but new auto slices are automatically created to fill the contents of the image.*

5. Press **Cmd+Z** (Mac) or **Ctrl+Z** (Windows) to undo the move you made in the last step.

Bounding box

6. Select the **Horizontal Type** tool from the **Toolbox**. In the **Layers** palette, click the **type** layer to select it. Click inside the **type** layer so you see the bounding box around the perimeter of the layer.

As you know from Chapter 6, "Creating Type," the editing box indicates the vector-based type is paragraph type.

7. Position your cursor over the middle node on the right side of the bounding box. Click and drag to resize the bounding box, as shown in the illustration here.

Notice that when you resize the bounding box, the layer-based slice updates automatically. In addition, the auto slices surrounding the layer-based slice update automatically. Layer-based slices offer a great deal of flexibility because they update each time you edit or change a layer. During the design process, you'll often have to make changes to your images. By using layer-based slices, you won't have to reslice images each time you make changes to them.

*Sometimes, you'll want to increase the size of a layer-based slice without affecting the size of the layer. In this example, **Slice 11** isn't aligned with the left edges of **Slice 17** and **Slice 23**, which creates a need for an extra slice–**Slice 10**. Also **Slice 12**, **Slice 18**, and **Slice 24** could be eliminated if **Slice 11**, **Slice 17**, and **Slice 23** extended to meet **Slice 06**. You can easily resize layer-based slices without affecting the size of the layer. You'll learn how in the next step.*

8. Select the **Slice Select** tool from the **Toolbox**. Click **Slice 11** to select it. In the **Slice** palette, click the arrow next to **Layer Based Dimensions** to expand that section of the **Slice** palette. Type **3** in the **Pad L** field, and press **Return** (Mac) or **Enter** (Windows).

*Notice **Slice 10** and **Slice 16** automatically combine to create a single auto slice. Although you changed the size of the layer-based slice, you didn't change the size of the actual layer. You can see the size of the layer if you have **Layer Edges** turned on. To turn on the **Layer Edges** option, choose **View > Show Layer Edges**.*

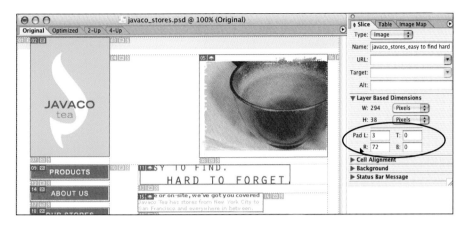

9. With **Slice 11** still selected, in the **Layer Based Dimensions** section of the **Slice** palette type **72** in the **Pad R** field, and press **Return** (Mac) or **Enter** (Windows).

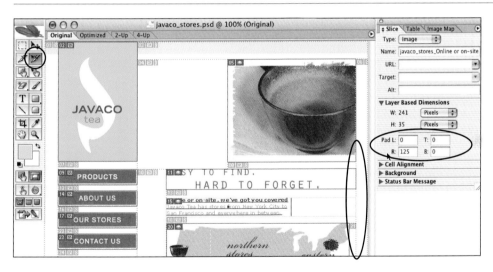

10. With the **Slice Select** tool still selected in the **Toolbox**, click **Slice 15** to select it. In the **Layer Based Dimensions** section of the **Slice** palette, type **125** in the **Pad R** field, and press **Return** (Mac) or **Enter** (Windows).

*Note: Depending on how much you resized the type layer in Step 7, 125 may be a few pixels too many or too few. Experiment until the edge of the slice is flush with the edge of **Slice 06**, as shown in the illustration here.*

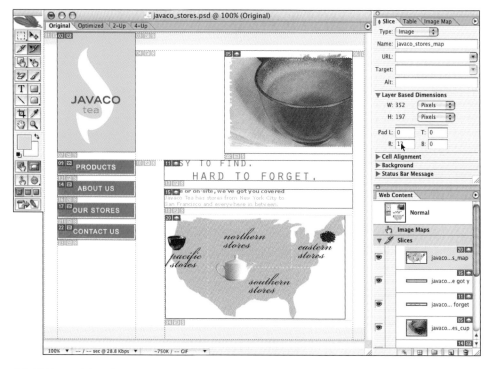

11. With the **Slice Select** tool still selected in the **Toolbox**, click **Slice 20** to select it. In the **Layer Based Dimensions** section of the **Slice** palette, type **13** in the **Pad R** field, and press **Return** (Mac) or **Enter** (Windows).

*By increasing the size of the slices, you eliminated some of the slices in the **javaco_stores.psd** image. Although you increased the size of the slices, the size of the layer remains the same, as you can see by the layer edges.*

12. Leave **javaco_stores.psd** open for the next exercise.

NOTE | Promoting Layer-Based Slices to User Slices

Layer-based slices don't have the flexibility of user slices. As a result, you may want to promote layer-based slices to user slices. Here's how:

Select the layer-based slice you want to promote to a user slice with the **Slice Select** tool or by selecting it in the **Web Content** palette. Choose **Slices > Promote to User Slice**. When you promote a layer-based slice to a user slice, the slice symbol updates automatically.

3. [IR] _____Renaming Slices

When you're slicing images, make sure you name slices correctly; the slice names will become the file-names when you save the slices. In this exercise, you'll learn two techniques for renaming slices. Later in this chapter, you'll see how slice names are used when you save sliced images.

1. If you followed the last exercise, **javaco_stores.psd** should still be open in ImageReady CS2. If it's not, go back and complete Exercise 2. Make sure the **Layers** palette, **Web Content** palette, and **Slice** palette are visible. If they're not, choose **Window > Layers**, **Window > Web Content**, and **Window > Slice**.

*In the **Web Content** palette, you'll notice that the slices are named using the filename and either the slice number or the layer name, depending on whether the slice is a user slice or a layer-based slice. Don't worry if the slice numbers don't match up exactly as shown here. Follow the exercise keeping the slice numbers you have in your image.*

The default slice naming convention for user slices is as follows: filename + underscore + slice number. The default slice naming convention for layer-based slices is as follows: file-name + underscore + layer name. Sometimes, you'll want to name your slices differently from the original filename.

***Note:** This example features user slices based on a flat image. If are working with layer-based slices from a layered image, the naming convention differs slightly: filename + underscore + layer name.*

*Next, you'll learn to rename slices using the **Web Content** palette.*

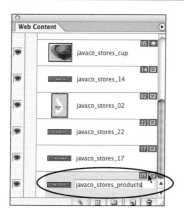

2. Scroll to the bottom of the **Web Content** palette so you can see the user slices. Double-click the **javaco_stores_09** slice name. When the bounding box appears, rename the slice as follows: **javaco_stores_products**. When you've finished, press **Return** (Mac) or **Enter** (Windows).

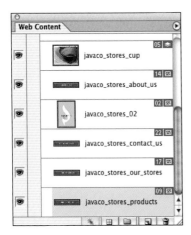

3. Using the technique you just learned, rename the other three slices for the buttons as follows: **javaco_stores_about_us**, **javaco_stores_our_stores**, and **javaco_stores_contact_us**.

Because these slice names will become filenames when you save the slices, do not use spaces in the slice name, because Web servers often have trouble reading filenames with spaces. Using an underscore (_) is a good substitute for a space.

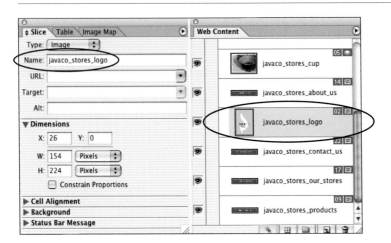

4. In the **Web Content** palette, click the **javaco_stores_02** slice to select it. Type **javaco_stores_logo** in the **Name** field of the **Slice** palette, and press **Return** (Mac) or **Enter** (Windows).

*So far, you've renamed user slices. What if you want to rename a layer-based slice? As you've seen, the layer name becomes part of the slice name; the slice name becomes part of the filename. Therefore, when you're naming layers in the **Layers** palette, you need to remember how the layer name will be used. By naming your layers properly in the **Layers** palette, you won't have to rename slices later on.*

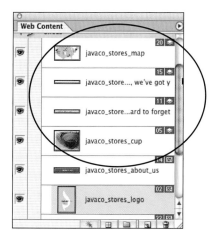

5. Scroll up in the **Web Content** palette so you can see the names of the layer-based slices.

*As you can see, two of the layer-based slice names require no changes (**javaco_stores_map** and **javaco_stores_cup**). However, the other two slice names contain spaces and apostrophes, which will be problematic when you save the files and view them in a Web browser.*

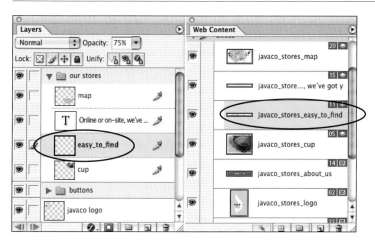

6. In the **Layers** palette, click the **easy to find...** layer to select it. Double-click the layer name. When the bounding box appears, type **easy_to_find**, and press **Return** (Mac) or **Enter** (Windows).

*Notice the slice name updated automatically in the **Web Content** palette when you changed the layer name.*

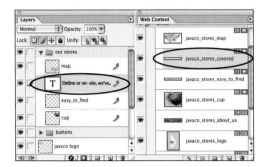

7. In the **Web Content** palette, double-click the **javaco_stores_we've got you...** slice. When the bounding box appears, rename the layer **javco_stores_covered**, and press **Return** (Mac) or **Enter** (Windows).

*Notice just the slice name changed—the layer name remained the same in the **Layers** palette. As you can see, you can choose to rename the layer and the corresponding layer-based slice at the same time, or you can just rename the layer-based slice.*

Tip: *You can also rename layer-based slices in the **Slice** palette using the technique you learned in Step 4.*

8. Leave **javaco_stores.psd** open for the next exercise.

TIP | Modifying the Default Slice Naming Settings

The default slice naming in ImageReady CS2 is as follows:

• **User slices:** filename + underscore + slice number

• **Layer-based slices:** filename + underscore + layer name

If you want to change the default slice naming settings, choose **File > Output Settings > Slices**. In the **Output Settings** dialog box, use the **Default Slice Naming** pop-up menus to choose your own slice naming convention.

4. [IR] _____Optimizing and Saving Slices

One of the benefits of slicing images is the ability to apply different optimization settings to each slice. In the last few exercises, you've learned different slicing techniques. In this exercise, you'll learn to apply different optimization settings to different slices to achieve the best overall file size and quality. Plus, you'll learn how to save the images and the required HTML table code so your sliced images appear correctly in a Web browser. If it sounds complicated, don't worry–ImageReady CS2 makes optimizing and saving sliced images, including the required HTML table code, a snap!

1. If you followed the last exercise, **javaco_stores.psd** should still be open in ImageReady CS2. If it's not, go back and complete Exercise 3. Make sure the **Optimize** palette is visible. If it's not, choose **Window > Optimize**.

Before you begin the optimization process, take a look at the different slices. Which ones are best optimized as JPEGs? Which ones are best optimized as GIFs? Which ones will require experimentation to determine the best format?

2. Inside the document window, click the **Optimized** tab. Select the **Slice Select** tool from the **Toolbox**. Click **Slice 05** to select it.

Slice 05 is the only slice that is best optimized as a JPEG. You'll start with it so you can optimize all the GIFs sequentially.

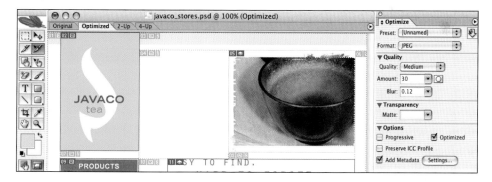

3. Using the techniques you learned in Chapter 7, "*Optimizing Images*," and Chapter 10 "*Creating Transparent Graphics*," specify optimization settings for **Slice 05**. In the **Toolbox**, make sure you toggle on and off the visibility of the slices using the **Toggle Slices Visibility** button so you can preview the optimization settings without the slices. (You can't get an accurate view of the optimized slices unless you turn off the slice visibility.)

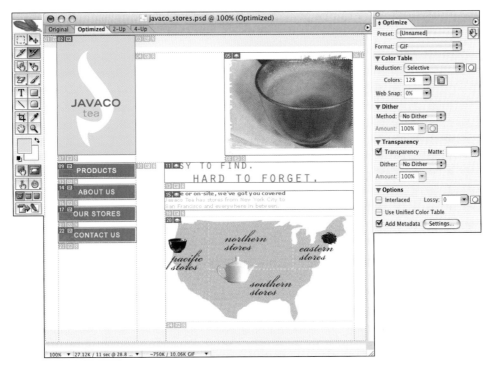

4. With the **Slice Select** tool still selected in the **Toolbox**, click **Slice 20** to select it. Match the settings in the **Optimize** palette to the ones shown in the illustration here.

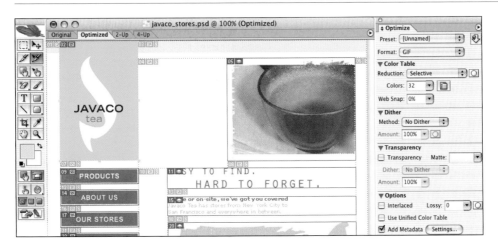

5. With the **Slice Select** tool still selected in the **Toolbox**, click **Slice 02** to select it. Match the settings in the **Optimize** palette to the ones shown in the illustration here.

6. With the **Slice Select** tool still selected in the **Toolbox**, click **Slice 09** to select it. Hold down the **Shift** key, and click **Slice 14**, **Slice 17**, and **Slice 22** to multiple-select all four slices. Choose **Slices > Link Slices for Optimization**.

*Notice the red link icon in the corner—it indicates the slices are linked for optimization. Because these four buttons look almost identical, they will all use the same optimization settings. Although you could specify the same settings for each slice, there's no need to make extra work for yourself. You can easily specify the same optimization settings for all four slices at the same time by using the **Link Slices for Optimization** option.*

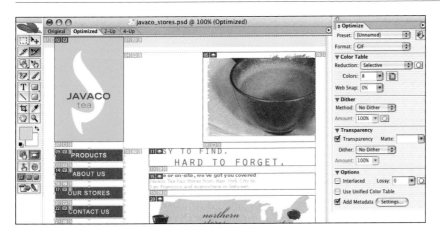

7. With **Slice 09**, **Slice 14**, **Slice 17**, and **Slice 22** selected and linked, match the optimization settings to the ones shown in the illustration here.

*Looking at the other two slices that need to be optimized—**Slice 11** and **Slice 15**—it's possible they may share the same optimization settings as the ones you specified in the last step.*

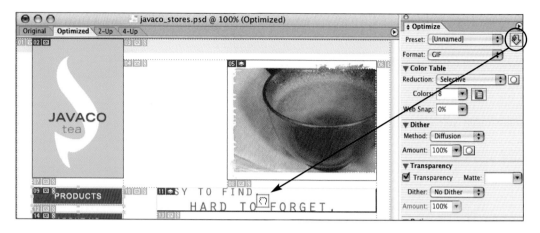

8. With **Slice 09**, **Slice 14**, **Slice 17**, and **Slice 22** still selected, drag the **Droplet** icon from the **Optimize** palette onto **Slice 11**.

9. With the **Slice Select** tool still selected in the **Toolbox**, click **Slice 11** to select it.

*Notice that the optimization settings you specified for **Slice 09**, **Slice 14**, **Slice 17**, and **Slice 22** were automatically applied to **Slice 11**. As you can see, the optimization settings you used for the buttons work perfectly for this slice, and you didn't have to specify the settings again in the **Optimize** palette.*

10. With **Slice 11** still selected, drag the **Droplet** icon from the **Optimize** palette onto **Slice 15**.

*As you can see, the **Droplet** feature lets you share optimization settings across multiple slices so you don't have to enter the same slice settings for multiple slices.*

At this point, all the user slices and layer-based slices should now be optimized. The only slices you have not optimized are the auto slices. Notice all the auto slices have a link icon. You can only specify one optimization setting for all the auto slices in an image. If you want to use different optimization settings for different auto slices, you must convert them to user slices, which you learned how to do in Exercise 1.

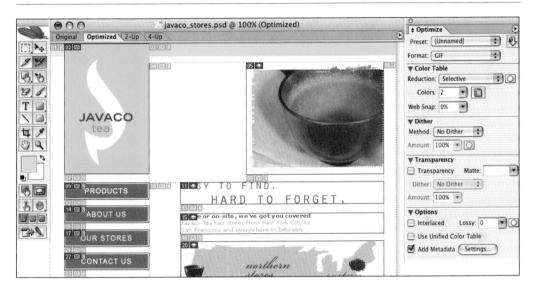

11. With the **Slice Select** tool still selected in the **Toolbox**, click **Slice 03** to select it. Match the settings in the **Optimize** palette to the ones shown in the illustration here.

12. Now that you've optimized all the slices, turn off the visibility of all the slices by clicking, in the **Toolbox**, the **Toggle Slices Visibility** button. Now you can view the image without the slices and make sure you're happy with all the optimization settings.

13. In the **Toolbox**, click the **Preview in Default Browser** button to preview the **javaco_stores.psd** image in a Web browser.

14. Close the Web browser, and return to ImageReady CS2. Choose **File > Save Optimized As**.

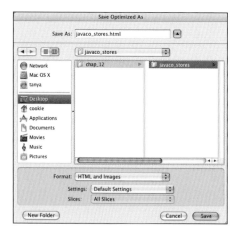

15. In the **Save Optimized As** dialog box, navigate to the **chap_12** folder you copied to your **Desktop**. Create a new folder called **javaco_stores**. Choose **HTML and Images** from the **Format** pop-up menu. Choose **All Slices** from the **Slices** pop-up menu. Click **Save**.

*Note: You don't have to save the HTML code with the images. If you prefer, you can choose **Images** from the **Format** pop-up menu, and create the HTML table code in an HTML editor, such as Adobe GoLive or Macromedia Dreamweaver. The choice is yours, but letting ImageReady CS2 create the code is easiest!*

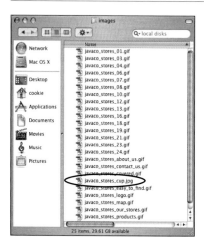

16. Browse to the **javaco_stores** folder in the **chap_12** folder on your **Desktop**.

*You'll see **javaco_stores.html** and a folder called **images**, which contains the sliced, optimized, and saved images! Pretty cool! Notice most of the images are GIFs, but one of the images is a JPEG. ImageReady CS2 remembered the settings you specified for each slice in the **Optimize** palette when it saved the slices.*

17. Double-click **javaco_stores.html** to open the sliced images in a Web browser.

The sliced images appear in the exact location as the original, unsliced image.

18. Close the Web browser and return to ImageReady CS2. Leave **javaco_stores.psd** open for the next exercise.

5. [IR]_____Applying Alt Text and Status Bar Messages

To make Web pages more accessible for all viewers, you should apply alt text to critical images on your Web sites, including sliced images. Alt text lets viewers see a text description of the images on a Web page. You can also apply status bar messages to slices. When a viewer positions his or her mouse over a slice on a Web page, the Web browser status bar changes to display the message you created. This is another helpful way to provide information about the contents of a slice.

1. If you followed the last exercise, **javaco_stores.psd** should still be open in ImageReady CS2. If it's not, go back and complete Exercise 4. Make sure the **Slice** palette is visible. If it's not, choose **Window > Slice**.

2. Select the **Slice Select** tool from the **Toolbox**. Click **Slice 20** to select it.

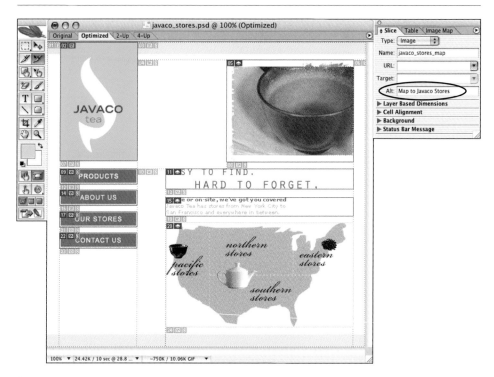

3. In the **Slice** palette, type **Map to Javaco Stores** in the **Alt** field. Press **Return** (Mac) or **Enter** (Windows) to apply the alt text to the slice.

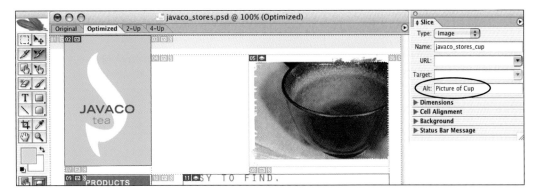

4. With the **Slice Select** tool still selected in the **Toolbox**, click **Slice 05** to select it. Type **Picture of Cup** in the **Alt** field of the **Slice** palette.

Alt text shows in a Web browser if the user turns off images in the Preferences or if he or she is accessing Web pages with a text-only Web browser. Some viewers turn off images when they surf the Web to speed up the downloading process. Sight-impaired visitors use screen-reading software to "read" the alt text to them out loud. Next, you'll learn to apply status bar messages to slices.

5. With the **Slice Select** tool still selected in the **Toolbox**, click **Slice 20** to select it. Click the arrow to expand the **Status Bar Message** section of the **Slice** palette.

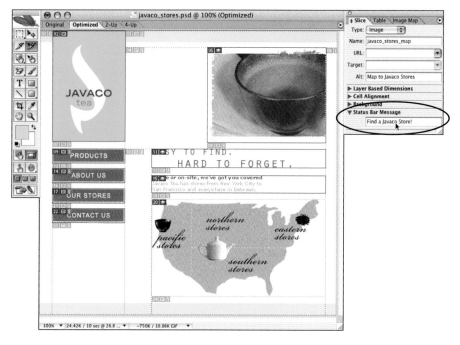

6. In the **Status Bar Message** field, type **Find a Javaco Store!** and press **Return** (Mac) or **Enter** (Windows).

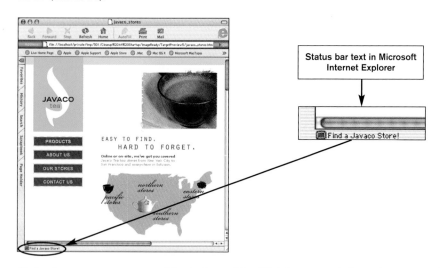

Status bar text in Microsoft Internet Explorer

Status bar messages appear at the bottom of the Web browser window when you position your mouse over the slice. Status bar messages are a great way to provide additional information to your viewers.

7. Leave **javaco_stores.psd** open for the next exercise.

6. [IR] _____Assigning URLs to Slices

When you assign a URL to a slice, the slice automatically becomes a hot spot users can click on. When users click on a hot spot, it links them to a specific URL. ImageReady CS2 makes it easy to assign URLs to slices. Here's a short exercise to show you how:

1. If you followed the last exercise, **javaco_stores.psd** should still be open in ImageReady CS2. If it's not, go back and complete Exercise 5. Make sure the **Slice** palette is visible. If it's not, choose **Window > Slice**.

2. Select the **Slice** tool from the **Toolbox**. Click **Slice 09** to select it.

3. In the **Slice** palette, type **http://www.lynda.com** in the **URL** field. Press **Return** (Mac) or **Enter** (Windows) to assign the URL.

*Notice the **URL** field is also a pop-up menu. The **URL** pop-up menu remembers the most recently used URLs and saves them in the pop-up menu for easy access.*

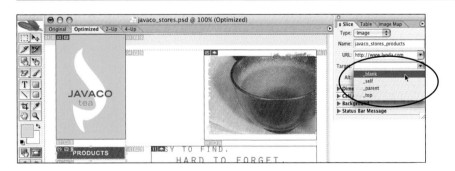

4. In the **Target** field, choose **_blank**, and press **Return** (Mac) or **Enter** (Windows).

***_blank** indicates you want the URL to open in a new Web browser window. If you want the URL to open in the same Web browser window, leave the **Target** field empty.*

5. In the **Toolbox**, click the **Preview in Default Browser** button. Click the **products** button.

*If you have a live Web connection, a new Web browser window will open automatically with the **lynda.com** Web site. This is a quick and easy way to assign URLs to slices without using an HTML editor.*

Note: *In order to test links, you must preview or open the file in a Web browser because there is no way to test a link in ImageReady CS2.*

*Because I linked to an external Web site, **lynda.com**, I included the **http://www** information. This type of link is called an **absolute link**. You can also link to Web pages inside the same Web site. This type of link is called a **relative link**. When you use relative links, you must know the file structure and how to link to the files. For more information about absolute and relative links, refer to the sidebar at the end of this exercise.*

6. Save and close **javaco_stores.psd**.

NOTE | Understanding Relative and Absolute Links

When you design Web sites, you'll use two kinds of links: relative and absolute. Here's a brief description of each to help you understand when and why to use them.

Relative links point to a page inside your Web site. For example, if you are designing a Web site, and you want to link from the Home page to the About Us page, you don't need to include the full **http://www** information. Instead, you include information about where you want to link to in relation to where you're linking from. For example—**about_us.html** (instead of **http://www.somedomain.com/about_us.html**). Because relative links can become complex to program when files are nested inside and outside of folders on the Web server, you might find it easier to create and manage them in an HTML editor, such as Adobe GoLive or Macromedia Dreamweaver.

Absolute links point to external Web sites. Absolute links always link to the same, defined location. For that reason, you must include the **http://www** information when you use absolute links.

Many HTML editors, including Adobe GoLive and Macromedia Dreamweaver, have site-management features, which help you manage absolute and relative links.

7. [IR] _____ Using Slice Sets

A slice set is a group of slices stored inside a folder in the Web Content palette. Slice sets keep your slices organized if you have lots of slices in an image. The benefit of using slice sets is you can create different slice configurations for different designs in the same file. In this exercise, you'll practice creating slice sets and adding slices to slice sets.

1. Open **javaco.psd** from the **chap_12** folder you copied to your **Desktop**. Make sure the **Layers** palette and the **Web Content** palette are visible. If they're not, choose **Window > Layers** and **Window > Web Content**.

*Take a look at the contents of the **Layers** palette. Turn on and off the visibility of the different layer sets so you can see how the file is constructed. As you can see, the buttons are contained in a layer set, and the contents for each of the pages of the Javaco Web site are also contained inside individual layer sets.*

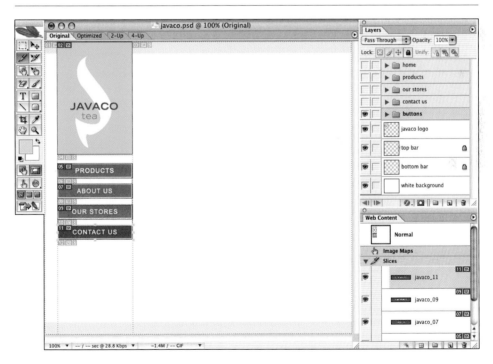

2. Select the **Slice** tool from the **Toolbox**. Using any of the techniques you learned in this chapter, create user slices for each of the following elements: **javaco tea** logo, **products** button, **about us** button, **our stores** button, and **contact us** button. When you've finished, make sure the slices in your image match the ones shown in the illustration here.

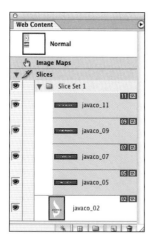

3. In the **Web Content** palette, click the **javaco_11** slice to select it. Hold down the **Shift** key and click the **javaco_05** slice to multiple-select the slices in-between. At the bottom of the **Web Content** palette, click the **New Slice Set** button.

The four slices you multiple-selected, which are the slices for the buttons in the Javaco tea Web page, are now contained inside a slice set, which is named ***Slice Set 1****.*

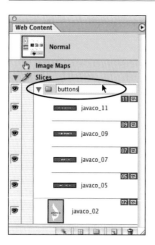

4. In the **Web Content** palette, double-click the **Slice Set 1** slice set name. When the bounding box appears, rename the slice set **buttons**, and press **Return** (Mac) or **Enter** (Windows). Click the arrow next to the **buttons** slice set to close the slice set.

Does this process seem familiar? Slice sets work almost the same as layer groups (Photoshop CS2) and layer sets (ImageReady CS2). As you can see, the skills you mastered in Chapter 5, "Working with Layers," are coming in handy!

5. In the **Layers** palette, turn on the visibility of the **home** layer set. With the **Slice** tool still selected in the **Toolbox**, use the techniques you learned earlier in this chapter to slice the elements of the Javaco home page, as shown in the illustration here.

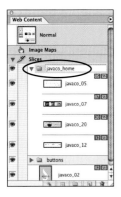

6. In the **Web Content** palette, click the **javaco_05** slice to select it. Hold down the **Shift** key, and click the **javaco_12** slice (or the last slice in the stacking order before the **buttons** slice set) to multiple-select the slices in-between. At the bottom of the **Web Content** palette, click the **New Slice Set** button to create a new slice set. Using the technique you learned in Step 4, rename the slice set **javaco_home**. When you've finished, click the arrow next to the **javaco_home** slice set to close the slice set.

*See how organized the **Web Content** palette is? Imagine how difficult it would be to navigate inside the **Web Content** palette if all the slices were at the same level. As you can see, just like layer groups (Photoshop CS2) and layer sets (ImageReady CS2), slice sets allow you to keep the **Web Content** palette organized.*

7. In the **Layers** palette, turn off the visibility of the **home** layer set, and turn on the visibility of the **products** layer set.

*Notice the slices you created for the **home** layer set are still visible for the **products** layer set. Unfortunately, the slices don't match the layers in the **products** layer set. Not to worry, you'll fix that in the next few steps!*

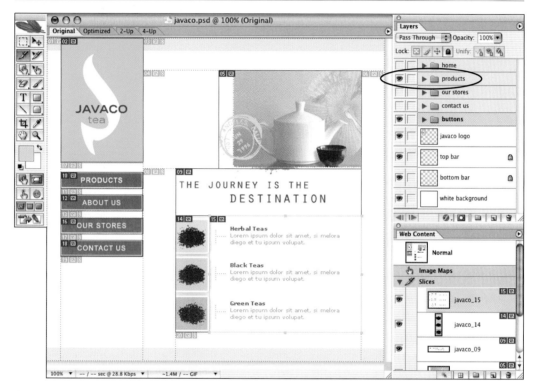

8. In the **Web Content** palette, turn off the visibility of the **javaco_home** slice set. With the **Slice** tool still selected in the **Toolbox**, slice the Javaco **products** page, as shown in the illustration here.

9. Using the techniques you learned in this chapter, group **Slice 05**, **Slice 09**, **Slice 14**, and **Slice 15** into a slice set. Rename the slice set **javaco_products**. When you've finished, click the arrow next to the **javaco_products** slice set to close the slice set.

10. In the **Layers** palette, turn off the visibility of the **products** layer set, and turn on the visibility of the **our stores** layer set. Just like in Step 7, the slices don't match the composition.

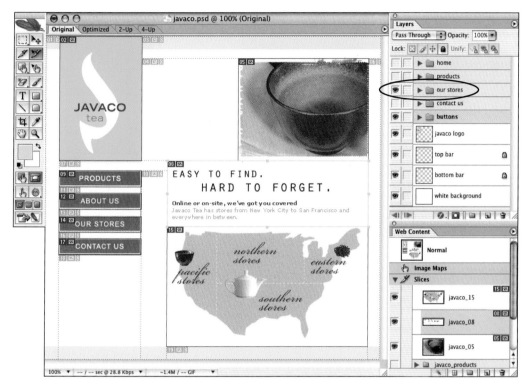

11. In the **Web Content** palette, turn off the visibility of the **javaco_products** slice set. With the **Slice** tool still selected in the **Toolbox**, slice the Javaco **our stores** page, as shown in the illustration here.

12. Using the techniques you learned in this chapter, group **Slice 05**, **Slice 08**, and **Slice 15** into a slice set. Rename the slice set **javaco_our_stores**. When you've finished, click the arrow next to the **javaco_our_stores** slice set to close the slice set.

13. In the **Layers** palette, turn off the visibility of the **our stores** layer set, and turn on the visibility of the **contact us** layer set. In the **Web Content** palette, turn off the visibility of the **javaco_our_stores** slice set.

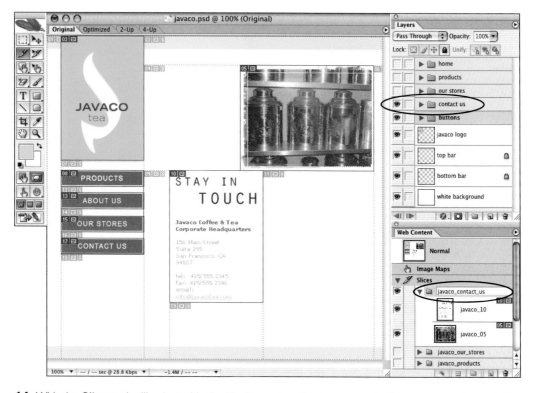

14. With the **Slice** tool still selected in the **Toolbox**, slice the Javaco **contact us** page, as shown in the illustration here. Using the techniques you learned in this chapter, group **Slice 05** and **Slice 10** into a slice set. Rename the slice set **javaco_contact_us**. When you've finished, click the arrow next to the **javaco_contact_us slice** set to close the slice set.

15. Go back and turn on and off the visibility of the different slice sets in the **Web Content** palette with their corresponding layer set in the **Layers** palette (for example, the **javaco_home** slice set and **home** layer slice set).

Notice the slice sets remembered the slices you created and didn't change when you created new slice sets. As you can see, slice sets not only offer an organizational benefit, but they also let you slice different compositions within the same file. If you have multiple Web pages in the same file, as in the illustration here, it's a huge time-saver to have different slice configurations for each page all in the same file because it saves you from reslicing over and over.

16. Close **javaco.psd**. You don't need to save your changes.

MOVIE | slices_sets.mov

To learn more about slice sets, including techniques for optimizing and saving the contents of slice sets, check out **slices_sets.mov** in the **movies** folder on the **PCS2Web HOT CD-ROM**.

You've finished another complex chapter! In this chapter, you learned the basics of working with slicing in ImageReady CS2. In Chapter 13, "Creating Rollovers," you'll take slicing to the next level by using slices to create rollovers.

13

Creating Rollovers

| Using Preset Rollover Styles | Optimizing and Saving Rollovers |

| Creating Rollovers from Layer Styles |

| Creating Rollovers from Layer Visibility |

| Creating Rollovers with Type | Creating Remote Rollovers |

| Creating Remote Rollovers with Selected States |

| Creating Animated Rollovers |

chap_13

PCS2Web HOT CD-ROM

In Chapter 9, "*Designing Navigation*," you learned how to create different buttons and navigation bars. In this chapter, you'll take navigation a step further and create interactive rollovers. A **rollover** is a type of Web graphic that changes when a user rolls his or her mouse over it or when it is clicked. Rollovers are one of the best ways to indicate a graphic is a link. To create a rollover, not only do you have to create the images for the different rollover states, you also have to create the required JavaScript and HTML code, which are required to make the rollover work on a Web page. The good news is when you create rollovers in ImageReady CS2, it creates the required JavaScript and HTML code for you!

In this chapter, you'll learn how to create simple rollovers using preset rollover styles, how to create rollovers from scratch with layer styles and layer visibility, how to create remote rollovers, and how to create animated rollovers. In addition, you'll learn how to optimize and save the images and required JavaScript and HTML code to make your rollovers work on a Web page. Sounds like a lot, but you'll be amazed at how easy it is to complete these complex tasks in ImageReady CS2!

About Rollovers

A rollover is an image on a Web page that changes in appearance when a user positions his or her mouse over it or clicks it. Each rollover appearance (or **state** in Web design lingo) is saved as a separate image. When you create rollovers, you also need to create the required JavaScript and HTML code to make the rollover work when it is placed inside a Web page. Fortunately, ImageReady CS2 saves the images and required JavaScript and HTML code in a single step!

You'll learn different techniques for creating rollovers in ImageReady CS2 throughout this chapter. Although you can't create rollovers in Photoshop CS2, you can open a rollover in Photoshop CS2 that was created in ImageReady CS2 and still retain the rollover information. The next time you open the rollover in ImageReady CS2, the rollover information will remain as part of the document.

About Rollover States

When you're creating rollovers in ImageReady CS2, you can specify a number of different rollover states. Here is a handy chart to help you understand them:

Rollover States in ImageReady CS2	
Rollover State	**Definition**
Normal	When a user loads a Web page, the default appearance of an image before or after a user activates a rollover state.
Over	When the user positions his or her mouse over a slice or image map region without clicking.
Down	When the user clicks over a slice or image map region. The Down state appears until the user releases the mouse.
Click	When the user clicks the mouse over a slice or image map region. The Click state appears until the user moves the mouse outside the rollover region.
Out	When the user moves the mouse outside the slice or image map region. If there is no defined Out state, the image will automatically return to the Normal state.
Up	When the user releases the mouse inside the slice or image map region. If there is no defined Up state, the image will automatically return to the Over state.
Custom	When a custom-programmed event occurs. This state is available if you want to create your own JavaScript event and add it to the HTML code.

continues on next page

Rollover States in ImageReady CS2 *continued*	
Rollover State	**Definition**
Selected	When the user clicks a slice or image map region, the Selected state appears until another rollover state is selected. Other rollover effects can occur while the Selected state is active. For example, a Selected state for one button and an Over state for another button can occur simultaneously. However, if a layer is used by both states, the layer attributes of the Selected state override those of the Over state. Use Default Selected State to activate the state initially when the document is previewed in ImageReady CS or loaded in a Web browser.
None	When you want to preserve the current state of an image for future use. Rollovers with a None state are not saved when you save rollovers.

About the Web Content Palette

When you're working with rollovers in ImageReady CS2, you'll need access to the Web Content palette. The Web Content palette not only stores information about rollovers, it also stores information about slices and image maps. As a result, you can see information about your rollovers, slices, and image maps in a single location.

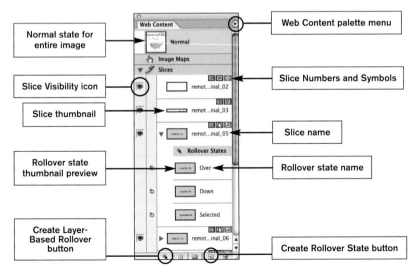

The Web Content palette lets you preview rollovers in an image. Similar to the Layers palette, the Web Content palette displays a thumbnail preview of the rollover, the rollover state, and lets you turn on and off the visibility of a rollover. The Web Content palette also offers a number of controls for creating and editing rollovers. It displays slice numbers and symbols, which are helpful when you're working with rollovers based on slices.

I. [IR] _____Using Preset Rollover Styles

In Chapter 9, "*Designing Navigation*," you learned how to apply layer styles to shapes by using the Styles palette in Photoshop CS2. What you didn't learn is that the Styles palette in ImageReady CS2 contains "rollover styles" that apply a layer style, create the rollover state(s), slice the image, and write the required JavaScript. As a result, you can create rollovers in no time flat. In this exercise, you'll learn how rollover styles are constructed, and you'll also learn how to identify rollover styles in the Styles palette and how to apply rollover styles to layers to create rollovers quickly and easily.

1. Open **javaco_round.psd** from the **chap_13** folder you copied to your **Desktop**. Make sure the **Layers** palette, the **Web Content** palette, and the **Styles** palette are visible. If they're not, choose **Window > Layers, Window > Web Content**, and **Window > Styles**.

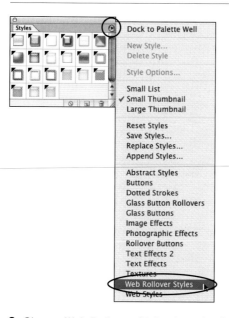

2. Choose **Web Rollover Styles** from the **Styles** palette menu. When the warning message appears, click **Replace** to replace the current styles in the **Styles** palette with the **Web Rollover Styles**.

Notice all the styles have a small black triangle in the upper-left corner, which indicates these styles are rollover styles. Rollover styles are different from regular styles because they have additional functionality. Not only do they apply a layer style to the layer, they also create a layer-based slice, create rollover state(s), and write the required JavaScript to make the rollover work in a Web browser.

3. In the **Layers** palette, click the arrow next to the **buttons** layer set to expand its contents. Click the **contact_us_btn** layer to select it.

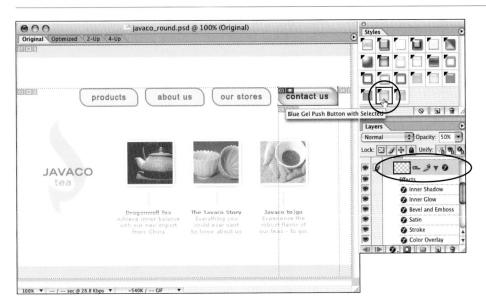

4. With the **contact_us_btn** layer selected in the **Layers** palette, in the **Styles** palette, click the **Blue Gel Push Button with Selected** style.

*Take a look at how this style affects the **contact us** button in the document window. Notice the **contact us** button layer is now a layer-based slice, and the rest of the image has been sliced automatically. Also take a look at the contents of the **Layers** palette. As you can see, ImageReady CS2 automatically added a series of layer styles to the layer. These layer styles are what make up the three-dimensional look of the button. All of these properties are part of the rollover style, including the layer-based slice, the required JavaScript code, and the visual elements that make up the button. You'll learn to make your own rollover styles from scratch in a later exercise. For now, just marvel at the power of preset rollover styles and the amount of information you can store within a rollover style!*

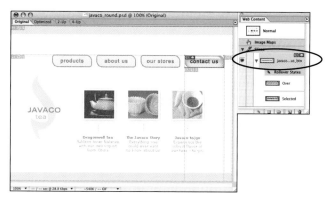

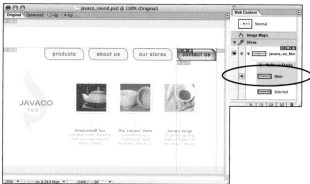

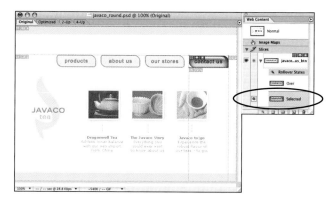

5. Take a look at the **Web Content** palette. Expand the **Slice 03** slice set so you can see the different rollover states ImageReady CS2 created automatically. Click the **Over** state and the **Selected** state so you can see how the button appears in the different states.

*The rollover style created a three-dimensional button with different shades of blue for the **Normal**, **Over**, and **Selected** states. As you can see, using rollover styles is an easy way to create rollovers in very little time!*

6. In the **Toolbox**, click the **Preview Document** button, and take a look at the **contact us** button in the document window. Position your mouse over the button, and notice it changes to the **Over** state. Next, click the button, and notice it changes to the **Selected** state.

*Using the **Preview Document** feature is a great way to preview the rollover states from within ImageReady CS2. By using it, you don't have to preview in a Web browser each time you want to see the different rollover states.*

7. In the **Toolbox**, click the **Preview Document** button to exit the preview mode.

*When you click the **Preview Document** button, you go into a preview mode in ImageReady CS2, which means you can no longer make changes to your image—you must exit the preview mode by clicking the **Preview Document** button. You'll know you've successfully exited the preview mode when the **Preview Document** button returns to white instead of gray.*

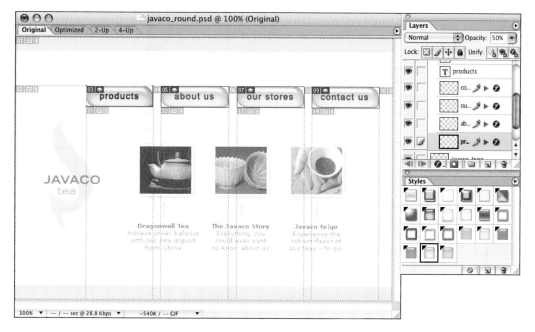

8. In the **Layers** palette, click the **our_stores_btn** layer to select it. Click the **Blue Gel Push Button with Selected** style in the **Styles** palette. Repeat this process for the **about_us_btn** layer and **products_btn** layer so all four buttons have the same rollover style. (You need to have consistency when you design Web navigation.)

9. In the **Toolbox**, click the **Preview Document** button, and take a look at the four buttons in the document window. Position your mouse over each button to view the **Over** state. Click each button to view the **Selected** state.

10. When you've finished, in the **Toolbox**, click the **Preview Document** button to exit the preview mode.

11. Leave **javaco_round.psd** open for the next exercise.

Next, you'll learn how to optimize and save rollovers.

2. [IR] _____Optimizing and Saving Rollovers

In the last exercise, you learned how to create rollovers from rollover styles in ImageReady CS2. In this exercise, you'll learn how to optimize and save rollovers, including the HTML and JavaScript code required to make rollovers work in a Web browser. Although this exercise is shown using the preset rollover styles you created in the last exercise, you can apply the skills you learn in this exercise to any type of rollover you create.

1. If you followed the last exercise, **javaco_round.psd** should be open in ImageReady CS2. If it's not, go back and complete Exercise 1. Make sure the **Web Content** palette and the **Optimize** palettes are visible. If they're not, choose **Window > Web Content** and **Window > Optimize**.

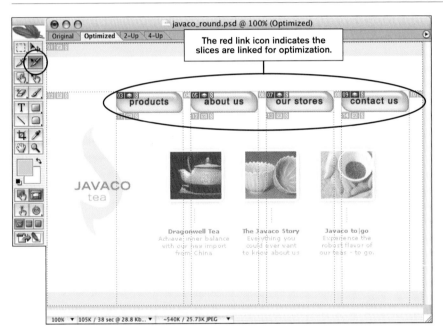

2. In the document window, click the **Optimized** tab. Select the **Slice Select** tool from the **Toolbox**. In the document window, click **Slice 03** to select it. Hold down the **Shift** key, and click **Slice 05**, **Slice 07**, and **Slice 09** to multiple-select all four slices. Choose **Slices > Link Slices for Optimization**.

Notice each slice now has a red link icon. The purpose of linking slices for optimization is to specify one optimization setting for all four slices.

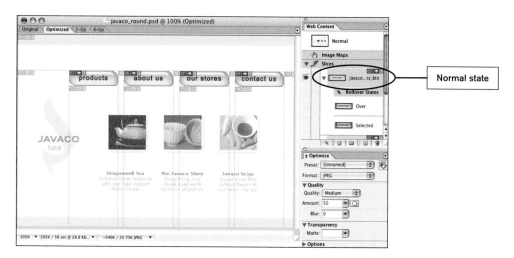

Normal state

3. In the **Web Content** palette, click the **Normal** state for the **javaco_round_products_btn** rollover (**Slice 03**). Using the techniques you learned in Chapter 7, "*Optimizing Images*," specify optimization settings in the **Optimize** palette. When you're happy with the settings you chose, click the **Over** and **Selected** states to ensure you're happy with the settings for those states, as well as the **Normal** state. (ImageReady CS2 uses the same optimization settings for all rollover states, regardless of the contents of each state.)

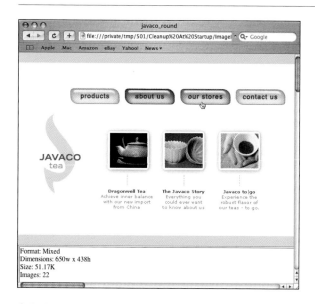

4. In the **Toolbox**, click the **Preview in Default Browser** button. When the image opens in your default Web browser, position your mouse over each of the buttons, and notice how each changes to the **Over** state. Click the image, and notice it changes to the **Selected** state. Scroll down and you'll see the JavaScript ImageReady CS2 generated automatically to make these rollovers work in your Web browser.

*Something that may not be immediately apparent is that when you save rollovers with **Selected** states, you need to save more than one HTML file. You need to save an HTML file for the original, **Normal** state when you first open the Web page, and you need to save an HTML page for each button in its **Selected** state. In this case, you need to save a total of five different HTML pages, and you need to make sure the buttons link to the proper pages. Don't stress–ImageReady CS2 has a handy option that will take care of these details for you.*

WARNING | Microsoft Internet Explorer Problem

In some versions of Microsoft Internet Explorer, you may find rollovers have an annoying black outline after you click them. This is not through any fault of ImageReady CS2. There are scripts within Adobe GoLive and Macromedia Dreamweaver that eliminate this issue. Unfortunately, there is nothing you can do with ImageReady CS2 to prevent the black outline.

---

5. Close the Web browser, and return to ImageReady CS2.

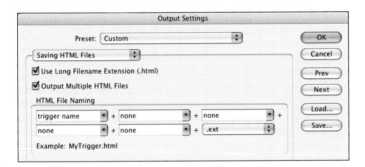

6. Choose **File > Output Settings > Saving HTML**. In the **Output Settings** dialog box, turn on the **Output Multiple HTML Files** option, and click **OK**.

*This option will tell ImageReady CS2 to save an HTML file for each of the **Selected** states, and it will make sure the buttons link properly from one to the next.*

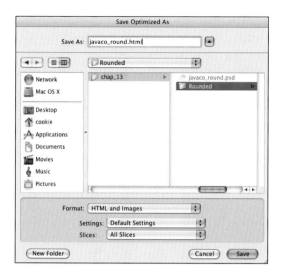

7. Choose **File > Save Optimized As**. In the **Save Optimized As** dialog box, navigate to the **chap_13** folder you copied to your **Desktop**. Create a new folder, and name it **Rounded**. Choose **HTML and Images** from the **Format** pop-up menu. Click **Save**.

*Note: You may see a warning message appear indicating some filenames may be truncated because they are over 31 characters. Click **OK** to acknowledge the warning. The names of some of your files may be cut a bit short if they exceed 31 characters. For the purposes of this exercise, you don't need to concern yourself with that limitation—just allow ImageReady CS2 to truncate the names where necessary. When you're designing your own Web pages, keep this limitation in mind, and keep your file, layer, and slice names as short as possible so your filenames don't get truncated when saved.*

8. Browse to the **Rounded** folder in the **chap_13** folder you copied to your **Desktop**.

*Notice ImageReady CS2 generated five HTML pages—one for the **Normal** state and one for each of the **Selected** states—which contain the JavaScript and HTML code required to make the rollovers work, and a folder called **images**, which contains images for the rollover states.*

9. Double-click the **javaco_round.html** file to view the file in your Web browser. Position your mouse over the image to see the **Over** state. Click the image to see the **Selected** state.

*Notice when you click one of the buttons to view the **Selected** state, the address bar in your Web browser changes to reflect the appropriate HTML page for the current **Selected** state.*

10. Return to ImageReady CS2. If you'd like, save your changes to keep the rollovers you created in this exercise as part of the file.

Next, you'll learn how to create rollovers from scratch!

3. [IR]_____Creating Rollovers from Layer Styles

In the last exercise, you learned how to create rollovers quickly and easily using rollover styles. In this exercise, you'll learn how to create rollovers from scratch using layer styles.

1. Open **javaco_stores.psd** from the **chap_13** folder you copied to your **Desktop**. Make sure the **Layers** palette, the **Web Content** palette, **Styles** palette, and **Optimize** palette are visible. If they're not, choose **Window > Layers, Window > Web Content, Window > Styles,** and **Window > Optimize**.

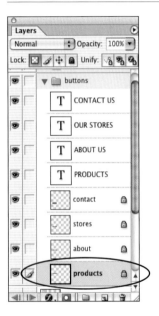

2. In the **Layers** palette, click the arrow next to the **buttons** layer set to expand the layer set. Click the **products** layer to select it.

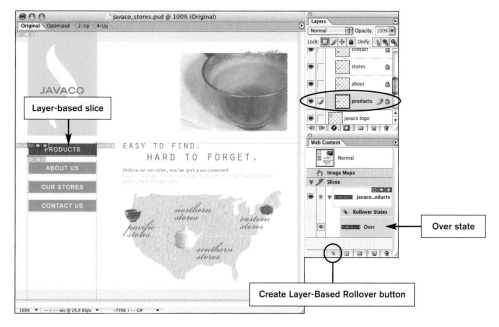

Layer-based slice

Over state

Create Layer-Based Rollover button

3. At the bottom of the **Web Content** palette, click the **Create Layer-Based Rollover** button.

*ImageReady CS2 automatically created two things: a layer-based slice for the products layer and a rollover in the **Web Content** palette, complete with an **Over** state. Right now, the **Over** state is identical to the **Normal** state. Not to worry, you'll change the **Over** state in the next step.*

4. Make sure the **Over** state is selected in the **Web Content** palette and the **products** layer still is selected in the **Layers** palette. Choose **Inner Shadow** from the **Layer Styles** pop-up menu.

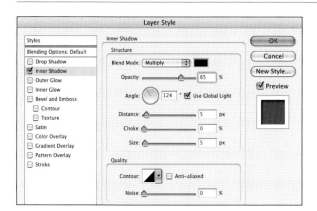

5. In the **Layer Style** dialog box, match the settings to the ones shown in the illustration here.

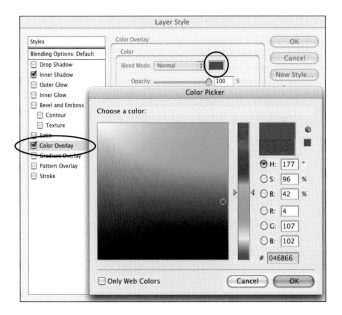

6. On the left side of the **Layer Style** dialog box, click the **Color Overlay** option. Click the color swatch to open the **Color Picker** dialog box. Choose a **medium blue**, and click **OK**. In the **Layer Style** dialog box, click **OK** to apply the **Inner Shadow** and **Color Overlay** layer styles to the **products** layer.

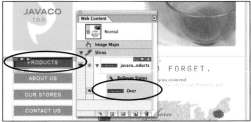

7. Click the **Normal** state. Click the **Over** state.

*Notice the changes you applied in the last two steps affect only the **Over** state. The **Normal** state remains unchanged.*

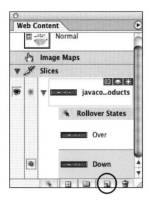

8. At the bottom of the **Web Content** palette, click the **Create Rollover State** button.

*Notice ImageReady CS2 automatically created a **Down** state. If you toggle between the **Over** and **Down** state, you'll notice they look identical. When you create a new rollover state, it automatically has the same properties as the previous state in the **Web Content** palette.*

9. With the **Down** state selected in the **Web Content** palette, and the **products** layer selected in the **Layers** palette, double-click the **Color Overlay** layer style to open the **Layer Style** dialog box.

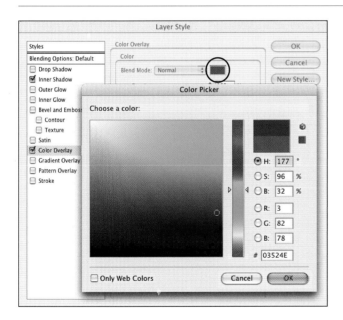

10. Click the color swatch to open the **Color Picker** dialog box. Choose a slightly **darker blue**, and click **OK**. In the **Layer Style** dialog box, click **OK**.

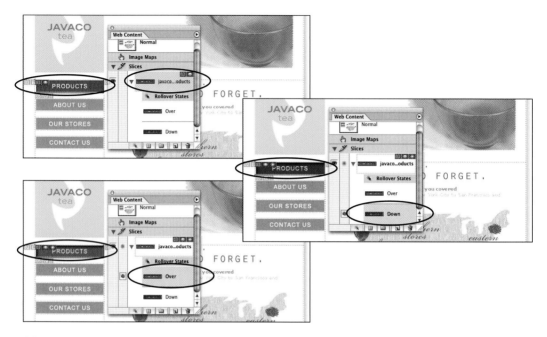

11. Toggle between the **Normal**, **Over**, and **Down** states in the **Web Content** palette, and notice that the change you made in the last step affects only the **Down** state.

12. With the **Down** state selected in the **Web Content** palette, at the bottom of the **Web Content** palette click the **Create Rollover State** button.

*Notice ImageReady CS2 automatically creates a **Selected** state.*

13. With the **Selected** state selected in the **Web Content** palette, and the **products** layer selected in the **Layers** palette, double-click the **Color Overlay** layer style to open the **Layer Style** dialog box.

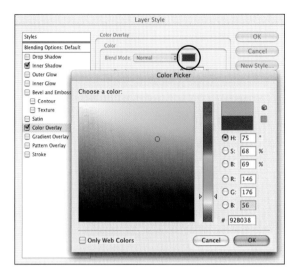

14. Click the color swatch to open the **Color Picker** dialog box. Choose a **light green**, and click **OK**. In the **Layer Style** dialog box, click **OK**.

15. Toggle between the **Normal**, **Over**, **Down**, and **Selected** states in the **Web Content** palette to see the rollover in all four states.

16. In the **Toolbox**, click the **Preview Document** button. Position your cursor over the **products** button to see the **Over** state. Click and hold the **products** button so you can see the **Down** state. When you release your mouse, you'll see the **Selected** state.

At this point, you may be wondering how you're going to remember the styles you applied to the ***products*** *button to create the states for the rollover. Not to worry, ImageReady CS2 provides a quick and easy way to solve that problem!*

17. Click the **Preview Document** button to exit the preview mode.

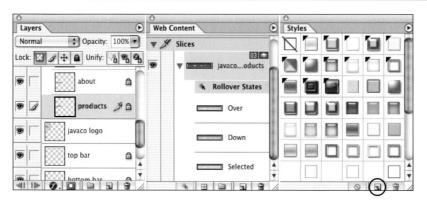

18. With the **products** layer still selected in the **Layers** palette, at the bottom of the **Styles** palette click the **Create New Style** button.

19. In the **Style Options** dialog box, type **Javaco Rollover** in the **Name** field, and turn on the **Include Layer Effects**, **Include Blending Options**, and **Include Rollover States** options. Click **OK**.

*The **Include Layer Effects** and **Include Rollover States** options are critical because these options ensure the rollovers states you created in this exercise are saved with the rollover style.*

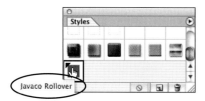

20. Scroll to the bottom of the **Styles** palette so you can see the style you created in the last step.

Notice the style has a small, black triangle in the upper-left corner. As you know from Exercise 1, this triangle indicates the style is a rollover style, not just a regular style.

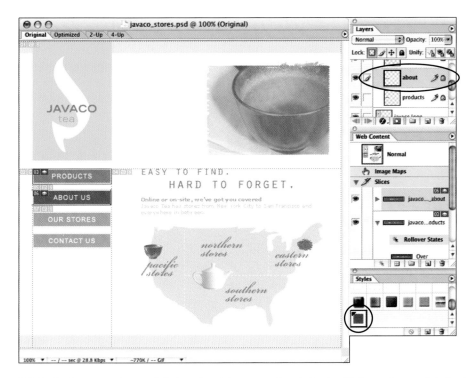

21. In the **Layers** palette, click the **about** layer to select it. In the **Styles** palette, click the **Javaco Rollover** style.

*Notice that a layer-based slice was automatically created for the **about** layer, and a new rollover was automatically created in the **Web Content** palette.*

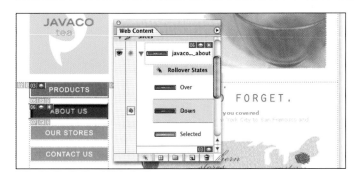

22. Click the arrow next to the **javaco_stores_about** rollover so you can see the different rollover states.

*As you can see, the rollover states are identical to the ones you created for the **products** button.*

23. In the **Layers** palette, click the **store** layer to select it. In the **Styles** palette, click the **Javaco Rollover** style.

*Just like in the **about** layer, ImageReady CS2 automatically created a layer-based slice and applied the rollover states you created for the **products** layer to the **about** layer.*

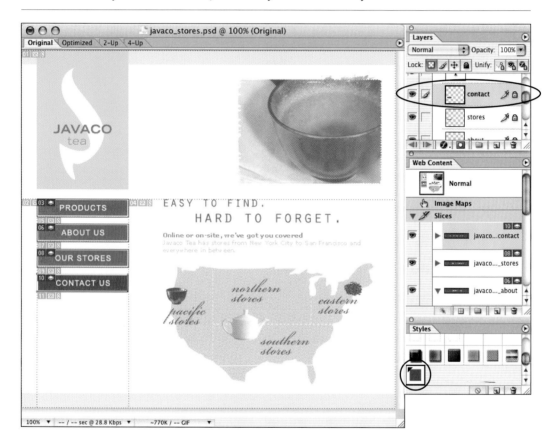

24. In the **Layers** palette, click the **contact** layer to select it. In the **Styles** palette, click the **Javaco Rollover** style.

*You should now have four layer-based slices—one for each of the four buttons. You should also have four rollovers in the **Web Content** palette—one for each button. Plus, each rollover should have identical states, which are based on the rollover states you created for the **products** button earlier in this exercise.*

25. In the **Toolbox**, click the **Preview in Default Browser** button.

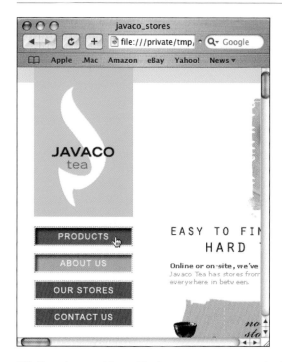

26. Experiment with positioning your cursor over the buttons and clicking the buttons so you can view the different rollover states.

As you can see, creating your own unique rollovers in ImageReady CS2 is very easy. Plus, by saving your own custom rollover styles, you can ensure your buttons have a consistent look and feel. If you'd like, use the techniques you learned in Exercise 2 to optimize the layer-based slices and save the images, JavaScript, and HTML code required to make rollovers work in a Web browser.

27. Close **javaco_stores.psd**. You don't need to save your changes.

MOVIE | Creating Rollovers from Layer Styles

To learn more about creating rollovers from layer styles, check out **rollovers_styles.mov** in the **movies** folder on the **PCS2Web HOT CD-ROM**.

4. [IR]_____Creating Rollovers from Layer Visibility

So far you've learned how to create rollovers by using preset rollover styles and by creating rollovers from layer styles. In this exercise, you'll learn how to create rollovers using the visibility of different layers.

1. Open **javaco.psd** from the **chap_13** folder you copied to your **Desktop**. Make sure the **Layers** palette and **Web Content** palette are visible. If they're not, choose **Window > Layers** and **Window > Web Content**.

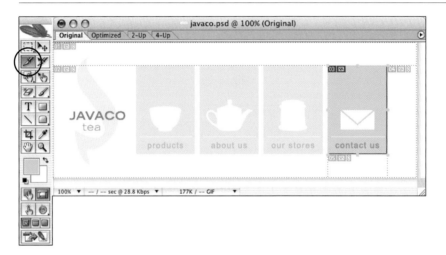

2. Select the **Slice** tool from the **Toolbox**. Click and drag to create a user slice around the **contact us** button, as shown in the illustration above.

3. In the **Web Content** palette, click the **Create Rollover State** button to create an **Over** state.

*Notice ImageReady CS2 automatically creates an **Over** rollover state, and the slice icons for the **Slice 03** slice update with the rollover icon.*

4. With the **Over** state still selected in the **Web Content** palette, expand the contents of the **contact** layer set in the **Layers** palette. Turn off the visibility of the **blue** and **contact blue** layers. Turn on the visibility of the **grey** and **contact green** layers.

5. At the bottom of the **Web Content** palette, click the **Create Rollover State** button to create a **Down** state.

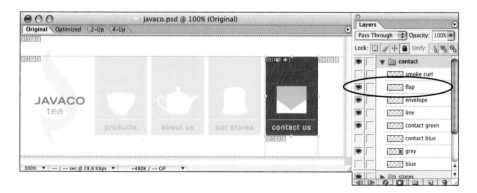

6. With the **Down** state selected in the **Layers** palette, turn on the visibility of the **flap** layer.

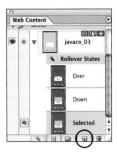

7. At the bottom of the **Web Content** palette, click the **Create Rollover State** button to create a **Selected** state.

8. With the **Selected** state still selected in the **Web Content** palette, turn on the visibility of the **smoke curl** layer in the **Layers** palette.

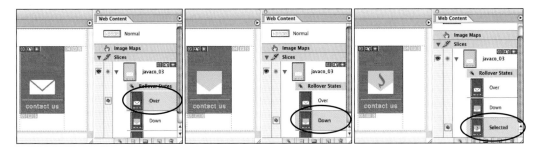

9. In the **Toolbox**, click the **Preview Document** button. Position your cursor over the **contact us** button to view the **Over** state. Click the **contact us** button to view the **Down** state. When you release your mouse, you'll see the **Selected** state.

As you can see, it's quite easy to create different rollover states using the visibility of different layers.

10. In the **Toolbox**, click the **Preview Document** button to exit the preview mode.

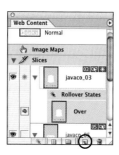
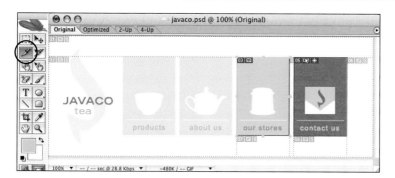

11. With the **Slice** tool selected in the **Toolbox**, click and drag to create a user slice around the **our stores** button, as shown in the illustration here.

12. At the bottom of the **Web Content** palette, click the **Create Rollover State** button to create an **Over** state.

13. With the **Over** state selected in the **Web Content** palette, close the **contact** layer set, and open the **stores** layer set. Turn off the visibility of the **blue** layer and the **stores blue** layer. Turn on the visibility of the **grey** and **stores green** layer.

14. At the bottom of the **Web Content** palette, click the **Create Rollover State** button to create a **Down** state. With the **Down** state selected in the **Web Content** palette, turn on the visibility of the **label** layer.

15. At the bottom of the **Web Content** palette, click the **Create Rollover State** button to create a **Selected** state. With the **Selected** state selected in the **Web Content** palette, turn on the visibility of the **smoke curl** layer.

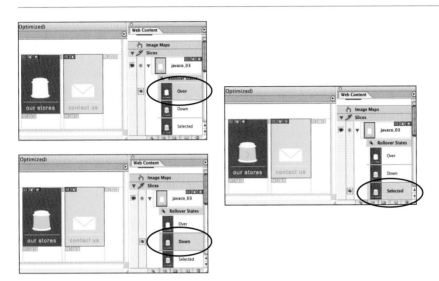

16. In the **Toolbox**, click the **Preview Document** button. Position your cursor over the **our stores** button to see the **Over** state. Click the **our stores** button to see the **Down** state. When you release your mouse, you'll see the **Selected** state.

17. When you've finished, click the **Preview Document** button to exit the preview mode.

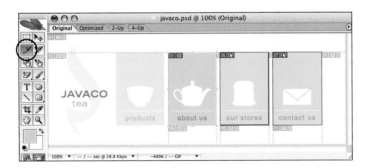

18. With the **Slice** tool selected in the **Toolbox**, click and drag to create a user slice around the **about us** button, as shown in the illustration here.

19. At the bottom of the **Web Content** palette, click the **Create Rollover State** button to create an **Over** state.

20. With the **Over** state selected in the **Web Content** palette, close the **stores** layer set, and open the **about** layer set in the **Layers** palette. Turn off the visibility of the **blue** and **about blue** layers, and turn on the visibility of the **grey** and **about green** layers in the **Layers** palette.

21. At the bottom of the **Web Content** palette, click the **Create Rollover State** button to create a **Down** state. With the **Down** state selected in the **Web Content** palette, turn on the visibility of the **circle** layer.

22. At the bottom of the **Web Content** palette, click the **Create Rollover State** button to create a **Selected** state. With the **Selected** state selected in the **Web Content** palette, turn on the visibility of the **smoke curl** layer in the **Layers** palette.

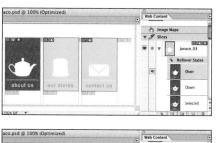

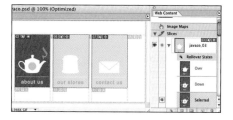

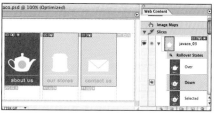

23. In the **Toolbox**, click the **Preview Document** button. Position your cursor over the **about us** button to view the **Over** state. Click the **about us** button to view the **Down** state. When you release your mouse, you'll see the **Selected** state.

24. In the **Toolbox**, click the **Preview Document** button to exit the preview mode.

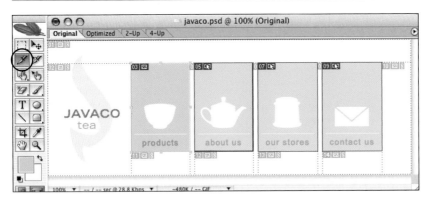

25. With the **Slice** tool selected in the **Toolbox**, click and drag to create a user slice around the **products** button, as shown in the illustration here.

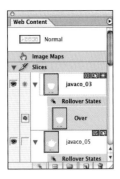

26. At the bottom of the **Web Content** palette, click the **Create Rollover State** button to create an **Over** state.

27. With the **Over** state selected in the **Web Content** palette, close the **about** layer set, and open the **products** layer set. Turn off the visibility of the **blue** and **products blue** layers in the **Layers** palette. Turn on the visibility of the **grey** and **products green** layer in the **Layers** palette.

28. At the bottom of the **Web Content** palette, click the **Create Rollover State** button to create a **Down** state. With the **Down** state selected in the **Web Content** palette, turn on the visibility of the **tea** layer in the **Layers** palette.

29. At the bottom of the **Web Content** palette, click the **Create Rollover State** button to create a **Selected** state. With the **Selected** state selected in the **Web Content** palette, turn on the visibility of the **smoke curl** layer in the **Layers** palette.

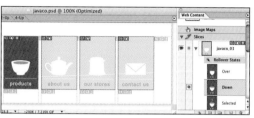

30. In the **Toolbox**, click the **Preview Document** button. Position your cursor over the **products** button to view the **Over** state. Click the **products** button to view the **Down** state. When you release your mouse, you'll see the **Selected** state.

31. In the **Toolbox**, click the **Preview Document** button to exit the preview mode.

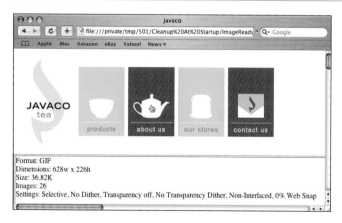

32. In the **Toolbox**, click the **Preview in Default Browser** button so you can view your handiwork in a Web browser. Position your cursor over each button to view the **Over** states, and click each button to view the **Down** and **Selected** states.

33. When you've finished, close the Web browser and return to ImageReady CS2. If you'd like, use the techniques you learned in Exercise 2 to optimize and save the HTML and images.

34. Close **javaco.psd**. You don't need to save your changes.

5. [IR]_____Creating Rollovers with Type

A popular technique for type-based navigation bars is changing the font properties to italic or bold italic to indicate rollover states. You may think it's as simple as changing the type properties for each rollover state, but it's a bit more complex than that. Here's an exercise to show you how.

1. Open **horizontal_nav.psd** from the **chap_13** folder you copied to your **Desktop**. Make sure the **Layers** palette and **Web Content** palette are visible. If they're not, choose **Window > Layers** and **Window > Web Content**.

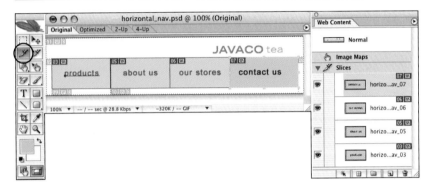

2. Select the **Slice** tool from the **Toolbox**. Create four user slices, as shown in the illustration here.

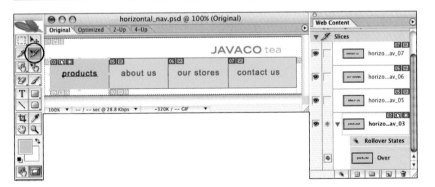

3. Select the **Slice Select** tool from the **Toolbox**. Click **Slice 03** to select it. In the **Web Content** palette, click the **Create Rollover State** button to create an **Over** state.

4. With the **Over** state selected in the **Web Content**, double-click the **T** icon of the **products** type layer to highlight the vector-based type. Choose **Italic** from the **Font Style** pop-up menu.

Note: When you double-click the layer, you may see a warning message indicating that editing the text layer may cause its layout to change. Click OK to acknowledge the warning.

5. Click the **Normal** state for the **horizontal_nav_03** slice in the **Web Content** palette. Click the **Over** state.

*Notice that the change you made to the vector-based type updates in both the **Normal** and **Over** states. Any change you make to vector-based type affects all rollover states, not just the one you have selected in the **Web Content** palette. Not to worry, in this exercise you'll learn a workaround to solve this problem.*

6. Press **Cmd+Z** (Mac) or **Ctrl+Z** (Windows) to undo to change you made to the type in Step 4. With the **products** layer selected in the **Layers** palette, choose **Duplicate Layer** from the **Layers** palette menu. Choose **Duplicate Layer** a second time from the **Layers** palette menu.

*Notice ImageReady CS2 automatically creates two new type layers—**products copy** and **products copy 2**—with identical properties.*

7. Double-click the **products copy** layer name. When the bounding box appears, rename the layer **products over**, and press **Return** (Mac) or **Enter** (Windows). Double-click the **products copy 2** layer name. When the bounding box appears, rename the layer **products selected**, and press **Return** (Mac) or **Enter** (Windows).

8. Click the **Normal** state for the **horizontal_nav_03** slice in the **Web Content** palette. Turn off the visibility of the **products over** and **products selected** layers in the **Layers** palette.

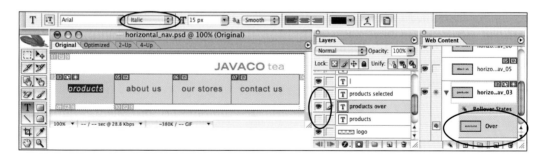

9. Click the **Over** state in the **Web Content** palette, turn off the visibility of the **products** layer in the **Layers** palette. Turn on the visibility of the **products over** layer in the **Layers** palette. Double-click the **T** icon of the **products over** type layer to highlight the type. Choose **Italic** from the **Font Style** pop-up menu.

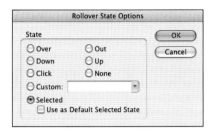

10. At the bottom of the **Web Content** palette, click the **Create Rollover State** button to create a **Down** state. Double-click the **Down** state to open the **Rollover State Options** dialog box. Select **Selected**, and click **OK**.

*For this exercise, you won't create a separate **Down** state—just an **Over** state and a **Selected** state.*

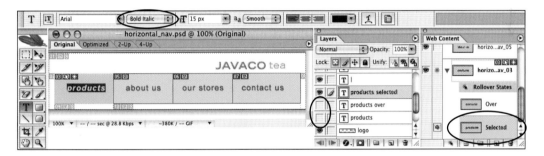

11. With the **Selected** state selected in the **Web Content** palette, turn off the visibility of the **products over** layer in the **Layers** palette, and turn on the visibility of the **products selected** layer. Double-click the **T** icon of the **products selected** type layer to highlight the type. Choose **Bold Italic** from the **Font Style** pop-up menu.

12. In the **Toolbox**, click the **Preview Document** button. Position your cursor over the word **products** to view the **Over** state. Click the word **products** to view the **Selected** state.

As you can see from this exercise, you have to use layer visibility to change the appearance of type for different rollover states. The easiest way to achieve such a result is to duplicate layers, as you've done in this exercise.

13. In the **Toolbox**, click the **Preview Document** button to exit the preview mode.

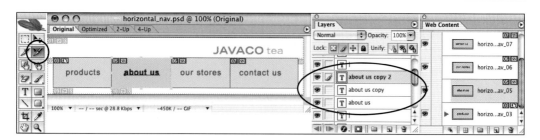

14. Select the **Slice Select** tool from the **Toolbox**. Click **Slice 05** to select it. In the **Layers** palette, click the **about us** layer to select it. Duplicate the **about us** layer in the **Layers** palette twice by choosing **Duplicate Layer** from the **Layers** palette menu twice.

*You should now have **about us**, **about us copy**, and **about us copy 2** layers in the **Layers** palette.*

15. Double-click the **about us copy** layer name. When the bounding box appears, rename the layer **about us over**. Double-click the **about us copy 2** layer name. When the bounding box appears, rename the layer **about us selected**.

16. With the **horizontal_nav_05** slice selected in the **Web Content** palette, turn off the visibility of the **about us over** and **about us selected** layers in the **Layers** palette.

17. At the bottom of the **Web Content** palette, click the **Create Rollover State** button to create an **Over** state. With the **Over** state selected in the **Web Content** palette, turn off the visibility of the **about us** layer, and turn on the visibility of the **about us over** layer in the **Layers** palette.

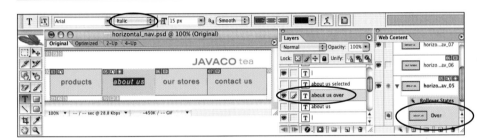

18. In the **Layers** palette, double-click the **T** icon of the **about us over** layer to highlight the vector-based type. Choose **Italic** from the **Font Style** pop-up menu.

19. At the bottom of the **Web Content** palette, click the **Create Rollover Style** button to create a **Down** state. Double-click the **Down** state to open the **Rollover State Options** dialog box. Select **Selected** and click **OK**.

20. With the **Selected** state selected in the **Web Content** palette, turn off the visibility of the **about us over** layer, and turn on the visibility of the **about us selected** layer in the **Layers** palette.

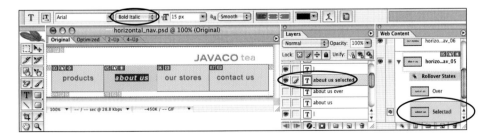

21. Double-click the **T** icon on the **about us selected** layer to highlight the vector-based type. Choose **Bold Italic** from the **Font Style** pop-up menu.

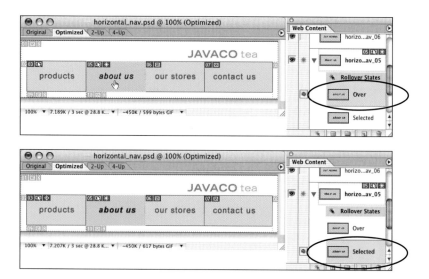

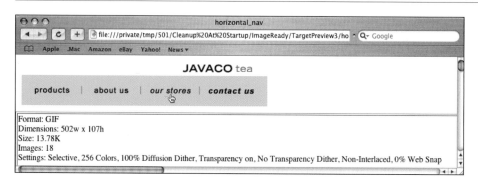

22. In the **Toolbox**, click the **Preview Document** button. Position your cursor over the words **about us** to see the **Over** state. Click the words **about us** to see the **Selected** state.

23. In the **Toolbox**, click the **Preview Document** button to exit the preview mode.

24. Using the techniques you learned in this exercise, create **Over** and **Selected** states for **our stores** and **contact us**. When you've finished, in the **Toolbox**, click the **Preview in Default Browser** button to view the results of your hard work in a Web browser.

25. Return to ImageReady CS2. If you'd like, use the techniques you learned in Exercise 2 to optimize and save the HTML and images.

26. Close **horizontal_nav.psd**. You don't need to save your changes.

6. [IR] _____Creating Remote Rollovers

The rollovers you've created so far have been replacement rollovers (which means the image representing the Normal state has been replaced with an image representing the Over, Down, or Selected states) or addition rollovers (which means something was added to the original image in the Over, Down, or Selected states). In this exercise, you'll learn how to combine addition rollovers with remote rollovers. When you create remote rollovers, additional visual information appears elsewhere on the Web page. Sound confusing? Here's an exercise to help you understand.

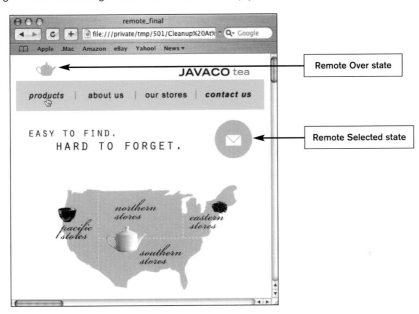

1. Open **remote_final.psd** from the **chap_13** folder you copied to your **Desktop**. Before you get started creating remote rollovers, take a moment to understand what remote rollovers are all about. In the **Toolbox**, click the **Preview in Default Browser** button. Position your mouse over the words **products**, **about us**, **our stores**, and **contact us**.

*When you position your mouse over one of these words, the appearance of the word changes to italic (via a technique you learned in Exercise 5). Also notice that when you position your mouse over the words, a small icon appears in the upper-left corner of the Web page. This icon represents a remote rollover for the **Over** state. Click each of the words **products**, **about us**, **our stores**, and **contact us**. Notice when you click each, another icon appears on the right side below the horizontal navigation bar. This icon represents a remote rollover for the **Selected** state. In this exercise, you'll learn how to create remote rollovers for **Over** states. In Exercise 7, you'll learn how to create remote rollovers for **Selected** states.*

2. Close **remote_final.psd**, and open **remote.psd** from the **chap_13** folder you copied to your **Desktop**. Make sure the **Layers** palette and **Web Content** palette are visible. If they're not, choose **Window > Layers** and **Window > Web Content**. Take a look at the contents of the **Layers** palette. Notice there are layer sets for each of the following: **products**, **about us**, **our stores**, and **contact us**.

*Notice each layer set contains **Normal**, **Over**, and **Selected** states for the type and includes **Over** and **Selected** states for the icon. In this exercise, you'll only use the layers labeled **over**. You'll use this same file in the next exercise and use the layers marked **selected**.*

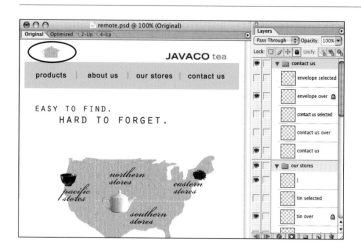

3. In the **Layers** palette, expand the contents of the **products**, **about us**, **our stores**, and **contact us** layer sets. Turn on the visibility of the **teapot over** layer in the **products** layer set, the **teacup over** layer in the **about us** layer set, the **tin over** layer in the **our stores** layer set, and the **envelope over** layer in the **contact us** layer set.

Don't worry about the appearance of the image in the document window—all four icons will be stacked on top of each other. The purpose of turning on all four layers is so you can see where to slice the image. You'll need to create a slice big enough to encompass the contents of these four layers since they will become the remote rollovers.

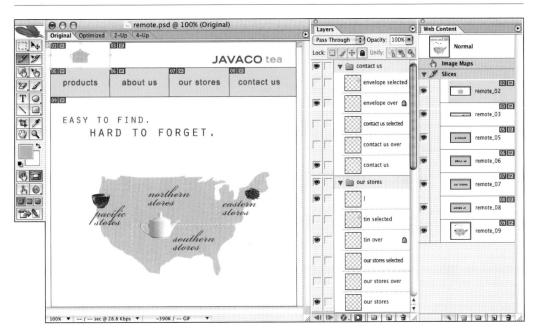

4. Select the **Slice** tool from the **Toolbox**. Using the **Slice** tool, slice the Web page, as shown in the illustration here.

*Note: The slice numbers on your computer should be identical to the ones shown in the illustration here because ImageReady CS2 automatically renumbers slices so they are numbered sequentially from left to right and top to bottom. That said, the stacking order of the slices in the **Web Content** palette on your computer may vary from the stacking order shown in the illustration here. The stacking order of the **Web Content** palette is based on the order in which you created the slices. I started from the bottom and worked to the top so the slices would appear sequentially in the **Web Content** palette. If you want to reorder your slices, simply drag and drop the slices inside the **Web Content** palette—the process is identical to the reordering of layers in the **Layers** palette, which you learned about in Chapter 5, "Working with Layers".*

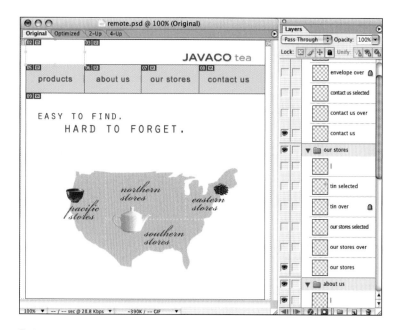

5. Now that you've sliced the image, you can turn off the visibility of the **teapot over** layer in the **products** layer set, the **teacup over** layer in the **about us** layer set, the **tin over** layer in the **our stores** layer set, and the **envelope over** layer in the **contact us** layer set. The purpose of turning on the visibility of these layers was to make sure the slice you created to contain these icons was an appropriate size—you want to be sure the full contents of the layer are contained inside the slice.

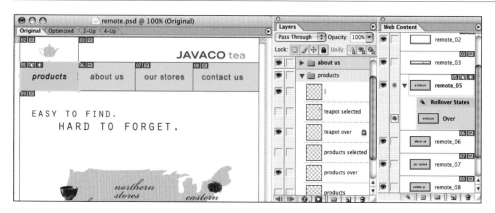

6. At the bottom of the **Web Content** palette, click the **remote_05** slice in the **Web Content** palette. Click the **Create Rollover State** button to create an **Over** state. With the **Over** state selected in the **Web Content** palette, turn off the visibility of the **products** layer in the **Layers** palette. Turn on the visibility of the **products over** and **teapot over** layers in the **Layers** palette.

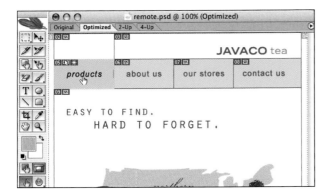

7. In the **Toolbox**, click the **Preview Document** button. Position your cursor over the word **products**.

*Notice the word **products** changes to the **Over** state, but you can't see the teapot icon above the word **products**. Remote rollovers require more than just turning on the visibility of the appropriate layer in the **Layers** palette to make them work. You'll learn how in the next steps.*

8. In the **Toolbox**, click the **Preview Document** button to exit the preview mode.

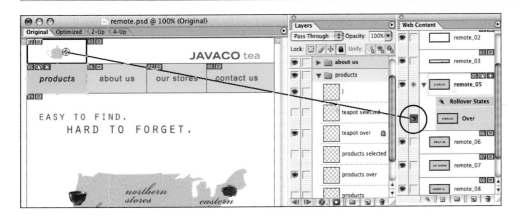

9. In the **Web Content** palette, click the **Over** state for the **remote_05** slice to select it. Click and drag the target icon next to the **Over** state onto **Slice 02**, as shown in the illustration here.

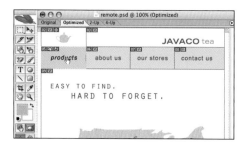

10. In the **Toolbox**, click the **Preview Document** button. Position your cursor over the word **products**.

*Notice this time, the teapot icon appears in the upper-left corner when you position your mouse over the word **products**. You've just learned how to create a remote rollover. Pretty easy, huh?*

11. In the **Toolbox**, click the **Preview Document** button to exit the preview mode.

12. Click the **Over** state for the **remote_05** slice in the **Web Content** palette to select it. At the bottom of the **Web Content** palette, click the **Create Rollover State** button to create a **Down** state.

*As you learned in previous exercises in this chapter, when you create a new state in the **Web Content** palette, it automatically takes on the properties of the previous state in the **Web Content** palette. Do you think the same will apply for remote rollover states?*

13. In the **Toolbox**, click the **Preview Document** button. Position your cursor over the word **products** to view the **Over** state. Click and hold to view the **Down** state.

*Notice when you click to invoke the **Down** state, the icon disappears, but the type remains the same as it was for the **Over** state. You've just learned a very important lesson. When you create a new state from an existing rollover state, it does not copy any remote states, such as the one in this example. If you want the remote state to be part of the new rollover state, you must specify it using the technique you learned in Step 9. Sound confusing? Follow the next few steps, and you'll understand.*

14. In the **Toolbox**, click the **Preview Document** button to exit the preview mode.

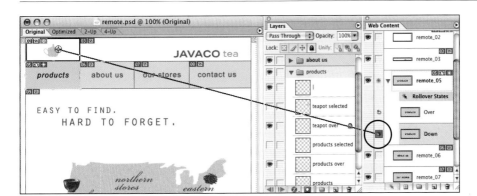

15. Click the **Down** state for the **remote_05** slice in the **Web Content** palette to select it. In the **Web Content** palette, click and drag the target icon next to the **Down** state onto **Slice 02**, as shown in the illustration here.

16. In the **Toolbox**, click the **Preview Document** button. Position your cursor over the word **products** to view the **Over** state. Click and hold the word **products** to view the **Down** state.

*As you can see, the remote state has now been applied to the **Down** state.*

17. In the **Toolbox**, click the **Preview Document** button to exit the preview mode.

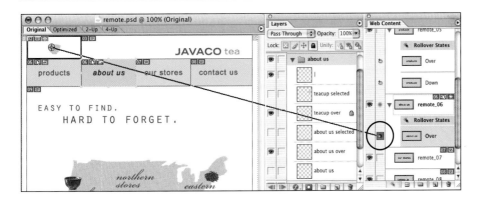

18. Click the **remote_06** slice in the **Web Content** palette to select it. Click the **Create Rollover State** button to create an **Over** state. With the **Over** state selected in the **Web Content** palette, turn off the visibility of the **about us** layer, and turn on the visibility of the **about us over** and **teacup over** layers in the **Layers** palette. In the **Web Content** palette, click and drag the target icon next to the **Over** state onto **Slice 02**, as shown in the illustration here.

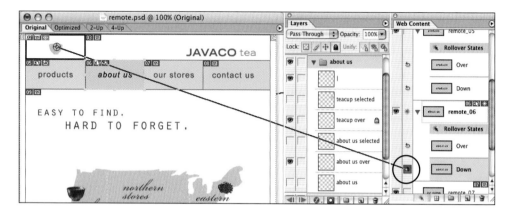

19. At the bottom of the **Web Content** palette, click the **Create Rollover State** button to create a **Down** state. With the **Down** state selected in the **Web Content** palette, click and drag the target icon next to the **Down** state onto **Slice 02**, as shown in the illustration here.

20. In the **Toolbox**, click the **Preview Document** button. Position your cursor over the words **about us** to view the **Over** state. Click the words **about us** to view the **Down** state. When you've finished, in the **Toolbox**, click the **Preview Document** button to exit the preview mode.

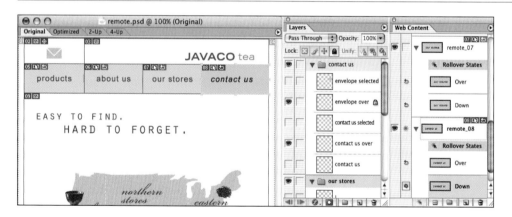

21. Repeat Steps 18 and 19 to create **Over** and **Down** states for the **remote_07** and **remote_08** slices in the **Web Content** palette. Make sure you use the appropriate layers from the **our stores** layer set (**about us over** and **tin over**) and the **contact us** layer set (**contact us over** and **envelope over**) to create the **Over** and **Down** states.

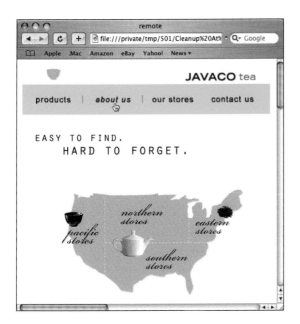

22. In the **Toolbox**, click the **Preview in Default Browser** button to view the results in a Web browser. Position your cursor over **products**, **about us**, **our stores**, and then **contact us** to view the **Over** states, then click and hold to view the **Down** states.

As you can see from this exercise, remote rollovers can be a very effective design element on your Web pages. And, ImageReady CS2 makes creating remote rollovers a snap!

23. Close the Web browser and return to ImageReady CS2. Leave **remote.psd** open for the next exercise.

In the next exercise, you'll take remote rollovers one step further and create remote rollovers for ***Selected*** *states.*

Creating Remote Rollovers with Selected States

In the last exercise, you learned how to create remote rollovers for Over states. In this exercise, you'll learn how to create remote rollovers for Selected states. In addition, you'll save the required HTML code and images for the pages.

1. If you followed the last exercise, **remote.psd** should still be open in ImageReady CS2. If it's not, go back and complete Exercise 6. Make sure the **Layers** palette and **Web Content** palette are visible. If they're not, choose **Window > Layers** and **Window > Web Content**.

2. Turn on the visibility of the **teapot selected** layer in the **products** layer set, the **teacup selected** layer in the **about us** layer set, the **tin selected** layer in the **our stores** layer set, and the **envelope selected** layer in the **contact us** layer set.

As you know from the last exercise, the purpose of turning on all four layers is to make sure you create a slice that contains all four layers. In this case, it's easy because all four layers share identical dimensions.

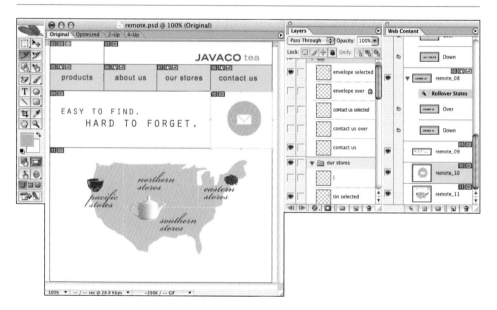

3. Select the **Slice** tool from the **Toolbox**. Create three additional user slices, as shown in the illustration here. Don't worry if the stacking order of the slices in the **Web Content** palette isn't identical to what you see here.

4. Turn off the visibility of the **teapot selected** layer in the **products** layer set, the **teacup selected** layer in the **about us** layer set, the **tin selected** layer in the **our stores** layer set, and the **envelope selected** layer in the **contact us** layer set.

5. In the **Web Content** palette, click the **Down** state of the **remote_05** slice to select it. At the bottom of the **Web Content** palette, click the **Create Rollover State** button to create a **Selected** state.

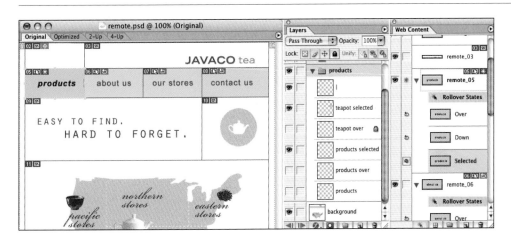

6. With the **Selected** state selected in the **Web Content** palette, turn off the visibility of the **products over** and **teapot over** layers in the **Layers** palette. Turn on the visibility of the **products selected** and **teapot selected** layer in the **products** layer set in the **Layers** palette.

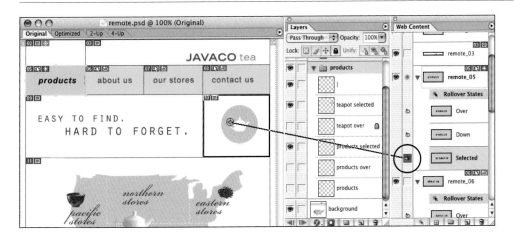

7. Click and drag the target icon next to the **Selected** state of the **remote_05** slice onto **Slice 10**, as shown in the illustration here.

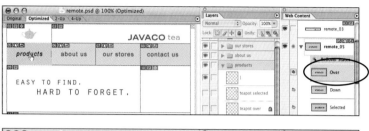

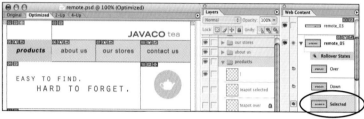

8. In the **Toolbox**, click the **Preview Document** button. Position your cursor over the word **products** to view the **Over** state. Click and hold to view the **Down** state. When you release your mouse, you'll see the **Selected** state.

---

9. In the **Toolbox**, click the **Preview Document** button to exit the preview mode.

---

10. In the **Web Content** palette, click the **Down** state of the **remote_06** slice to select it. At the bottom of the **Web Content** palette, click the **Create Rollover State** button to create a **Selected** state.

---

11. With the **Selected** state selected in the **Web Content** palette, turn off the visibility of the **about us** over and **teacup over** layers in the **about us** layer set. Turn on the visibility of the **about us selected** and **teacup selected** layers in the **about us** layer set.

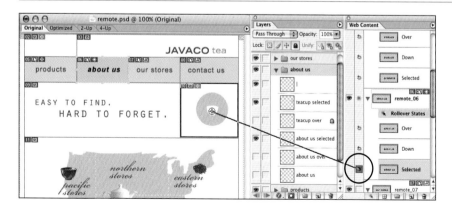

12. Click and drag the target icon next to the **Selected** state for the **remote_06** slice onto **Slice 10**, as shown in the illustration here.

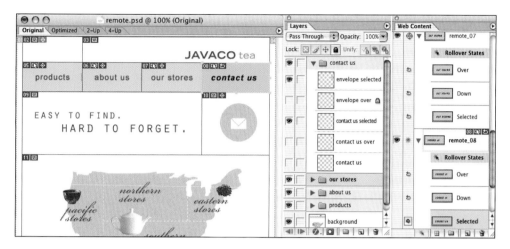

13. Repeat Steps 10,11, and 12 to create **Selected** states for the **remote_07** and **remote_08** slices in the **Web Content** palette. Make sure you use the appropriate layers from the **our stores** layer set (**about us selected** and **tin selected**) and the **contact us** layer set (**contact us selected** and **envelope selected**) to create the **Over** and **Down** states.

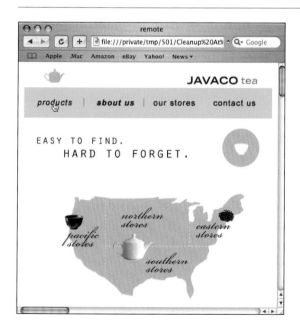

14. In the **Toolbox**, click the **Preview in Default Browser** button. Position your cursor over the words **products**, **about us**, **our stores**, and **contact us** to view the **Over** states. Click and hold to view the **Down** states. When you release your mouse, you'll see the **Selected** states.

15. When you've finished, close the Web browser and return to ImageReady CS2.

*Any time you create rollovers with **Selected** states, you need to generate more than just one HTML file—you must create one HTML file for each **Selected** state. Fortunately, ImageReady CS2 offers a helpful option to make this process quick and easy. You'll learn how in the following steps.*

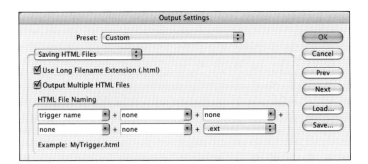

16. Choose **File > Output Settings > Saving HTML**. In the **Output Settings** dialog box, turn on the **Output Multiple HTML Files** option, and click **OK**.

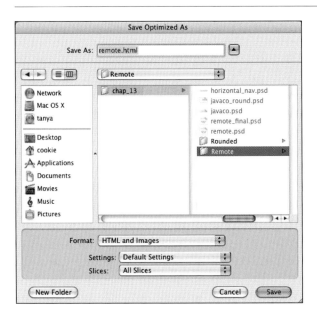

17. Choose **File > Save Optimized As**. In the **Save Optimized As** dialog box, navigate to the **chap_13** folder on your **Desktop**. Create a new folder called **Remote**. Choose **HTML and Images** from the **Format** pop-up menu. Click **Save** to save the multiple HTML files and images.

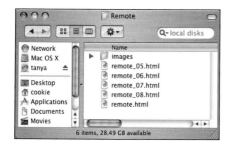

18. Browse to the **Remote** folder in the **chap_13** folder on your **Desktop**.

*Notice there are a number of HTML files—one for each of the slices with **Selected** states you created in this exercise. As you can see, by using the **Output Multiple HTML Files** option, you don't have to manually save each file from within ImageReady CS2.*

19. Double-click the **remote.html** file. Position your cursor over the words **products**, **about us**, **our stores**, and **contact us** to view the **Over** states. Click and hold to view the **Down** states. When you release your mouse, you'll see the **Selected** states.

Note: *If you look carefully at the address bar, you'll see the HTML file change from **remote.html** to **remote_05.html**, **remote_06.html**, **remote_07.html**, or **remote_08.html**, depending on which **Selected** state is currently active.*

20. Return to ImageReady CS2. Close **remote.psd**. You don't need to save your changes.

8. [IR]_____Creating Animated Rollovers

In ImageReady CS2, you can create animated rollovers. If you've never created an animated rollover in ImageReady CS2 before, you may find this process a bit peculiar. Not to worry, the steps in this exercise will make more sense once you've finished the entire exercise. Note: Although Photoshop CS2 now supports animation, you must use ImageReady CS2 to create animated rollovers because Photoshop CS2 doesn't allow you to create rollovers.

1. Open **animated.psd** from the **chap_13** folder you copied to your **Desktop**. Make sure the **Layers** palette, the **Web Content** palette, and the **Animation** palette are visible. If they're not, choose **Window > Layers**, **Window > Web Content**, and **Window > Animation**.

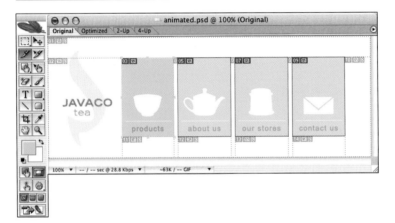

2. Select the **Slice** tool from the **Toolbox**. Click and drag to create four user slices, as shown in the illustration here.

3. In the **Web Content** palette, click the **animated_03** slice to select it. At the bottom of the **Web Content** palette, click the **Create Rollover State** button to create an **Over** state.

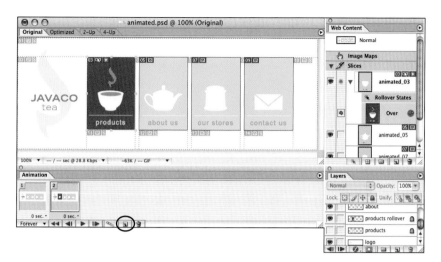

4. With the **Over** state selected in the **Web Content** palette, at the bottom of the **Animation** palette click the **Duplicate Current Frame** button. With **Frame 2** selected in the **Animation** palette, turn off the visibility of the **products** layer, and turn on the visibility of the **products rollover** layer.

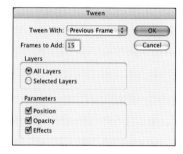

5. At the bottom of the **Animation** palette, click the **Tween** button to open the **Tween** dialog box. Match the settings in the **Tween** dialog box to the ones shown in the illustration here. Click **OK**.

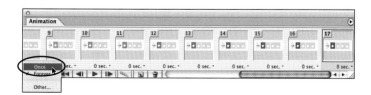

6. Choose **Once** from the **Looping** pop-up menu.

Because this animation will appear as part of the navigation for a Web page, you want to limit the looping to once; otherwise it will be annoying for your viewers.

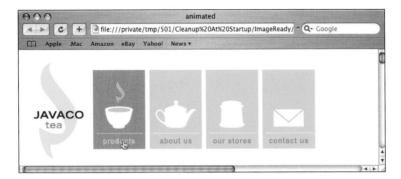

7. In the **Toolbox**, click the **Preview in Default Browser** button. Position your cursor over the **products** button to view the animated rollover. Pretty cool!

8. Close the Web browser and return to Image Ready CS2.

9. With the **Over** state still selected in the **Web Content** palette, click the **Create Rollover State** button to create a **Down** state.

*Notice when you create the **Down** state, the animation does not copy from the **Over** state to the **Down** state. If you want the animation to play again on the **Down** state you have to re-create it. Animation is something you should use minimally because it can easily distract from your main message. For this reason, you'll leave the **Down** state as it is—without any animation.*

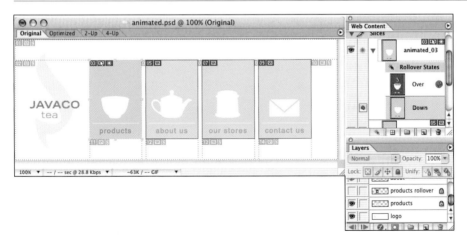

10. With the **Down** state selected in the **Web Content** palette, turn off the visibility of the **products rollover** layer, and turn on the visibility of the **products** layer in the **Layers** palette.

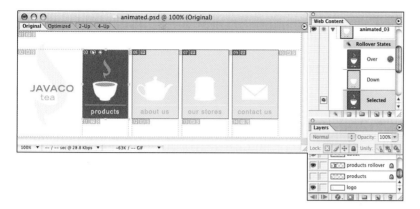

11. With the **Down** state still selected in the **Web Content** palette, click the **Create Rollover Button** to create a **Selected** state. Turn off the visibility of the **products** layer, and turn on the visibility of the **products rollover** layer in the **Layers** palette.

12. In the **Toolbox**, click the **Preview in Default Browser** button.

13. Position your cursor over the products button to view the animated **Over** state. Click and hold to view the **Down** state. When you release your mouse, you'll see the **Selected** state.

14. Close the Web browser and return to ImageReady CS2.

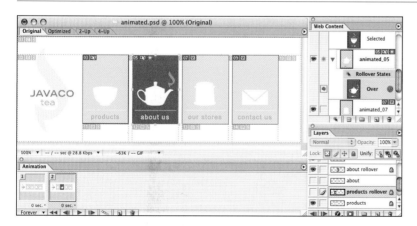

15. In the **Web Content** palette, click the **animated_05** slice. At the bottom of the **Web Content** palette, click the **Create Rollover State** button to create an **Over** state. With the **Over** state selected in the **Web Content** palette, at the bottom of the **Animation** palette click the **Duplicate Current Frame** button. With **Frame 2** selected in the **Animation** palette, turn off the visibility of the **about** layer, and turn on the visibility of the **about rollover** layer in the **Layers** palette.

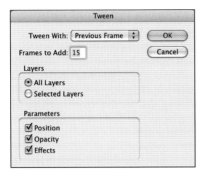

16. At the bottom of the **Animation** palette, click the **Tween** button to open the **Tween** dialog box. Match the settings to the ones shown in the illustration here. Click **OK**. Choose **Once** from the **Looping** pop-up menu at the bottom of the **Animation** palette.

17. With the **Over** state selected in the **Web Content** palette, at the bottom of the **Web Content** palette click the **Create Rollover State** button to create a **Down** state.

18. With the **Down** state selected in the **Web Content** palette, turn off the visibility of the **about rollover** layer, and turn on the visibility of the **about** layer in the **Layers** palette.

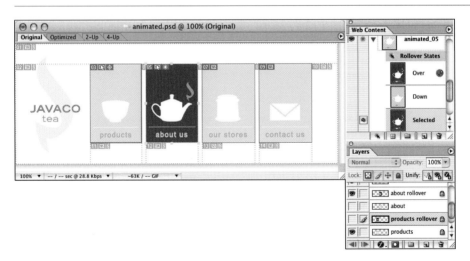

19. With the **Down** state selected in the **Web Content** palette, at the bottom of the **Web Content** palette click the **Create Rollover State** button to create a **Selected** state. Turn off the visibility of the **about** layer, and turn on the visibility of the **about rollover** layer in the **Layers** palette.

*Notice the only rollover state with an animation is the **Over** state.*

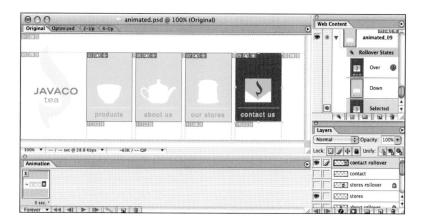

20. Repeat Steps 15 through 19 to create **Over**, **Down**, and **Selected** states for the **animated_07** and **animated_09** slices. Make sure you use the appropriate layers in the **Layers** palette—the **stores** layer and the **stores rollover** layer for the **animated_07** slice, and the **contact** layer and the **contact rollover** layer for the **animated_09** slice.

21. When you've finished, in the **Toolbox**, click the **Preview in Default Browser** button. Position your mouse over each of the buttons to view the animated **Over** states. Click and hold each of the buttons to view the **Down** states. When you release your mouse, you'll see the **Selected** states.

As you can see from this exercise, ImageReady CS2 gives you a lot of flexibilty to create animated rollovers. Keep in mind, animation should be used minimally and tastefully when you design Web sites—so don't get carried away!

22. Close the Web browser and return to ImageReady CS2. Close **animated.psd**. You don't need to save your changes.

You've just finished an exceptionally complex chapter! In this chapter, you learned to create different kinds of rollovers in ImageReady CS2. You'll use these skills again and again when you design your own Web graphics. In the next chapter, "Creating Image Maps," you'll learn how to create image maps in ImageReady CS2.

14

Creating Image Maps

| Creating an Image Map with the Image Map Tools |
| Creating an Image Map from Layers |
| Renaming, Optimizing, and Saving Image Maps |
| Assigning URLs and Applying Alt Text To Image Maps |
| Creating Image Map-Based Rollovers |

chap_14

PCS2Web HOT CD-ROM

Most buttons and navigation bars on Web pages are composed of individual images that link to individual URLs. When you're designing Web graphics, you'll often want one image to link to multiple URLs. For example, if you have a map of the United States, you may want each state to link to a different URL. With image maps, you can create multiple links from a single graphic.

In the past, you had to create image maps in HTML editors or special-ized image map editing software. Fortunately, ImageReady CS2 makes it easy to create image maps without the need for other applications. In this chapter, you'll learn different techniques for creating image maps in ImageReady CS2. Although you can't create image maps in Photoshop CS2, you can open an image map created in ImageReady CS2 in Photoshop CS2 and still keep the image map information. The next time you open the image map in ImageReady CS2, the image map information will remain as part of the document.

Server-Side and Client-Side Image Maps

There are two types of image maps—server-side image maps and client-side image maps. In the early days of the Web, it was only possible to create server-side image maps. Today, server-side image maps are no longer used due to the difficulty involved in creating them, the extra bandwidth required to load them, and because server-side image maps do not meet current accessibility recommendations. As a result, this chapter will only focus on creating client-side image maps.

In this chapter, you'll learn different techniques for creating client-side image maps, including creating image maps with the Image Map tool, creating image maps from layers, creating image maps from type layers, and creating rollovers from image maps.

NOTE | Creating Server-Side Image Maps in ImageReady CS2

This chapter focuses on creating client-side image maps in ImageReady CS2. If you need to create server-side image maps in ImageReady CS2, here's how:

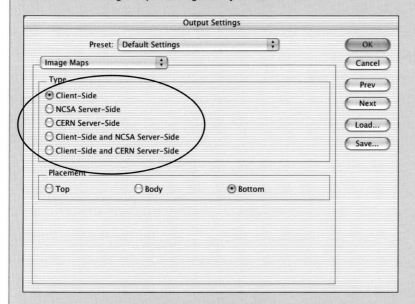

In ImageReady CS2, choose **File > Output Settings > Image Maps**. The **Output Settings** dialog box opens automatically. In the **Type** section of the **Output Settings** dialog box, choose the type of server-side image map you want to create. When you build server-side image maps in ImageReady CS2, the program will create an HTML file, an image file, and a separate map definition file, which you'll store on the Web server.

What Does an Image Map Look Like?

The required HTML code for client-side image maps contains **map** and **usemap** tags, plus the coordinates for the image map regions. The coordinates plot the dimensions and location of the hot spots in an image map.

What's a hot spot? A **hot spot** is a clickable area on a Web page that links to another Web page. Moving your cursor over a hot spot changes the cursor to a hand, which indicates you can click on it and link to another Web page.

Here is an example of an image map (a single graphic containing more than one clickable area—one for each region of the United States), including the required HTML code created in ImageReady CS2.

*In the HTML code, you can see the two types of **area shape** elements (**poly** [polygon] and **circle**), **coords** (coordinates), and a series of comma-separated numbers. The numbers describe the coordinates of the hot spots around each shape.*

Creating Image Maps in ImageReady CS2

Creating image maps in ImageReady CS2 is a snap! There are two ways to create image maps in ImageReady CS2. You can use the image map tools, or you can create image maps from layers.

There are four image map tools in ImageReady CS2. Here's a handy chart to help you understand them:

Image Map Tools in ImageReady CS2	
Tool	Description
Rectangle Image Map tool	Use to create a rectangular image map.
Circle Image Map tool	Use to create a circular image map.
Polygon Image Map tool	Use to create an irregularly shaped image map.
Image Map Select tool	Use to select an image map.

About the Web Content and Image Map Palettes

When you're working with image maps in ImageReady CS2, you'll need to access the Web Content palette and the Image Map palette. Here is an overview of the palettes and their roles in the image map creation process.

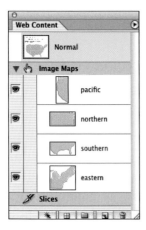

With the Web Content palette, you can preview the image maps in an image. Similar to the Layers palette, the Web Content palette displays a thumbnail preview of the image map and lets you turn on and off the visibility of an image map. The Web Content palette also displays information about slices and rollovers, which you learned about in Chapter 12, "*Slicing*," and Chapter 13, "*Creating Rollovers*."

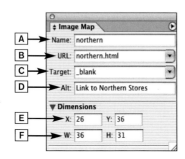
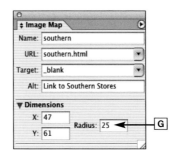

In the Image Map palette, you can specify different options for image maps. It is context-sensitive and changes depending on the current image map. If you're working with a tool-based image map, the palette displays dimension information. If you're working with a layer-based image map, it displays layer-based settings. Here's a handy chart to help you understand the controls in the Image Map palette:

Image Map Palette Controls		
A	Name field	Specify a name for the currently selected image map.
B	URL pop-up menu	Specify a URL you want the currently selected image map to link to.
C	Target pop-up menu	Choose one of the following target types when you specify a URL for an image map: _blank, _self, _parent, or _top.
D	Alt field	Specify the text you want viewers to see when images are turned off in a Web browser.
E	X and Y Coordinates fields	Specify the left edge (X) and top edge (Y) of an image map.
F	Width and Height fields (available only for image maps created with the Rectangle Image Map tool and the Polygon Image Map tool)	Specify the width and height of an image map.
G	Radius field (available only for image maps created with the Circle Image Map tool)	Specify the radius of an image map area.
H	Shape pop-up menu (available only for layer-based image maps)	Specify the shape of an image map area (rectangle, circle, or polygon).
I	Quality pop-up menu (available only for the polygonal layer-based image maps)	Specify the accuracy of polygon vertices.

I. [IR] _____Creating an Image Map with the Image Map Tools

Using the image map tools is the best way to create image maps when you're working with flattened images or images on a single layer. In this exercise, you'll learn how to create and modify an image map with the image map tools.

1. Open **our_stores.psd** from the **chap_14** folder you copied to your **Desktop**. Make sure the **Web Content** palette and the **Image Map** palette are visible. If they're not, choose **Window > Web Content** and **Window > Image Map**.

Because the map in this image is on a single layer, you'll use the image map tools to create an image map and its associated hot spots. If the image was separated into layers, you'd have the option to create the image map from the image map tools or from layers, which you'll learn about in the next exercise.

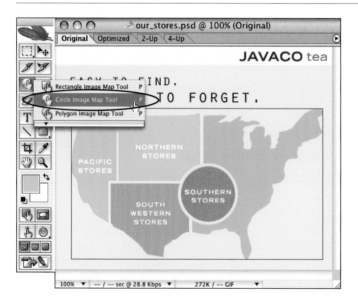

2. Select the **Circle Image Map** tool from the **Toolbox**.

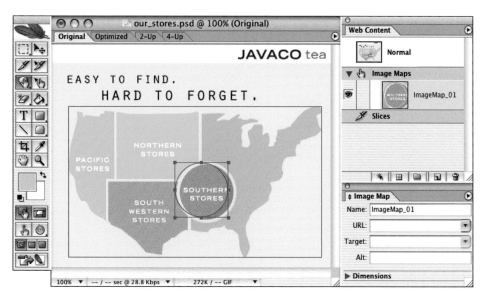

3. Click and drag over the **Southern Stores** graphic to create a circular image map.

*Tip: To draw a circular image map from the center out, hold down the **Option** (Mac) or **Alt** (Windows) key while dragging.*

*Notice that when you create an image map, it automatically appears in the **Image Maps** section of the* **Web Content** *palette. Also, notice that the image map is automatically given the name **ImageMap_01**, which is reflected both in the **Web Content** palette and in the **Name** section of the **Image Map** palette. You'll learn how to rename image maps later in this chapter.*

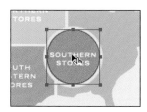

4. Position your cursor inside the circle you created in the last step. Notice that when you position your cursor inside the circle it changes to the **Image Map Selection** tool. Click and drag to reposition the image map directly over the circle in the map. Alternately, you can use the arrow keys on your keyboard to nudge it into place.

NOTE | Resizing Image Maps

If you create an image map with one of the image map tools, you can resize it easily. Here's how:

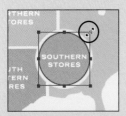

With one of the image map tools selected in the **Toolbox**, position your mouse over one of the nodes on the perimeter of the image map. You'll notice the cursor change from the **image map** cursor to the **resize** cursor. When the cursor changes to the resize cursor, click and drag to resize the image map.

5. In the **Toolbox**, click the **Preview in Default Browser** button. In the Web browser, position your cursor over the **Southern Stores** graphic.

*Notice that the cursor changes to a hand, indicating the image is a hot spot. If you take a look at the HTML code, you'll see the code that makes up the image map. The coordinates indicate the hot spot area you created in this exercise using the **Circle Image Map** tool.*

---

6. Return to Image Ready CS2.

*Next, you'll use the **Polygon Image Map** tool to create an image map for the other regions on the map.*

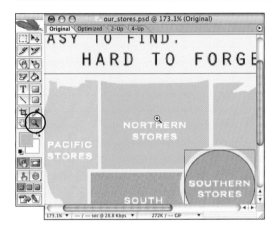

7. Select the **Zoom** tool from the **Toolbox**. Click and drag around the **Northern Stores** graphic so you can accurately see the edges. Zooming in will make it easier for you to work with the **Polygon Image Map** tool.

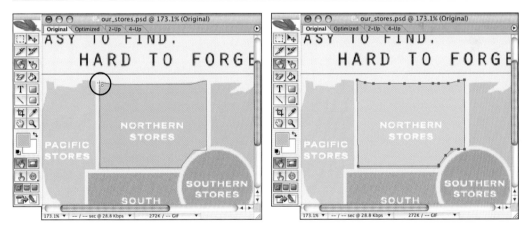

8. Select the **Polygon Image Map** tool from the **Toolbox**. Click the upper-left corner of the **Northern Stores** graphic. Click and drag your cursor around the border of the graphic, clicking when you need to create a contour in the line. When you finish outlining the shape, position your cursor over the spot in the upper-left corner where you began. When the cursor changes to a small circle, click to close the path.

*You may find the **Polygon Image Map** tool difficult to work with. If you don't draw the shape perfectly, don't worry. You'll learn how to adjust the shape in the next step.*

9. With the **Polygon Image Map** tool still selected in the **Toolbox**, position your mouse over one of the nodes on the path. When the cursor changes to the white arrow and white hand, click and drag the node into position.

As you can see, you can simply reposition the nodes to adjust the shape.

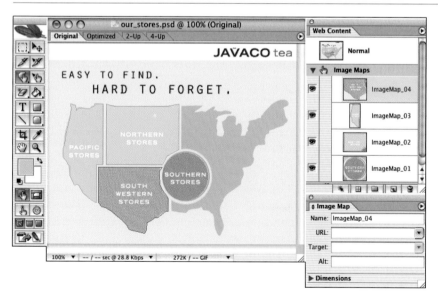

10. Using the **Polygon Image Map** tool, create image map areas for the **Pacific Stores** and **Southwestern Stores** graphics, as shown in the illustration here.

```
Format: GIF
Dimensions: 432w x 334h
Size: 12.44K
Settings: Selective, 256 Colors, 100% Diffusion Dither, Transparency on, No Transparency Dither, Non-Interlaced, 0% Web Snap


<html>
<head>
<title>our_stores</title>
<meta http-equiv="Content-Type" content="text/html; charset=iso-8859-1">
</head>
<body bgcolor="#FFFFFF" leftmargin="0" topmargin="0" marginwidth="0" marginheight="0">
<!-- ImageReady Slices (our_stores.psd) -->
<img src="images/our_stores.gif" width="432" height="334" border="0" alt="" usemap="#our_stores_Map">
<map name="our_stores_Map">
<area shape="poly" alt="" coords="211,279, 205,280, 199,283, 196,286, 191,289, 187,289, 182,292, 180,295, 178,296, 1
<area shape="poly" alt="" coords="96,103, 83,99, 82,99, 80,104, 74,109, 60,107, 51,107, 48,103, 40,99, 40,115, 30,15
<area shape="poly" alt="" coords="102,103, 117,104, 199,104, 213,103, 227,100, 227,175, 218,180, 209,187, 202,195, 1
<area shape="circle" alt="" coords="240,221,41" href="#">
</map>
<!-- End ImageReady Slices -->
</body>
</html>
```

11. In the **Toolbox**, click the **Preview in Default Browser** button. Position your cursor over each area of the map.

*Notice there are now four hot spots in the image—one for **Southern Stores**, one for **Northern Stores**, one for **Southwestern Stores**, and one for **Pacific Stores**.*

12. Return to ImageReady CS2. Close **our_stores.psd**. You don't need to save your changes.

Next, you'll learn how to create layer-based image maps. Later in this chapter, you'll learn how to rename, optimize, and save image maps.

2. [IR]——————Creating an Image Map from Layers

In the last exercise, you learned how to create image maps with the image map tools. In this exercise, you'll learn how to create image maps from layers. Layer-based images are a great way to create image maps because they create hot spots the same size as the layer. Creating image maps from layers is often easier than using the image map tools to trace around the edges of irregularly shaped images because layer-based image maps match the exact size and shape of the layer. Plus, if you change the contents of a layer or move a layer, the image map updates automatically.

1. Open **javaco_stores.psd** from the **chap_14** folder you copied to your **Desktop**. Make sure the **Layers** palette, the **Web Content** palette, and the **Image Map** palette are visible. If they're not, choose **Window > Layers, Window > Web Content**, and **Window > Image Map**.

*Notice each region on the map is on a separate layer–**eastern, southern, northern,** and **pacific**.*

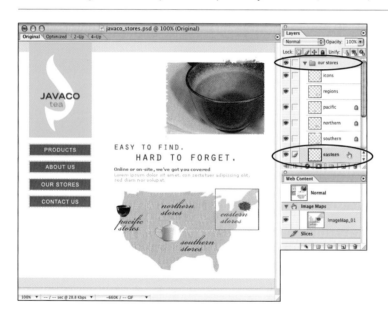

2. In the **Layers** palette, click the arrow to expand the contents of the **our stores** layer set. Click the **eastern** layer to select it. Choose **Layer > New Layer Based Image Map Area**.

*Notice the hand symbol to the right of the **eastern** layer name in the **Layers** palette. The hand symbol indicates the **eastern** layer has an image map associated with it. Also notice, just like when you created an image map with the image map tools in the last exercise, when you create a layer-based image map area, it automatically appears in the **Image Maps** section of the **Web Content** palette, and it is automatically given a name–in this case, **ImageMap_01**. You'll learn how to rename image maps in the next exercise.*

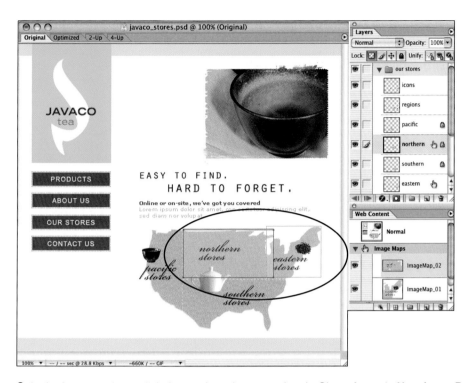

3. In the **Layers** palette, click the **northern** layer to select it. Chose **Layer > New Layer Based Image Map Area**.

Notice that you have a conflict with the image maps—they overlap! By default, layer-based image maps are rectangular. Not to worry, you can easily fix this issue.

4. Select the **Image Map Select** tool from the **Toolbox**. Click the image map you created for the **eastern** layer to select it.

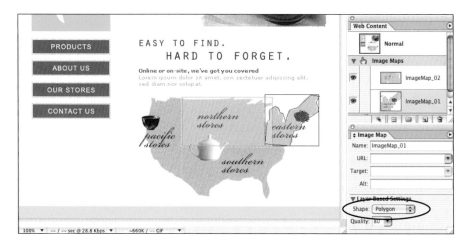

5. Click the arrow to expand the contents of the **Layer Based Settings** section of the **Image Map** palette. Choose **Polygon** from the **Shape** pop-up menu.

Notice the edges of the image map automatically take the shape of the layer. Although it mostly covers the entire layer, there are still a few areas that aren't part of the image map. You'll fix that in the next step.

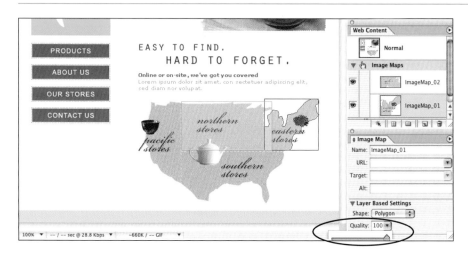

6. In the **Image Map** palette, set the **Quality** to **100** using the **Quality** slider.

Notice the image map now perfectly hugs the edges of the layer. Pretty cool!

7. With the **Image Map Select** tool still selected in the **Toolbox**, click the image map you created for the **northern stores** section of the map. Choose **Polygon** from the **Shape** pop-up menu, and set the **Quality** to **100** in the **Layer Based Settings** section of the **Image Map** palette.

8. Using the techniques you learned in this exercise, create layer-based image maps areas for the **southern** and **pacific** layers in the **Layers** palette. Be sure to change the shape to **Polygon** and adjust the **Quality** to **100%** so the image map accurately hugs the edges of the layer.

9. In the **Toolbox**, click the **Preview in Default Browser** button. Notice that your cursor changes to the hand when you position it over each geographic region on the map.

10. Return to ImageReady CS2. In the **Layers** palette, click the **pacific** layer to select it. Select the **Move** tool from the **Toolbox**. Click and drag to reposition the layer, as shown in the illustration here.

Notice the image map area moves with the layer.

11. In the **Toolbox**, click the **Preview in Default Browser** button. Position your cursor over the **pacific stores** region. Notice the cursor changes to the hand, indicating it is a link.

Just like layer-based slices, layer-based image map areas update automatically when you move or resize the contents of a layer. As you can see, when you're working with a layered file, such as the one in this exercise, you'll find it most beneficial to work with layer-based image maps.

12. Return to ImageReady CS2. Press **Cmd+ Z** (Mac) or **Ctrl+Z** (Windows) to undo the move you made in Step 10.

13. Leave **javaco_stores.psd** open for the next exercise.

3. [IR] _____ Renaming, Optimizing, and Saving Image Maps

In the last two exercises, you learned how to create image maps by using the image map tools and by creating layer-based image map areas. Next, you'll learn how to rename, optimize, and save image maps, including the required HTML code to make the image map work in a Web browser.

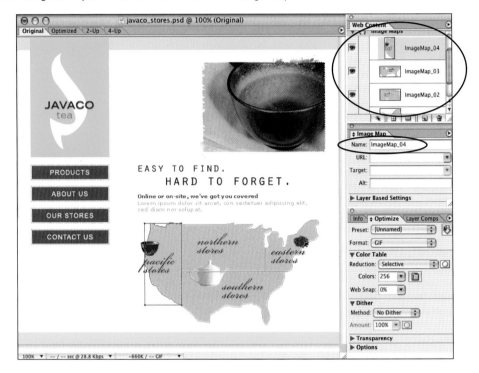

1. If you followed the last exercise, **javaco_stores.psd** should still be open in Image Ready CS2. If it's not, go back and complete Exercise 2. Make sure the **Web Content** palette, **Image Map** palette, and **Optimize** palette are visible. If they're not, choose **Window > Web Content**, **Window > Image Map**, and **Window > Optimize**.

_Take a look at the names for the image map areas in the **Web Content** palette. Notice they all have generic names—**ImageMap_01**, **ImageMap_02**, **ImageMap_03**, and **ImageMap_04**. ImageReady CS2 automatically generated these names when you created the image map areas. Regardless of whether you create image maps using the image map tools or create layer-based image map areas, ImageReady CS2 will generate these generic names. In the next steps, you'll learn how to rename them. The image map names are important because they will help you identify them in the HTML code._

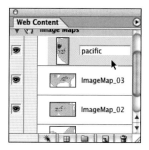

2. In the **Web Content** palette, double-click the **ImageMap_04** image map name. When the bounding box appears, type **pacific**, and press **Return** (Mac) or **Enter** (Windows).

Notice when you press ***Return*** *(Mac) or* ***Enter*** *(Windows) the image map name updates in the* ***Web Content*** *palette and in the* ***Name*** *field of the* ***Image Map*** *palette.*

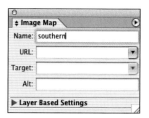

3. In the **Web Content** palette, click **ImageMap_03** to select it. Type **southern** in the **Name** field of the **Image Map** palette, and press **Return** (Mac) or **Enter** (Windows).

4. Using the techniques you learned in Steps 2 and 3, rename **ImageMap_02** to **northern** and **ImageMap_01** to **eastern**.

Next, you'll optimize and save the image map.

5. Click the **Optimized** tab in the document window. Using the techniques you learned in Chapter 7, "*Optimizing Images*," specify appropriate optimization settings in the **Optimize** palette. In the **Toolbox**, click the **Image Maps Visibility** button so you can accurately see the optimization settings.

Note: You can only specify one optimization setting for the entire image map, so make sure you're happy with the optimization settings for the entire image map, not just one area.

6. Choose **File > Save Optimized As**. In the **Save Optimized As** dialog box, navigate to the **chap_14** folder you copied to your **Desktop**. Create a new folder called **javaco_stores**. Choose **HTML and Images** from the **Format** pop-up menu. Click **Save**.

Note: You don't have to save the HTML code with the image map. If you prefer, you can choose Images from the Format pop-up menu and create the HTML code in an HTML editor such as Adobe GoLive or Macromedia Dreamweaver. The choice is yours, but it's easiest to let ImageReady CS2 create the code.

7. Browse to the **javaco_stores** folder in the **chap_14** folder you copied to your **Desktop**.

*Notice the folder contains the **javaco_stores.html** file, which contains the code required to make the image map work in a Web browser. Notice the **images** folder contains only one image. Even though the image map is divided into four image map areas, only one image is required to make the image map work in a Web browser.*

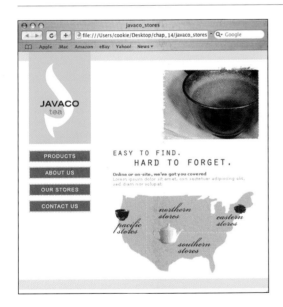

8. Double-click **javaco_stores.html** to open the file in a Web browser. Position your cursor over each region of the map.

Notice the cursor changes to a hand, indicating a hot spot or a clickable area.

9. Close the Web browser and return to ImageReady CS2. Leave **javaco_stores.psd** open for the next exercise.

4. [IR] _____Assigning URLs and Applying Alt Text to Image Maps

Now that you've learned how to create, rename, optimize, and save image maps, it's time to learn how to assign URLs and apply alt text to image map areas.

1. If you followed the last exercise , **javaco_stores.psd** should still be open in ImageReady CS2. If it's not, go back and complete Exercise 3. Make sure the **Web Content** palette and **Image Map** palette are visible. If they're not, choose **Window > Web Content** and **Window > Image Map**.

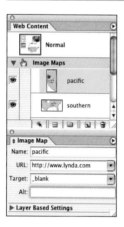

2. In the **Web Content** palette, click the **pacific** image map area to select it. In the **Image Map** palette, type **http://www.lynda.com** (or type a URL of your choice) in the **URL** field. Choose **_blank** from the **Target** field.

*Choosing the **_blank** option will open the link in a new browser window.*

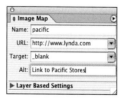

3. In the **Image Map** palette, type **Link to Pacific Stores** in the **Alt** field.

As you know from Chapter 12, "Slicing," alt text shows in a Web browser if the user turns off images in the Preferences or if they are accessing Web pages with a text-only Web browser. Some viewers turn off images when they surf the Web to speed up the downloading process. Sight-impaired visitors use screen-reading software to "read" the alt text to them out loud.

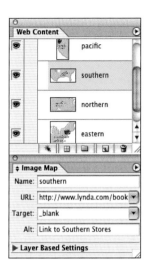

4. In the **Web Content** palette, click the **southern** image map area to select it. In the **Image Map** palette, type **http://www.lynda.com/books** (or type a URL of your choice) in the **URL** field. Choose **_blank** from the **Target** field. Type **Link to Southern Stores** in the **Alt** field.

5. In the **Web Content** palette, click the **northern** image map area to select it. In the **Image Map** palette, type **http://www.lynda.com** (or type a URL of your choice) in the **URL** field. Choose _blank from the **Target** field. Type **Link to Northern Stores** in the **Alt** field.

6. In the **Web Content** palette, click the **eastern** image map area to select it. In the **Image Map** palette, type **http://www.lynda.com/books** (or type a URL of your choice) in the **URL** field. Choose **_blank** from the **Target** field. Type **Link to Eastern Stores** in the **Alt** field.

7. In the **Toolbox**, click the **Preview in Default Browser** button.

8. Position your cursor over the areas of the image map.

Notice the cursor changes to the hand, which indicates a hot spot or a clickable area. If you like, click on the hot spots to open up the URLs you specified in Steps 2 through 6.

9. Return to ImageReady CS2. Close **javaco_stores.psd**. You don't need to save your changes.

5. [IR] _____Creating Image Map-Based Rollovers

In Chapter 13, *"Creating Rollovers,"* you learned how to create rollovers from slices. You can also create rollovers from image maps. You use this technique when the shape triggering the rollover is not a rectangle or a square (slice-based rollovers can only be created from rectangles and squares). Here's an exercise to show you how.

1. Open **stores.psd** from the **chap_14** folder you copied to your **Desktop**. Make sure the **Layers** palette, the **Web Content** palette, and the **Image Map** palette are visible. If they're not, choose **Window > Layers, Window > Web Content**, and **Window > Image Map**.

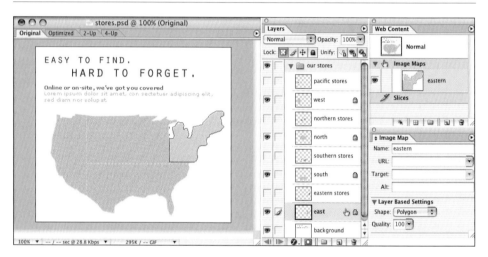

2. In the **Layers** palette, click the arrow to expand the contents of the **our stores** layer set (if it's not expanded already). In the **Layers** palette, click the **east** layer to select it. Choose **Layer > New Layer Based Image Map Area**. In the **Image Map** palette, type **eastern** in the **Name** field, choose **Polygon** from the **Shape** pop-up menu of the **Layer Based Settings** section, and set the **Quality** to **100**.

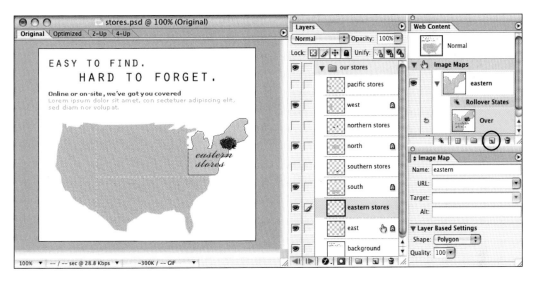

3. With the **eastern** image map area selected in the **Web Content** palette, click the **Create Rollover State** button to create an **Over** state. With the **Over** state selected, turn on the visibility of the **eastern stores** layer in the **Layers** palette.

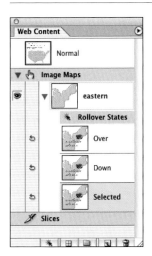

4. With the **Over** state selected in the **Web Content** palette, click the **Create Rollover State** button to create a **Down** state. With the **Down** state selected, click the **Create Rollover State** button to create a **Selected** state.

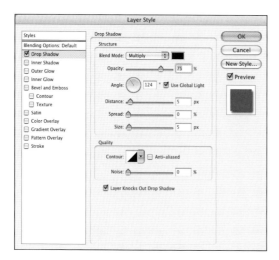

5. With the **Selected** state selected in the **Web Content** palette, and the **eastern stores** layer selected in the **Layers** palette, choose **Drop Shadow** from the **Layer Styles** pop-up menu at the bottom of the **Layers** palette. In the **Layer Style** dialog box, match the settings to the ones shown in the illustration here. Click **OK**.

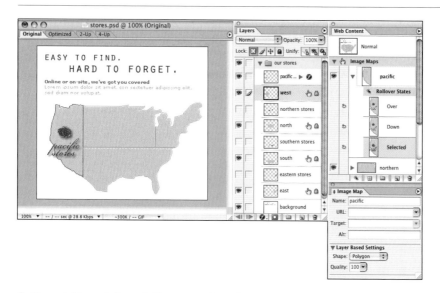

6. Repeat Steps 2 through 5 to create layer-based image map areas and rollovers with **Over**, **Down**, and **Selected** states. Be sure to name the image map areas correctly (**southern**, **northern**, and **pacific**) and to turn on the visibility of the appropriate layers for the rollovers states (**southern stores** for the **south** image map area, **northern stores** for the **north** image map area, and **pacific stores** for the **pacific** image map area).

7. In the **Toolbox**, click the **Preview in Default Browser** button. Position your cursor over the image map areas to view the **Over** states. Click to view the **Down** states (which are the same as the **Over** states). When you release your mouse, you'll see the **Selected** states.

As you can see, you're combining the knowledge you acquired in Chapter 13, "Creating Rollovers," with the skills you learned in this chapter.

Note: *Although you created rollover-based image maps from layer-based image map areas in this exercise, you can also create rollover-based image maps using the image map tools. Aside from the process of creating the image map areas, the process for creating rollover-based image maps is identical to what you learned in this exercise.*

8. Close the Web browser and return to ImageReady CS2. If you'd like, use the techniques you learned in Exercises 3 and 4 to optimize and save the images and HTML, assign URLs, and apply alt text.

You've just finished another chapter! Creating image maps is fairly simple once you get the hang of it. Up next, you'll learn how to create Web Photo Galleries.

15

Creating Web
Photo Galleries

| Creating a Web Photo Gallery |
| Customizing a Web Photo Gallery |
| Creating a Collaborative Web Photo Gallery |

chap_15

PCS2Web HOT CD-ROM

The Web Photo Gallery feature in Photoshop CS2 lets you take a folder of images and publish them easily as a Web page. This feature automatically optimizes the images and writes the required HTML code without you having to write a line of code. The Web Photo Gallery feature is a quick and easy way for anyone to display their work; for architects to show renderings to clients, for photographers to display proofs, or for families to share personal photos on the Web. You can also use one of the feedback templates, which provides an interface for clients and contacts to approve and comment on images in a Web Photo Gallery, without having to do any complicated programming! In this chapter, you'll learn how to create a Web Photo Gallery and you'll learn how to customize Web Photo Galleries to suit your unique needs.

Understanding Web Photo Galleries

New to Photoshop CS2, you can now create a Web Photo Gallery directly from Adobe Bridge. Adobe Bridge is an excellent interface for creating a Web Photo Gallery because it lets you preview and organize images before you create the Web Photo Gallery. This will save you time spent opening and editing images.

You can customize Web Photo Galleries using several appearance options. In this example, I created a Web Photo Gallery using the **Centered Frame 1 – Feedback** style. The feedback styles allow others to approve and comment on images in a Web Photo Gallery without any extra programming required. In an upcoming exercise, you'll learn how easy it is to create, customize, and use the feedback styles with the Web Photo Gallery feature in Photoshop CS2.

When you create a Web Photo Gallery, Photoshop CS2 performs the following tasks automatically:

- Copies, resizes, and optimizes the images
- Creates thumbnails of the images
- Writes the required HTML code for the Web site
- Includes file information you specify, such as the filename, who created the image, a description of the file, and copyright information
- Generates Next, Previous, and Home buttons to help you navigate around the Web page

Photoshop CS2 provides numerous options for customizing your Web Photo Gallery. You'll learn about these options in the next two exercises. If you want to make further modifications to your Web Photo Gallery, you can edit the files in an HTML editor, such as Adobe GoLive or Macromedia Dreamweaver.

I. [PS] _____Creating a Web Photo Gallery

In this exercise, you'll learn how to create a Web Photo Gallery in Photoshop CS2 using images provided on the **PCS2Web HOT CD-ROM**. When you've finished the exercise, try it on a folder of your own images. You'll be amazed at how easy it is to create an entire Web site with minimal effort!

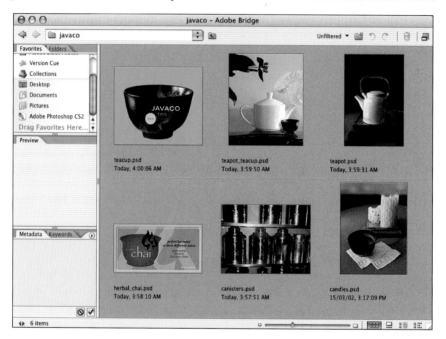

1. In Photoshop CS2, choose **File > Browse** to open **Adobe Bridge**. Navigate to the **javaco** folder in the **chap_15** folder you copied to your **Desktop**. You'll see six images in the **javaco** folder inside the Adobe Bridge **Preview Panel**.

2. Choose **Tools > Photoshop > Web Photo Gallery** to open the **Web Photo Gallery** dialog box.

Tip: _You can also open the **Web Photo Gallery** dialog box by choosing **File > Automate > Web Photo Gallery** from Photoshop CS2. I prefer to access the Web Photo Gallery feature from Adobe Bridge because it's a more visual interface and lets me preview and organize my images before creating a Web Photo Gallery._

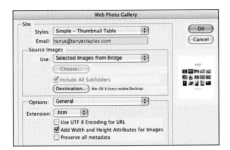

3. Choose **Simple – Thumbnail Table** from the **Styles** pop-up menu. In the **Email** field, type an e-mail address. Choose **Selected Images from Bridge** from the **Use** pop-up menu.

4. Click the **Destination** button. In the **Select a destination location** dialog box, navigate to the **simple** folder in the **chap_15** folder you copied to your **Desktop**. Click **Choose** (Mac) or **OK** (Windows).

5. Click **OK** in the **Web Photo Gallery** dialog box.

Now you can sit back and watch Photoshop CS2 do all the work for you! Photoshop CS2 resizes and optimizes the images, creates the HTML for the Web site, and displays the Web Photo Gallery in your default Web browser. This process can take seconds or minutes depending on the speed of your computer and the number of images in the source folder.

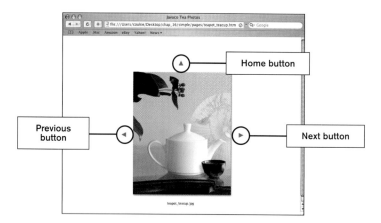

6. Click one of the thumbnail images to view the larger version.

*Notice when you view a larger version of the image, you no longer see the thumbnails. Instead, you see **Previous**, **Next**, and **Home** buttons.*

---

7. Experiment with the **Previous** and **Next** buttons to navigate through the images in the Web Photo Gallery. When you're finished, click the **Home** button to return to the **Home** page.

8. Click the e-mail address at the bottom of the **Home** page.

Your default e-mail application (in my case, Apple Mail) opens automatically and creates a new message with the e-mail address in the To field. This is an easy way to have clients, contacts, or friends contact you when they have viewed the images in your Web Photo Gallery. Photoshop CS2 also offers features your clients, contacts, or friends can use to provide collaborative feedback, as you'll learn about later in this chapter.

---

9. Close the e-mail application and the Web browser. Take a look at the contents of the **simple** folder in the **chap_15** folder you copied to your **Desktop**.

As you can see, the Web Photo Gallery feature took care of saving and optimizing all the required images and writing and saving the required HTML code to make the pages work. How cool is that? The Web Photo Gallery feature is a quick, easy way to put images online without having to design and build complex Web sites. In the next exercise, you'll learn how to customize a Web Photo Gallery.

---

10. Return to Adobe Bridge so you're ready for the next exercise.

2. [PS] _____Customizing a Web Photo Gallery

If you want to change the content or appearance of a Web Photo Gallery, you can use the customization features in the Web Photo Gallery dialog box.

1. If you followed the last exercise, Adobe Bridge should still be open with the content of the **javaco** folder in the **Preview Panel**. If not, go back and complete Step 1 from Exercise 1.

2. Choose **Tools > Photoshop > Web Photo Gallery** to open the **Web Photo Gallery** dialog box.

Notice the **Web Photo Gallery** dialog box has the same settings you specified in the last exercise. The settings in the **Web Photo Gallery** dialog box are sticky—Photoshop CS2 remembers the settings you last used.

3. Choose **Dotted Border – Black on White** from the **Styles** pop-up menu. Click the **Destination** button. Navigate to the **custom** folder in the **chap_15** folder you copied to your **Desktop**. Click **Choose** (Mac) or **OK** (Windows).

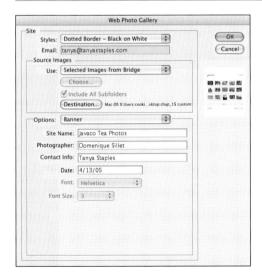

4. Choose **Banner** from the **Options** pop-up menu. Type **Javaco Tea Photos** in the **Site Name** field, **Domenique Sillet** in the **Photographer** field, and type any name in the **Contact Info** field.

Notice the **Font** and **Font Size** options are dimmed. The customization options vary depending on the style. In this case, you can't customize the font of the banner using the **Dotted Border – Black on White** style.

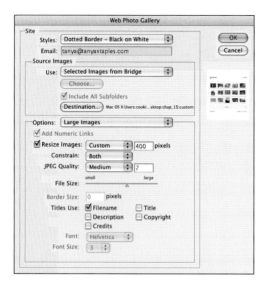

5. Choose **Large Images** from the **Options** pop-up menu. **Large Images** lets you customize how the large images appear in the **Web Photo Gallery**, including the **Size**, **JPEG Quality**, and **Title**. Match the settings to the ones shown in the illustration here or choose your own custom settings.

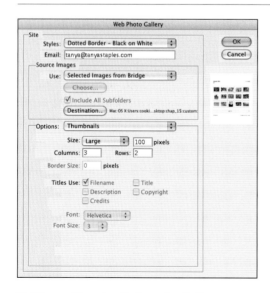

6. Choose **Thumbnails** from the **Options** pop-up menu. Using **Thumbnails** you can customize how the thumbnail images appear in the Web Photo Gallery, including the **Size**. In this case, because the Web Photo Gallery is based on a table, you can also specify the size of the table. Match the settings to the ones shown in the illustration here, or choose your own custom settings.

7. Choose **Custom Colors** from the **Options** pop-up menu.

For this particular style, you can't customize colors (the options are dimmed). For others, you can customize the background, banner, text, active link, link, and visited link by clicking the color swatch to open the Color Picker dialog box.

8. Click **OK** in the **Web Photo Gallery** dialog box to create the custom Web Photo Gallery using the **Dotted Border – Black on White** style and to open it in your default Web browser.

*As you can see, the settings you specified in the last few steps have been reflected in this Web Photo Gallery. Experiment by clicking the thumbnails, the e-mail address, and the **Previous**, **Next**, and **Home** buttons.*

9. Close the Web browser and return to Adobe Bridge.

Understanding the Web Photo Gallery Settings

The Photoshop CS2 Web Photo Gallery dialog box contains many settings. Here is an overview:

Web Photo Gallery Settings	
Setting	**Description**
Site Settings	
Styles pop-up menu	Choose a preset site layout for your Web Photo Gallery.
Email field	Specify an e-mail address.
Source Images Settings	
Use pop-up menu	Specify the images you want to use in the Web Photo Gallery. You can choose a folder of images or selected images in Adobe Bridge.
Choose button	Choose the folder of images to use for the Web Photo Gallery.
Include All Subfolders check box	Include subfolders in the Web Photo Gallery.
Destination button	Specify where to save the Web Photo Gallery on your computer.
General Options	
Extension pop-up menu	Specify the HTML file extension—HTM or HTML.
Banner Options	
Site Name field	Specify the name of the Web Photo Gallery.
Photographer field	Specify the name of the individual(s) who created the images.
Contact Info field	Specify contact information, such as a Web site address.
Date field	Specify the date the images were created or posted.
Font pop-up menu	Choose a font for the Web Photo Gallery.
Font Size pop-up menu	Choose a font size for the Web Photo Gallery.
Large Images Options	
Resize Images pop-up menu	Choose the size of the large images (Small, Medium, Large, or Custom).
Constrain pop-up menu	Choose if you want to constrain the width and/or height of the images when they are resized.
	continues on next page

Web Photo Gallery Settings *continued*	
Setting	**Description**
	Large Images Options *(continued)*
JPEG Quality pop-up menu	Choose the quality of JPEG optimization (Low, Medium, High, or Maximum).
File Size slider	Specify a file size (large or small).
Border Size field	Specify a border size for the large images.
Titles Use check boxes	Specify if you want the filename, title, description, copyright, or credit information to appear next to the large images.
Font pop-up menu	Chooose a font for the large image label.
Font Size pop-up menu	Choose a font size for the large image label.
	Thumbnails Options
Size pop-up menu	Choose the size of the thumbnail images (Small, Medium, Large, or Custom).
Columns and Rows fields	Specify how many columns and rows of thumbnail images to include in the Web Photo Gallery.
Border Size field	Specify a border size for the thumbnail images.
Titles Use check boxes	Specify if you want the filename, title, description, copyright, or credit information to appear next to the thumbnail images in the Web Photo Gallery.
Font pop-up menu	Choose a font for the thumbnail label.
Font Size pop-up menu	Choose a font size for the thumbnail label.
	Custom Colors Options
Background	Specify a color for the background in Web Photo Gallery.
Banner	Specify a color for the banner in the Web Photo Gallery.
Text	Specify a color for the text in the Web Photo Gallery.
Active Link	Specify a color for active links in the Web Photo Gallery.
Link	Specify a color for links in the Web Photo Gallery.
Visited Link	Specify a color for visited links in the Web Photo Gallery.

3. [PS]_____Creating a Collaborative Web Photo Gallery

Photoshop CS2 includes Web Photo Gallery styles that let clients approve or provide feedback about images in a Web Photo Gallery. Collaborating through the Web Photo Gallery interface is easy because it doesn't require any extra programming.

1. If you followed the last exercise, Adobe Bridge should still be open with the content of the **javaco** folder in the **Preview Panel**. If not, go back and complete Step 1 from Exercise 1.

2. Choose **Tools > Photoshop > Web Photo Gallery** to open the **Web Photo Gallery** dialog box.

3. Choose **Centered Frame 1 – Feedback** from the **Styles** pop-up menu.

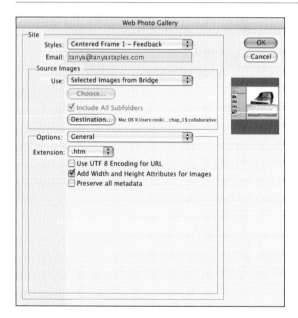

4. Click the **Destination** button. Navigate to the **collaborative** folder in the **chap_15** folder you copied to your **Desktop**. Click **Choose** (Mac) or **OK** (Windows).

5. Using the techniques you learned in the last exercise, customize the Web Photo Gallery as you wish. When you've finished, click **OK** to create the Web Photo Gallery and to open it in your default Web browser.

Note: Only a style with the word Feedback *in the title provides the collaborative functionality you'll learn about in this exercise.*

6. Take a look at the Web Photo Gallery Photoshop CS2 created. Click the thumbnails to view the larger images.

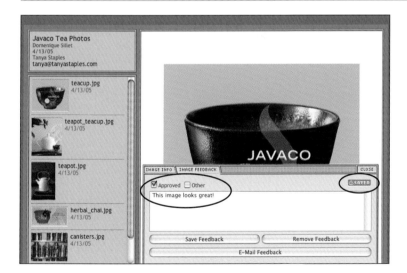

7. Click the **Image Feedback** (Mac) or **Feedback** (Windows) button. Turn on the **Approved** option and type a message in the **Feedback** field. Click the **Save Feedback** button.

Notice a Saved icon appears in the upper-right corner of the Image Feedback window.

Note: *If you're using Microsoft Internet Explorer with Windows XP, a warning message may appear. Click the warning bar and choose **Allow blocked content**.*

8. Click the **E-Mail Feedback** button. In the **JavaScript** dialog box, type a name and click **OK**.

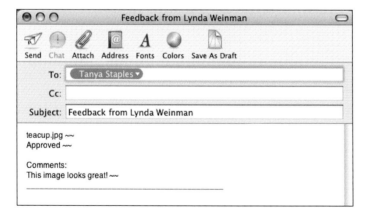

*As soon as you click OK, a new message opens in your default e-mail application. The e-mail address you specified in the **Web Photo Gallery** dialog box is automatically entered in the To field. The title automatically reflects who the feedback is from, and the content of the message shows the name of the image, the approved status, and the feedback comments.*

9. Close the e-mail you created in the last step. Close the Javaco Tea Photos Web Photo Gallery. Close the Web browser and return to Adobe Bridge.

You've finished another chapter! As you can see, creating a Web Photo Gallery is a fast, easy way to put images online. Plus, with the feedback styles, you can get easy approval and comments from clients without having to design and program complex Web sites. Next, you'll learn about the automation features in Photoshop CS2 and ImageReady CS2.

16
Automation

| Creating Actions in ImageReady CS2 |
| Creating Droplets in ImageReady CS2 |

chap_16

PCS2Web HOT CD-ROM

Photoshop CS2 and ImageReady CS2 offer many practical and creative tools to help you design Web graphics. This chapter shows you how to automate tasks. Automating tasks is a huge timesaver—who wants to repeat the same operations over and over when Photoshop CS2 or ImageReady CS2 can do the work for you?

Photoshop CS2 and ImageReady CS2 both offer **actions**, which allow you to store a series of operations as a recording and play the recording back over a single image or multiple images in the same folder.

Both programs also let you save actions as **droplets**. You can drag and drop a single image or a folder of images onto a droplet to perform an action. For example, if you create an action to resize and optimize images, you can save it as a droplet, then drag a folder of images onto the droplet and instantly resize and optimize all the images at the same time!

In this chapter, you'll learn how to use actions and droplets. This is the stuff computers were made for. Enjoy!

What Are Actions?

An *action* is a series of commands you can play back on a single image or on a folder of images. For example, you can create an action that opens, crops, optimizes, and saves images.

Most of the commands and tool operations in Photoshop CS2 and ImageReady CS2 can be recorded as actions. Photoshop CS2 and ImageReady CS2 both allow stops, which let actions stop so you can perform tasks that can't be recorded; they also allow modal controls, which let you enter values in a dialog box while playing an action.

If you want to apply an action to a single image, click the **Play** button at the bottom of the **Actions** palette. If you want to apply the action to a series of images, you can save the action as a droplet. You'll learn how in the next few exercises.

Using Predefined Actions

Photoshop CS2 and ImageReady CS2 include predefined actions, which you can access in the Actions palette. Using the predefined actions in Photoshop CS2 or ImageReady CS2 is easy. Simply open an image, in the **Actions** palette click to select the action you want to play, and click the **Play** button.

I. [IR] _____Creating Actions

Actions are a great way to automate repetitive tasks, such as creating and optimizing thumbnails for a Web page, which you'll learn to do in this exercise. Actions are good for hundreds of other things; this example was developed to teach you the basics of recording your own actions. You'll create an action that resizes a copy of an image to thumbnail size and saves it as an optimized JPEG. For this exercise, you'll use ImageReady CS2, but it works the same way in Photoshop CS2. In Exercise 2, you'll apply the action to a whole folder of images using the droplet feature.

1. Open **candles.psd** from the **action** folder in the **chap_16** folder you copied to your **Desktop**. Make sure the **Actions** palette and **Optimize** palette are visible. If they're not, choose **Window > Actions** and **Window > Optimize**.

2. At the bottom of the **Actions** palette, click the **Create New Action** button.

3. In the **New Action** dialog box, type **Optimized Thumbnails** in the **Name** field. Choose **F2** from the **Function Key** pop-up menu, and turn on the **Shift** option. Click **Record**.

You can now start performing the steps you want to include in your action. First, you'll resize the image, then you'll optimize and save the image.

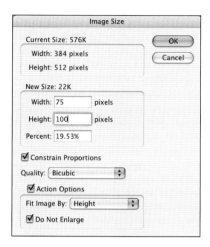

4. Choose **Image > Image Size**. Type **100** in the **Height** field. Make sure the **Constrain Proportions** option is turned on. Turn on the **Action Options** option, and choose **Height** from the **Fit Image By** pop-up menu. Turn on the **Do Not Enlarge** option. Click **OK**.

*The purpose of specifying the **Height** at **100** pixels and choosing **Height** from the **Fit Image By** pop-up menu is to ensure all the thumbnails are the same height. You can also choose **Width**, **Width and Height**, or **Percent**. By turning on the **Do Not Enlarge** option, if you perform the action on images smaller than 100 pixels in height, ImageReady CS2 will not make the image larger to match the 100 pixels you specified in this step.*

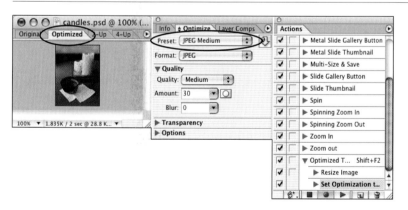

5. In the document window, click the **Optimized** tab. In the **Optimize** palette, choose **JPEG Medium** from the **Preset** pop-up menu, or specify an optimization setting of your choice using the techniques you learned in Chapter 7, "*Optimizing Images*."

6. Choose **File > Save Optimized As**. Navigate to the **action** folder in the **chap_16** folder you copied to your **Desktop**. Name the file **candles.jpg**. Click **Save**.

7. In the **Actions** palette, click the **Stop** button to stop the recording.

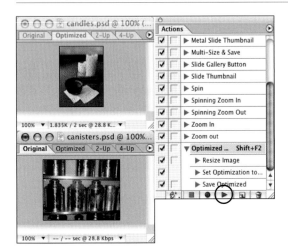

8. Open **canisters.psd** from the **actions** folder in the **chap_16** folder you copied to your **Desktop**. Press **Shift+F2**, or click the **Play Selection** button to play the **Optimized Thumbnails** action you created in this exercise.

Notice the action automatically resized the image. Next, you'll see how the action optimized and saved the image.

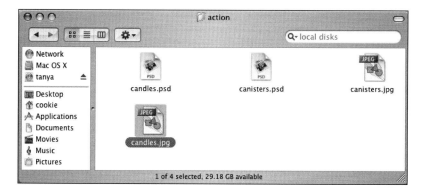

9. Navigate to the **actions** folder in the **chap_16** folder you copied to your **Desktop**.

*Notice there are two JPEGs: candles.jpg was created when you recorded the **Optimized Thumbnails** action, and canisters.jpg was created when you played the **Optimized Thumbnails** action in Step 8.*

10. Double-click **candles.jpg** and **canisters.jpg** to open the images.

*Notice that the images have the same height—100 pixels—and both images are optimized using the settings you specified in the **Optimize** palette. As you can see, recording these steps into an action can save you valuable time performing the same task over and over. Although this is a very simple example, it shows the power of actions. Most tasks in Photoshop CS2 and ImageReady CS2 can be recorded as actions.*

11. Close **candles.psd**, **candles.jpg**, **canisters.psd**, and **canisters.jpg**. You don't need to save your changes.

Next, you'll learn how to create droplets so you can perform actions on multiple images.

NOTE | Recording Actions in Photoshop CS2

Now that you've learned how to create an action in ImageReady CS2, you might wonder if you can do the same thing in Photoshop CS2. You can indeed! Photoshop CS2 also includes an **Actions** palette, and the process for recording actions is identical.

Editing Actions

Once you've created an action in Photoshop CS2 or ImageReady CS2, you can always make changes to it later. Here's a handy chart that outlines how to add, delete, or move steps in an action:

Editing Actions

Operation	Method
Add	To add a step to an action, choose **Start Recording** from the **Actions** palette menu. Perform the operations you want to add. At the bottom of the **Actions** palette, click the **Stop** button. The steps you recorded will be automatically added to the end of the action. If you want to add steps to the middle of an action, click the action you want to come after the insertion and begin the recording process.
Delete	To delete a step from an action, click the step to select it in the **Actions** palette. Drag the step to the **Trash** icon at the bottom of the **Actions** palette or choose **Delete** from the **Actions** palette menu.
Move	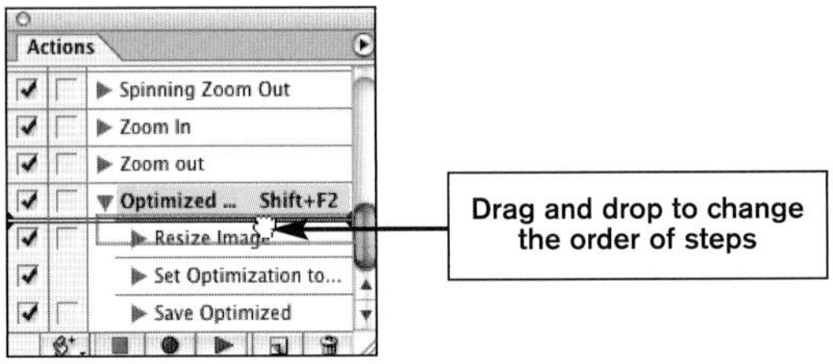 Drag and drop to change the order of steps To move a step inside an action, click the step to select it, then drag and drop the step until a black line appears where you want the step moved.
Turn On/Off Step	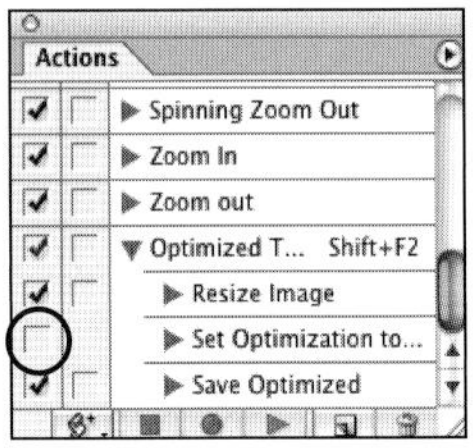 To turn on or off a step, click the **Toggle item on/off** check box in the **Actions** palette. When you play an action with a step turned off, it will skip over that step.

continues on next page

Editing Actions *continued*	
Operation	**Method**
Turn On/Off Dialog Box	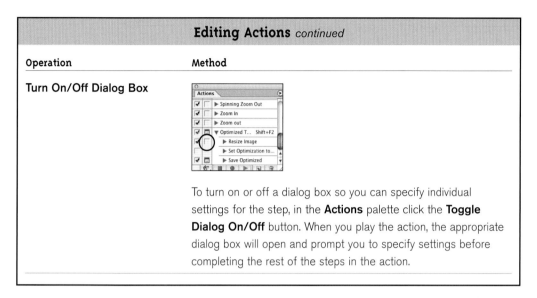
	To turn on or off a dialog box so you can specify individual settings for the step, in the **Actions** palette click the **Toggle Dialog On/Off** button. When you play the action, the appropriate dialog box will open and prompt you to specify settings before completing the rest of the steps in the action.

About Droplets

A droplet is a small application created by Photoshop CS2 or ImageReady CS2 that applies an action to a folder of images or to a series of selected images.

When you create a droplet, Photoshop CS2 and ImageReady CS2 create a small application, which contains the commands of the action you used to create the droplet. To apply the droplet, drag and drop a single image, a series of selected images, or a folder of images onto the droplet icon.

The process for creating droplets in Photoshop CS2 and ImageReady CS2 is identical. Here are a few other fun facts about droplets to keep in mind as you learn to use them:

- You can create droplets from actions in the Actions palette in Photoshop CS2 or ImageReady CS2.
- You can save droplets to your Desktop or any location on your computer.
- You can use a droplet without first opening Photoshop CS2 or ImageReady CS2. The application will launch automatically when you drag a folder or series of files onto the droplet.
- You can share droplets between Mac and Windows computers because they are cross-platform.

Note: If you create a droplet on a Mac, make sure you add the .exe file extension so Windows computers will recognize it.

2. [IR] _____ Creating Droplets

In the last exercise, you learned how to create an action and apply it to a single image. In this exercise, you'll learn how to create a droplet, which lets you apply an action to a folder or series of images. For this exercise, you'll use ImageReady CS2, but it works similarly in Photoshop CS2.

1. If you followed the last exercise, you should have the **Optimized Thumbnails** action in the **Actions** palette. If not, go back and complete Exercise 1. Make sure the **Actions** palette is visible. If it's not, choose **Window > Actions**.

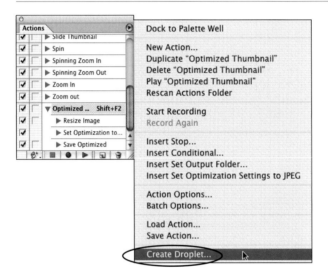

2. In the **Actions** palette, click the **Optimized Thumbnail** action to select it. Choose **Create Droplet** from the **Actions** palette menu.

3. In the **Save This Action as a Droplet** dialog box, navigate to your **Desktop**. Type **opt_thumb.exe** in the **Save As** field. Click **Save**.

Note: On a Windows computer, ImageReady CS2 will automatically apply the .exe extension. Adding this extension is important in case you want to share actions with others.

4. Browse to your **Desktop**, and open the **chap_16** folder. Drag the **droplet** folder onto the **opt_thumb.exe** droplet, as shown in the illustration here.

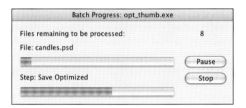

*You can watch the progress of the action in the **Batch Process** dialog box. If you need to pause or stop the action, click **Pause** or **Stop**.*

5. Open the **droplet** folder in the **chap_16** folder on your **Desktop**.

The droplet worked! Notice each PSD file has an associated JPG file. If you want to view the results, double-click the JPG files to open them in ImageReady CS2.

As you can see, creating droplets is a great feature if you want to perform the same action to more than one image or to an entire folder of images.

TIP | Changing the Save Location for Droplets

By default, droplets created in ImageReady CS2 save optimized images in the same folder as the original images. If you want to save the optimized images in a different folder, you can specify a different location easily. Here's how:

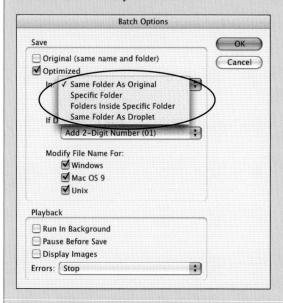

Choose **Batch Options** from the **Actions** palette menu. Choose one of the following options from the **In** pop-up menu: **Same Folder As Original** (which is the default setting), **Specific Folder**, **Folders Inside Specific Folder**, or **Same Folder as Droplet**.

NOTE | Creating Droplets in Photoshop CS2

In the last exercise, you learned how to create droplets in ImageReady CS2. You can also create droplets in Photoshop CS2. Here's how:

1. In the **Actions** palette, click an action to select it.

2. Choose **File > Automate > Create Droplet**.

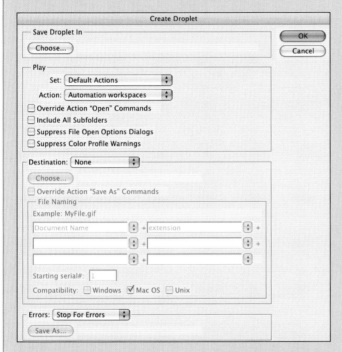

3. In the **Create Droplet** dialog box, click **Choose** to choose where you want to save the droplet. Choose a set and an action from the **Set** and **Action** pop-up menus. Choose the destination in the **Destination** section. Specify the file naming convention you want to use. When you're happy with the settings in the **Create Droplet** dialog box, click **OK**.

4. Browse to the location where you saved the droplet. Click and drag a single image, series of selected images, or a folder of images onto the droplet.

Although this was a short, simple chapter, it introduced some powerful automation concepts. As you can see, by using actions and droplets you don't have to perform repetitive tasks over and over. You can automate simple tasks (as you did in this chapter), or you can automate more complex tasks. Next, you'll learn about another powerful feature—data sets.

I7

Creating Data-Driven Graphics

| Defining Visibility Variables and Creating Data Sets |
| Defining Text Replacement Variables |
| Defining Pixel Replacement Variables |
| Previewing and Exporting Data Sets |
| Importing Data Sets from Text Files |

chap_I7

PCS2Web HOT CD-ROM

In the early days of Web design, designers and developers built Web sites page-by-page and graphic-by-graphic. Today, there are alternative ways to create graphics—by using data-driven templates and dynamic content. For example, if you need to create 25 Web banners that are the same size, use the same font, and have a same-sized image in the same position, you can build a data set with different variables to generate the Web banners for you. All you have to do is assemble the template and specify the data!

In this chapter, you'll learn how to specify variables and create data sets in Photoshop CS2. Plus, you'll learn how to populate data sets from spreadsheets and text files. If you don't know what these terms and buzzwords mean, not to worry—they will all be explained here. In Chapter 20, "*Integrating with GoLive and Dreamweaver*," you'll learn how to manipulate data sets in Adobe GoLive. Although data sets have been part of ImageReady for the past few versions, they are a new addition in Photoshop CS2.

Buzzwords and Definitions

Before you begin working with data sets, here is an overview of common terms you'll need to understand:

Data-driven: Data-driven refers to the process of feeding content to a template so data changes from page to page without having to create each page individually. When you work with data-driven templates, you design an overall page layout that accepts data and formats it according to the template. Usually, templates and data are text-based; however, you can create templates that are image-based. In this chapter, you'll learn how to create image-based data-driven templates using Photoshop CS2 and ImageReady CS2.

Dynamic content: Dynamic content refers to data or text content that changes from page to page. Dynamic content is generated on the fly and populates data-driven templates.

Dynamic graphics: Dynamic graphics refers to graphics or images that change from page to page. Dynamic graphics are generated on the fly and populate data-driven templates. In this chapter, you'll learn how to create data sets that let you create Web pages with dynamic graphics.

Variables: Variables determine which images in a template are dynamic. There are three types of variables in Photoshop CS2 and ImageReady CS2: **Text Replacement** variables, which replace vector-based type; **Visibility** variables, which replace images using layer visibility; and **Pixel Replacement** variables, which replace pixels in a layer with pixels from a different file. You'll learn how to create all three types of variables in this chapter.

Data sets: Data sets store all the variables for a template. Once you define data sets, you can output images as PSD files, optimized images (JPEGs or GIFs), or Macromedia Flash (SWF) files. **Note:** You can only export data sets as PSD files in Photoshop CS2. If you want to export data sets as optimized images or as Macromedia Flash files, you must use ImageReady CS2.

I. [PS]_____Understanding Data Sets

The best way to understand data sets and variables is to take a look at a file containing them. This exercise will introduce you to the concept of data sets and variables by showing a file with Visibility variables and Text Replacement variables. You can also create Pixel Replacement variables, which you'll learn about later in this chapter.

1. Open **banner.psd** from the **chap_17** folder you copied to your **Desktop**.

Notice the image contains one vector-based type layer and four pixel-based layers with graphics. The visibility of some of the pixel-based layers is turned off.

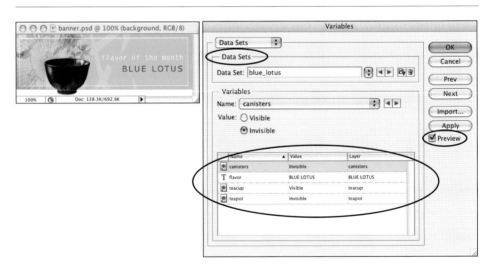

2. Choose **Image > Variables > Data Sets**. Make sure the **Preview** option is turned on.

*In the **Variables** dialog box, notice **blue_lotus** is selected in the **Data Set** pop-up menu. Take a look at the contents of the **Variables** chart. Notice the **canisters** variable is invisible, the **teacup** variable is visible, and the **teapot** variable is invisible. These are examples of **Visibility** variables because they are based on the visibility of the respective layers in the **Layers** palette.*

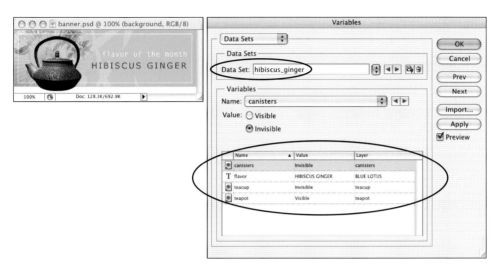

3. Choose **hibiscus_ginger** from the **Data Set** pop-up menu.

*Notice the difference between the **Visibility** variables in the **hibiscus_ginger** data set and the **blue_lotus** data set you looked at in the last step. As you can see, with the **hibiscus_ginger** data set, the **canisters** variable is invisible, the **teacup** variable is invisible, and the **teapot** variable is visible. The image in this data set changed from the teacup to the teapot because of the change to the **Visibility** variables.*

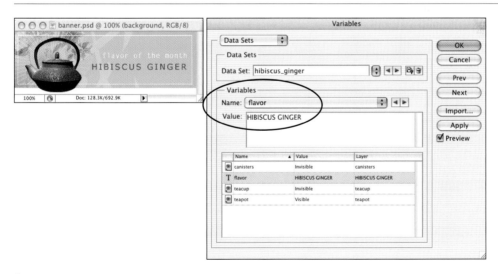

4. Choose **flavor** from the **Name** pop-up menu.

*Notice the **Value** field contains the words **HIBISCUS GINGER**, which are the same words in the image.*

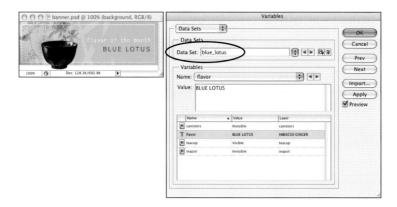

5. With **flavor** still selected in the **Name** pop-up menu, choose **blue_lotus** from the **Data Set** pop-up menu.

*Notice the **Value** field contains the words **BLUE LOTUS**, which are the same words in the image. The **HIBISCUS GINGER** and **BLUE LOTUS** are examples of a **Text Replacement** variable because the text has been replaced using the value specified in the variable.*

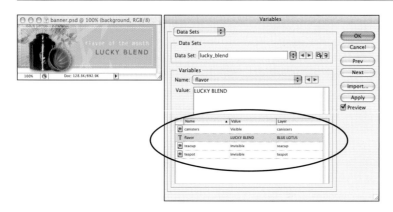

6. Choose **lucky_blend** from the **Data Set** pop-up menu.

*Notice the **canisters** variable is visible, the **teacup** variable is invisible, and the **teapot** variable is invisible. Also notice the text has been replaced with the words **LUCKY BLEND**.*

As you can see from this exercise, it's easy to produce multiple images that use a common format using data sets and variables.

7. Click **Cancel** to close the **Variables** dialog box. Close **banner.psd**. You don't need to save your changes.

Now that you've had a chance to look at an image with data sets and variables, it's time to learn how to create them.

2. [PS] _____Defining Visibility Variables and Creating Data Sets

Over the next four exercises, you'll learn how to create data sets and variables. In this exercise, you'll define Visibility variables and create the data sets. In Exercise 3, you'll define Text Replacement variables. In Exercise 4, you'll define Pixel Replacement variables. Note: Although you'll use Photoshop CS2 for this exercise, the process works similarly in ImageReady CS2.

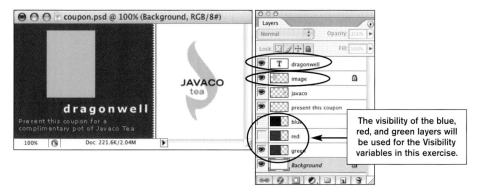

The visibility of the blue, red, and green layers will be used for the Visibility variables in this exercise.

1. Open **coupon.psd** from the **coupon** folder in the **chap_17** folder you copied to your **Desktop**. Make sure the **Layers** palette is visible. If it's not, choose **Window > Layers**.

*First, take a minute to see how the image is constructed and to get an idea of what layers will become variables. As you can see, the image contains three similar-looking layers— green, red, and blue. If you toggle the visibility of these layers, you'll see the solid background color on the left side of the image change. You'll define these layers as **Visibility** variables in this exercise. Also notice there is a type layer in the image—**dragonwell**. In Exercise 3, you'll define this layer as a Text Replacement variable. Finally, notice the **image** layer. Currently, this layer contains a solid-colored rectangle. In Exercise 4, you'll define this layer as a **Pixel Replacement** variable. Sound complicated? Not to worry, the next few exercises will help you understand.*

2. Choose **Image > Variables > Define** to open the **Variables** dialog box.

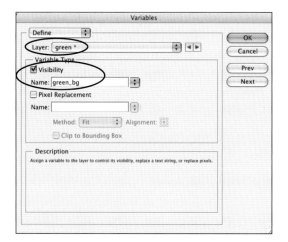

3. Choose **green** from the **Layer** pop-up menu to define the layer as a **Visibility** variable. Turn on the **Visibility** option. Type **green_bg** in the **Name** field.

*When you choose a layer from the **Layer** pop-up menu, you must define what type of variable you want it to be. Because the **green** layer is a pixel-based layer, you have two options: **Visibility** and **Pixel Replacement**.*

*Once you specify a name in the **Name** field, you'll see an asterisk appear next to the layer name in the **Layer** pop-up menu. The asterisk indicates you have successfully defined the layer as a variable.*

Note: *You cannot use spaces or special characters in the **Name** field.*

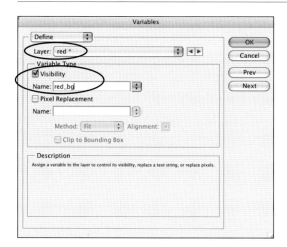

4. Choose **red** from the **Layer** pop-up menu. Turn on the **Visibility** option to define the layer as a **Visibility** variable. Type **red_bg** in the **Name** field.

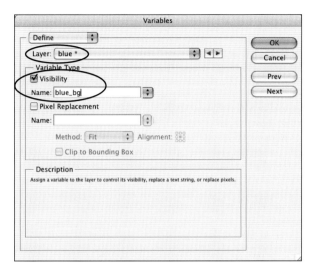

5. Choose **blue** from the **Layer** pop-up menu. Turn on the **Visibility** option to define the layer as a **Visibility** variable. Type **blue_bg** in the **Name** field.

*You've just successfully defined the **Visibility** variables. Next, you'll create the data sets to contain these **Visibility** variables.*

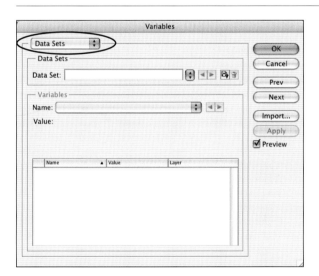

6. Choose **Data Sets** from the pop-up menu at the top of the **Variables** dialog box. The contents of the **Variables** dialog box will automatically change, as shown in the illustration here.

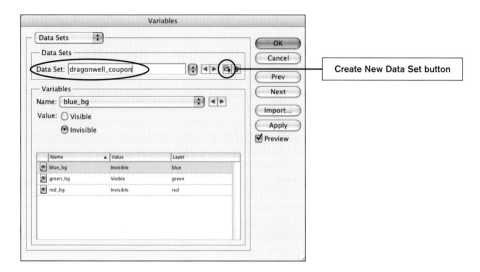

7. Click the **Create New Data Set** button. Type **dragonwell_coupon** in the **Data Set** field.

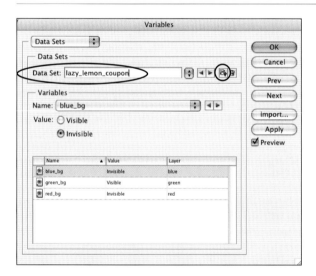

8. Click the **Create New Data Set** button to create another data set. Type **lazy_lemon_coupon** in the **Data Set** field.

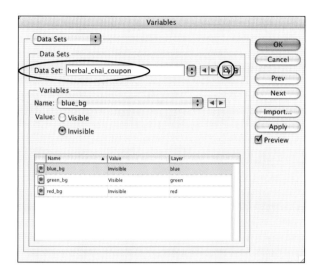

9. Click the **Create New Data Set Button** to create a third data set. Type **herbal_chai_coupon** in the **Data Set** field.

You just successfully created three new data sets. The number of data sets you create dictates the total number of images you'll generate from this file. Next, you'll specify which variables you want to be turned on in each data set using the **Visibility** *variables you defined earlier in this exercise.*

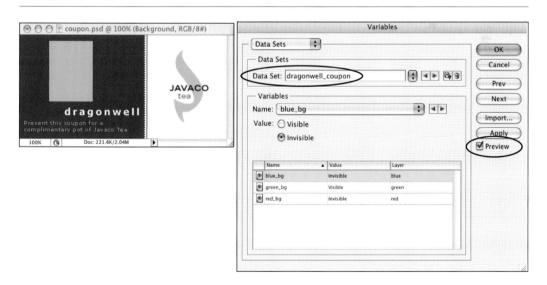

10. Choose **dragonwell_coupon** from the **Data Set** pop-up menu. Reposition the **Variables** dialog box so you can see its contents and the contents of the document window. Make sure the **Preview** option is turned on in the **Variables** dialog box.

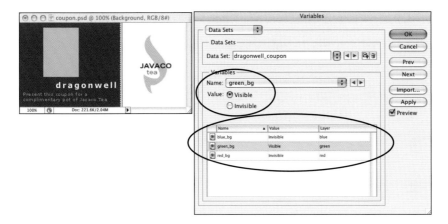

11. Choose **green_bg** from the **Name** pop-up menu.

Notice the visibility status of the three variables you defined earlier in this exercise—blue_bg is invisible, green_bg is visible, and red_bg is invisible.

Because the visibility of the green layer is turned on in the Layers palette, the green_bg variable is automatically visible. Likewise, because the visibility of the blue and red layers is turned off in the Layers palette, the blue_bg and red_bg variables are automatically invisible. For the dragonwell_coupon data set, that's fine. However, for the other two data sets, you'll want to use the other Visibility variables to change the background color, which you'll learn how to do in the next few steps.

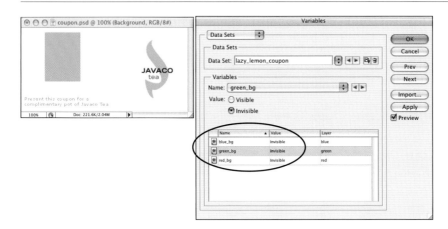

12. Choose **lazy_lemon_coupon** from the **Data Set** pop-up menu. **green_bg** should still be selected in the **Name** pop-up menu. Click the **Invisible** option.

Notice there is no background because all three Visibility variables—blue_bg, green_bg, and red_bg—are invisible. You'll fix this in the next step.

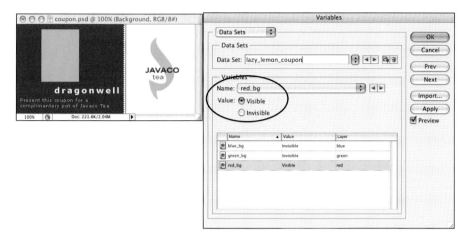

13. Choose **red_bg** from the **Name** pop-up menu. Click the **Visible** option.

Notice the background in the image automatically changes to red.

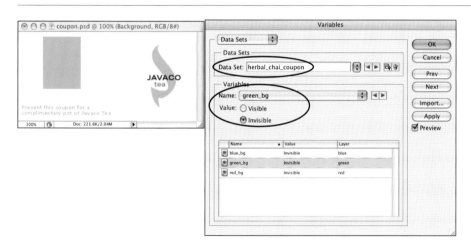

14. Choose **herbal_chai_coupon** from the **Data Set** pop-up menu. Choose **green_bg** from the **Name** pop-up menu, and click the **Invisible** option.

15. Choose **blue_bg** from the **Name** pop-up menu, and click the **Visible** option. Make sure the **Value** of the **red_bg** is set to **Invisible**. If it's not, choose **red_bg** form the **Name** pop-up menu, and click the **Invisible** option.

16. Use the **Prev** and **Next** buttons next to the **Data Set** pop-up menu to view the three data sets you created with the respective **Visibility** variables.

*Notice each data set has a different colored background, which is a result of the **Visibility** variables you defined in this exercise.*

17. Click **OK** to close the **Variables** dialog box.

18. Leave **coupon.psd** open for the next exercise.

*In the next exercise, you'll learn how to create **Text Replacement** variables for the vector-based type layer in the **coupon.psd** file.*

3. [PS] Defining Text Replacement Variables

In the last exercise, you defined Visibility variables to change the color of the background in the **coupon.psd** file. You also created data sets—one for each of the images you want to generate. In this exercise, you'll learn how to create Text Replacement variables for vector-based type layers. Text replacement variables allow you to create and format one vector-based type layer and use those properties to create different strings of text with the same properties. It sounds confusing, but you'll understand how easy it is after you follow this exercise. Note: Although you'll use Photoshop CS2 for this exercise, it works similarly in ImageReady CS2.

1. If you followed the last exercise, **coupon.psd** should still be open in Photoshop CS2. If it's not, go back and complete Exercise 2.

2. Choose **Image > Variables > Define** to open the **Variables** dialog box.

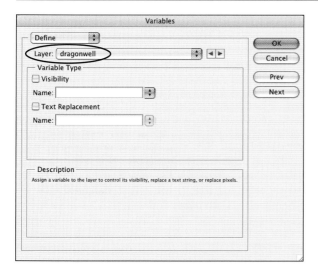

3. Choose **dragonwell** from the **Layer** pop-up menu.

*Notice when the **dragonwell** layer is selected in the **Layer** pop-up menu you have two **Variable Type** options—**Visibility** and **Text Replacement**. When you worked with pixel-based layers in the last exercise, you instead had **Visibility** and **Pixel Replacement** as options. The **Variable Type** section of the **Variables** dialog box is context-sensitive based on the type of layer you have selected in the **Layer** pop-up menu. Photoshop CS2 automatically recognizes the **dragonwell** layer as a vector-based type layer and provides two options—**Visibility** and **Text Replacement**. You can't use **Pixel Replacement** variables with type layers—you can only use them with pixel-based layers.*

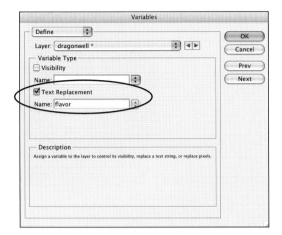

4. Turn on the **Text Replacement** option. Type **flavor** in the **Name** field.

The word flavor *won't ever appear in the image—this is just a name to describe what the contents of the **Text Replacement** variable will contain. You'll specify the flavor names to populate the **Text Replacement** variable later in this exercise.*

5. Choose **Data Sets** from the pop-up menu at the top of the **Variables** dialog box. The contents of the dialog box will automatically change.

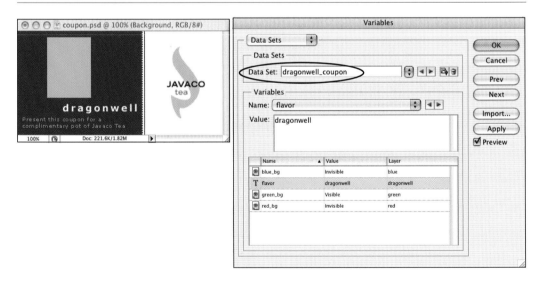

6. Choose **dragonwell_coupon** from the **Data Set** pop-up menu. Choose **flavor** from the **Name** pop-up menu to choose the **Text Replacement** variable you defined in this exercise.

*Notice the **Value** field contains the word **dragonwell**. The **Value** field is automatically populated by the vector-based type layer you used to define the **Text Replacement** variable. Not to worry, you don't have to use **dragonwell** for the other two data sets—you can use any text you want! You'll learn how in the next steps.*

7. Choose **lazy_lemon_coupon** from the **Data Set** pop-up menu. With **flavor** still selected in the **Name** pop-up menu, type **lazy lemon** in the **Value** field, and click **Apply**.

Notice the contents of the document window update automatically with the words lazy lemon. *Also notice the type options, such as **Font**, **Font Size**, **Font Style**, and so on, remain the same. Very cool!*

8. Choose **herbal_chai_coupon** from the **Data Set** pop-up menu. With **flavor** still selected in the **Name** pop-up menu, type **herbal chai** in the **Value** field, and click **Apply**.

9. Use the **Prev** and **Next** buttons next to the **Data Set** pop-up menu to view the three data sets you created with the respective **Visibility** and **Text Replacement** variables.

*Each data set should have a different colored background and a different flavor. These changes are a result of the **Visibility** variables you defined in the last exercise and the **Text Replacement** variables you defined in this exercise.*

10. Click **OK** to close the **Variables** dialog box.

11. Leave **coupon.psd** open for the next exercise.

*Next, you'll learn how to define **Pixel Replacement** variables to add a photograph to each data set.*

4.  [PS/IR] Defining Pixel Replacement Variables

In the last two exercises, you learned how to define Visibility variables and Text Replacement variables. You also learned how to create data sets. In this exercise, you'll learn how to create Pixel Replacement variables. Pixel Replacement variables allow you to replace the contents of a layer with the contents of another image. Note: Although you'll use Photoshop CS2 for this exercise, the process works the same way in ImageReady CS2.

1. If you followed the last exercise, **coupon.psd** should still be open in Photoshop CS2. If it's not, go back and complete Exercise 3.

2. Choose **Image > Variables > Define** to open the **Variables** dialog box.

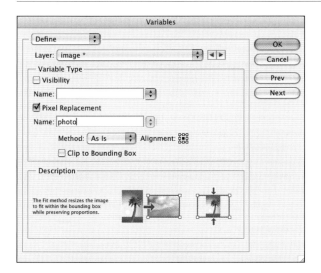

3. Choose **image** from the **Layer** pop-up menu. Turn on the **Pixel Replacement** option, and type **photo** in the **Name** field. Choose **As Is** from the **Method** pop-up menu. Make sure the middle square of the **Alignment** diagram is selected, as shown in the illustration here. If it's not, click it to select it.

*Note: The **Method** and **Alignment** options are available at the bottom of the **Variables** dialog box in Photoshop CS2, as shown in the illustration above. In order to access the **Method** and **Alignment** options in ImageReady CS2, at the bottom of the **Variables** dialog box, click the **Pixel Replacement Options** button to open the **Pixel Replacement Options** dialog box. The options work the same in Photoshop CS2 and ImageReadyCS2—the only difference is how you access the options.*

NOTE | Understanding Pixel Replacement Options

Wondering what the different Pixel Replacement options are all about? Here's a chart to help you understand.

Pixel Replacement Options	
Option	**Description**
Fit	Scales the image to fit the height. (**Note:** This may leave undesirable gaps on the sides of the image when you put the image into a Web page.)
Fill	Fills the entire layer with the image while constraining the proportions. (**Note:** This may cause part of the image to be cut off when you put the image into a Web page.)
As Is	Makes no modifications to the image.
Conform	Scales the image without keeping the original proportions of the image.
Alignment	Aligns the image on a Web page based on which square you click in the **Alignment** diagram.
Clip to	Clips areas of the image that do not fit. (**Note:** This option is available when the **Fill** or **As Is** options are selected in the **Method** pop-up menu.)

4. Choose **Data Sets** from the pop-up menu at the top of the **Variables** dialog box. The contents of the **Variables** dialog box will automatically change.

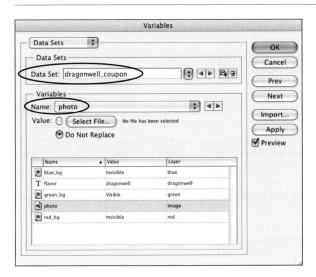

5. Choose **dragonwell_coupon** from the **Data Set** pop-up menu. Choose **photo** from the **Name** pop-up menu.

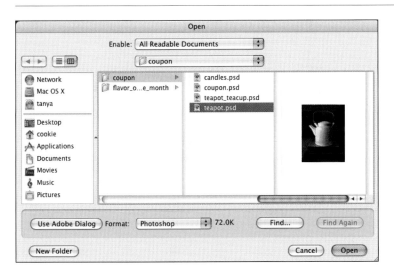

6. Click the **Select File** button to open the **Open** dialog box. You should automatically see the contents of the **coupon** folder in the **chap_17** folder you copied to your **Desktop**. If not, navigate to the **coupon** folder in the **chap_17** folder you copied to your **Desktop**. Click **teapot.psd** to select it. Click **Open**.

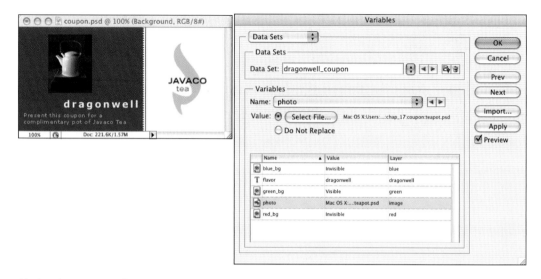

*Notice the contents of the image layer are automatically replaced with the contents of the **teapot.psd** file.*

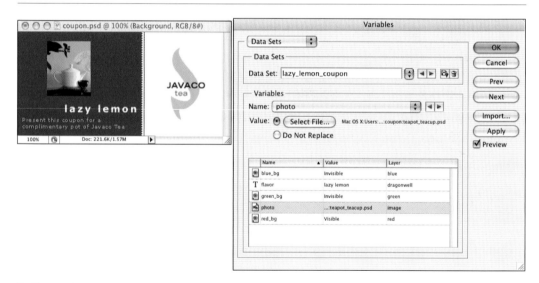

7. Choose **lazy_lemon_coupon** from the **Data Set** pop-up menu. Click the **Select File** button to open the **Open** dialog box. In the **coupon** folder in the **chap_17** folder you copied to your **Desktop**, click **teapot_teacup.psd** to select it. Click **Open**.

The contents of the image layer are automatically replaced with the contents of the
***teapot_teacup.psd** file.*

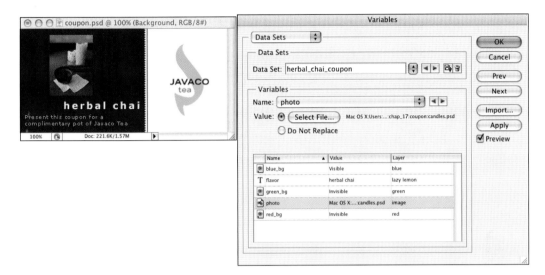

8. Choose **herbal_chai_coupon** from the **Data Set** pop-up menu. Click the **Select File** option to open the **Open** dialog box. In the **coupon** folder in the **chap_17** folder you copied to your **Desktop**, click **candles.psd** to select it. Click **Open**.

*The contents of the image layer are automatically replaced with the contents of the **candles.psd** file.*

9. Use the **Prev** and **Next** buttons next to the **Data Set** pop-up menu to view the three data sets you created with the respective **Visibility**, **Text Replacement**, and **Pixel Replacement** variables.

As you can see, if you're designing multiple images based on the same layout or template, data sets are a quick and easy way to create a series of images.

10. Click **OK** to close the **Variables** dialog box.

11. Leave **coupon.psd** open in Photoshop CS2.

Next, you'll learn how to preview and export the images you created from the data sets and variables.

5. [IR] _____Previewing and Exporting Data Sets

In the last three exercises, you created data sets and defined Visibility, Text Replacement, and Pixel Replacement variables. In this exercise, you'll learn how to preview and export the images you generated. Although you used Photoshop CS2 for the past three exercises, you'll use ImageReady CS2 for this exercise. ImageReady CS2 makes it easier to preview the images and lets you export optimized versions of the images. In Photoshop CS2, you can only export PSDs.

1. If you followed the last exercise, **coupon.psd** should still be open in Photoshop CS2. If it's not, go back and complete Exercise 3. Click the **Edit in ImageReady CS2** button at the bottom of the Photoshop CS2 **Toolbox** to open **coupon.psd** in ImageReady CS2. In ImageReady CS2, make sure the **Optimize** palette is visible. If it's not, choose **Window > Optimize**.

First, you'll preview the images you created from the data sets and variables you created in the last three exercises.

2. In the **Toolbox**, click the **Preview Document** button.

*Notice that the contents of the **Options** bar update automatically to show a **Data Set** pop-up menu and **Prev** and **Next** buttons.*

3. On the **Options** bar, choose a data set from the **Data Set** pop-up menu, or click the **Prev** and **Next** buttons to view the three different images you generated. When you've finished, click the **Preview Document** button to exit the preview mode.

4. Click the **Optimized** tab in the document window. Using the techniques you learned in Chapter 7, "*Optimizing Images*," specify optimization settings in the **Optimize** palette. This is a tricky example because it contains both flat graphical content and photographic content. Experiment with different GIF and JPEG settings until you find the best quality image with the smallest file size.

5. When you're satisfied with the optimization settings, in the **Toolbox**, click the **Preview Document** button, and use the **Next** and **Prev** buttons on the **Options** bar to view the settings on each image you generated with the data sets. When you've finished, in the **Toolbox**, click the **Preview Document** button to exit the preview mode.

You can only specify one optimization setting for all images generated from the data sets. Therefore, make sure you're satisfied with the optimization settings for each image.

6. Choose **File > Export > Data Sets as Files**.

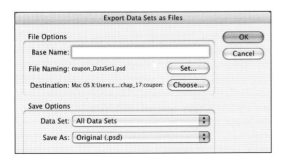

7. In the **Export Data Sets as Files** dialog box, leave the **Base Name** field blank.

8. Click the **Set** button to open the **Data Set File Naming** dialog box. Match the options to the ones shown in the illustration here. Click **OK**.

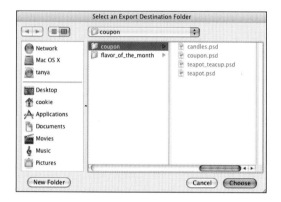

9. In the **Select an Export Destination Folder** dialog box, click the **Choose** button. Navigate to the **coupon** folder in the **chap_17** folder you copied to your **Desktop**. Click **Choose** (Mac) or **OK** (Windows).

10. Choose **All Data Sets** from the **Data Set** pop-up menu.

11. Choose **Optimized** from the **Save As** pop-up menu.

*Notice additional options appear when you choose **Optimized** from the **Save As** pop-up menu.*

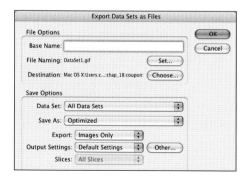

12. Choose **Images Only** from the **Export** pop-up menu, and choose **Default Settings** from the **Output Settings** dialog box. Click **OK**.

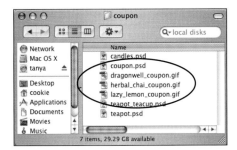

13. Browse to the **coupon** folder in the **chap_17** folder you copied to your **Desktop**.

Notice there are three GIF files—*dragonwell_coupon.gif*, *lazy_lemon_coupon.gif*, and *herbal_chai_coupon.gif*. If you'd like, double-click to open the image(s) you generated.

As you can see from the exercises in this chapter, data sets offer an easy way to generate multiple images from the same layout or template. Although you created only three final images in these exercises, you can see the power of the data sets feature.

14. Return to ImageReady CS2. Close **coupon.psd**. You don't need to save your changes.

6. [PS] _____ Importing Data Sets from Text Files

In the last few exercises, you learned how to manually define variables and create data sets. Manually defining variables and data sets works well if you're working with only a few images. What if you have to generate tens or hundreds of images based on the same layout or template? With Photoshop CS2 and ImageReady CS2, you can import data sets from text files and spreadsheets. Here's an exercise to show you how. Note: Although you'll use Photoshop CS2 for this exercise, the process works similarly in ImageReady CS2.

1. Open **flavor_of_the_month.psd** from the **flavor_of_the_month** folder in the **chap_17** folder you copied to your **Desktop**. Make sure the **Layers** palette is visible; if it's not, choose **Window > Layers**.

*Take a look at the contents of this file. Notice there is a type layer with the word **LEMONGRASS** and a pixel-based layer with an image of two hands holding a teacup. In this exercise, you'll define the type layer as a **Text Replacement** variable and the pixel-based layer as a **Pixel Replacement** variable. Instead of setting up all the data sets manually, you'll import the data sets from a text file.*

Before you import the text file, you need to understand how to build a file Photoshop CS2 and ImageReady CS2 will recognize.

2. In Microsoft Excel, open **flavor_of_the_month.xls** from the **flavor_of_the_month** folder in the **chap_17** folder you copied to your **Desktop**.

*If don't have Microsoft Excel, open the **flavor_of_the_month.txt** file in a text editor, such as NotePad or TextEdit. You can also build a properly formatted file in a text editor.*

*Take a look at how the file has been constructed. Notice there are two headings—**flavor** and **photo**. These headings will become the **Text Replacement** and **Pixel Replacement** variables. Also, notice under each heading are a series of words. The words under the **flavor** heading will become the values for the **Text Replacement** variable. The words under the **photo** heading are the images that will be used for the **Pixel Replacement** variable.*

Note: *If you store the images inside the same folder as the text file, you can use a relative path (just the filename). If you store the images in a different folder from the text file, you must specify the full path where the file is stored.*

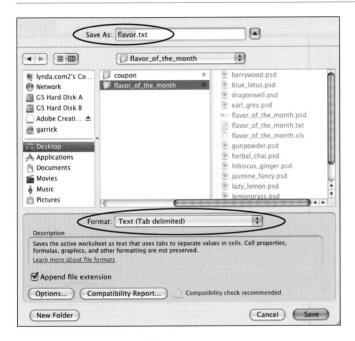

3. Choose **File > Save As**. In the **Save As** dialog box, choose **Text (Tab delimited)** or **CSV (Comma Separated Variable)** from the **Save Type As** pop-up menu. Name the file **flavor.txt** or **flavor.csv**, and click **Save**.

In order for Photoshop CS2 and ImageReady CS2 to successfully import data sets, you must save a tab-delimited text file or a comma-separated variable file.

*If you don't have Microsoft Excel, not to worry, you can use the **flavor_of_the_month.txt** file provided in the **flavor_of_the_month** folder in the **chap_17** folder you copied to your **Desktop** for the rest of the exercise.*

4. Return to Photoshop CS2. Choose **Image > Variables > Define** to open the **Variables** dialog box.

*Before you can import the text file, you must set up variables in Photoshop CS2 that are identical to the names of the variables you specified in the text file (**flavor** and **photo** in this case).*

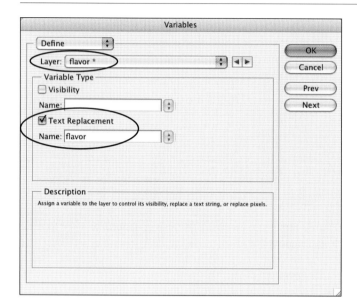

5. Choose **flavor** from the **Layer** pop-up menu. Turn on the **Text Replacement** option. Type **flavor** in the **Name** field.

*It may seem odd to you to create variables with the same names as the variables in the spreadsheet. The purpose of this step and the following step is to tell Photoshop CS2 which layer to replace with the contents of the spreadsheet. You must use the same names when you define the variables as the ones you used in the spreadsheet (in this case **flavor** and **photo**).*

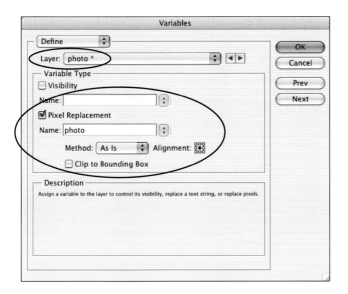

6. Choose **photo** in the **Layer** pop-up menu. Turn on the **Pixel Replacement** option. Type **photo** in the **Name** field. Choose **As Is** from the **Method** pop-up menu.

7. Choose **Data Sets** from the pop-up menu at the top of the **Variables** dialog box.

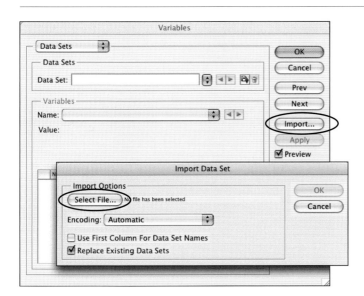

8. Click the **Import** button to open the **Import Data Set** dialog box. Click the **Select File** button to open the **Load** dialog box.

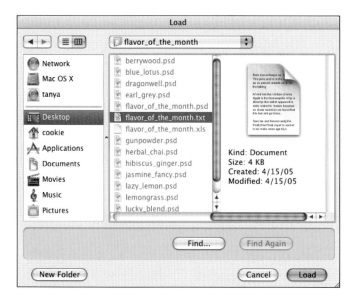

9. Navigate to the **flavor_of_the_month** folder in the **chap_17** folder you copied to your **Desktop**. Choose the **flavor.txt** file you saved in Step 3, or choose the **flavor_of_the_month.txt** file provided for you. Click **Load** (Mac) or **Open** (Windows).

10. Choose **Automatic** from the **Encoding** pop-up menu. Turn on the **Use First Column For Data Set Names** and the **Replace Existing Data Sets** options. Click **OK**.

*The **Use First Column For Data Set Names** will name the data sets using the names in the first column of the spreadsheet. This option is helpful because you won't have to rename the data after you import it. If you don't turn on this option, Photoshop CS2 will generate a generic name—Data Set 1, Data Set 2, and so on—which can be difficult to work with when you have a lot of data sets because they aren't very descriptive.*

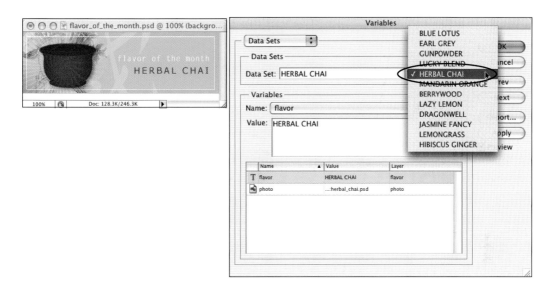

11. Use the **Prev** and **Next** buttons next to the **Data Set** pop-up menu to browse through the different data sets or choose a data set from the **Data Set** pop-up menu. Make sure the **Preview** option is turned on in the **Variables** dialog box, and position the **Variables** dialog box so you can see the results in the document window.

As you can see, it was very easy to create twelve data sets—one for each month of the year—by importing them from a text file. Although you could manually create these data sets as you did in previous exercises, you can see the huge time-saving benefit to importing data sets from a text file— especially if you need to create a large number of images.

12. In the **Variables** dialog box, click **OK** to accept your changes. If you'd like, use the techniques you learned in Exercise 5 to preview and export the data sets.

13. Close **flavor_of_the_month.psd**. You don't need to save your changes.

That's a wrap! You may not put these skills to work right away, but they are the workflow of the future. Next up: learning to integrate Photoshop CS2 and ImageReady CS2 with Adobe Illustrator and Adobe Acrobat.

18

Integrating with Illustrator and Acrobat

| Exporting Photoshop Files from Illustrator CS2 |
| Embedding Illustrator CS2 Files as Smart Objects |
| Creating PDFs from Photoshop CS2 |
| Saving PDFs with Password Protection | Creating Multipage PDFs |
| Creating PDF Presentations |

chap_18

PCS2Web HOT CD-ROM

When you're designing Web graphics, you'll often need to use more than one program. This chapter's exercises provide information about how to integrate with Illustrator CS2 and Adobe Acrobat. You'll learn how to export Illustrator CS2 files as Photoshop files while keeping editable layers. You'll also learn how to use the new Smart Objects feature in Photoshop CS2 to embed vector-based content created in Illustrator CS2 into a layered Photoshop file. The benefit of this workflow is that you can edit the vector-based Smart Object in Illustrator CS2 and have it update automatically in Photoshop CS2. It sounds terribly complicated, but you'll quickly see the benefits of this powerful new feature.

In this chapter you'll also learn how to create PDFs directly from Photoshop CS2. Photoshop CS2 has a new PDF engine with many new options for generating PDFs, which you'll learn about in detail. You'll also learn how to create multipage PDFs and PDF presentations directly from Photoshop CS2.

I. [PS] ——————Exporting Photoshop Files from Illustrator CS2

Sometimes you'll design a vector-based graphic in Illustrator CS2 and want to use that graphic in Photoshop CS2. You can use many techniques to take content created in Illustrator CS2 and bring it into Photoshop CS2. For example, if you don't want to edit the layered content from Illustrator CS2, you can simply copy and paste the content into Photoshop CS2. If you want to edit the content in Photoshop CS2, you'll want to export the Illustrator CS2 content as a Photoshop file. Here's an exercise to show you how.

1. In Illustrator CS2, open **logo.ai** from the **chap_18** folder you copied to your **Desktop**. Make sure the **Layers** palette is visible. If it's not, choose **Window > Layers**.

*Notice the file contains four layers—**text**, **smoke**, **cup**, and **circles**. You could copy and paste the contents of this image into Photoshop CS2, but you wouldn't be able to retain the layer information. In this exercise, you'll learn how to export Illustrator CS2 files as Photoshop files, which will preserve the same layer structure as you have in the original file.*

2. Choose **File > Export** to open the **Export** dialog box. Navigate to the **chap_18** folder you copied to your **Desktop**. Choose **Photoshop (psd)** from the **Format** pop-up menu. Click **Export** (Mac) or **Save** (Windows).

Notice the file extension automatically changes to .psd, indicating the file will be exported as a Photoshop file.

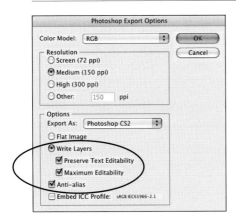

3. As soon as you click **Export**, the **Photoshop Export Options** dialog box opens and provides a number of options. Match the options to the ones shown in the illustration here. Click **OK**.

*Make sure you choose **Write Layers** and turn on the **Preserve Text Editability** and **Maximum Editability** options. These options are what will create a layered file you can open and edit in Photoshop CS2.*

4. In Photoshop CS2, open **logo.psd** from the **chap_18** folder you copied to your **Desktop**. Make sure the **Layers** palette is visible. If it's not, choose **Window > Layers**.

*Notice the structure of the layers in the **Layers** palette is identical to the original structure in Illustrator CS2. Also notice if you expand the contents of the text layer group, you'll see the text from Illustrator CS2 was automatically converted to a vector-based type layer in Photoshop CS2. If you want, you can edit the vector-based type layer using the techniques you learned in Chapter 6, "Creating Type."*

Exporting PSD files from Illustrator CS2 while keeping the layers intact makes it easy for you to create Web graphics that rely heavily on layers, such as rollovers, animations, and so on.

5. Close **logo.psd** and **logo.ai**. You don't need to save your changes.

NOTE | Learning Illustrator CS2

The purpose of the last exercise was to show you how to bring content from Illustrator CS2 into Photoshop CS2. If you're interested in learning more about how to use Illustrator CS2, check out the **Adobe Illustrator CS 2 Essential Training** video training with **Jeff Van West** available at **http://www.lynda.com**.

2. [PS] **Embedding Illustrator CS2 Files as Smart Objects**

In Chapter 9, "*Designing Navigation*," you learned about the benefit of using Smart Objects. In addition to defining layers as Smart Objects in Photoshop CS2, you can paste or place content from Illustrator CS2 as a Smart Object. When you want to edit the content, you can do so in Illustrator CS2. It sounds confusing, but you'll see how cool the Smart Objects feature is as you follow this exercise.

1. In Illustrator CS2, open **javaco_tea_logo.ai** from the **chap_18** folder you copied to your **Desktop**.

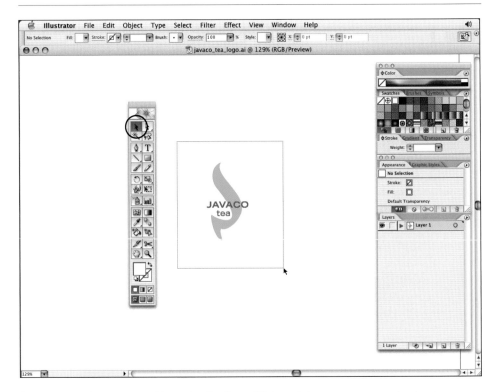

2. Select the **Selection** tool from the **Toolbox**. Click and drag to create a selection box around the **javaco tea** logo, as shown in the illustration here.

*When you release your mouse, the contents of the **javaco tea** logo should be fully selected, as shown in the illustration here.*

3. Choose **Edit > Copy**. When you've finished, close **javaco_tea_logo.ai**, leaving Illustrator CS2 open.

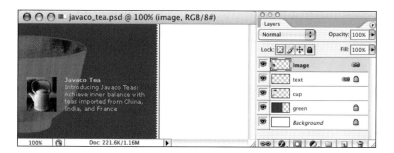

4. In Photoshop CS2, open **javaco_tea.psd** from the **chap_18** folder you copied to your **Desktop**. Make sure the **Layers** palette is visible. If it's not, choose **Window > Layers**.

5. In the **Layers** palette, click the **image** layer to select it. Choose **Edit > Paste**.

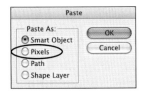

6. When the **Paste** dialog box appears, select **Smart Object**, and click **OK**.

*Notice the content you copied in Illustrator CS2 has been pasted into the center of the **javaco_tea** document. If you look at the **Layers** palette, you'll see a new entry called **Vector Smart Object**. Right now, the **javaco tea** logo you pasted from Illustrator CS2 has an X through it. Because content created in Illustrator CS2 is vector-based, you must rasterize it when you bring it into Photoshop CS2 by pasting as a Smart Object. Fortunately, you can resize the content before you rasterize the content, which will allow you to keep the crisp edges.*

Click and drag to resize the javaco tea logo.

7. Hold down the **Shift** key, and click and drag one of the resize handles to resize the **javaco tea** logo you pasted from Illustrator CS2.

*Holding down the **Shift** key constrains the bounding box and allows you to maintain the same aspect ratio when you resize.*

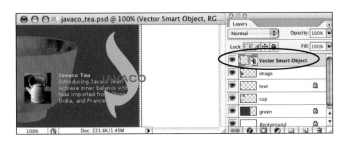

8. When you've finished resizing, position your cursor inside the bounding box and double-click.

*As soon as you double-click, the bounding box disappears, and the **Vector Smart Object** icon updates in the **Layers** palette to the **Smart Object** icon.*

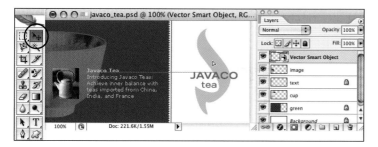

9. With the **Vector Smart Object** layer selected in the **Layers** palette, select the **Move** tool from the **Toolbox**. Click and drag to reposition the **javaco tea** logo, as shown in the illustration here.

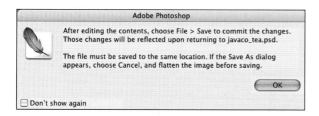

10. In the **Layers** palette, double-click the **Vector Smart Object** icon. A warning dialog box will appear, indicating you must choose **File > Save** to commit the changes. Click **OK** to acknowledge the warning.

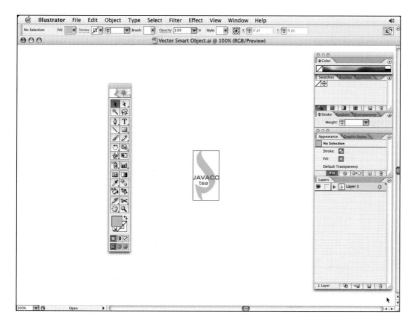

*As soon as you click **OK**, the **Vector Smart Object** will automatically open in Illustrator CS2.*

11. In Illustrator CS2, select the **Direct Selection** tool (the white arrow) from the **Toolbox**. Click the edge of the smoke curl to select the path.

12. Click and drag the nodes on the path to reshape the smoke curl, as shown in the illustration here. Don't worry if yours doesn't exactly match what you see here.

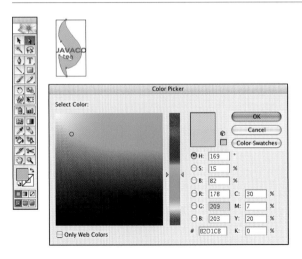

13. With the path still selected, in the **Toolbox** double-click the **Foreground Color** swatch to open the **Color Picker** dialog box. Choose a **light blue**, and click **OK**.

*Notice as soon as you click **OK**, the smoke curl updates with the color you chose in the **Color Picker** dialog box.*

14. In Illustrator CS2, choose **File > Save**. Close **Vector Smart Object.ai**, and return to Photoshop CS2.

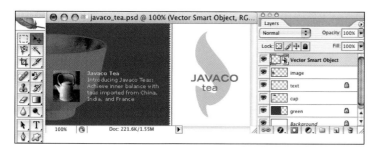

*As soon as you return to Photoshop CS2, you'll see the **javaco_tea.psd** file update automatically with the changes you made to the **Vector Smart Object** in Illustrator CS2. Very cool! Because Photoshop CS2 recognizes the content you pasted as a **Vector Smart Object**, you can edit the **Smart Object** in Illustrator CS2 while maintaining the vector-based properties. Further, if you need to make changes to the file, you don't have to copy and paste the revised content into Photoshop CS2— the **Vector Smart Object** updates the content automatically.*

15. Close **javaco_tea.psd**. You don't need to save your changes.

3. [PS] _____Creating PDFs from Photoshop CS2

PDF (**P**ortable **D**ocument **F**ormat) is used to exchange documents when the formatting of the document is critical, but the recipient may not have the application the document was created with (in this case, Photoshop CS2 or ImageReady CS2). Sure, you could send a GIF or a JPEG, but PDF has some advanced security features you may find useful.

For the past few versions, you've been able to save PDFs directly from Photoshop without the need for Adobe Acrobat. Photoshop CS2 boasts a brand-new PDF engine that provides many more options for saving PDFs, including advanced compression, output, and security settings.

In this exercise, you'll learn the basics of saving Photoshop files as PDFs. In the next exercise, you'll learn how to save PDFs with password protection. Later in this chapter, you'll also learn how to save multiple-page PDFs and PDF presentations from Photoshop CS2.

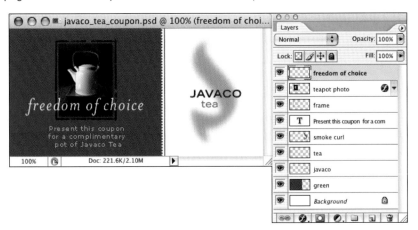

1. Open **javaco_tea_coupon.psd** from the **chap_18** folder you copied to your **Desktop**.

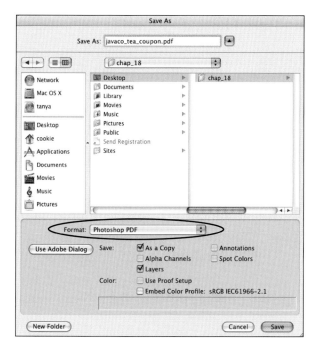

2. Choose **File > Save As**. In the **Save As** dialog box, navigate to the **chap_18** folder you copied to your **Desktop**. Choose **Photoshop PDF** from the **Format** pop-up menu. Turn on the **As a Copy** option. In the **Save As** field, name the file **javaco_tea_coupon.pdf**. Click **Save**.

*You'll find the **As a Copy** option helpful because it won't overwrite the current file you have open in Photoshop CS2.*

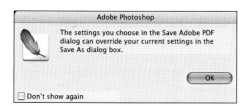

3. A warning dialog box will appear, indicating the settings you choose in the **Save Adobe PDF** dialog box can override the current settings in the **Save As** dialog box. Click **OK** to acknowledge the warning and to open the **Save Adobe PDF** dialog box.

*The **Save Adobe PDF** dialog box contains a number of advanced options. If you've used previous versions of Photoshop, this dialog box will look new to you. Photoshop CS2 includes a number of new options for saving PDFs.*

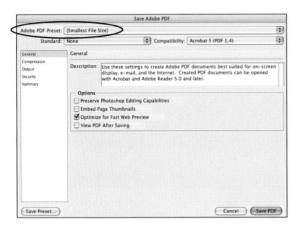

4. Choose **Smallest File Size** from the **Adobe PDF Preset** pop-up menu, and leave the other options in the dialog box the same.

*Notice the **Description** field updates automatically to reflect the settings you specified. **Smallest File Size** is best to use when you need to put content on the Web because it optimizes the image for fast Web preview.*

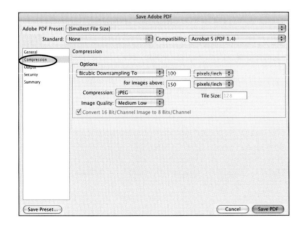

5. On the left side of the **Save Adobe PDF** dialog box, click **Compression**.

*Notice the contents of the **Save Adobe PDF** dialog box automatically change to reflect the **Compression** options. The **Compression** settings are designed to help you create the best quality images with the smallest file size when you want to use the saved PDF on the Web or when you want to share it with another user electronically. If you want to print the saved PDF, skip the **Compression** settings and go directly to the **Output** settings. Because the scope of this book focuses exclusively on creating images for the Web, you'll learn how to best create PDFs for the Web using the **Compression** settings. If you need to create a PDF for print, refer to the **Saving PDF Files** section of the Photoshop CS2 online Help.*

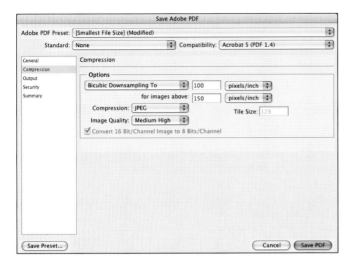

6. Match the settings in the **Compression** section of the **Save Adobe PDF** dialog box to the ones shown in the illustration here.

For more information about these ***Compression*** *settings, refer to the chart at the end of this exercise.*

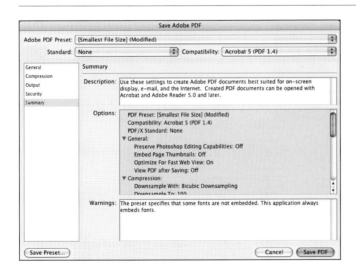

7. On the left side of the **Save Adobe PDF** dialog box, click **Summary**.

You'll see an overview of the settings you specified in the ***Save Adobe PDF*** *dialog box.*

8. Click **Save PDF**.

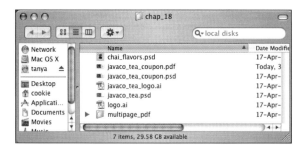

9. Browse to the **chap_18** folder you copied to your **Desktop**. Double-click the **javaco_tea_coupon.pdf** file you saved in the last step.

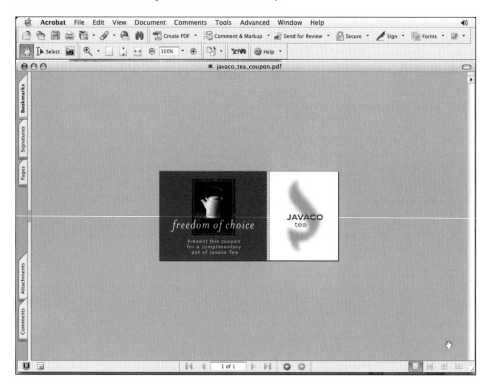

*Depending on what programs you have installed on your computer, **javaco_tea_coupon.pdf** will open in Adobe Acrobat or Adobe Reader. If you don't have a program that will open a PDF file, you can download Adobe Reader for free from Adobe's Web site at **http://www.adobe.com**.*

10. Close **javaco_tea_coupon.pdf**, and return to Photoshop CS2. Close **javaco_tea_coupon.psd**.

Understanding Adobe PDF Compression Options

When you're saving images as PDFs to share electronically or on the Web, either as single images, multi-page documents, or PDF presentations, you'll want to compress and downsample the image(s). The PDF engine in Photoshop CS2 provides many compression options. Here' a chart to help you understand.

Save As PDF Compression Options	
Term	**Description**
Downsampling	When you save PDFs for the Web, downsampling allows you to achieve higher compression settings, which makes for smaller images. Downsampling decreases the number of pixels in an image. For example, if you have an image with 300 ppi (pixels per inch), you may want to downsample it to 72 ppi, which is typically the resolution used for Web graphics. When you downsample an image, you decrease the number of pixels, which reduces the file size. In order to decrease the number of pixels, Photoshop CS2 must make some guesses about which pixels to keep and which ones to discard based on the number and range of colors in the image. This process is called *interpolation.* Photoshop CS2 provides four interpolation options in the Downsampling pop-up menu. Here's an overview of each option:
	Do Not Downsample: Turns off downsampling. Use this option if you are outputting PDFs for print and do not want to reduce the number of pixels in your image.
	Average Downsampling: Samples the colors of pixels in an area and replaces the pixels with the average pixel color.
	Subsampling: Chooses a pixel color in the middle of an area and uses that color for the entire area. You'll find Subsampling often produces undesirable results because it produces poor transitions between colors.
	Bicubic Downsampling: Averages the pixels by weighing the number and color of pixels. You'll find Bicubic the slowest but most precise interpolation method because it produces the smoothest transitions between colors.
Compression	You can choose one of the following compression methods to compress PDFs:
	None: Use this option if you do not want to compress the PDF.
	JPEG: JPEG is a lossy compression method, which means it eliminates pixel data during the compression process. For most images, JPEG compression produces smaller file sizes than ZIP compression.
	continues on next page

Save As PDF Compression Options *continued*	
Term	**Description**
Compression *(continued)*	**ZIP:** ZIP compression works best on images with single colors or repeating patterns. ZIP compression can be lossy or lossless, depending on which setting you choose from the Image Quality pop-up menu. For example, if you have an 8-bit image, and you choose 8-bit image quality, you'll apply lossless compression. If you have an 8-bit image, and you apply 4-bit compression, you'll apply lossy compression.
	JPEG2000: JPEG2000 is a newer international compression standard than JPEG, and it provides lossless compression, which can result in better image quality because it does not discard pixels during the compression process.
Image Quality	Image Quality options change, depending on which Compression method you choose. Here's an overview:
	• For JPEG and JPEG2000 compression, you can choose from Low, Medium Low, Medium, Medium High, and High. Low produces the poorest quality and the smallest file size. High produces the best quality and the largest file size.
	• For ZIP compression, you can choose from 4-bit or 8-bit. The bit-depth of the original image will determine the image quality. For example, if you have an 8-bit image, and you choose 8-bit image quality, you'll produce the best quality image. If you have an 8-bit image, and you apply 4-bit compression, you'll produce the poorest quality.
Tile Size	If you choose JPEG2000 compression, you can specify the number of tiles used to compress the file. The lower the tile size, the lower the quality. The higher the tile size, the higher the quality.
Convert 16 Bit/Channel Image to 8 Bits/Channel	Converts 16-bit images to 8-bit images. This option is only available if the original image is 16-bit, if you choose ZIP from the Compression pop-up menu, and if you choose Acrobat 5, Acrobat 6, or Acrobat 7 from the Compatibility pop-up menu.

[PS] _____**Saving PDFs with Password Protection**

One of the benefits of the PDF file format is the capability to password-protect specific commands, such as opening, editing, and printing. In this exercise, you'll learn how to set up password protection when you save PDF files from Photoshop CS2.

1. Open **chai_flavors.psd** from the **chap_18** folder you copied to your **Desktop**.

2. Choose **File > Save As**. In the **Save As** dialog box, navigate to the **chap_18** folder you copied to your **Desktop**. Choose **Photoshop PDF** from the **Format** pop-up menu. Turn on the **As a Copy** option. In the **Save As** field, name the file **chai_flavors.pdf**. Click **Save**.

---

3. A warning dialog box will appear, indicating the settings you choose in the **Save Adobe PDF** dialog box can override the current settings in the **Save As** dialog box. Click **OK** to acknowledge the warning and to open the **Save Adobe PDF** dialog box.

---

4. Choose **Smallest File Size** from the **Adobe PDF Preset** pop-up menu.

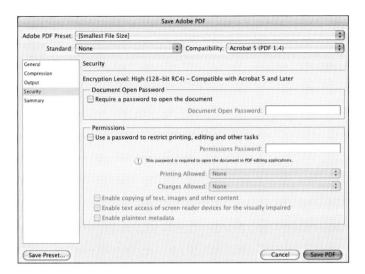

5. On the left side of the **Save Adobe PDF** dialog box, click **Security**.

Notice the contents of the Save Adobe PDF dialog box update automatically with the Security options.

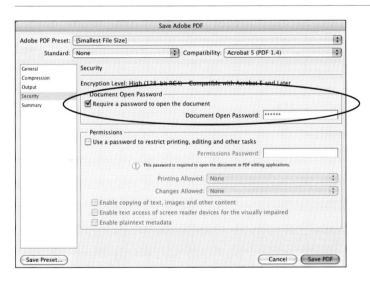

6. Turn on the **Require a password to open the document** option. Type **javaco** in the **Document Open Password** field.

You'll find this option helpful if you want to restrict who can open a document. The only way a user can open the document is by providing the required Document Open Password you specified in this step. The Document Open Password is required in any application you open the PDF, including Adobe Reader and Adobe Acrobat.

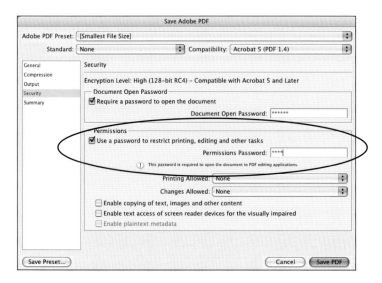

7. Turn on the **Use a password to restrict printing, editing and other tasks** option. Type **chai** in the **Permissions Password** field.

Users will only be prompted for this password if they try to edit the file using a PDF editing application, such as Adobe Acrobat.

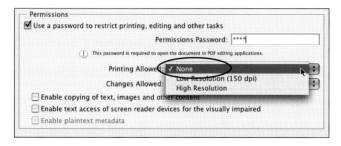

8. Take a look at the options in the **Printing Allowed** pop-up menu. As you can see, you can specify **None** (which allows no printing) **Low Resolution** printing, and **High Resolution** printing. Choose **None**.

*Choosing **None** is an excellent way to prevent users from printing a document.*

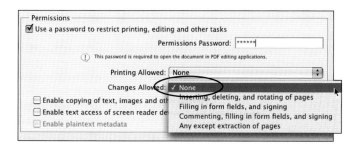

9. Take a look at the options in the **Changes Allowed** pop-up menu. As you can see, you have a lot of control over what type of editing users can perform when they open the PDF. Choose **None**.

Notice there are two other options at the bottom of the ***Save Adobe PDF*** *dialog box—****Enable copying of text, images and other content*** *and* ***Enable text access of screen reader devices for the visually impaired****. Depending on the level of access you want users to have to the content in your document, you can choose to leave these options turned off, or you can turn them on.*

10. Click **Save PDF**.

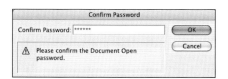

11. In the **Confirm Password** dialog box, type **javaco** to confirm the **Document Open** password. Click **OK**.

12. In the **Confirm Password** dialog box, type **chai** to confirm the **Permissions** password. Click **OK**.

13. Browse to the **chap_18** folder you copied to your **Desktop**. Double-click **chai_flavors.pdf** to open the file. When you open the file, you'll be prompted for a **Document Open** password. Type **javaco**, and click **OK**.

As soon as you type the correct password, the file will open automatically. You won't be able to print the file because you disabled printing.

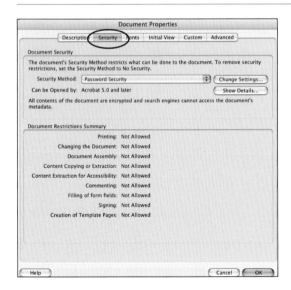

14. If you have the file open in Adobe Acrobat, choose **File > Document Properties** to open the **Document Properties** dialog box. Click **Security**. Click the **Change Settings** button.

*Notice **Password Security** is automatically selected in the **Security Method** pop-up menu.*

15. In the **Password** dialog box, type **chai** in the **Enter Password** field, and click **OK**.

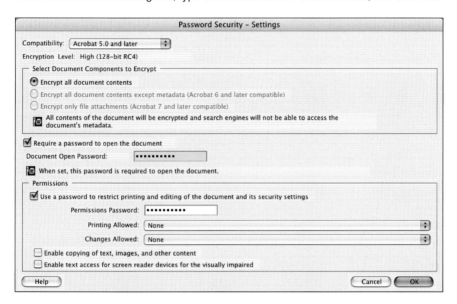

The **Password Security – Settings** dialog box will open automatically, which will let you change the security options you specified in Photoshop CS2.

16. Close **chai_flavors.pdf**, and return to Photoshop CS2. Close **chai_flavors.psd**.

Note: In order to open the **chai_flavors.pdf** file in Photoshop CS2, you'll need access to the **Document Open** and **Permissions** passwords.

NOTE | Learning Adobe Acrobat 7

The purpose of the last two exercises was to show you how to create PDFs in Photoshop CS2. If you're interested in learning more about how to use Adobe Acrobat 7, check out the **Learning Adobe Acrobat 7** video training with **Garrick Chow** available at: **http://www.lynda.com**.

5. [PS] Creating Multipage PDFs

In the last exercise, you learned how to create PDFs from a single image in Photoshop CS2. You can also create multipage PDFs from a series of images. Here's an exercise to show you how.

1. In Photoshop CS2, choose **File > Automate > PDF Presentation** to open the **PDF Presentation** dialog box. Click the **Browse** button so you can select the files you want to use in the multipage PDF.

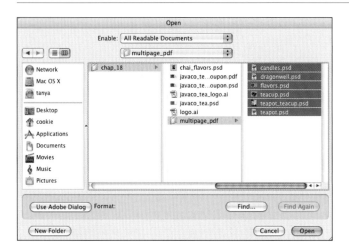

2. In the **Open** dialog box, navigate to the **multipage_pdf** folder in the **chap_18** folder you copied to your **Desktop**. Click **candles.psd** to select it. Hold down the **Shift** key, and multiple-select the entire contents of the **multipage_pdf** folder, as shown in the illustration here. Click **Open**.

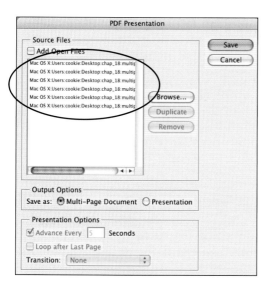

*Notice the **Source Files** box now contains the six images you just specified.*

---

3. Select **Multi-Page Document** from the **Save As** section if it's not already selected. Click **Save**.

*Wondering about the **Presentation Options**? You'll learn how to create a PDF presentation in the next exercise.*

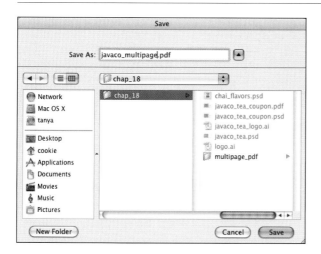

4. In the **Save** dialog box, navigate to the **chap_18** folder you copied to your **Desktop**. Type **javaco_multipage.pdf** in the **Save As** field. Click **Save**.

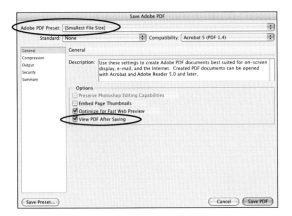

5. In the **Save Adobe PDF** dialog box, choose **Smallest File Size** from the **Adobe PDF Preset** pop-up menu. Turn on the **View PDF After Saving** option. (If you'd like, use the techniques you learned in Exercises 3 and 4 to customize the **Compression** and **Security** settings.) Click **Save PDF**.

This option will automatically open the file in Adobe Acrobat or Adobe Reader when you save the file.

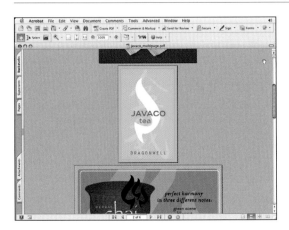

6. As soon as Photoshop CS2 finishes generating the file, **javaco_multipage.pdf** will open automatically in Adobe Acrobat or Adobe Reader. Use the scroll bar to navigate through the pages.

Notice each image is on its own page. Wondering why the images are all different sizes? When you create a multipage PDF, the individual pages are automatically created with the same pixel dimensions as the original images. Because some of the images were smaller than others, some of the pages in the PDF are smaller than others.

7. Close **javaco_multipage.pdf** and return to Photoshop CS2.

Next, you'll learn how to create a PDF presentation.

6. [PS] _____Creating PDF Presentations

In this exercise, you'll learn how create a PDF presentation complete with transitions!

1. In Photoshop CS2, choose **File > Browse** to open Adobe Bridge.

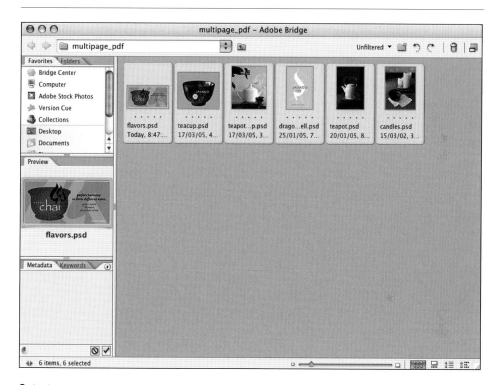

2. In Adobe Bridge, navigate to the **multipage_pdf** folder in the **chap_18** folder you copied to your **Desktop**. Using the **Shift** key or the **Cmd** (Mac) or **Ctrl** (Windows) key, multiple-select any or all of the images in the **multipage_pdf** folder.

3. Choose **Tools > Photoshop > PDF Presentation**.

*Note: You can also create a PDF presentation directly from Photoshop CS2 by choosing **File > Automate > PDF Presentation**. However, accessing this control from Adobe Bridge is helpful because it provides a visual interface to organize and select the images you want to use in the presentation.*

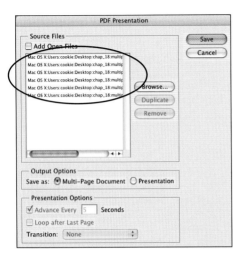

4. In the **PDF Presentation** dialog box, you'll notice that the images you selected in Adobe Bridge automatically appear in the **Source Files** box.

*Note: If you want to add any additional files, click **Browse** to locate them. If you want to remove any files, in the **Source Files** box click the unwanted file(s), and click **Remove**.*

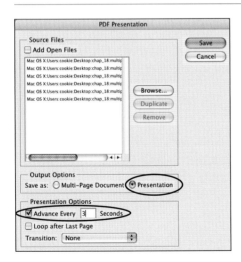

5. Click the **Presentation** option. Turn on the **Advance Every** option, and type **3** in the **Seconds** field. This option controls how quickly the pages advance from one to the next. Leave the **Loop after Last Page** option turned off.

*If you want the presentation to play continuously, turn on the **Loop after Last Page** option. If you want the presentation to play only once, leave this option turned off.*

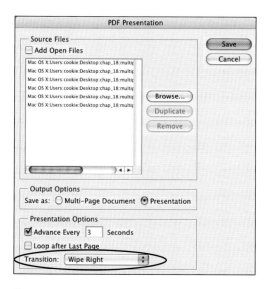

6. Choose **Wipe Right** from the **Transition** pop-up menu. Click **Save**.

*As you can see, you can choose from a number of different transitions. I like **Wipe Right** because it transitions smoothly from one slide to the next.*

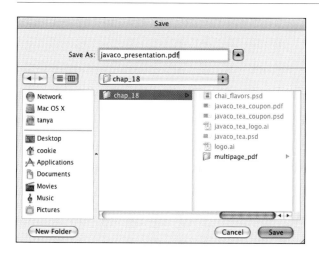

7. In the **Save** dialog box, navigate to the **chap_18** folder you copied to your **Desktop**. Name the file **javaco_presentation.pdf**, and click **Save**.

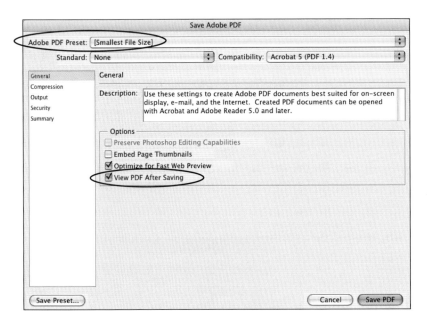

8. In the **Save Adobe PDF** dialog box, choose **Smallest File Size**. Turn on the **View PDF After Saving** option if it's not automatically turned on from the last exercise. (If you'd like, use the techniques you learned in Exercises 3 and 4 to customize the compression and security settings.) When you've finished, click **Save PDF**.

9. As soon as Photoshop CS2 finishes generating the file, **javaco_presentation.pdf** will automatically open and begin playing in Adobe Acrobat or Adobe Reader. If you want to navigate through the presentation more quickly, use the **Page Down** key to move forward and the **Page Up** key to move backwards.

As you can see, taking a series of images and converting them into a PDF presentation is very easy. You don't need any additional presentation software to create a simple, effective presentation.

10. Press the **Esc** key to exit the presentation and to return to Adobe Acrobat or Adobe Reader.

11. Close **javaco_presentation.pdf**.

12. Return to Adobe Bridge. Quit Adobe Bridge, and return to Photoshop CS2.

You've just finished another chapter. Next, you'll learn integration techniques with Macromedia Flash.

19

Integrating with Macromedia Flash

| Exporting Images to Macromedia Flash (SWF) |

| Exporting Images with Type and Shape Layers |

| Exporting Images with Layer Styles |

| Exporting Macromedia Flash (SWF) Files for the Web |

chap_19

PCS2Web HOT CD-ROM

When you're designing Web graphics in Photoshop CS2 or ImageReady CS2, you may want to take the content you created and bring it into Macromedia Flash. Unfortunately, even though you can import a Photoshop file into Macromedia Flash, it won't recognize the layers, which makes editing the contents of the file in Macromedia Flash almost impossible. Fortunately, ImageReady CS2 includes an **Export to Macromedia Flash** feature, which allows you to bring a layered file into Macromedia Flash.

The purpose of this chapter is to show you different techniques for exporting content from Photoshop CS2 and ImageReady CS2 to best maintain the correct appearance, structure, and maximum editability of layered Photoshop files. In this chapter, you'll also learn how to export files as Macromedia Flash files so they can be used directly on the Web without the need to use Macromedia Flash.

Importing Photoshop Files into Macromedia Flash

When you need to take content created in Photoshop CS2 or ImageReady CS2 into Macromedia Flash, your first instinct may be to import the Photoshop file directly into Flash. After all, both programs support layers, so why wouldn't Flash recognize the layers in a Photoshop file? Provided you have QuickTime installed on your computer, you can easily import the contents of a Photoshop file into Macromedia Flash. Unfortunately, the content will come in as a single bitmap, and the layered content you worked so hard to create in Photoshop CS2 and ImageReady CS2 will be lost. Here's an example:

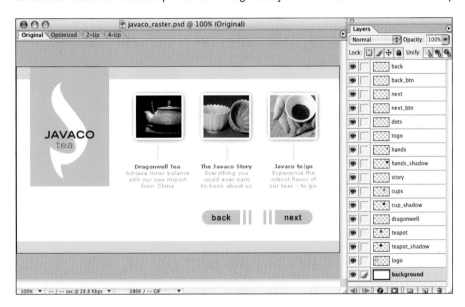

The illustration here shows a layered file in Photoshop CS2. As you can see, the file was constructed using a number of layers, including pixel-based layers, layer styles, vector-based shape layers, and vector-based type layers.

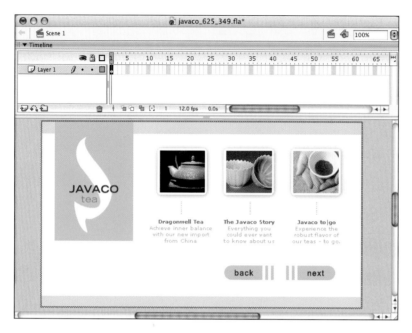

The illustration here shows the same file imported in Macromedia Flash MX 2004 Professional using the **File > Import > Import to Stage** command. As you can see, although the content looks identical to what you saw in Photoshop CS2, none of the layers from the layered Photoshop file were retained on import.

If you just want to import a flattened bitmap into Flash, this technique may be acceptable. If you want manipulate the contents of your layered Photoshop file in Macromedia Flash (which you inevitably will at some point), you can export the file as a Macromedia Flash (SWF) file from ImageReady CS2. At first glance, this may seem like the perfect solution. However, there are a few issues you'll need to work around, especially when your file contains vector-based type layers, vector-based shape layers, and layer styles. Not to worry, this chapter will show you techniques to work around these challenges.

I. [IR] _____**Exporting Images to Macromedia Flash (SWF)**

One way you can successfully import content created in Photoshop CS2 or ImageReady CS2 into Macromedia Flash is to use the **Export to Macromedia Flash (SWF)** feature in ImageReady CS2. Here's an exercise to show you how it works.

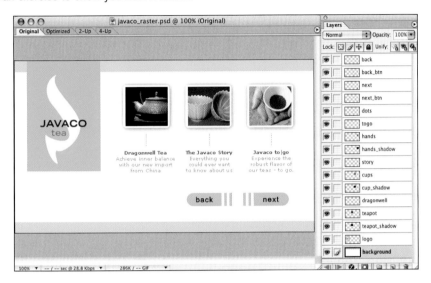

1. Open **javaco_raster.psd** from the **chap_19** folder you copied to your **Desktop**.

*Take a look at the **Layers** palette. Notice each element of this page is on a separate, pixel-based layer. Next, you'll export the file as a Macromedia Flash file.*

2. Choose **File > Export > Macromedia Flash (SWF)** to open the **Macromedia Flash (SWF) Export** dialog box.

*In the **Macromedia Flash (SWF) Export** dialog box, you'll see a number of options. Because your objective is to take the file directly into Macromedia Flash, you need to concern yourself with only two options—**Preserve Appearance** and **Format**. Later in this chapter, you'll learn how to export Macromedia Flash files to use directly on the Web, and you'll learn about the other options in this dialog box.*

3. Choose **Lossless-32** from the **Format** pop-up menu.

***Lossless-32** is the best format to use when you plan to import content into Macromedia Flash because it is the only format that maintains original layer transparency and does not compress the file. As a result, you'll keep the same level of transparency you had in your original Photoshop file, and you won't lose any pixel data during the export process.*

| 565 |

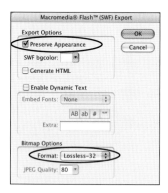

4. Turn on the **Preserve Appearance** option. Click **OK**.

*By turning on **Preserve Appearance**, you're instructing ImageReady CS2 to maintain the exact appearance of the file.*

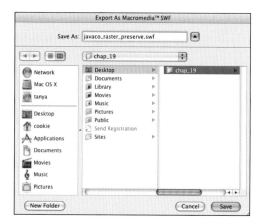

5. In the **Export As Macromedia SWF** dialog box, navigate to the **chap_19** folder you copied to your **Desktop**. Name the file **javaco_raster_preserve.swf**, and click **Save**.

6. When you click **Save**, a warning message appears, indicating text or shape layers were flattened because **Preserve Appearance** was checked. Click **OK** to acknowledge the warning. However, keep this warning message in mind because it will have an impact on how the layers come into Macromedia Flash, which you will soon witness for yourself.

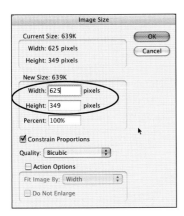

7. Choose **Image > Image Size**, and take note of the dimensions of the file. As you can see, the file is **625** pixels wide and **349** pixels high.

*Before you go to Macromedia Flash, you need to determine the image size of the **javaco_raster.psd** file so you can create a blank file with the same dimensions in Macromedia Flash. Creating a document with the same dimensions in Macromedia Flash will make it easy to import the contents of the **javaco_raster_preserve.swf** file.*

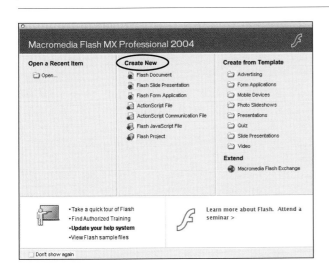

8. Launch Macromedia Flash, and choose **Flash Document** from the **Create New** section of the **Macromedia Flash MX Professional 2004 Welcome Screen**.

*A new file will open automatically. Before you import the contents of the **javaco_raster_preserve.swf** file, you need to make sure the Macromedia Flash document has the same dimensions as the **javaco_raster.psd** file.*

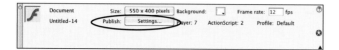

9. In Macromedia Flash, click the **Document Properties** button in the **Properties** palette.

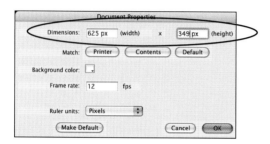

10. In the **Document Properties** dialog box, type **625 px** in the **width** field and **349 px** in the **height** field. Click **OK**.

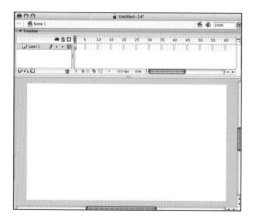

*The Macromedia Flash document should now be the same size as the original **javaco_raster.psd** file. Next, you'll save this blank Macromedia Flash file—you'll use it many times as you work through the exercises in this chapter.*

11. Choose **File > Save As**. In the **Save As** dialog box, navigate to the **chap_19** folder you copied to your **Desktop**. Name the file **javaco.fla** and click **Save**.

.fla is the native Macromedia Flash extension.

12. Choose **File > Import > Import to Stage**. In the **Import** dialog box, navigate to the **chap_19** folder you copied to your **Desktop**. Click **javaco_raster_preserve.swf** to select it, and click **Import** (Mac) or **Open** (Windows).

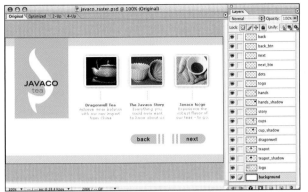

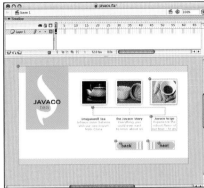

13. Press **Cmd+A** (Mac) or **Ctrl+A** (Windows) to select all.

Notice blue outlines appear around some, but not all, of the original layers. Although the imported image looks the same, some, but not all, of the layers were preserved. Remember the warning dialog box you saw after you saved the Macromedia Flash file? When you use the **Preserve Appearance** *option, you risk flattening some layers to maintain the exact appearance, regardless of whether they are type or shape layers. Next, you'll export the same file but with the* **Preserve Appearance** *option turned off.*

14. Choose **File > Revert**. Click **OK** (Mac) or **Revert** (Windows) to revert the **javaco.fla** file to a blank document.

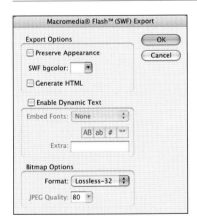

15. In ImageReady CS2, choose **File > Export > Macromedia Flash**. In the **Macromedia Flash (SWF) Export** dialog box, turn off **Preserve Appearance**, and click **OK**.

16. In the **Export As Macromedia SWF** dialog box, navigate to the **chap_19** folder you copied to your **Desktop**. Name the file **javaco_raster_no_preserve.swf**, and click **Save**.

17. In Macromedia Flash, choose **File > Import > Import to Stage**. Navigate to the **chap_19** folder you copied to your **Desktop**. Click **javaco_raster_no_preserve.swf**, and click **Import** (Mac) or **Open** (Windows).

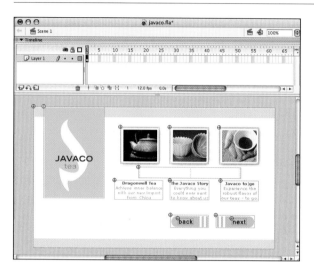

18. Press **Cmd+A** (Mac) or **Ctrl+A** (Windows) to select all.

Notice this time, blue lines appear around all of the original layers, indicating the layers have been retained on import. Plus, the file looks almost identical to the original Photoshop file in ImageReady CS2.

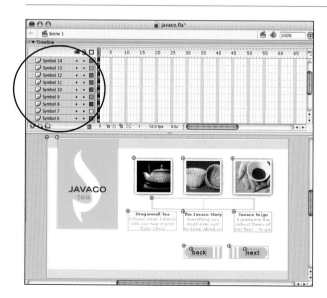

19. Choose **Modify > Timeline > Distribute to Layers**.

*All the layers from the original Photoshop file have now been converted to layers. Unfortunately, the layer names haven't been retained—they layers are named **Symbol 1**, **Symbol 2**, **Symbol 3**, and so on. If you want to rename the layers, the process is identical to renaming layers in Photoshop CS2. Double-click the layer name. When the bounding box appears, type the new layer name, and press **Return** (Mac) or **Enter** (Windows).*

*Although turning off **Preserve Appearance** may seem like the perfect solution because it maintains all the layers, you will run into problems when you work with vector-based type, shape, and layer styles. The next two exercises will provide an overview of the issues and help provide workarounds for those scenarios.*

20. Choose **File > Revert**. Click **OK** to revert the **javaco.fla** file to a blank document. Leave **javaco.fla** open for the next exercise.

21. Return to ImageReady CS2. Close **javaco_raster.psd**. You don't need to save your changes.

NOTE | Understanding Preserve Appearance

In this exercise, you exported layered Photoshop files as Macromedia Flash (SWF) files. First, you exported the file with Preserve Appearance turned on, which resulted in a loss of layers. Next, you exported the file with Preserve Appearance turned off, which maintained the layer structure of the original Photoshop file. This begs the question—what is Preserve Appearance?

Preserve Appearance rasterizes all content in a Photoshop file so it will look identical when you open the exported SWF file in Macromedia Flash. As a result, you'll maintain the exact appearance of the file, including layer styles, which Macromedia Flash cannot understand. Although the file will look identical, you'll compromise editability because it will drop some pixel-based layers, flatten layer styles, and rasterize vector-based type and shape layers. If you leave Preserve Appearance turned off, you'll maintain the original layer structure and vector-based content, but you'll lose the layer styles because Macromedia Flash cannot understand them. Fortunately, there are workarounds to these issues, which you'll learn about in the next two exercises.

TIP | Exporting Animations to Macromedia Flash

In this exercise, you learned how to export layered files from ImageReady CS2 to the Macromedia Flash format. If you create an animation in Photoshop CS2 or ImageReady CS2, and you want to bring it into Macromedia Flash, you can use the same techniques you learned in this chapter.

Just like with exporting images, the only two options in the **Export to Macromedia Flash** dialog box you need to concern yourself with are **Format** and **Preserve Appearance**. Use the **Lossless-32** format because it will maintain the original transparency, and it will not compress the file, which means you won't lose any pixel data during the export process. If you want to retain the layers, leave **Preserve Appearance** turned off.

NOTE | Learning Macromedia Flash

The purpose of this chapter is to show you how to effectively take content from Photoshop CS2 or ImageReady CS2 into Macromedia Flash. If you're interested in learning more about how to use Macromedia Flash, check out the following resources available from **http://www.lynda.com**:

- **Macromedia Flash MX 2004 HOT**
  by Rosanna Yeung, developed with Lynda Weinman
  lynda.com/books and Peachpit Press
  ISBN: 0321202988

- **Macromedia Flash MX 2004 Beyond the Basics HOT**
  by Shane Rebenschied, developed with Lynda Weinman
  lynda.com/books and Peachpit Press
  ISBN: 0321228537

- **Learning Flash MX 2004 video training**
  with Shane Rebenschied

- **Intermediate Flash MX 2004 video training**
  with Shane Rebenschied

- **Audio and Video Integration in Macromedia Flash MX 2004 video training**
  with Shane Rebenschied

2. [IR] Exporting Images with Type and Shape Layers

Macromedia Flash is a vector-based application. Although Photoshop CS2 is a bitmap-based application, it does offer some vector-based features, specifically vector-based type and vector-based shapes, which you learned about in earlier chapters. In this exercise, you'll learn how to export Photoshop files so you can edit vector-based content created in Photoshop CS2 and ImageReady CS2 in Macromedia Flash.

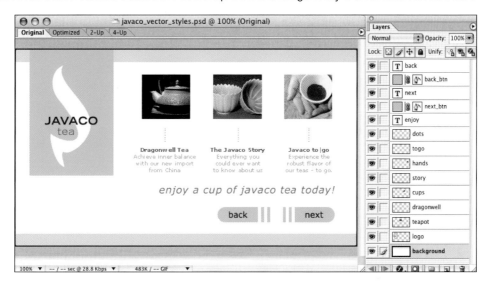

1. In ImageReady CS2, open **javaco_vector_styles.psd** from the **chap_19** folder you copied to your **Desktop**. Make sure the **Layers** palette and **Character** palette are visible. If they're not, choose **Window > Layers** and **Window > Character**.

*In the **Layers** palette, you'll see a series of pixel-based layers, two vector-based shape layers, which make up the **next** and **back** buttons, and three vector-based type layers. Because Macromedia Flash is a vector-based application, you'll often want to take vector-based content created in Photoshop CS2 or ImageReady CS2 into Macromedia Flash so you can continue to edit it. In this exercise, you'll learn how to export this file so you can maintain the vector-based content and edit it in Macromedia Flash.*

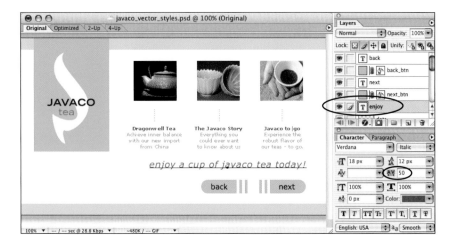

2. In the **Layers** palette, click the **enjoy** type layer to select it. In the **Character** palette, take a look at the **Tracking** setting for the type layer.

*Notice the **Tracking** is set to **50**.*

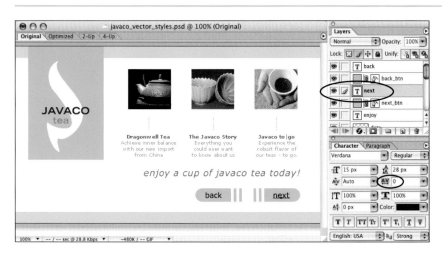

3. In the **Layers** palette, click the **next** type layer to select it. In the **Character** palette, take a look at the **Tracking** setting for the **next** type layer. Click the **back** type layer to select it. Take a look at the **Tracking** setting for the **back** type layer.

*Notice the **Tracking** is set to **0** for both the **next** and **back** type layers, which means no tracking has been applied. Although the tracking setting for the type layers may seem irrelevant now, it will become important later on in this exercise. For now, remember the settings for each of the three type layers in the image.*

4. In ImageReady CS2, choose **File > Export > Macromedia Flash SWF** to open the **Macromedia Flash (SWF) Export** dialog box.

*As you know from the last exercise, because you're taking content from ImageReady CS2 directly into Macromedia Flash (rather than using it directly on the Web), there are only two options you need to think about—**Preserve Appearance** and **Format**.*

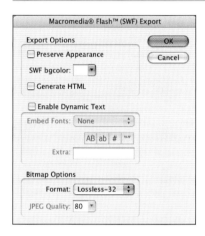

5. Turn off the **Preserve Appearance** option. Make sure **Lossless-32** is selected in the **Format** pop-up menu. Click **OK**.

*In the last exercise, when you turned on **Preserve Appearance** the file looked exactly the same as it did in ImageReady CS2, but not all the layers were maintained. When you turned off **Preserve Appearance**, the layers were all kept intact. Because your goal is to keep the layers so you can edit the vector-based content in Macromedia Flash, you'll leave **Preserve Appearance** turned off for this exercise. If you weren't concerned about the editability but wanted to have the content look the same as it does in ImageReady CS2, you'd turn on the **Preserve Appearance** option.*

*As you know from the last exercise, any time you export to SWF for purposes of taking content into Macromedia Flash, **Lossless-32** is the best format to choose because it maintains the transparency of the layers and does not compress the file, which means you won't lose any pixel data during the export process.*

6. In the **Export As Macromedia SWF** dialog box, navigate to the **chap_19** folder you copied to your **Desktop**. Name the file **javaco_vector_styles.swf**, and click **Save**.

7. In Macromedia Flash, you should have **javaco.fla** open from the last exercise. If not, open **javaco_625_349.fla** from the **chap_19** folder you copied to your **Desktop**. Both the **javaco.fla** file and the **javaco_625_349.fla** file have the same dimensions as the Photoshop file.

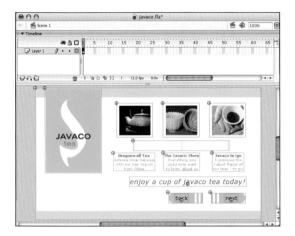

8. Choose **File** > **Import** > **Import to Stage**. Navigate to the **chap_19** folder you copied to your **Desktop**. Click the **javaco_vector_styles.swf** file to select it. Click **Import** (Mac) or **Open** (Windows). Press **Cmd+A** (Mac) or **Ctrl+A** (Windows) to select all.

Notice each layer from the Photoshop file is now its own separate object in Macromedia Flash, even though it is on the same layer. This is indicated by the blue bounding box around each object.

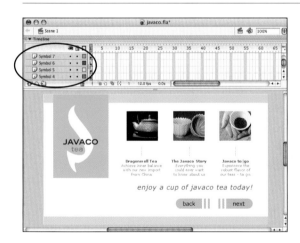

9. Choose **Modify** > **Timeline** > **Distribute to Layers**. Press **Esc** to deselect the layers.

*You now have a layered file in Macromedia Flash that matches the structure of the layered Photoshop file. Although each layer has a generic layer name (**Symbol 1**, **Symbol 2**, **Symbol 3**, and so on), you can easily rename a layer by double-clicking the layer name. When the bounding box appears, type the new layer name and press **Return** (Mac) or **Enter** (Windows).*

Next, you'll see how the vector-based type and shape layers were maintained.

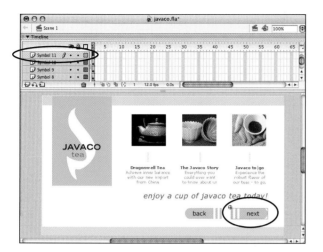

10. Click **Symbol 11** (the **next** button) to select it.

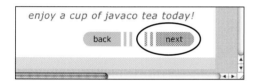

11. Choose **Modify > Break Apart**.

*The **next** button now has a series of dots over it. Not to worry, this isn't a permanent part of the button—it's simply the visual cue Macromedia Flash uses to indicate a vector is editable.*

12. Position your cursor off the **next** button and click, and you'll see the dots over the **next** button disappear.

 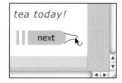 

13. Position your cursor at the edge of the **next** button. When the cursor changes, as shown in the illustration here, click and drag to reshape the button. Don't worry if the shape in your document doesn't exactly match the one shown in the illustration here.

*You can reshape the **next** button because Macromedia Flash recognizes the content of the layer as vector-based content—just like it was in ImageReady CS2.*

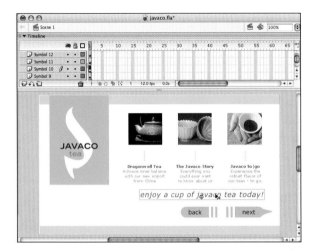

14. Click **Symbol 10** (the **enjoy a cup of javaco tea today!** type) to select it. Position your cursor inside the layer, and double-click to go into editing mode.

15. Click the characters of the **enjoy a cup of javaco tea today!** type.

Notice each character is a separate text block. Although it's still editable, vector-based text, having each separate character as its own text block won't make for easy editing.

16. At top of the document window, click the arrow to exit the editing mode.

17. Click **Symbol 14** (the **back** button label) to select it. Position your cursor inside the layer, and double-click to go into editing mode.

18. Click the characters on the **back** layer. When you've finished, at the top of the document window click the arrow to exit the editing mode.

*Notice all the characters are contained inside the same text block, which is a much easier editing scenario than having each character as its own text block. Wondering why the characters in the **back** button label are contained in a single text box and the characters in the **enjoy a cup of javaco tea today!** slogan are separated into individual text boxes? Do you remember when you looked at the tracking settings in the **Character** palette for the type layers at the beginning of this exercise? The **enjoy...** type layer used a **Tracking** setting of **50**; the **back** and **next** type layers had a **Tracking** setting of **0**. Because Photoshop CS2 and ImageReady CS2 use a different text-rendering engine than Macromedia Flash, some of the advanced type formatting features, such as tracking, cause characters to be separated into individual text boxes in order to maintain the correct formatting and appearance.*

At this point, you need to make some decisions about what's most important to you—do you want the type to look the same as it did in ImageReady CS2, or do you want to edit the text easily in Macromedia Flash? If you want to do basic editing in Macromedia Flash, such as changing color, you may be perfectly happy leaving the type in separate text boxes. If you do want to edit the type in Macromedia Flash, you'll find it easier to have the text in a single text box. In order to do that, you should use minimal formatting options when you create type in ImageReady CS2 and apply advanced formatting using the type features in Macromedia Flash. Follow the next few steps and you'll understand.

19. Choose **File > Revert**. Click **OK** to revert the **javaco.fla** file to a blank document.

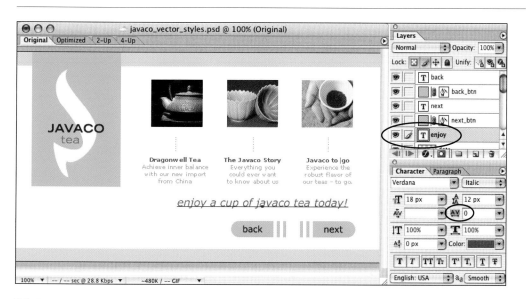

20. Return to ImageReady CS2. In the **Layers** palette, click the **enjoy** type layer to select it. In the **Character** palette, choose **0** from the **Tracking** pop-up menu.

21. Choose **File > Export > Macromedia Flash (SWF)**. In the **Macromedia Flash (SWF) Export** dialog box, make sure **Preserve Appearance** is turned off and **Lossless-32** is selected from the **Format** pop-up menu. Click **OK**.

22. In the **Export As Macromedia SWF** dialog box, navigate to the **chap_19** folder you copied to your **Desktop**. Name the file **javaco_vector_styles_no_track.swf**, and click **Save**.

23. In Macromedia Flash, choose **File > Import > Import to Stage**. In the **Import** dialog box, navigate to the **chap_19** folder you copied to your **Desktop**. Click **javaco_vector_styles_no_track.swf** to select it, and click **Import** (Mac) or **Open** (Windows).

24. Press **Cmd+A** (Mac) or **Ctrl+A** (Windows) to select all. Choose **Modify > Timeline > Distribute to Layers**.

25. Click **Symbol 10** to select it. Position your cursor inside the layer, and double-click inside to go into editing mode.

26. At the top of the document window, click the arrow to exit the editing mode.

Notice the type is now contained inside a single text box, which will make for much easier editing.

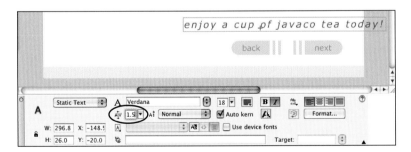

27. If you want to adjust the tracking in Macromedia Flash, type a value in the **Tracking** field on the **Text** palette, which is automatically visible when you edit vector-based type.

*Keep in mind, because Macromedia Flash uses a different text-rendering engine than Photoshop CS2 or ImageReady CS2, you may have to experiment with the tracking values. In this example, I typed **1.5** in the **Tracking** field, which closely matches the type in ImageReady CS2 when **Tracking** was set to **50**.*

28. If you'd like, experiment with the other options in the **Text** palette. When you've finished, at the top of the document window click the arrow to exit the editing mode.

29. Choose **File > Revert**. Click **OK** (Mac) or **Revert** (Windows) to revert the **javaco.fla** file to a blank document. Leave **javaco.fla** open for the next exercise.

30. Return to ImageReady CS2. Leave **javaco_vector_styles.psd** open for the next exercise.

WARNING | Type Layer Compatibility Issues

If you export a Photoshop file with vector-based type you created in an older version of Photoshop or ImageReady (any version other than CS2), you may get an error message during the **Export to Macromedia Flash** process. Because ImageReady CS2 doesn't automatically prompt you to update type layers when you open Photoshop files, you'll have to update the type layers manually. If you get this warning message, do the following for each of the type layers in the file:

1. Double-click the **T** icon of the type layer to highlight the type.

2. Without making any changes to the type, on the **Options** bar click the **Commit Current Edits** button.

The type layer will automatically be updated and you can now successfully export the file to Macromedia Flash.

---

3. [IR] _____Exporting Images with Layer Styles

In the last exercise, you learned how to effectively export layered files with vector-based type and shapes to Macromedia Flash while preserving the vector-based content. What if you work with layer styles? Layer styles introduce a new problem when exporting layered Photoshop CS2 and ImageReady CS2 files to Macromedia Flash. This exercise will identify the issues and provide workarounds to help you maintain the effect of layer styles when exporting files to the Macromedia Flash format.

1. If you followed the last exercise, **javaco_vector_styles.psd** should still be open in ImageReady CS2. If it's not, go back and complete Exercise 2. Make sure the **Layers** palette is visible. If it's not, choose **Window > Layers**.

In the last exercise, you exported this file to the Macromedia Flash format by turning off **Preserve Appearance**, *which allowed you to maintain editability with the vector-based type and shape layers. In this exercise, you'll introduce a new challenge—layer styles.*

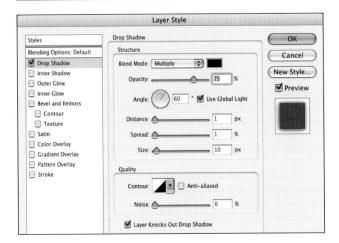

2. In the **Layers** palette, click the **teapot** layer to select it. Choose **Drop Shadow** from the **Layer Styles** pop-up menu. In the **Layer Style** dialog box, match the settings to the ones shown in the illustration here. Click **OK**.

3. Hold down the **Option** (Mac) or **Alt** (Windows) key and click and drag the **Drop Shadow** layer style into the **cups** layer. Repeat this step for the **hands** layer. You now have the same drop shadow layer style on the **teapot**, **cups**, and **hands** layers.

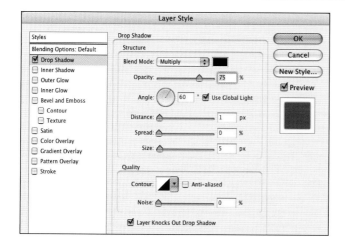

4. In the **Layers** palette, click the **enjoy** type layer to select it. Choose **Drop Shadow** from the **Layer Styles** pop-up menu. In the **Layer Style** dialog box, match the settings to the ones shown in the illustration here. Click **OK**.

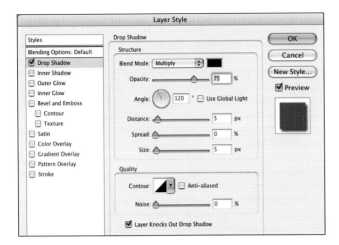

5. In the **Layers** palette, click the **next_btn** shape layer to select it. Choose **Drop Shadow** from the **Layer Styles** pop-up menu. In the **Layer Style** dialog box, match the settings to the ones shown in the illustration here.

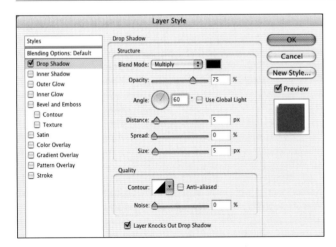

6. In the **Layers** palette, click the **back_btn** shape layer to select it. Choose **Drop Shadow** from the **Layer Styles** pop-up menu. In the **Layer Style** dialog box, match the settings to the ones shown in the illustration here.

Now that you have a series of layer styles attached to different types of layers—pixel-based layers and vector-based type and shape layers—it's time to look at what happens when you export a file with layer styles to the Macromedia Flash format.

7. Choose **File > Export > Macromedia Flash (SWF)**. In the **Macromedia Flash (SWF) Export** dialog box, leave the **Preserve Appearance** option turned off, and make sure **Lossless-32** is selected in the **Format** pop-up menu. Click **OK**.

*Based on what you learned in the last two exercises, you know that in order to maintain the layers as individual objects, you need to export Photoshop files with **Preserve Appearance** turned off.*

8. In the **Export As Macromedia SWF** dialog box, navigate to the **chap_19** folder you copied to your **Desktop**. Name the file **javaco_vector_styles_pres.swf** and click **Save**.

9. In Macromedia Flash, **javaco.fla** should still be open from the last exercise. If it's not, open **javaco_625_349.fla** from the **chap_19** folder you copied to your **Desktop**.

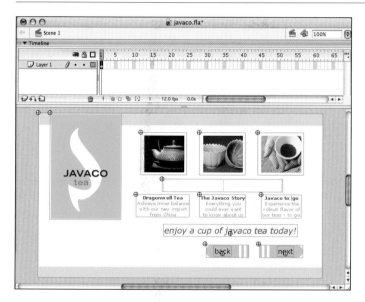

10. Choose **File > Import > Import to Stage**. In the **Import** dialog box, navigate to the **chap_19** folder you copied to your **Desktop**. Choose **javaco_vector_styles_pres.swf**, and click **Import** (Mac) or **Open** (Windows). When the file has imported successfully, press **Cmd+A** (Mac) or **Ctrl+A** (Windows) to select all.

As you can see, the layers were retained. Unfortunately, the layer styles were dropped during the import process.

11. Choose **File > Revert**. Click **OK** (Mac) or **Revert** (Windows) to revert the **javaco.fla** file to a blank document.

12. Return to ImageReady CS2. Choose **File > Export > Macromedia Flash (SWF)**. In the **Macromedia Flash (SWF) Export** dialog box, turn on the **Preserve Appearance** option, and make sure **Lossless-32** is selected in the **Format** pop-up menu. Click **OK**. In the **Export As Macromedia SWF** dialog box, navigate to the **chap_19** folder you copied to your **Desktop**. Name the file **javaco_vector_styles_no_pres.swf**, and click **Save**. A warning message appears, indicating text or shape layers were flattened because **Preserve Appearance** was checked. Click **OK** to acknowledge the warning, but keep this warning message in mind.

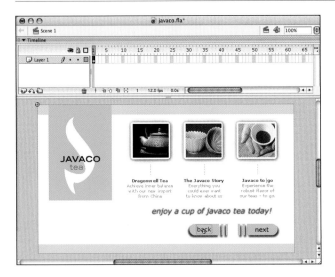

13. In Macromedia Flash, choose **File > Import > Import to Stage**. In the **Import** dialog box, navigate to the **chap_19** folder you copied to your **Desktop**. Click **javaco_vector_styles_no_pres.swf** to select it, and click **Import** (Mac) or **Open** (Windows). When the file has imported successfully, press **Cmd+A** (Mac) or **Ctrl+A** (Windows) to select all.

*With the **Preserve Appearance** option on, you lost the layers, but you retained the layer styles. Unfortunately, the only way you can keep layer styles when you export Photoshop files to Macromedia Flash is to turn on **Preserve Appearance**. What if you want to retain the layers, including the vector-based content, and keep the layer styles, too?*

There are two ways to address this problem: you can merge the layer style with the layer it is attached to; or you can put the contents of the layer style into its own layer. Ultimately, you need to decide how much editability you want to have in Macromedia Flash. If you want to work with the layer and the layer style at the same time, go with the first option. If you want to work with the layer style independent of the layer it's attached to, go with the second option. In the next few steps, you'll learn both techniques.

14. Choose **File > Revert**. Click **OK** (Mac) or **Revert** (Windows) to revert the **javaco.fla** file to a blank document.

15. Return to ImageReady CS2. In the **Layers** palette, click the **logo** layer to select it. At the bottom of the **Layers** palette, click the **New Layer** button to create a new layer above the **logo** layer.

16. In the **Layers** palette, click the **teapot** layer to select it. Choose **Layer > Merge Down**, or use the shortcut key **Cmd+E** (Mac) or **Ctrl+E** (Windows). The contents of the **teapot** layer, including the layer style, will automatically be merged into **Layer 1**. Double-click the **Layer 1** layer name. When you see the bounding box, rename the layer **teapot**, and press **Return** (Mac) or **Enter** (Windows).

17. In the **Layers** palette, toggle the visibility of the **teapot** layer.

As you can see, the shadow is now a permanent part of the layer. If you compare the shadow in the **teapot** *layer to the shadow in the* **cups** *or* **hands** *layer, you'll notice it looks identical, but it is no longer a layer style. It has been merged with the layer.*

18. In the **Layers** palette, click the **dragonwell** layer to select it. At the bottom of the **Layers** palette, click the **New Layer** button to create a new layer, **Layer 1**, above the **dragonwell** layer. Click the **cups** layer to select it. Press **Cmd+E** (Mac) or **Ctrl+E** (Windows) to merge the contents of the **cups** layer, including the layer style, into **Layer 1**. Double-click the **Layer 1** layer name. When the bounding box appears, rename the layer **cups**, and press **Return** (Mac) or **Enter** (Windows).

19. In the **Layers** palette, click the **story** layer to select it. At the bottom of the **Layers** palette, click the **New Layer** button to create a new layer, **Layer 1**, above the **story** layer. Click the **hands** layer to select it. Press **Cmd+E** (Mac) or **Ctrl+E** (Windows) to merge the contents of the **hands** layer, including the layer style, into **Layer 1**. Double-click the **Layer 1** layer name. When the bounding box appears, rename the layer **hands**, and press **Return** (Mac) or **Enter** (Windows).

20. In the **Layers** palette, click the **dots** layer to select it. At the bottom of the **Layers** palette, click the **New Layer** button to create a new layer, **Layer 1**, above the **dots** layer. Click the **enjoy** type layer to select it. Press **Cmd+E** (Mac) or **Ctrl+E** (Windows) to merge the contents of the **enjoy** layer, including the layer style, into **Layer 1**.

Did you notice the problem with this technique? You lost the vector-based type layer when you merged the layers. Any time you merge a vector-based layer and a layer style, you automatically convert the contents of the layer to a pixel-based layer. If you want to edit the vector-based type in Macromedia Flash, merging layers isn't the answer. Fortunately, there is another workaround. You can put the contents of the layer style into its own layer, which will be independent of the vector-based type layer. Follow the next few steps, and you'll understand.

21. Press **Cmd+Z** (Mac) or **Ctrl+Z** (Windows) twice—once to undo the **Merge Layers** command, and once to undo the **New Layer** command.

22. At the bottom of the ImageReady CS2 **Toolbox**, click the **Edit in Photoshop** button.

In order to put the contents of a layer style onto its own layer, you must use Photoshop CS2.

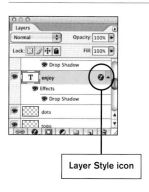

Layer Style icon

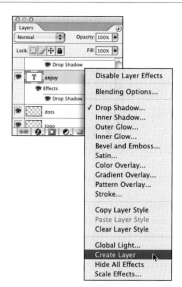

23. Ctrl+click (Mac) or **right-click** (Windows) the **Layer Style** icon next to the **enjoy** layer name. Choose **Create Layer** from the contextual menu. A warning message appears, indicating some aspects cannot be reproduced with layers. Click **OK** to acknowledge the warning.

For some of the more complex layer styles, you won't be able to place the contents into a separate layer. Fortunately, drop shadows work fine if you place them on their own layers.

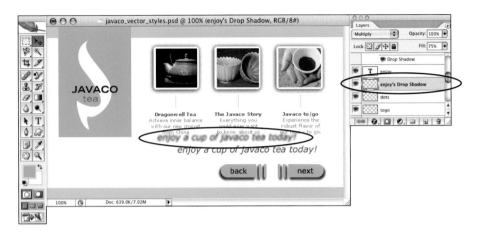

24. Click the **enjoy's Drop Shadow** layer to select it. Toggle the visibility of **enjoy's Drop Shadow**. With the visibility turned on, select the **Move** tool from the **Toolbox**. Click and drag.

*As you can see, the drop shadow is now independent of the **enjoy** layer. By default, when you created the new layer, Photoshop CS2 automatically named the layer **enjoy's Drop Shadow**. You can change this long layer name if you want to, using the techniques you learned in Chapter 5, "Working with Layers."*

25. Press **Cmd+Z** (Mac) or **Ctrl+Z** (Windows) to undo the move you made with the **Move** tool so the drop shadow is properly positioned below the **next** button.

*Next, you'll move onto the **next_btn** and **back_btn** vector-based shape layers. As with the vector-based type layers, if you use the merge layer style technique you learned earlier in this exercise, you'll lose the vector-based shape layer, and you won't be able to edit the shape in Macromedia Flash. In order to keep the vector-based properties, you need to put the shadow on its own layer.*

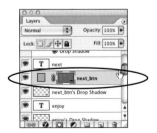

26. Ctrl+click (Mac) or **right-click** (Windows) the layer style icon next to the **next_btn** layer name. Choose **Create Layer** from the contextual menu. A warning message appears, indicating some aspects cannot be reproduced with layers. Click **OK** to acknowledge the warning.

*In the **Layers** palette, you should now have a **next_btn's Drop Shadow** layer, which contains the contents of the drop shadow layer style.*

27. Ctrl+click (Mac) or **right-click** (Windows) the layer style icon next to the **back_btn** layer name. Choose **Create Layer** from the contextual menu. A warning message appears, indicating some aspects cannot be reproduced with layers. Click **OK** to acknowledge the warning.

*In the Layers palette, you should now have a **back_btn's Drop Shadow** layer, which contains the contents of the drop shadow layer style.*

---

28. At the bottom of the Photoshop CS2 **Toolbox,** click the **Edit in ImageReady CS2** button to open **javaco_vector_styles.psd** in ImageReady CS2.

Next, you'll export the file to Macromedia Flash and see the results of your hard work.

---

29. Choose **File > Export > Macromedia Flash (SWF)**. In the **Macromedia Flash (SWF) Export** dialog box, leave **Preserve Appearance** turned off, and make sure **Lossless-32** is selected in the **Format** pop-up menu. Click **OK**. In the **Export As Macromedia SWF** dialog box, navigate to the **chap_19** folder you copied to your **Desktop**. Name the file **javaco_vector_styles_shadows.swf**. Click **Save**.

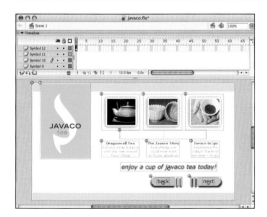

30. In Macromedia Flash, choose **File > Import > Import to Stage**. In the **Import** dialog box, navigate to the **chap_19** folder you copied to your **Desktop**. Click the **javaco_vector_styles_shadows.swf** file to select it. Click **Import** (Mac) or **Open** (Windows). When the file has imported successfully, press **Cmd+A** (Mac) or **Ctrl+A** (Windows) to select all. Choose **Modify > Timeline > Distribute to Layers**.

As you can see, you've maintained the original layer structure, and you've maintained the shadows. Phew!

---

31. Close **javaco.fla**. You don't need to save your changes.

32. Return to ImageReady CS2. Close **javaco_vector_styles.psd**. You don't need to save your changes.

TIP | PSD2FLA Plug-In by Media Lab

So far in this chapter, you've learned how to get layered content from Photoshop CS2 into Macromedia Flash using the ImageReady CS2 Export to Macromedia Flash SWF feature. As you saw in the exercises, you often need to make some compromises in order to maintain the layer structure of the original Photoshop file.

There is a commercial solution available that converts Photoshop files to the Macromedia Flash format: the PSD2FLA plug-in, which you can download from **http://www.medialab.com**. Unlike the Export to Macromedia Flash feature in ImageReady CS2, the PSD2FLA plug-in exports files as FLA files, the native Macromedia Flash format. As a result, you can open the exported file in Macromedia Flash, while maintaining the original layer structure, rather than importing an SWF.

Note: You can download a trial version of the **PSD2FLA** plug-in from **http://www.medialab.com**. When you open the exported file in Macromedia Flash, you'll see a series of blue lines through the image. To eliminate these blue lines, you can purchase an unlock key from **http://www.medialab.com**.

Here's how it works:

Once you have the PSD2FLA plug-in installed, open a file in Photoshop CS2, and choose **File > Export > PSD2FLA**. The **PSD2FLA** dialog box will open automatically.

Turn on the **Open in Flash After Export** option so the file will automatically open in Macromedia Flash.

Turn on the **Export Hidden Layers** option if you want all layers, including those with the visibility turned off, exported. If you don't want to export layers with the visibility turned off, turn off the **Export Hidden Layers** option.

continues on next page

TIP | PSD2FLA Plug-In by Media Lab *continued*

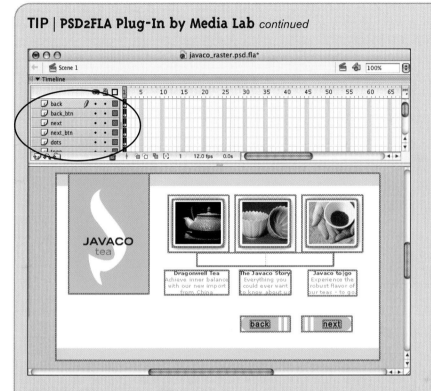

Click **OK**. When you click **OK**, the file will open automatically in Macromedia Flash with all the layers intact. Even better, the layer names you specified in the **Layers** palette were maintained. If you look at the filename, you'll see the **.fla** extension has been added, indicating it is a Macromedia Flash file, not an SWF file.

Note: When you export files with vector-based shape and type layers, they will automatically be converted to pixel-based layers. When you export files with layer styles, they will be merged with the layer on export.

NOTE | More About Photoshop and Flash Integration

If you're interested in learning more in-depth techniques for taking content from Photoshop CS2 and ImageReady CS2 into Macromedia Flash, check out the **Photoshop and Flash Integration** video training with **Michael Ninness**, available from **http://www.lynda.com**.

4. —————————Exporting Macromedia Flash (SWF) Files for the Web

So far in this chapter, you've learned techniques for successfully taking layered content created in Photoshop CS2 and ImageReady CS2 into Macromedia Flash. Occasionally, you may want to export an SWF file from ImageReady CS2 to use directly on the Web without taking it into Macromedia Flash. When you want to save directly for the Web, there are a few options in the Export As Macromedia SWF dialog box you need to consider, including generating HTML, background color, and format.

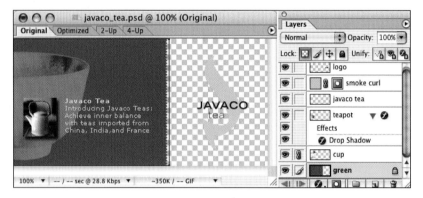

1. Open **javaco_tea.psd** from the **chap_19** folder you copied to the **Desktop**. Make sure the **Layers** palette is visible. If it's not, choose **Window > Layers**.

*Take a look at the contents of the **Layers** palette. Notice the file is constructed of pixel-based layers (one with a layer style), and one vector-based shape layer. Also notice the area surrounding the **javaco tea** logo is transparent. The good news is, because you're exporting directly for the Web, you don't need to retain the layers in the exported Macromedia Flash file. Therefore, you don't have to worry about the complex workarounds you learned about earlier in this chapter.*

2. Choose **File > Export > Macromedia Flash (SWF)**.

3. In the **Macromedia Flash (SWF) Export** dialog box, turn on the **Preserve Appearance** option.

*Because the purpose of this exercise is to take content from ImageReady CS2 to the Macromedia Flash format to use directly on the Web, your first priority is making sure the file looks exactly the same as it did in ImageReady CS2. As you know from previous exercises, the best way to ensure your file looks exactly as it did in ImageReady CS2 is to turn on the **Preserve Appearance** option.*

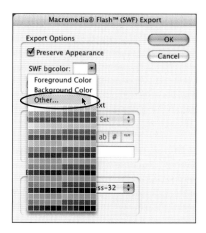 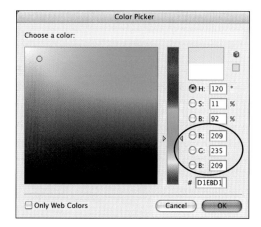

4. Choose **Other** from the **SWF bgcolor** pop-up menu to open the **Color Picker** dialog box. In the **Color Picker** dialog box, specify **R: 209**, **G: 235**, and **B: 209**. Click **OK**.

5. Turn on the **Generate HTML** option.

*When you use Macromedia Flash files on the Web, your viewers need the Macromedia Flash browser plug-in in order to view the files. If you turn on the **Generate HTML** option, ImageReady CS2 will automatically generate the HTML required to make the file work in a Web browser, including the browser plug-in detection code, which ensures viewers have the Macromedia Flash plug-in installed on their computers. If they don't, they will automatically be directed to Macromedia's Web site, where they can download the plug-in for free. As you can imagine, if you don't know HTML, writing that piece of code is quite complex, so you might as well let ImageReady CS2 do the work for you.*

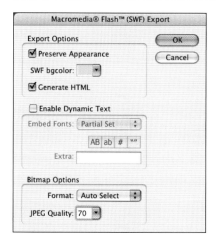

6. Choose **Auto Select** from the **Format** pop-up menu. Type **70** in the **JPEG Quality** field.

When you're exporting Macromedia Flash files for the Web, you can choose one of three formats: *JPEG*, which is best for continuous-tone images or photographs because, as the name suggests, it is based on the JPEG file format; *Lossless-8*, which is best for flat, graphical content because it is based on the GIF file format; and *Auto Select*, which automatically determines the best format based on the content in the file. If you choose *JPEG* or *Auto Select*, you have access to the *JPEG Quality* option.

Like optimizing JPEGs, the higher the quality, the better the image quality and the larger the file size; the lower the quality, the poorer the image quality and the smaller the file size. As you learned in Chapter 7, "Optimizing Images," you need to experiment in order to produce the highest quality image with the smallest file size. Unfortunately, the Macromedia Flash (SWF) Export dialog box does not provide a preview option, so you'll have to export the file, take a look at the exported file, and determine if you're happy with the quality and image size. If not, you'll have to go back to the Export to Macromedia Flash (SWF) dialog box, specify a different Quality setting, and re-export the file.

7. In the **Macromedia Flash (SWF) Export** dialog box, click **OK**. In the **Export As Macromedia SWF** dialog box, navigate to the **chap_19** folder you copied to your **Desktop**. Create a new folder and name it **javaco_tea**. Leave the filename as the default, **javaco_tea.swf**, and click **Save**.

8. When you click **Save**, a warning message appears, indicating text or shape layers were flattened because **Preserve Appearance** was checked. Again, because your goal is to use the file directly on the Web without going into Macromedia Flash, you don't need to worry if you've lost any layers or the editability of the vector-based shape layer. Click **OK** to acknowledge the warning.

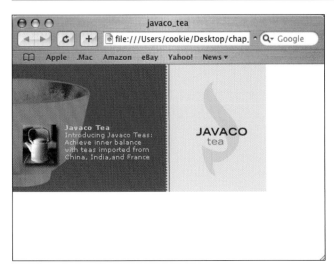

9. Browse to the **javaco_tea** folder in the **chap_19** folder you copied to your **Desktop**. Double-click **javaco_tea.html**.

*javaco_tea.html will automatically open in your default Web browser. You may find it odd that the color you specified as the **SWF bgcolor** is only covering the areas where the original ImageReady CS2 image was transparent, not the entire background of the Web page. Although it's labeled **bgcolor** in the **Macromedia Flash (SWF) Export** dialog box, it works more like the matte color feature when you're optimizing JPEGs in Photoshop CS2 and ImageReady CS2 in that it fills transparent pixels with the color you specified in the **Matte Color** pop-up menu. If you want to specify a background color, do so using the **Output Settings**, which you learned about in Chapter 8, "Creating Web Backgrounds."*

10. Close the Web browser, and return to ImageReady CS2. Close **javaco_tea.psd**. You don't need to save your changes.

WARNING | Exporting SWF Animations for the Web

Although you can export animations from ImageReady CS2 to the Macromedia Flash format, use caution when you export Macromedia Flash files to use on the Web. As you know, you need to maintain the best image quality and the smallest file size.

If you're optimizing a simple animation built with layer visibility, and you choose **Auto Select**, **JPEG**, or **Lossless-8** from the **Format** pop-up menu, you'll be able to create an animation that looks good with a relatively small file size.

However, if you're working with a more complex animation that involves tweening, you'll run into some trouble when you export the animation. If you choose **Auto Select**, **JPEG**, or **Lossless-8**, you'll see muddy, black frames when you play the animation because those formats can't handle the transparency and transitions in the file. In order to export a quality animation with tweening as an SWF file, you must use the **Lossless-32** format. Unfortunately, it also significantly increases the file size and makes it too big to use on the Web.

If you build an animation in Photoshop CS2 or ImageReady CS2, and you want to export it as a Macromedia Flash file to use on the Web, export the file using the techniques you learned in Exercise 1. Then, open the file in Macromedia Flash, and publish the final file from there. The result will be a much higher quality animation with a significantly smaller file size.

You've finished this chapter! Although this chapter had only four exercises, they were filled with complex ideas and workarounds. Next up: integrating with GoLive and Dreamweaver.

20

Integrating with GoLive and Dreamweaver

| Using Smart Objects in GoLive CS2 |
| Editing and Updating Smart Objects in GoLive CS2 |
| Working with Variables in GoLive CS2 |
| Importing Rollovers into Dreamweaver MX 2004 |

chap_20

PCS2Web HOT CD-ROM

When you're designing Web sites, you may choose to design the graphical elements, such as static graphics, image maps, and rollovers, in Photoshop CS2 or ImageReady CS2 and then lay out the site in an HTML editor, such as GoLive or Dreamweaver. In this chapter, you'll learn how to take the graphics you created in Photoshop CS2 and ImageReady CS2 and bring them into GoLive CS2 and Dreamweaver MX 2004.

You may or may not have the programs described in this chapter, and you may or may not know how to use them. Some sections in this chapter are intended for advanced users who know how to perform tasks in other applications without much coaching. Most books cover only a single program, but since Web design and development almost always involves more than one program, I had a feeling this chapter might be useful to many readers. Enjoy! ;-)

Using Content from Photoshop CS2 and ImageReady CS2
in GoLive CS2 or Dreamweaver MX 2004

Throughout this book, you may have been wondering, "How do I get this into an HTML editor?"
You can insert any optimized image generated from Photoshop CS2 and ImageReady CS2 into an
HTML editor, and it will work beautifully. Likewise, if you open an HTML file that was generated by
Photoshop CS2 or ImageReady CS2 in any HTML editor, you'll maintain the slices, rollovers, image
maps, animations, and any other content you created.

The "gotcha" comes when you need to take interactive content, such as a rollover, created in
ImageReady CS2 and insert it into a file you created in GoLive CS2 or Dreamweaver MX 2004. In
this chapter, you'll learn how to import rollovers into GoLive CS2 and Dreamweaver MX 2004. You'll
also learn about how to work with the Smart Objects feature in GoLive CS2, which lets you embed
content created in Photoshop CS2 and provides an easy way to update the content. You'll also learn
how to integrate the data sets and variables you created in Photoshop CS2 or ImageReady CS2
with GoLive CS2.

I. [IR]_____Using Smart Objects in GoLive CS2

In Chapter 9, "*Designing Navigation*," and Chapter 18, "*Integrating with Illustrator and Acrobat*," you learned how to use the new Smart Objects feature in Photoshop CS2. GoLive also has a Smart Objects feature, which has been around for a few versions. With Smart Objects in GoLive CS2, you can embed content, update the original file, and have the embedded content update automatically, just like in Photoshop CS2. In this exercise, you'll learn how to embed rollovers and static graphics created in Photoshop CS2 and ImageReady CS2 as Smart Objects in GoLive CS2. In the next exercise, you'll learn how to edit the content of a Smart Object in Photoshop CS2 and ImageReady CS2 and, in turn, automatically update the Smart Objects in GoLive CS2. It sounds far more complicated than it is, so follow the next two exercises, and you'll see the power of Smart Objects in GoLive CS2!

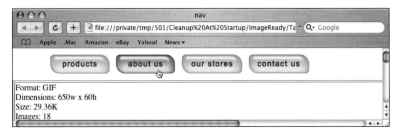

1. In ImageReady CS2, open **nav.psd** from the **chap_20** folder you copied to your **Desktop**. In the **Toolbox**, click the **Preview in Default Browser** button. Position your cursor over the buttons to view the **Over** states.

*Notice the buttons change color when you view the **Over** state.*

2. When you've finished, return to ImageReady CS2, and close **nav.psd**.

*The purpose of opening and previewing the file in a Web browser is to familiarize yourself with the contents of the file. Later in this exercise, you'll embed this file as a **Smart Object** in GoLive CS2, so you need to know what the buttons and associated **Over** states look like.*

3. Open **content.psd** from the **chap_20** folder you copied to your **Desktop**. Take a look at the contents of the file.

*Again, the purpose of this step is to familiarize yourself with the content in the file. Like in **nav.psd**, you'll embed the contents of this file as a **Smart Object** in GoLive CS2, so you need to know what the file looks like.*

4. Close **content.psd**, and close ImageReady CS2.

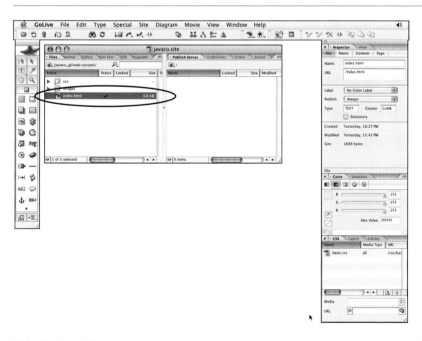

5. In GoLive CS2, open **javaco.site** from the **javaco_gl** folder in the **chap_20** folder you copied to your **Desktop**. The GoLive CS2 site window will open automatically. In the **Site** window, double-click the **index.html** file to open it.

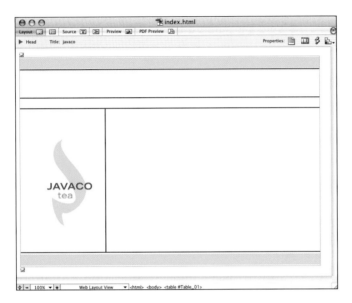

6. Take a look at the contents of the **index.html** file.

*There is a blue bar at the top and bottom, a javaco logo on the left, and three empty table cells. In this exercise, you'll fill one of the table cells with the contents of **nav.psd**, and you'll fill one of the table cells with the contents of **content.psd**.*

7. In the **Toolbox**, choose **Smart** from the **Objects** flyout. The contents of the **Toolbox** will change automatically.

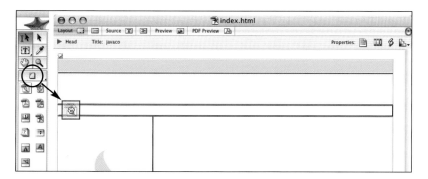

8. Click and drag the **Smart Photoshop Object** onto the second, empty horizontal table cell, as shown in the illustration here.

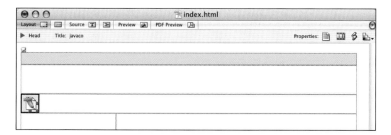

*When you release your mouse, you'll se a **Smart Photoshop Object** icon appear in the empty table cell, as shown in the illustration here. Next, you'll link a Photoshop file to the **Smart Photoshop Object** you just created.*

9. The **Smart Photoshop Object** should automatically be selected. If it's not, click the **Smart Photoshop Object** icon to select it. Make sure the **Inspector** palette is visible. If it's not, choose **Window > Inspector**. Click the **Browse** button to open the **Open** dialog box.

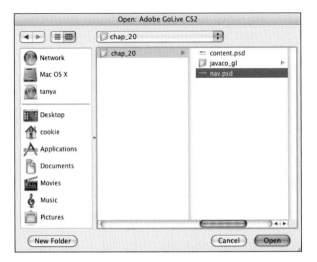

10. In the **Open** dialog box, navigate to the **chap_20** folder you copied to your **Desktop**. Click the **nav.psd** file to select it, and click **Open**. The **Variable Settings** dialog box will open automatically.

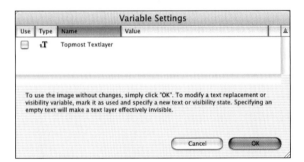

11. In the **Variable Settings** dialog box, click **OK**. The **Save For Web** dialog box will open automatically.

*Note: Because **nav.psd** does not contain any data sets or variables, you don't need to make changes in the **Variable Settings** dialog box. In Exercise 4, you'll learn how to import variables from Photoshop CS2 into ImageReady CS2.*

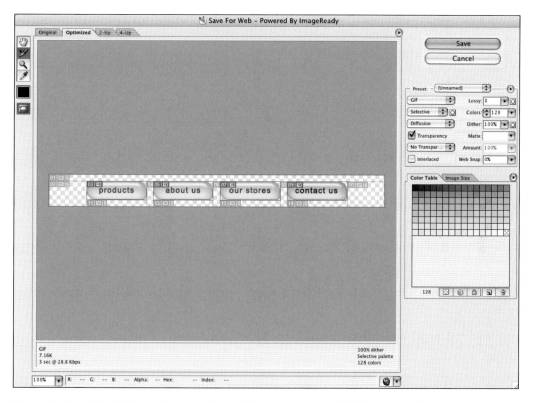

12. In the **Save For Web** window, use the techniques you learned in Chapter 7, "*Optimizing Images*," to optimize the contents of the **nav.psd** file. The **Save For Web** dialog box works the same in GoLive CS2 as it did in Photoshop CS2, so you shouldn't have any problem optimizing the file. When you've finished, click **Save**. The **Save** dialog box will open automatically.

*Optimizing the images at this point may seem peculiar to you. Because you're embedding a Photoshop file as part of the **Smart Object**, you must optimize the file as a JPEG or GIF so GoLive CS2 can display the image(s) properly in a Web browser.*

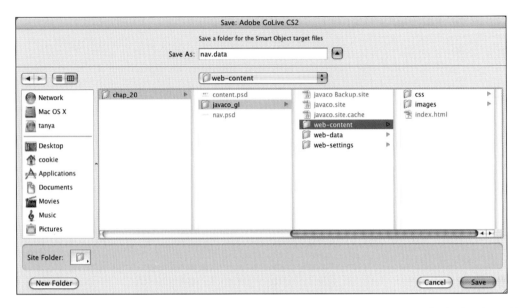

13. In the **Save** dialog box, navigate to the **web-content** folder in the **javaco_gl** folder in the **chap_20** folder you copied to your **Desktop**. Click **Save**.

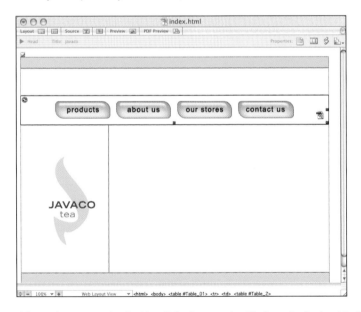

*After a few seconds, GoLive CS2 inserts the file into the **index.html** file. When it's finished, the contents of your **index.html** file should match the illustration here. As you can see, the buttons look the same as they did in ImageReady CS2. Next, you'll preview the image to view the **Over** states.*

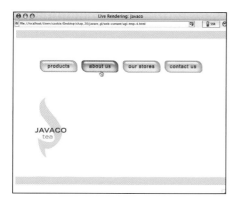

14. Press **Cmd+T** (Mac) or **Ctrl+T** (Windows) to preview the Web page. Position your cursor over the buttons to view the **Over** states.

*The rollovers work beautifully! Next, you'll embed the contents of the **content.psd** file into the* **index.html** *file.*

15. When you've finished previewing the file, close the preview window, and return to the **index.html** file.

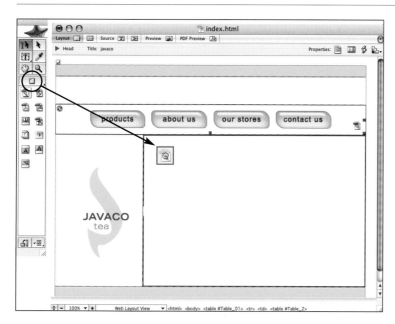

16. Click and drag the **Smart Photoshop Object** icon onto the large, empty table cell, as shown in the illustration here.

*When you release your mouse, you'll see a **Smart Photoshop Object** icon inside the table cell.*

17. In the **Inspector** palette, click the **Browse** button to open the **Open** dialog box. Navigate to the **chap_20** folder you copied to your **Desktop**. Click the **content.psd** file to select it, and click **Open**.

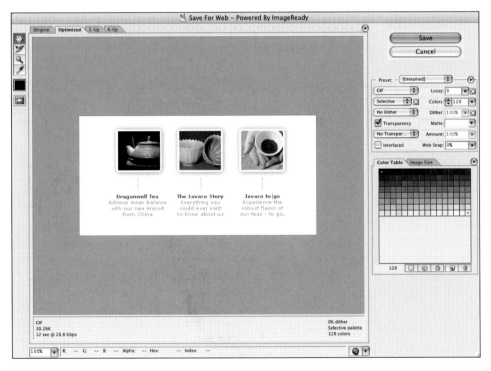

18. In the **Variable Settings** dialog box, click **OK**. In the **Save For Web** dialog box, use the techniques you learned in Chapter 7, "*Optimizing Images*," to optimize the image. When you've finished, click **Save**. In the **Save** dialog box, navigate to the **web-content** folder in the **javaco_gl** folder in the **chap_20** folder you copied to your **Desktop**. Click **Save**.

*The contents of the **content.psd** file should now appear inside the table cell. Notice the contents of the **Smart Photoshop Object** extend beyond the blue, horizontal bars at the top and bottom of the **index.html** page, indicating it is too big for the table cell. You could go back to Photoshop CS2 or ImageReady CS2 to adjust the size, but there is an even easier way without leaving GoLive CS2.*

19. The **Smart Photoshop Object** should automatically be selected. If it's not, click inside the table cell to select it. In the **Inspector** palette, click the **Crop** button to go into crop mode.

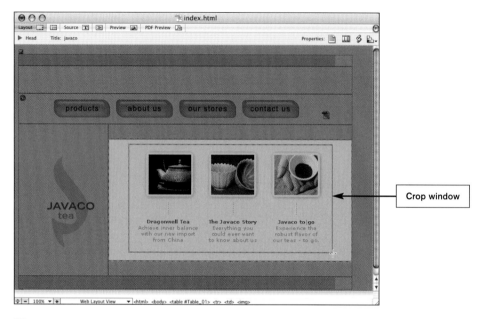

20. Click and drag to create a crop window, as shown in the illustration here.

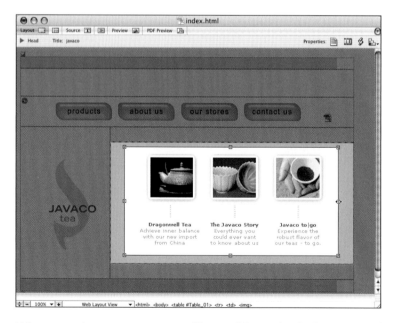

When you release your mouse, you'll see editing nodes in the corners of the image. If you'd like, position your cursor over the nodes, and resize the crop window.

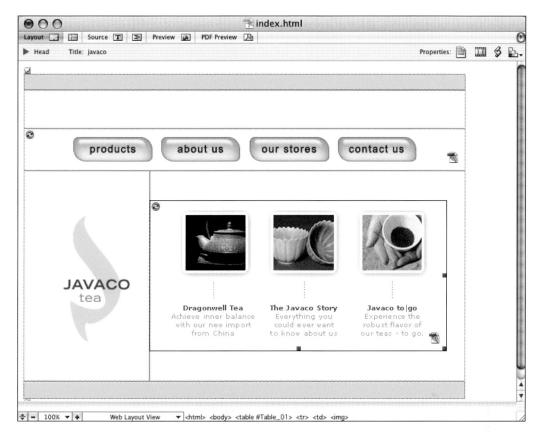

21. When you're satisfied with the size and shape of the crop window, position your cursor inside the crop window, and double-click to apply the changes.

Now you can see the image fits nicely inside the table cell.

22. Press **Cmd+T** (Mac) or **Ctrl+T** (Windows) to preview the Web page. When you've finished, close the preview window.

23. Leave **index.html** open for the next exercise.

*In the next exercise, you'll learn how to edit the contents of the **Smart Object** in Photoshop CS2 and ImageReady CS2 and automatically update the **Smart Object** in GoLive CS2.*

NOTE | Learning GoLive CS2

The purpose of the last exercise was to show you how import rollovers from ImageReady CS2 into GoLive CS2. If you're interested in learning more about how to use GoLive CS2, check out the **Adobe GoLive CS2 Essential Training** video training with **Garrick Chow** available at **http://www.lynda.com.**

2. [IR]   Editing and Updating Smart Objects in GoLive CS2

In the last exercise, you learned how to create Smart Objects in GoLive CS2 using content created in Photoshop CS2 and ImageReady CS2. In this exercise, you'll unleash the true power of working with Smart Objects by editing the content in Photoshop CS2 and ImageReady CS2 and automatically updating the Smart Object in GoLive CS2.

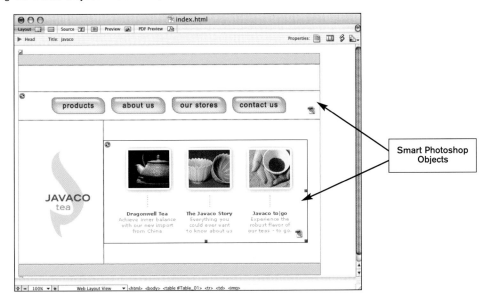

1. If you followed the last exercise, **index.html** should still be open in GoLive CS2 with the two **Smart Photoshop Objects** you created in the last exercise. If it's not, go back and complete Exercise 1.

2. Position your cursor at the edge of the table cell with the content from **nav.psd**, and click to select the contents of the table cell.

3. Ctrl+click (Mac) or **right-click** (Windows) and choose **Source Link > Edit Original** from the contextual menu.

*In a few seconds, **nav.psd** will automatically open in ImageReady CS2. **Note:** Because this image was last edited and saved in ImageReady CS2, it will automatically open in ImageReady CS2. If the image was last edited and saved in Photoshop CS2, it would open in Photoshop CS2.*

4. In ImageReady CS2, make sure the **Layers** palette and **Web Content** palette are visible. If they're not, choose **Window > Layers** and **Window > Web Content**.

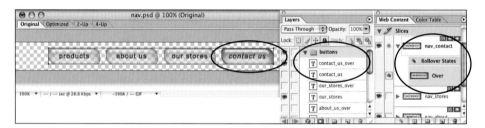

5. In the **Layers** palette, expand the contents of the **buttons** layer set. In the **Web Content** palette, expand the contents of the **nav_contact** rollover. Click the **Over** state to select it. In the **Layers** palette, turn off the visibility of the **contact_us** layer, and turn on the visibility of the **contact_us_over** layer.

Notice the type changes from regular to italic.

6. Repeat Step 5 to change the text in the **Over** state of the **nav_stores**, **nav_about**, and **nav_products** buttons. When you've finished, in the **Toolbox** click the **Preview in Default Browser** button to preview the changes you made. When you position your cursor over the buttons, you should see the color change, and the font style should change from regular to italic.

7. Close the Web browser and return to ImageReady CS2.

8. Choose **File > Save**, and return to GoLive CS2, leaving ImageReady CS2 open.

*The **Smart Object** will update automatically. It may take a few seconds for the **Smart Photoshop Object** to update.*

9. Press **Cmd+T** (Mac) or **Ctrl+T** (Windows) to preview the changes. Position your cursor over each button to view its revised **Over** state. When you've finished, close the preview window.

*Notice the changes you made in ImageReady CS2 are automatically reflected, and you didn't have to do a thing to inform GoLive CS2 of the changes you made. Although this is a very simple example, it gives you an idea of the power of the **Smart Objects** feature. Imagine having these buttons on multiple pages based on the **nav.psd** file. Defining the buttons as **Smart Objects** would ensure all buttons update if you make a change to the file in Photoshop CS2 or ImageReady CS2.*

10. Close **index.html** and **javaco.site**. You don't need to save your changes.

*As you can see, embedding content created in Photoshop CS2 and ImageReady CS2 as a **Smart Object** in GoLive CS2 is very powerful. Although you used a rollover as the example, you can apply the same techniques to image maps, animations, or any other content you create in Photoshop CS2 or ImageReady CS2.*

3. [PS] _____Working with Variables in GoLive CS2

In Chapter 17, "*Creating Data-Driven Graphics*," you learned how to define variables and create data sets in Photoshop CS2 and ImageReady CS2. Data sets become much more powerful when you work with them in GoLive CS2–especially if you embed them as Smart Objects, which you'll do in this exercise. Hold on to your hats–this is an amazing feature!

1. In Photoshop CS2, open **flavor_of_the_month.psd** from the **chap_20** folder you copied to your **Desktop**. Make sure the **Layers** palette is visible. If it's not, choose **Window > Layers**.

First, you'll define the variables in Photoshop CS2. You'll define the vector-based type layer as a **Text Replacement** *variable, and you'll define the* **teapot, red_cup,** *and* **hands** *layers as* **Visibility** *variables. When you bring the files into GoLive CS2, you'll be able to create different configurations of the Web banner using these variables.*

2. Choose **Image > Variables > Define** to open the **Variables** dialog box.

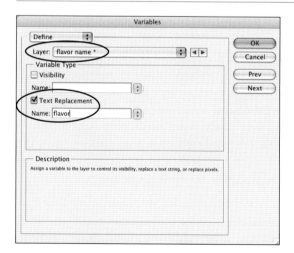

3. In the **Variables** dialog box, choose **flavor name** from the **Layer** pop-up menu. Turn on the **Text Replacement** option, and type **flavor** in the **Name** field.

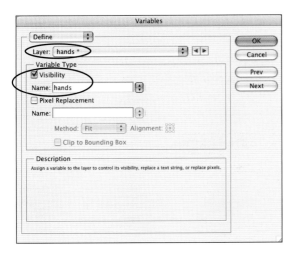

4. Choose **hands** from the **Layer** pop-up menu. Turn on the **Visibility** option, and type **hands** in the **Name** field.

5. Choose **red_cup** from the **Layer** pop-up menu. Turn on the **Visibility** option, and type **red_cup** in the **Name** field. Choose **teapot** from the **Layer** pop-up menu, turn on the **Visibility** option, and type **teapot** in the **Name** field.

Now that you've defined the variables, you need to create a data set to store the variables.

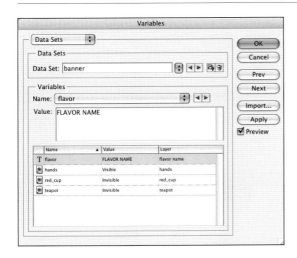

6. Choose **Data Sets** from the pop-up menu at the top of the **Variables** dialog box. To the right of the **Data Set** pop-up menu, click the **Create New Data Set Based on Current Data Set** button. In the **Data Set** field, type **banner**. Click **OK** to close the **Variables** dialog box.

7. Choose **File > Save As**. In the **Save As** dialog box, navigate to the **chap_20** folder you copied to your **Desktop**. Name the file **flavor_of_the_month_variables.psd**. Click **Save**. Close **flavor_of_the_month_variables.psd**.

*Next, you'll embed the contents of the **flavor_of_the_month.psd** file into GoLive CS2 so you can see the true power of this feature.*

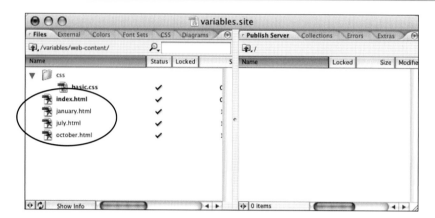

8. In GoLive CS2, open the **variables.site** file from the **variables** folder in the **chap_20** folder you copied to your **Desktop**. The **variables.site** file will automatically open in the **Site** window.

*Take a look at the contents of the site window. Notice there are four HTML files—**index.html**, **january.html**, **july.html**, and **october.html**. In the next few steps, you'll embed a different iteration of the flavor of the month Web banner into each page as a **Smart Photoshop Object**. Plus, you'll change the appearance of each using the variables you defined earlier in this exercise.*

9. Double-click **january.html** to open the file.

10. If it's not selected already, in the **Toolbox** choose **Smart** from the **Objects** flyout. The contents of the **Toolbox** will change automatically.

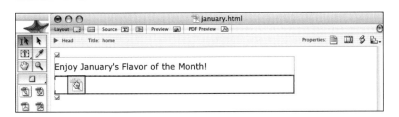

11. Click and drag the **Smart Photoshop Object** icon from the **Toolbox** into the empty table cell, as shown in the illustration here.

12. Make sure the **Inspector** palette is visible. If it's not, choose **Window > Inspector**. If the **Smart Photoshop Object** is not already selected, click the **Smart Photoshop Object** icon to select it. In the **Inspector** palette, click the **Browse** button. The **Open** dialog box will open automatically.

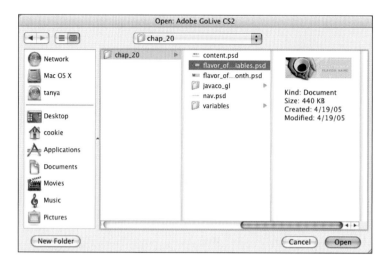

13. In the **Open** dialog box, navigate to the **chap_20** folder you copied to your **Desktop**. Choose the **flavor_of_the_month_variables.psd** file and click **Open**.

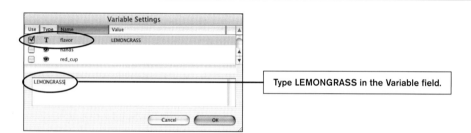

Type LEMONGRASS in the Variable field.

14. In the **Variable Settings** dialog box, turn on the **flavor** variable, and type **LEMONGRASS** in the **Variable** field, as shown in the illustration here.

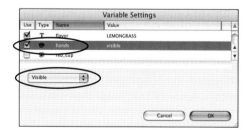

15. Turn on the **hands** variable. **Visible** should automatically be selected from the **Visibility** pop-up menu. If it's not, choose **Visible**, as shown in the illustration here.

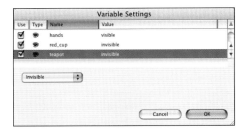

16. Turn on the **red_cup** variable, and choose **Invisible** from the **Visibility** pop-up menu. Turn on the **teapot** variable, and choose **Invisible** from the **Visibility** pop-up menu. Click **OK**.

17. In the **Save For Web** dialog box, use the techniques you learned in Chapter 7, "*Optimizing Images*," to optimize the image. When you've finished, click **Save**.

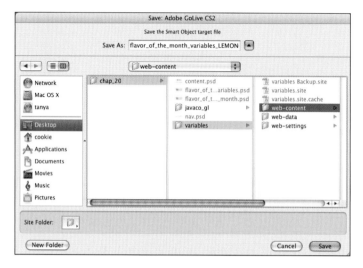

18. In the **Save** dialog box, navigate to the **web-content** folder in the **variables** folder in the **chap_20** folder you copied to your **Desktop**. Click **Save**.

*In a few seconds, you'll see the contents of the **flavor_of_the_month_variables.psd** file appear in the **january.html** file. As you can see, the flavor name, **LEMONGRASS**, is using the vector-based type properties from the original Photoshop CS2 file, but it is using the flavor name you specified in the **Variable Settings** dialog box. Also notice the visibility of the **hands** layer is turned on, which is a result of the visibility settings you specified in the **Variable Settings** dialog box. How cool is that?*

19. Choose **File > Save** to save your changes to **january.html**. Close **january.html**, and return to the **variables.site** window.

20. In the **variables.site** window, double-click the **july.html** file to open it. Click and drag the **Smart Photoshop Object** icon from the **Toolbox** onto the empty table cell in the **july.html** file. When you've finished, in the **Inspector** palette click the **Browse** button to open the **Open** dialog box. Navigate to the **chap_20** folder you copied to your **Desktop**. Choose **flavor_of_the_month_variables.psd**, and click **Open**.

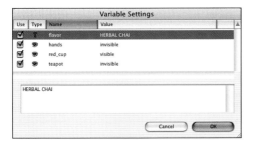

21. In the **Variable Settings** dialog box, turn on the **flavor** variable, and type **HERBAL CHAI** in the **Variable** field. Turn on the **hands** option, and choose **Invisible** from the pop-up menu. Turn on the **red_cup** variable, and choose **Visible** from the **Visibility** pop-up menu. Turn on the **teapot** variable, and choose **Invisible** from the **Visibility** pop-up menu. Click **OK**.

22. In the **Save For Web** dialog box, use the techniques you learned in Chapter 7, "*Optimizing Images*," to optimize the image. When you've finished, click **Save**.

23. In the **Save** dialog box, navigate to the **web-content** folder in the **variables** folder in the **chap_20** folder you copied to your **Desktop**. Click **Save**.

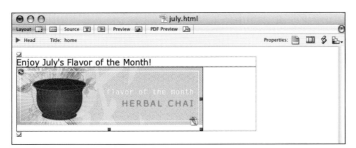

*In a few seconds, you'll see the contents of the **flavor_of_the_month_variables.psd** file appear in the **july.html** file. As you can see, the flavor name, **HERBAL CHAI**, is using the vector-based type properties from the original Photoshop CS2 file, but it is using the flavor name you specified in the **Variable Settings** dialog box. Also notice the visibility of the **red_cup** layer is turned on, which is a result of the visibility settings you specified in the **Variable Settings** dialog box.*

24. Choose **File > Save** to save your changes to **july.html**. Close **july.html**, and return to the **variables.site** window.

25. In the **variables.site** window, double-click the **october.html** file to open it. Click and drag the **Smart Photoshop Object** icon from the **Toolbox** onto the empty table cell in the **october.html** file. When you've finished, in the **Inspector** palette click the **Browse** button to open the **Open** dialog box. Navigate to the **chap_20** folder you copied to your **Desktop**. Choose **flavor_of_the_month_variables.psd**, and click **Open**.

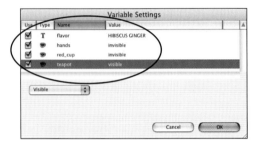

26. In the **Variable Settings** dialog box, turn on the flavor option, and type **HIBISCUS GINGER**. Turn on the **hands** variable, and choose **Invisible** from the **Visibility** pop-up menu. Turn on the **red_cup** variable, and choose **Invisible** from the **Visibility** pop-up menu. Turn on the **teapot** option, and choose **Visible** from the **Visibility** pop-up menu. Click **OK**.

27. In the **Save For Web** dialog box, dialog box, use the techniques you learned in Chapter 7, "*Optimizing Images*," to optimize the image. When you've finished, click **Save**.

28. In the **Save** dialog box, navigate to the **web-content** folder in the **variables** folder in the **chap_20** folder you copied to your **Desktop**. Click **Save**.

*In a few seconds, you'll see the contents of the **flavor_of_the_month_variables.psd** file appear in the **october.html** file. As you can see, the flavor name, **HIBISCUS GINGER**, is using the vector-based type properties from the original Photoshop CS2 file, but it is using the flavor name you specified in the **Variable Settings** dialog box. Also notice the visibility of the **teapot** layer is turned on, which is a result of the visibility settings you specified in the **Variable Settings** dialog box.*

29. Choose **File > Save** to save your changes to **october.html**, and leave it open in GoLive CS2.

*As you can see, using the data set and variables you created in Photoshop CS2 earlier in this exercise, you were able to create three different Web banners on three different Web pages without having to do any additional image editing in Photoshop CS2—the **Variables** feature in GoLive CS2 took care of it for you!*

*What if you create a series of Web banners but then decide you don't like the font style or the color of the Web banner? Because you embedded the banner as a **Smart Photoshop Object**, all you have to do is make the changes to the original Photoshop CS2 file, and it will update all the Web banners at the same time. Follow the next few steps, and it will all become clear.*

30. Ctrl+click (Mac) or **right-click** (Windows) the **Smart Photoshop Object** in the **october.html** file and choose **Source Link > Edit Original** from the contextual menu.

flavor_of_the_month_variables.psd will automatically open in Photoshop CS2.

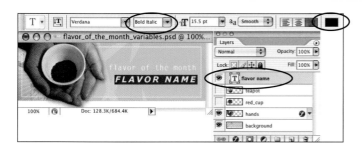

31. In Photoshop CS2, double-click the **T** icon of the **flavor name** type layer in the **Layers** palette to highlight the contents of the type layer. On the **Options** bar, choose **Bold Italic** from the **Font Style** pop-up menu. Click the color swatch to open the **Color Picker** dialog box. Select a **dark blue**, and click **OK**.

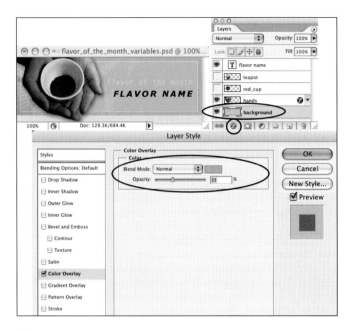

32. In the **Layers** palette, click the **background** layer to select it. Choose **Color Overlay** from the **Layer Style** pop-up menu. Click the color swatch to open the **Color Picker** dialog box, select a **light blue-gray**, and click **OK**. Decrease the **Opacity** setting to **35%**. Click **OK**.

33. Choose **File > Save** to save the changes you made in the last two steps and return to GoLive CS2.

In a few seconds, you'll see the type reflects the changes you made in Step 31, and the background reflects the changes you made in Step 32.

*What about the other the Web banners in the **january.html** file and the **july.html** file? Follow the next few steps, and you'll find out!*

34. Choose **File > Save** to save the changes to **october.html**. Close **october.html** and return to the **variables.site** window. Double-click **january.html** to open it.

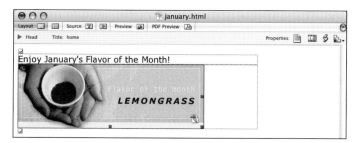

It may take a few seconds to open and update the file, but when it does, you'll see the type reflects the changes you made in Step 31, and the background reflects the changes you made in Step 32.

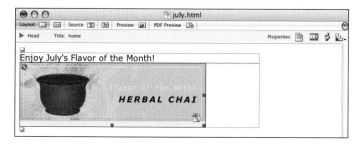

*If you open **july.html**, you'll see the same result.*

*Because you used the same Photoshop file for the **Photoshop Smart Object** in the **january.html**, **july.html**, and **october.html** files, you have to make the changes just once in the original Photoshop file. It will automatically update each instance the file is used within a site without impacting the variables you set up. How cool is that?*

*As you can see, combining the **Smart Objects** and **Variables** feature in GoLive CS2 with content created in Photoshop CS2 and ImageReady CS2 produces very powerful results! This is what dynamic content is all about!*

35. Save and close **january.html** and/or **july.html** to return to the **variables.site** window. Save your changes and close GoLive CS2.

4. [IR]_____**Importing Rollovers into Dreamweaver MX 2004**

In this exercise, you'll learn how to import rollovers created in ImageReady CS2 into Dreamweaver MX 2004. If all you want to do is use the HTML and images from ImageReady CS2 in their original form, you can simply open the HTML file generated from ImageReady CS2 in Dreamweaver MX 2004. However, if you want to import rollovers created in ImageReady CS2 into an existing file, it's a bit trickier. Here's an exercise to show you how.

1. Before you get started with the exercise, you need to install an extension called **ImageReadyHTML.mxp** from the **software** folder in the **chap_20** folder you copied to your **Desktop**.

This extension is a Macromedia Extension Manager file written by Massimo Foti for ***lynda.com***. *This extension converts code from ImageReady CS2 to native Dreamweaver MX 2004 code.*

Before you install the extension, you must have the Macromedia Extension Manager installed on your computer. You can install the Macromedia Extension Manager from the Dreamweaver MX 2004 CD-ROM.

To install the extension, copy the ***ImageReadyHTML.mxp*** *file from the* ***software*** *folder in the* ***chap_20*** *folder you copied to your* ***Desktop***. *Double-click the file, and follow the instructions onscreen.*

If you want to be sure it's installed correctly, open Dreamweaver MX 2004, and take a look at the ***Insert*** *bar. Make sure* ***Common*** *is selected from the pop-up menu. If the* ***ImageReadyHTML.mxp*** *file is installed correctly, you'll see an* ***ImageReady HTML*** *icon on the* ***Insert*** *bar.*

NOTE | What Is the ImageReadyHTML.mxp File?

lynda.com commissioned well-known Dreamweaver Extension developer **Massimo Foti** to create an extension for Dreamweaver to convert ImageReady rollover code into a native Dreamweaver behavior. The folks at **lynda.com** saw this as an opportunity to support customers who might be using these two products together. **lynda.com** offers the **ImageReady HTML** extension for free from the **lynda.com** Web site. You can find it (and other helpful files) at: **http://www.lynda.com/files/**.

*After you successfully install the ImageReady HTML extension, you need to define your **Site** settings before you import the rollovers from Dreamweaver.*

2. In Dreamweaver MX 2004, choose **Site > Manage Sites**. In the **Manage Sites** dialog box, click the **New** button, and choose **Site** from the pop-up menu.

In the next few steps, Dreamweaver MX 2004 will guide you through the process of defining a site.

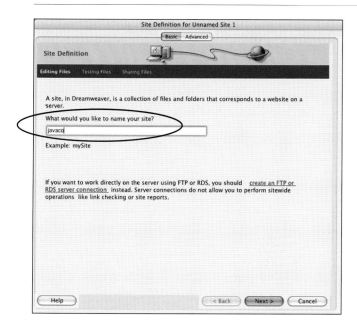

3. In the **Site Definition: Editing Files** dialog box, type **javaco** in the **What would you like to name your site?** field. Click **Next**.

4. In the **Site Definition: Editing Files, Part** 2 dialog box, select the **No, I do not want to use a server technology** option. Click **Next**.

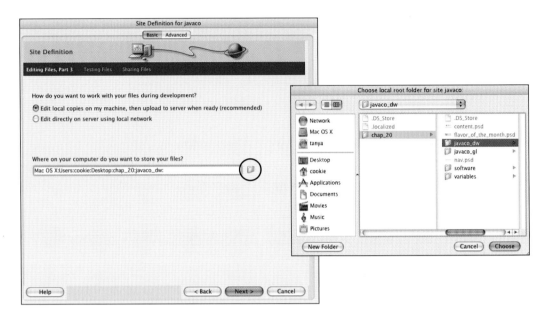

5. In the **Site Definition: Editing Files, Part 3** dialog box, select the **Edit local copies on my machine, then upload to server when ready** option if it's not already selected. Click the **folder** icon next to the **Where on your computer do you want to store your files?** field. In the **Choose local root folder** dialog box, navigate to the **chap_20** folder you copied to your **Desktop**. Click the **javaco_dw** folder, and click **Choose** (Mac) or **Select** (Windows). Click **Next**.

6. In the **Site Definition: Sharing Files** dialog box, choose **None** from the **How do you connect to your remote server?** pop-up menu. Click **Next**.

7. In the **Site Definition: Summary** dialog box, review the settings. When you've finished, click **Done**.

8. In the **Manage Sites** dialog box, notice there is now an entry called **javaco**. Make sure **javaco** is selected, and click **Done**.

9. Make sure the **Files** palette is visible. If it's not, choose **Window > Files**. The **Files** palette contains the **javaco** site you defined in this exercise. Double-click the **index.html** file to open it.

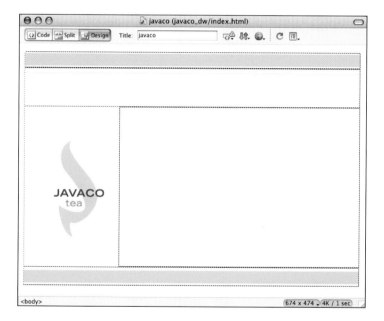

*The **index.html** file was created ahead of time so you can simulate the workflow of importing rollovers created in ImageReady CS2 into Dreamweaver MX 2004. If you followed Exercise 1, you'll notice this file looks very similar to the file you worked with in GoLive CS2.*

*Next, you'll create an empty file so you can import the rollovers from ImageReady CS2. Wondering why you can't import them directly into the **index.html** file? When you import rollovers from ImageReady CS2 using the ImageReady HTML extension, you don't have any control over where the content is placed inside the HTML file. If you import it into an empty HTML file, you can copy and paste it into the exact location in the **index.html** file.*

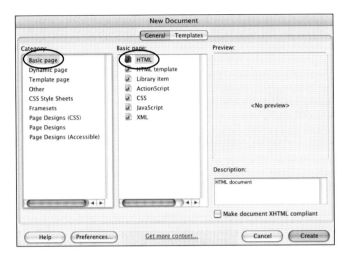

10. Choose **File > New**. In the **New Document** dialog box, select **Basic page** from the **Category** options, and select **HTML** from the **Basic page** options. Click **Create**.

11. Choose **File > Save As**. Navigate to the **javaco_dw** folder in the **chap_20** folder you copied to your **Desktop**. Name the file **rollover_import.html**. Click **Save**.

12. Make sure **Common** is selected in the **Insert** bar pop-up menu. Click the **ImageReady HTML** button to open the **ImageReady HTML** dialog box.

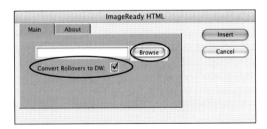

13. In the **ImageReady HTML** dialog box, make sure the **Convert Rollovers to DW** option is turned on. Click **Browse**.

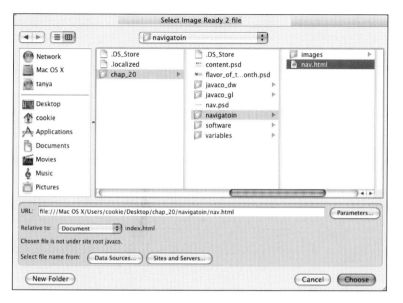

14. In the **Select ImageReady 2 File** dialog box, navigate to the **navigation** folder in the **chap_20** folder you copied to your **Desktop**. Select **nav.html**, and click **Choose** (Mac) or **OK** (Windows).

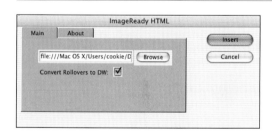

15. In the **ImageReady HTML** dialog box, click **Insert**. A warning message will appear, indicating the process may take a few minutes. Click **OK** to proceed.

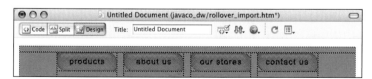

The contents of the **nav.html** file should now be visible inside the **rollover_import.html** file, as shown in the illustration here.

16. Choose **Edit > Copy**.

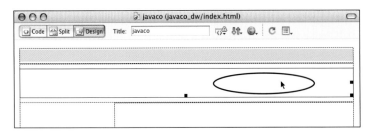

17. Choose **Window > index.html**. In the **index.html** file, click the empty table cell below the blue bar to select it. Choose **Edit > Paste HTML**.

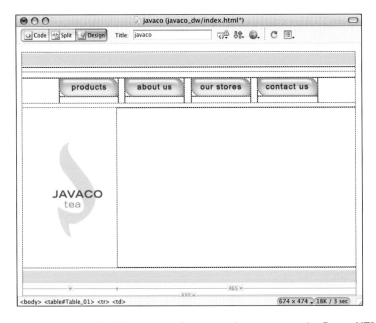

*Dreamweaver MX 2004 takes a few seconds to process the **Paste HTML** command. When it's finished, the rollovers should be pasted in the table cell you selected, as shown in the illustration here.*

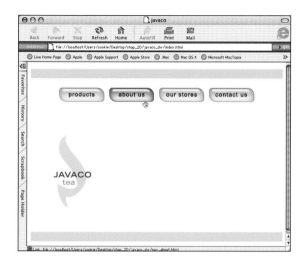

18. Press **F12** to preview the file in a Web browser. You'll be prompted to save your changes. Click **Save**. Position your cursor over the buttons to view the **Over** states.

It worked! The rollovers behave the same way they did originally in ImageReady CS2. As you can see, the ImageReady HTML extension makes it easy to bring rollovers created in ImageReady CS2 into Dreamweaver MX 2004!

NOTE | Learning Dreamweaver MX 2004

The purpose of the last exercise was to show you how to import rollovers from ImageReady CS2 into Dreamweaver MX 2004. If you're interested in learning more about how to use Dreamweaver MX 2004, check out the following resources available at: **http://www.lynda.com**:

Macromedia Dreamweaver MX 2004 HOT
by Garo Green, developed with Lynda Weinman
lynda.com/books and Peachpit Press
ISBN: 032120297X

Learning Macromedia Dreamweaver MX 2004 video training
with Garo Green

Intermediate Macromedia Dreamweaver MX 2004 video training
with Garo Green and Daniel Short

Congratulations! You just finished the last chapter—and a complex one at that! Now it's time to start designing your own Web graphics. Enjoy! ;-)

A

Troubleshooting FAQ and Technical Support

Appendix A

_____
HOT

PCS2Web HOT CD-ROM

If you've run into any problems following the exercises in this book, this Troubleshooting FAQ (Frequently Asked Questions) should help. This document will be maintained and expanded upon at this book's companion Web site: **http://www.lynda.com/ info/books/pscs2web/**.

If you don't find what you're looking for here or in the companion Web site, please send an email to **pscs2webhot@lynda.com**.

If you have a question related to Photoshop CS2 or ImageReady CS2 that is not related to a specific exercise in this book, visit the Adobe Photoshop support Web site: **http://www.adobe.com/support/ products/photoshop.html**.

Q: I'm using a Windows computer, and all the files on the **PCS2Web HOT CD-ROM** are locked even though I transferred them to my hard drive. What should I do?

A: Unfortunately, some versions of the Windows operating system treat files copied from a CD-ROM to be read-only files, which means you can't make changes to any of the files until you remove the read-only property. For specific instructions about how to do this, take a look at the Introduction.

Q: When I open some of the exercise files, I get a warning message asking if I want to update text layers. What should I do?

A: Text created or saved from previous versions of Photoshop require you to update text layers. When the warning message appears, click **Update** to update the text layers in the file and continue with the exercise.

Q: If I create a CMYK image for print, can I use it on the Web?

A: You can't use CMYK images for the Web. You'll have to convert CMYK images to RGB first. To convert CMYK images to RBG in Photoshop CS2, choose **Image > Mode > RGB Color**. You may see some color shifting during this process because CMYK and RGB are different color spaces, and you cannot achieve an exact color translation when you convert the files.

Q: Sometimes when I'm in the **Save For Web** dialog box I see an orange warning triangle. What should I do?

A: Choose **Repopulate Views** from the **Save For Web** menu to refresh all views. The warning icon will disappear.

Q: When I work with layered images in ImageReady CS2, I often see an outline around the edges of the selected layers. Sometimes it's helpful, but sometimes it's distracting. What are these lines, and how can I turn then off?

A: ImageReady CS2 has a feature called layer edges, which let you see where the edges in a layer begin and end. Layer edges can be helpful when you need to visualize the size of a layer. To turn the layer edges off, choose **View > Show > Layer Edges**.

Q: When I click the **Optimized** tab in the ImageReady CS2 document window, I see a checkerboard pattern instead of the background of the image. What is this?

A: If you're having trouble seeing an image when you click the **Optimized** tab, make sure **Auto Regenerate** is turned on in the **Optimize** palette menu. Remember, the checkerboard pattern indicates a file is a transparent GIF.

Q: When I'm optimizing a GIF in ImageReady CS2, sometimes I don't see any color swatches in the **Color Table** palette. Why not?

A: At the lower left of the **Color Table** palette, click the yellow triangle to regenerate the color table.

Q: Every time I save a file I get this annoying box asking me where I want to update it.

A: You're in luck! There is a simple way to fix this in both programs. Choose **Photoshop > Preferences > General** (Mac) or **Edit > Preferences > General** (Windows). Turn on the **Auto-Update Open Documents** option. Click **OK**, and you'll never have to see that pesky box again! These steps work for both Photoshop CS2 and ImageReady CS2.

Q: Not to complain, but I get sick of zooming in and out. Is there a quick way to get a large view of an image or to return to 100%?

A: In the **Toolbox**, if you double-click the **Hand** tool, the image will expand to fill your screen. If you double-click the **Zoom** tool in the **Toolbox**, the image will change to **100%**. The trick is to double-click the tool, not inside your image.

Q: When I'm working in ImageReady CS2, it's taking forever for the program to accept my edits, and it's driving me crazy. What do I do?

A: It sounds like you're working in the **Optimized** tab, which tells ImageReady CS2 to constantly optimize your graphic while you're editing it. Switch over to the **Original** tab. It will go faster—I promise.

Q: Is there a quick, one-step way to hide all the palettes? Sometimes I find it overwhelming to have them all visible onscreen.

A: Photoshop CS2 and ImageReady CS2 have a handy keyboard shortcut to toggle the visibility of the palettes on and off. Just press the **Tab** key! It's a beautiful thing!

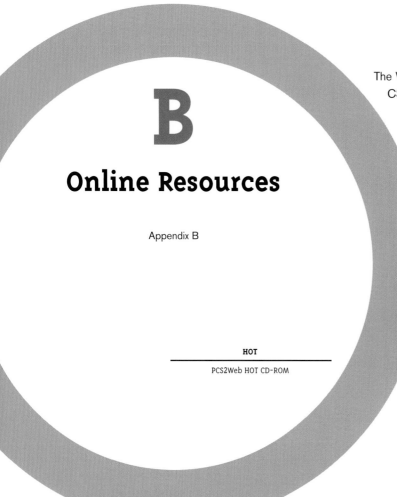

B

Online Resources

Appendix B

The Web is full of great resources for Photoshop CS2 users. There are a variety of newsgroups, listservs, and third-party Web sites that can help you get the most out of the new skills you've developed by following the exercises in this book. This appendix lists some of the best resources for learning and extending Photoshop CS2 and ImageReady CS2.

Adobe User-to-User Forums

Adobe has set up several discussion boards (newsgroups) for Photoshop CS2 and ImageReady CS2. This is a great place to ask questions and get help from thousands of Photoshop CS2 and ImageReady CS2 users. The newsgroup is composed of beginning to advanced users, so you should have no problem finding the type of help you need. You can access all of the Adobe User Forums at **http://www.adobe.com/support/forums/main.html**. You will need to register to log in, read, and post messages. Here are some of the forums that might interest you:

- Adobe Photoshop and Adobe Image Ready for Mac
- Adobe Photoshop and Adobe ImageReady for Windows

Adobe Design Forums

Adobe also offers a number of design forums to help you find information about design.

You can access the design forums at **http://www.adobe.com/support/forums/main.html**. Here are a few design forums that might interest you:

- Animation
- Typography
- Print Web/Web Print Workflow
- Design Discussion

Adobe Studio

Adobe also offers a design resource Web site, which provides resources for graphics professionals. You can check out the Adobe Studio Web site at **http://studio.adobe.com**.

National Association of Photoshop Professionals (NAPP)

The **National Association of Photoshop Professionals** (NAPP) is an organization dedicated to providing Photoshop CS2 and ImageReady CS2 users with the latest education, training, and news. Membership with NAPP provides you with access to the **Resource Center**, which provides useful tutorials, tips, and news about Photoshop CS2 and ImageReady CS2. Members also receive a subscription to *Photoshop User* magazine, help with technical questions, and special offers on training, videos, and seminars. NAPP also holds a useful conference twice a year called Photoshop World.

For more information about NAPP, visit their Web site at **http://www.photoshopuser.com**.

Planet Photoshop

Planet Photoshop also offers tutorials, user forums, education materials, books, seminars, and more to help you learn Photoshop CS2 and ImageReady CS2.

For more information about Planet Photoshop, visit their Web site at **http://www.planetphotoshop.com**.

Index

Learn More for Less

@ the lynda.com Online Movie Library:

ONLY **$25**/mo FOR UNRESTRICTED ACCESS.

- Self-paced learning.
- 24/7 access.
- Over 33 of the latest software titles and technologies.
- Over 3,300 QuickTime Movies and growing monthly.
- Affordable pricing.
- Month-to-month option.
- Free online samples.

Visit http://movielibrary.lynda.com/

lynda.com™

Hands-on Training Books, CDs, & Online Movie Library.